A MIDWIFE'S TALE

DATE DUE

OC 1 03			
OC 2 03			
MR 16 05			
AP 07 05			

DEMCO 38-296

ALSO BY
LAUREL THATCHER ULRICH

*Good Wives: Image and Reality in the Lives
of Women in Northern New England,
1650–1750*

A MIDWIFE'S TALE

The Life of Martha Ballard,
Based on Her Diary,
1785–1812

Laurel Thatcher Ulrich

Vintage Books
A Division of Random House, Inc.
New York

FIRST VINTAGE BOOKS EDITION, JUNE 1991

Copyright © 1990 by Laurel Thatcher Ulrich
Maps copyright © 1990 by Karen Hansen

Library of Congress Cataloging-in-Publication Data
Ulrich, Laurel.
A midwife's tale : the life of Martha Ballard, based on her diary, 1785-1812 / Laurel Thatcher Ulrich.—1st Vintage Books ed.
p.   cm.
Includes bibliographical references (p.   ) and index.
ISBN 0-679-73376-0
1. Ballard, Martha, 1735-1812.   2. Hallowell (Me.)—Biography.   3. Augusta (Me.)—Biography.   4. Kennebec River Valley (Me.)—Social life and customs.   5. Midwives—Maine—Hallowell—Biography.   6. Midwives—Maine—Augusta—Biography.   I. Title.
[F29.H15U47 1991]
974.1′6—dc20
[B]   90-55674
CIP

Design by Dorothy Schmiderer Baker

Manufactured in the United States of America
3579D864

for Gael

Contents

Maps and Illustrations

Tables and Graphs

A MIDWIFE'S TALE

Martha Ballard
her diary

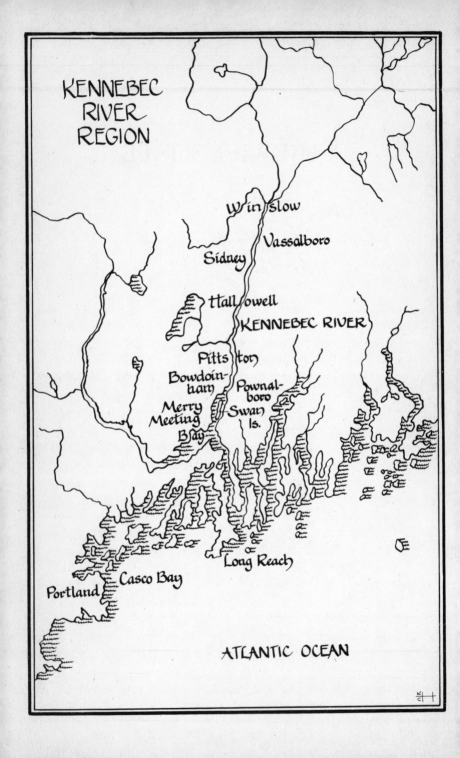

INTRODUCTION

"a great sea A going"

Eight months of the year Hallowell, Maine, was a seaport. From early April to late November, ocean-going vessels sailed up the Kennebec, forty-six miles from the open Atlantic, bringing Pennsylvania flour, West Indian sugar, and English cloth and hardware, returning with shingles, clapboards, hogshead and barrel staves, white ash capstan bars, and pine boards destined for Boston or Bristol or Jamaica.[1] In late autumn, ice blockaded the river, sometimes so suddenly that though a man had been expecting it for weeks, he was caught unprepared. One year, on November 25, after the last ships had sailed from the town, Jonathan Ballard pushed off from his father's sawmill with a raft of boards destined for Long Reach on the coast. He got no farther than Bumberhook Point, three miles below, before the Kennebec closed around him. It didn't open again until April 1.[2]

Hallowell folks remembered openings and closings of the river the way people in other towns remembered earthquakes or drought. In 1785, the year of the long winter, the ice was still firm enough on April 22 to hold a sleigh bearing the body of Samuel Howard, one of the original settlers of the town, to his burying place at Fort Western. Not until May 3 did the first vessels arrive from "the westward," bringing corn and pork to the straitened town.[3] People both welcomed and feared the opening of the river. In bad years ice jams made ponds of fields and rafts of fences, backing up water in the mill creeks that cut through the steep banks on both sides. In good years, the opening water sent mill hands flying through April nights, ripping logs and securing lumber unlocked by the spring thaw. Sometimes the greatest danger was not from the river itself, though high water might pitch a man from a raft to his death before his fellows could reach him, but from the raging creeks on the shore.[4]

In 1789, the river opened on April 7 in a heavy rain that took away the bridge over Ballard's brook, made a breach in the mill dam, and washed out the underpinning of the north side of the house. "But we are yet alive & well for which we ought to be thankful," Martha Ballard told her diary. She was fifty-four years old, a midwife. She and her family had lived at the mills since 1778, seven years after the incorporation of the town. Though she knew little of the sea, she had traveled much on the Kennebec, by water, by ice, and, during those treacherous seasons when the river was neither one nor the other, by faith.

The year Old Lady Cony had her stroke, Martha Ballard crossed the river in a canoe on December 2, pushing through ice in several places. On December 30 of another year, summoned by a woman in labor, she walked across, almost reaching shore before breaking through to her waist at Sewall's Eddy. She dragged herself out, mounted a neighbor's horse, and rode dripping to the delivery. Necessity and a fickle river cultivated a kind of bravado among Hallowell folks. "People Crost the river on a Cake of ice which swong round from the Eddy East side & stopt at the point below Mr Westons," Martha wrote on December 15 of one year. On April 1 of another she reported walking across on the ice after breakfast, adding drily in the margin of the day's entry, "the river opened at 4 hour pm"[5]

Martha Moore was born in 1735 in the small town of Oxford, near the Connecticut border in Worcester County, Massachusetts, but the real story of her life begins in Maine with the diary she kept along the Kennebec. Without the diary her biography would be little more than a succession of dates. Her birth in 1735. Her marriage to Ephraim Ballard in 1754. The births of their nine children in 1756, 1758, 1761, 1763, 1765, 1767, 1769, 1772, and 1779, and the deaths of three of them in 1769. Her own death in 1812. The *American Advocate* for June 9, 1812, summed up her life in one sentence: "Died in Augusta, Mrs. Martha, consort of Mr. Ephraim Ballard, aged 77 years."[6] Without the diary we would know nothing of her life after the last of her children was born, nothing of the 816 deliveries she performed between 1785 and 1812. We would not even be certain she had been a midwife.

In the spring of 1789, Martha faced a flooding river and a rising tide of births. She attended seven deliveries in March and another seven before the end of April, twice her monthly average. On April 23 she went down the Kennebec to visit several families on the west side of the river opposite Bumberhook. This is how she told her story:

[*April 23*] Clear & very Pleasant. I sett out to go to Mr Bullins. Stept out of the Canue & sunk in the mire. Came back & Changd my Cloaths. Maid another attempt & got safe there. Sett out for home. Calld at Capt Coxes & Mr Goodins. Was Calld in at Mrs Husseys. Tarried all night. A sever storm before morn.

[*April 24*] A sever Storm of rain. I was Calld at 1 hour pm from Mrs Husseys by Ebenzer Hewin. Crosst the river in their Boat. A great sea A going. We got safe over then sett out for Mr Hewins. I Crost a stream on the way on fleeting Loggs & got safe over. Wonder full is the Goodness of providence. I then proseeded on my journey. Went beyond Mr Hainses & a Larg tree blew up by the roots before me which Caused my hors to spring back & my life was spared. Great & marvillous are thy sparing mercies O God. I was assisted over the fallen tree by Mr Hains. Went on. Soon Came to a stream. The Bridg was gone. Mr Hewin

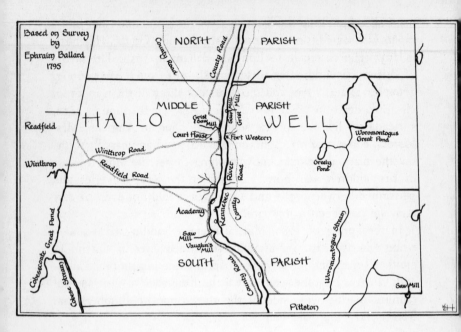

took the rains waded thro & led the horse. Asisted by the same allmighty power I got safe thro & arivd unhurt. Mrs Hewins safe delivd at 10 h Evn of a Daughter.

After great deliverances came small annoyances. In the margin of that day's narrative, she wrote, "My Cloak was burnt while there so that it is not wareable." In all the excitement, someone had apparently allowed the midwife's sodden wrap to hang too near the fire. The story continued:

[*April 25*] Rainy. I came from Mr Hewins to Mr Pollards. My hors mired & I fell off in the mud but blessed be God I receivd no hurt. Mr Hewins attended me to Mrs Husseys. We arivd at 11 hour morning. Mrs Norcross was in Travill. Her women were immediately Calld & Shee was Safe Delivrd at 5 hour 30 minutes Evening of a fine son. Her Husband & Mrs Delino & her Childn went on board bound for Nantucket Early this morn.

[*April 26*] A very Cold morn. Snowd. I took my leav of Mrs Hussey & family. Came to Mr Herseys. He & William Howard brot me from fort Western by water. I left my patients Cleverly & found my famely well. It is the greatest freshet in this river that has been this many years.

Reading such a story, we can easily imagine Martha as an archetypical pioneer. Indeed, the rhythms of her story echo the seventeenth-century captivity narratives that gave New England its first frontier heroines. One thinks of Mary Rowlandson crossing the Ware River in Vermont on a makeshift raft in the early spring of 1676 or of Hannah Swarton traveling into Maine "over Steep and hideous Mountains one while, and another while over Swamps and Thickets of Fallen Trees."[7] The religious language in Martha Ballard's diary strengthens the affinity with her Puritan progenitors. Dramatizing the dangers of her journey, she both glorified God and gave meaning and dimension to her own life. Mr. Hewins led her horse and Mr. Hains walked beside her, but Providence rescued her from the violence of the spring freshet.

"A great sea A going"—Martha knew how to suggest an entire landscape, or in this case a riverscape, in a phrase. Her description of the river crossing is part psalm, part tale.[8] She understood instinctively, if not self-consciously, the importance of repetition and the uses of convention. Notice how in the April 24 passage she alternated spare, but vivid, action sentences with formulaic religious phrases:

I Crost the stream on the way on fleeting Loggs & got safe over. *Wonder full is the Goodness of providence.* I then proseeded on my journey. Went beyond Mr Hainses & a Larg tree blew up by the roots before me which Caused my hors to spring back & my life was spared. *Great & marvillous are thy sparing mercies O God.* I was assisted over the fallen tree by Mr Hains. Went on. Soon Came to a stream. The Bridg was gone. Mr Hewin took the rains waded thro & led the horse. *Asisted by the same allmighty power* I got safe thro & arivd unhurt.

Here the religious sentiments become a kind of refrain, punctuating and accentuating each stage in the narrative. Such a passage reveals a storyteller, if not a writer, at work.

There are other passages of similar quality in the diary. Yet most of Martha's entries are more mundane. The structure of her diary derives from two workaday forms of record-keeping, the daybook and the interleaved almanac. In eighteenth-century New England, farmers, craftsmen, shopkeepers, ship's captains, and perhaps a very few housewives kept daybooks, running accounts of receipts and expenditures, sometimes combining economic entries with short notes on important family events and comments on work begun or completed. Other early diarists used the blank pages bound into printed almanacs to keep their own tally on the weather, adding brief entries on gardening, visits to and from neighbors, or public occurrences of both the institutional and the sensational sort. Martha Ballard did all these things.

The extant diary, which begins in January of 1785, may have been preceded by an almanac of some sort, since she ruled the margins of her homemade booklets and numbered the days of the month and week, using a "dominical letter" for Sundays, according to the almanac form. Whatever its origins, the diary functioned as a kind of daybook. Martha recorded debts contracted and "rewards" received, and some of the time she noted numbers of yards "got out" of the loom and varieties of beans put into the ground. Her midwifery accounts are even more methodical. She carefully labeled and numbered each delivery, adding an XX to the margin when the fee was paid.

Those few historians who have known about the diary have not known quite what to do with it. In his *History of Augusta* published in 1870, James W. North quoted several passages, including the one for April 24, 1789, but he pronounced most of the entries "brief and with some exceptions not of general interest." Although Charles Elventon Nash devoted more than a third of his 600-page *History of Augusta* to an abridgment of the journal, carefully extracting birth records and a sample of almost everything else except unsavory medical details or anything tainted with sex, he too found much of it "trivial and unimportant ... being but a repetition of what has been recited many times." Curiously, a feminist history of midwifery published in the 1970s repeated the old dismissal: "Like many diaries of farm women, it is filled with trivia about domestic chores and pastimes."[9]

Yet it is in the very dailiness, the exhaustive, repetitious dailiness, that the real power of Martha Ballard's book lies. To extract the river crossings without noting the cold days spent "footing" stockings, to abstract the births without recording the long autumns spent winding quills, pickling meat, and sorting cabbages, is to destroy the sinews of this earnest, steady, gentle, and courageous record. Martha sometimes slipped the folded half-sheets from which she constructed her diary into her bag when she crossed the river or waded through snow to sit out a tedious labor, and when she felt overwhelmed or enlivened by the very "trivia" the historians have dismissed, she said so, not in the soul-searching manner of a Puritan nor with the literary self-consciousness of a sentimentalist, but in a plain, matter-of-fact, and in the end unforgettable voice. For more than twenty-seven years, 9,965 days to be exact, she faithfully kept her record. Martha was not an introspective diarist, yet in this conscientious recording as much as in her occasional confessions, she revealed herself. "And now this year is come to a close," she wrote on December 31, 1800, "and happy is it if we have made a wise improvement of the time." For her, living was to be measured in doing. Nothing was trivial.

Because so few New England women of her generation left writing in any form, one searches for an explanation for the diary. Though her grandmother, Hannah Learned, was able to muster a clear but labored signature on the one surviving document bearing her name, her mother, Dorothy Moore, signed with a mark.[10] On the male side of the family, however, there is a record of education. Martha's uncle Abijah Moore, who graduated from Yale in 1726, was the first college graduate from the town of Oxford. Martha's younger brother, Jonathan Moore, was the second. Jonathan graduated from Harvard College in 1761, serving for a time as librarian of the college before accepting a call as pastor of the First Congregational Church in Rochester, Massachusetts. Throughout her life Martha Ballard corresponded with "Brother Jonathan."[11]

Although her handwriting is crude in comparison with her brother's and less certain than that of her husband, who was a surveyor and mapmaker as well as a miller, her ability to write cursive in any form is itself evidence that someone in Oxford in the 1740s was interested in educating girls.[12] Judging from the diary, that education was quite conventional. Although Martha occasionally "perrused" newspapers, she mentioned only one book other than the Bible. On June 25, 1786, a Sunday, she wrote, "I have Red in Mr Marshalls gospel ~~mistry~~ Mystery of Sanctification." The book was Walter Marshall's *Gospel-Mystery of Sanctification*, a work of popular piety first published in London in 1692, though reprinted many times in the eighteenth century. Her concern with the spelling of the title is intriguing; normally, she showed little interest in such matters. Obviously having the book in her hand elevated her consciousness, though it had little effect on the rest of the passage. *Read* remained *Red*.

Martha's choice of reading material was conservative, at least on that Sunday in 1786. She was aware of more modern forms of English literature, however. Her younger sister, Dorothy Barton, had two daughters named after characters in the novels of Samuel Richardson. *Pamela* and *Clarissa Harlowe* Barton were frequent visitors to and sometime inhabitants of the Ballard house, as was their sister *Parthenia*. Classical or pseudo-classical names were still rare in New England in the 1760s, though they became more popular after the Revolution. The Ballards succumbed to the same impulse and displayed an uncharacteristic bit of whimsy when they named their third daughter *Triphene*.[13]

By Oxford standards, the Moores were well educated and ambitious. The family also seems to have had a medical bent. Martha's uncle Abijah Moore was a physician, as were two of her brothers-in-law, including Stephen Barton, the father of Pamela, Parthenia, and Clarissa.[14] The one hint that Martha herself was involved in caring for the sick in Oxford comes from a Barton family story recorded many years later. It survives in two versions.

One explains that during the pre-Revolutionary boycotts, when Stephen Barton was on a committee to see that no tea was bought in the town, he "was wont to put on his hat and go without while his sympathetic wife and her sister, Martha Moore Ballard, made a cup of tea in the cellar for some sick mother in the neighborhood whose sufferings patriotism and loyalty failed to heal."[15] The other version comes from Dorothy and Stephen's granddaughter, a woman christened Clarissa Harlowe Barton, but known to millions of Americans by her nickname, Clara. Clara Barton, the founder of the American Red Cross, later recalled being entertained by her "interesting, precise and intelligent grandmother Barton, telling us of the tea parties she and her sister Aunt Ballard held in the cellar when grandfather was out or *up* and didn't know what was going on in his own disloyal and rebellious home." Although the neighborly ministrations of the first story become "tea parties" in this one, both emphasize Dorothy Barton's independence. According to Clara, the two sisters "hung blankets inside the cellar door to prevent the savory fumes of the tea from reaching the loyal and official olfactories of 'Pater familias.' "[16] Martha's rebellion may have been less serious than her sister's. As we shall see, Ephraim Ballard was himself a reluctant supporter, at best, of the Revolution.

The best evidence of the practical side of Martha's education comes from the diary itself. When it opened in 1785, she knew how to manufacture salves, syrups, pills, teas, and ointments, how to prepare an oil emulsion (she called it an "oil a mulge"), how to poultice wounds, dress burns, treat dysentery, sore throat, frostbite, measles, colic, "hooping Cough," "Chin cough," "St. Vitas dance," "flying pains," "the salt rhume," and "the itch," how to cut an infant's tongue, administer a "clister" (enema), lance an abscessed breast, apply a "blister" or a "back plaster," induce vomiting, assuage bleeding, reduce swelling, and relieve a toothache, as well as deliver babies.[17]

She later wrote that she delivered her first baby in July of 1778, less than a year after her arrival in Maine. This statement should not be taken entirely at face value. She no doubt officiated as a midwife for the first time in 1778, but she had probably assisted in dozens of births in Oxford. This was the era of "social childbirth," when female relatives and neighbors, as well as midwives, attended births. Most midwives began as observers, gradually assuming a more active role, until one day, when the old midwife was delayed or willing, they "performed." For Martha, moving to Maine probably accelerated this process. In Oxford, even if she had the ability to practice she may have had little opportunity, since there were many older women in the town. Her own Grandmother Learned was alive until 1777.[18] In Hallowell, by contrast, she was one of the older women in a young and rapidly growing town.

Giving birth to nine babies was also a part of her preparation as a midwife. As one eighteenth-century midwifery manual expressed it, "There is a tender regard one woman bears to another, and a natural sympathy in those that have gone thro' the Pangs of Childbearing; which, doubtless, occasion a compassion for those that labour under these circumstances, which no man can be a judge of."[19] Martha's "natural" sympathy had also been developed through death. Between 1767 and 1770, Oxford lost 12 percent of its population in one of the worst diphtheria epidemics in New England's history. One hundred forty-four persons died, mostly children ages two to fourteen. Martha's uncle and aunt, Richard and Mary Moore, buried eight of their eleven children. Martha and Ephraim lost three of their six children in less than ten days.[20] A row of tiny headstones in the burying ground behind the Oxford Congregational Church commemorates the Moore deaths. There are no Ballard stones. Martha memorialized her little girls in the diary she kept along the Kennebec.

June 17, 1786: "this is 17 years since the Death of my Daughter Triphene who Deceast AE 4 years & 3 months."

July 1, 1788: "It is 19 years this Day since the Death of my Daughter Dorothy." (Dorothy had been two.)

July 5, 1789: "20 years since my daughter Martha's death." (Martha was "8 years & 2 months & 28 days" when she died.)

Both of the Ballard sons, Cyrus, twelve, and Jonathan, six, survived the throat distemper. Of the four daughters, only Lucy, age ten, remained. "It was a very hott day & Continued so thro the sumer," Martha recalled in one of the entries remembering Triphene's death.[21] She had reason to feel the heat in that summer of sorrow. She was seven and a half months pregnant when the first of her daughters died.

On August 6, 1769, amidst death, she gave birth. The baby was named Hannah, for Mother Ballard. Two years later another baby girl was born. She became Dorothy, or "Dolly," for Grandmother Moore, for her Aunt Dorothy Barton, and for the sister who had died of diphtheria. Perhaps there would have been another Triphene or Martha in 1773, but in that year Ephraim Ballard was in Maine searching out a new home. As a consequence, the last Ballard baby, named Ephraim for his father, was born in Hallowell in 1779.[22]

When Ephraim Ballard ascended the Kennebec in 1775 in search of new land, he was doing what his great-grandfather had done more than a century before when he left Lynn, Massachusetts, to build mills in the new town of Andover and what his own father had done when he left Andover for Billerica and then Oxford. The Ballards had been millers for four generations in New England, and in three of those four they helped to settle new towns.[23]

The French and Indian wars first led Oxford men to Maine. Martha's cousin Nathan Moore, a veteran of the invasion of Canada, was settled in Vassalboro on the Kennebec by 1768.[24] Another cousin, Ebenezer Learned, also a veteran, became a proprietor of the new township of Livermore on the Androscoggin River, though he continued to live in Oxford. Ephraim went to Maine for the first time as a surveyor and agent for Cousin Ebenezer, though his interest soon turned from the Androscoggin to the Kennebec.[25] By 1775 his brother Jonathan, his brother-in-law Thomas Towne, Martha's brother Ebenezer Moore, and her brother-in-law Stephen Barton had all settled on lands laid out by the Kennebec Proprietors.[26] Removing to Maine became another way of remaining in Oxford.

In 1775, there were six incorporated townships along the

Kennebec above Long Reach—Pownalboro, Gardinerstown, Hallowell, Winthrop, Vassalboro, and Winslow—the town names reflecting the family connections and political power of the Kennebec Proprietors, also known as the Plymouth Company because they traced their land claims to seventeenth-century Pilgrim grants. Unlike the pioneer settlements of early Massachusetts, these Maine towns were laid out by merchant speculators, who, having no intention of migrating themselves, gave away some of the land to early settlers, looking for a return on their investment from later land sales and rents and from the proceeds of mills, ships, and stores run by hired agents, who were themselves often paid in land. In 1775 the Kennebec Proprietors owned more than 600,000 acres of wild land, though the exact boundaries of their grants were in dispute. Here indeed was work for a good surveyor, and opportunity perhaps to acquire land and mills.[27]

On April 6, 1775, Ephraim secured a lease from Silvester Gardiner of Boston, one of the wealthiest of the Kennebec Proprietors, to "Fort Hallifax and all the land adjoining." The Fort, originally built by the Massachusetts government, stood on a peninsula between the Kennebec and Sebasticook rivers. Surrounded by 400 acres of timber, it was described by one contemporary as "a great Salmon fishery in the summer and a bass fishery in the Winter."[28]

It was an impressive site, but the timing was bad. In April of 1775, as Ephraim was sailing up the Kennebec toward the Fort, Martha was in Oxford watching her cousin Ebenezer Learned muster troops to meet the Lexington and Concord alarm. In June, when Ephraim applied to the Lincoln County Court for a tavern license, the Oxford Minutemen were at Bunker Hill.[29] When an advance party of Benedict Arnold's army reached Fort Halifax in September of 1775, they disdained the accommodations of the Fort, not only because it was in a "ruinous state" but because the proprietor (who was without question Ephraim Ballard) was reputed a "rank tory." Still, they were pleased with the man's willingness to exchange "a barrel of smoke-dried salmon for a barrel of pork, upon honest terms."[30]

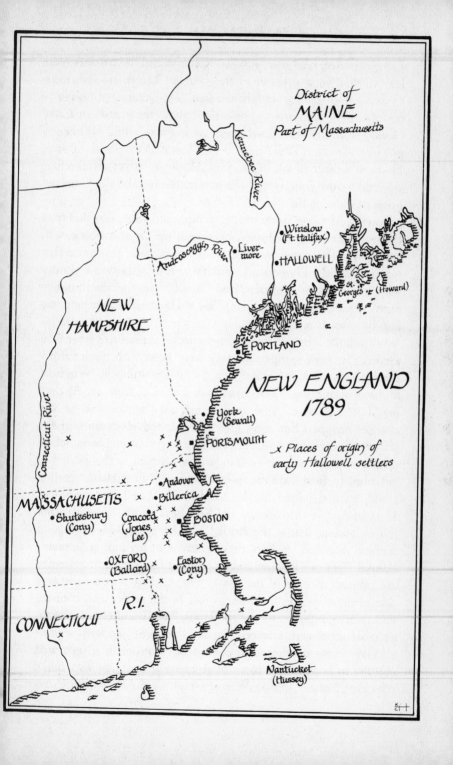

District of
MAINE
Part of Massachusetts

Kennebec River

Winslow
(Ft. Halifax)

Liver-
more

HALLOWELL

Androscoggin River

St.
Georges (Howard)

NEW
HAMPSHIRE

PORTLAND

NEW ENGLAND
1789

York
(Sewall)

PORTSMOUTH

x *Places of origin of*
early Hallowell settlers

Connecticut River

Andover

Billerica

MASSACHUSETTS

Shutesbury
(Cony)

Concord
(Jones,
Lee)

BOSTON

OXFORD
(Ballard)

Easton
(Cony)

R.I.

CONNECTICUT

Nantucket
(Hussey)

A year later, relations between Ephraim and the patriots were less cordial. In a petition to the General Court, the Winslow Committee of Safety complained that "Mr Ballard with a Number of People (supposed to be unfriendly to the grand American Cause) from the next Town were cutting and haling Mill Logs" on Fort lands. (The "next Town" was Vassalboro, where Ephraim's brother and a bevy of Moore relatives lived.) The General Court empowered the committee to take the Gardiner property "under their care."[31]

Having lost one Tory property, Ephraim went downriver to Hallowell and acquired another, taking up the management of land and mills owned by John Jones, a longtime resident of the Kennebec and a Plymouth Company agent. Jones was a loyalist who had already been declared "inimical to the liberties and privileges of the United States" by a Hallowell town meeting, but he was foresighted enough to deed his property to his wife's relatives before fleeing to Canada.[32] Ephraim's lease was secure. His own sympathies may have been with his landlord, but he knew how to make peace with a revolution. When he too was accused of "Treasonable & Enimical Conduct Against the United States of America," he not only managed to get the charges dropped but soon after was elected moderator of the Hallowell town meeting. According to a treasurer's account, he contributed 200 pounds (a standard assessment in this period of inflation) toward the support of a soldier at Fort Halifax.[33]

Martha had joined her husband in Hallowell in October of 1777. "I first set my feet on the Kenebeck shore ... at Mr John Jones' landing below the Hook," she later recalled, adding, "I spent 1 year and 17 days, then removed to his mill at Boman's brook."[34] Jones's landing and his mills at Bowman's Brook were in opposite corners of the town. The landing was on the east side of the river in the southern half of the settlement, the section usually referred to as "the Hook," for Bumberhook Point, its most prominent feature. The mills were on the west side of the river in the northern half of the town (the part that separated in 1797 to become the town of Augusta). This area was called "the Fort," after old Fort Western, built by the Plymouth Company in 1754 as part of its line of defense on the Kennebec. Since 1769, the Fort had been owned by James Howard, who used it as a dwelling house and store. (The restored Fort is now a museum owned and maintained by the city of Augusta.)

In 1777 there were 100 families in Hallowell, spread out along ten miles of river. Most people still lived in their first log houses, though a few, perhaps including John Jones, had managed to build frame houses and barns. The settlers had come from more than thirty different towns, some from Rhode Island and Nantucket, a few from New Hampshire, several from the British Isles, most from Massachusetts and Maine. They had come in small clusters of kin. There were two Howard brothers with their progeny, three Sewall cousins, two generations of Conys, strings of Savages and Clarks, and so on. Although most of the Ballard and Moore relatives were in other Kennebec towns, Ephraim's nephew and namesake, Ephraim Towne, was also a tenant of John Jones in Hallowell. In 1778, Towne married his cousin Lucy Ballard, Martha and Ephraim's oldest daughter.[35]

Letters from John Jones to Towne provide the only glimpse we have of these years. "I have had an acompt of what you have met with or had your House serched for me," Jones wrote in the autumn of 1778. "I am very sorry that they should trouble themselves concerning me. I hant dun them no ronge. I sincear wish Everybody would miend their own business." When Kennebec patriots continued to mind Jones's business, he joined the British resistance at Fort George. His military forays into the region gave new point to his old nickname, "Black Jones." In one exploit he kidnapped Colonel Charles Cushing of Pownalboro, dragging him from his house barefoot in the night. His letters to Towne say less about politics, however, than about their common interest in the farm. "I am afraid there will be a famin for bread if the war continues," he wrote in February of 1779. He urged his tenant to "buy sum oxen or furrow cows" while he could, to set out apple trees on the hill behind the barn, and to "git a Salmon net maide, for Provisons is intolerable Dear." When shearing time came he hoped Towne would take care of his wool, though "if you need any of it before I come you or your father Ballard may use what you stand in need of."[36]

Ten years later, Jones had not yet come. He made an attempt in 1785, the first year Martha kept her diary, but was soon spirited out of town. "A gang went to Samuel Duttuns & took John Jones, brought him to Pollards, tarried till morn when they Set out with him for Wiscasset," Martha wrote.[37] Characteristically, she offered no judgment on the behavior either of Jones or of his attackers. Nor does her diary open in time to record what may have been a last vigilante action against her own family. In 1784 Lucy and Ephraim Towne moved from Hallowell to Winslow, the place where Ephraim Ballard had had his first encounter with the Revolution. According to an oral tradition preserved in the Towne family, the young couple transported their household goods upriver on a flatboat, leaving their furniture on the wharf overnight. "Somebody tied one of the chairs to the top of a birch tree," their great-granddaughter recalled, "and when they went to get the furniture in the morning, here was a chair in the top of a tree."[38] In her mouth the incident is an amusing but inexplicable event. Was tying furniture in trees some species of frontier humor, a folk form of welcome? The political context suggests otherwise. Apparently somebody in Winslow resented Ephraim Towne's association with John Jones, and perhaps, too, with that "rank tory" who had once cut timber at Fort Halifax.

When the diary opened, there were seven Ballards living in John Jones's house on Bowman's Brook—Martha and Ephraim and five unmarried children—Cyrus, Jonathan, Hannah, Dolly, and Ephraim. There were usually one or two hired helpers as well. All these people crowded into an unfinished house that had two rooms on the main floor (Martha called them simply the "east room" and the "west room") and two unfinished chambers above, which were unusable in winter. In addition there were a "seller," a barn, and various "yards," some fenced, some defined only by their proximity to a significant structure or natural barrier, as in "I sowd parsnip & Carrot seed *in the gardin by the Barn.*" Or "I howd the Beans & Cucumbers *in the yard by the Brook.*" Or "Houghed the plants *before the door.*" Or "Cutt Aulders and maid a sort of a fence part round *the yard By the mill Pond.*"[39]

Housework extended from the west room to the yards. Martha Ballard and her daughters bleached newly spun thread on the grass and hung laundry on such fences as they had, though there were risks in such a practice. "Hannah washt Daniels Blankett & our swine tore it into strips," Martha wrote on one fateful day. (No matter, the girls cut up the remnants and made a warm petticoat for one of Lucy's children.) There were no sheep yet, but Ephraim owned a horse and a pair of oxen and Martha milked both a red and a "speckled" cow. Chickens pecked in a dooryard cluttered with wood chips and animal droppings, giving a comforting domesticity to a setting that was still wilderness beyond the clearings for hay and corn. "There was a moose by our gardin this afternoon," Martha wrote into the margin of her diary on one April day. In November of 1787, she noted, "Hannah & Dolly were fritened by a Baire between here & Neighbor Savages." In such a setting an errant calf—or a neighbor's child—might wander "up the crik" and disappear.[40]

Yet for all its wildness there was a motion, a life, in Hallowell that had been missing in Oxford. There were ships on the river and a continuous movement of settlers through the town and into the back country. Ephraim's mill was a ram against the wilderness, an engine for transforming woods into towns. On good days the saw kept a steady rhythm, the vertical blade moving up and down 120 times a minute, striking a rapid trochee ("Faaa-sher, Faaa-sher") that echoed through the trees as log after log inched along the wooden track. Weather and the changing seasons, as much as the availability of timber, regulated the operation, too much water being as much of a problem as too little. "Our saw mills go Briskly," Martha wrote on one day after a heavy rain, but on another, "The mills have been stopt from going by the freshet."[41]

Ephraim and his sons operated a gristmill as well as a sawmill, both perhaps housed in the same building, the saw or saws in the story above, the grinding mechanism below. There is a fitting symbolism in the division of responsibility for the two. Cyrus, the quiet older son who into his forties moved in and out of his father's household, never marrying, never achieving full independence, was assigned the grinding. Jonathan, the flamboyant and rebellious younger brother, did the rafting and ripping. One wonders if Cyrus was impaired in some way, though his mother never wrote of it in her diary. His shoulders, at least, were powerful, since it was his job to "pick mill," that is, to work with a mallet and chisel to restore and maintain grooves on the granite millstones. "Son Town" too had a role in the family operation. Having carried away the eldest daughter to Winslow, he returned every week or so, rafting logs to the mill.[42]

When conditions were right the mills went day and night, though mechanical and human failure as well as the weather could bring silence. "The cornmill ceast grinding till finisht repairing," Martha would write, or "Thee sweap of one of the mills got off thee Crank so neither of them were tended this night." Still the sounds of sawing were as much a part of spring on Bowman's Brook as the songs of birds, such an omnipresent part of Martha's world that she usually did not notice them unless they were gone, as one May evening, after the hired hand had gone to bed ill and Jonathan had returned late from two days on the river searching for logs that had gone adrift, when she noted quietly, "The mill Lies still."[43]

Perhaps it was a sense of history or a craving for stability, perhaps only a practical need to keep birth records, that first motivated Martha to keep a diary. "Thee number of childn I have Extracted since I came to Kennebeck I find by written acount & other Calculations to be 405," she wrote on December 31, 1791. The demands of a practice that averaged almost forty births a year even in the prediary period may eventually have made a "written account" essential. The diary opens on January 1, 1785, with short, choppy entries nineteen to the page. Gradually the entries become fuller and more regular. (The diary's overall average is six entries per page.) From the beginning she ruled a margin at the left of her page where she entered the day of the month. Soon she added a second column for the day of the week. By the end of 1787 she had added a right-hand margin where she summarized each day's events. A year or two later she began keeping a running head at the top of each page. Such changes suggest that she too could get lost in a stream of days. One delivery, one April day, could so easily fuse with another.

April 24, 1785: "I was Calld at 2 O Clock in the Morn to go to thee hook to Mrs Blake in travil."

April 18, 1786: "A rainy day. I was calld to Mr Gillmans at the hook to see his wife in Travil."

April 22, 1787: "I Was calld to Mr Welmans at 9 this morn. His wife Safe Delivd at 7 Evn of a son . . . it raind this Evinng."

April 28, 1788: "Rain, Snow & Haill & Cold [but this time no deliveries!]"

And then on April 24, 1789, the dramatic encounter with the spring freshet. "A sever Storm of rain. I was Calld at 1 h pm from Mrs Husseys by Ebenzer Hewin. . . ."

Both the difficulty and the value of the diary lie in its astonishing steadiness. Consider again that sequence of entries for April 23 through 26, 1789. The central story—Martha's crossing and recrossing of the Kennebec—is clear enough, but on first reading the reader is unlikely to notice a subplot being played out at the Hussey house while Martha was traveling through the April storm to the Hewins delivery. In fact, it is not even apparent at first that she has left one pregnant woman to attend another. Recall that she initially crossed the river on April 23 "to go to Mr Bullins," that a few hours later as she was about to return home after stopping in at "Capt Coxes & Mr Goodins," she was "Calld in at Mrs Husseys." She "Tarried all night" at the Husseys', leaving about one the next afternoon when Ebenezer Hewins came through the storm to fetch her to his wife's delivery. She did not, however, return home after leaving the Hewins house, which was on the same side of the river as her own, but crossed the Kennebec once again to the Husseys.

In the entry for November 25 we find out why: "Mr Hewins attended me to Mrs Husseys. We arivd at 11 h morn. Mrs Nor-

22

April 89

7 3 a heavy rain the river opend and
the Bridg over this Crick went away
the undermining ap. of North side our
house fell in but we are yet alive
& well for which we ought to be
thankfull part of y Jam gone also

a heavy
rain
the river
opend
I have be
at home

8 4 Snowd y morn a very raw cold day
mr Smiley came here to work
mrs Williams & Jan Robbins went
from here I paid her 1/6

at home

9 5 I went to hamlins his infant sick from
there to Esqr Husseys

at Esqr
Husseys

10 6 at Jitsys my Cox there a rain
Jno Capen here q th will at home

11 7 at Jitoys Cap Norcross came
home I way called from there by
mr True y morn ½ past 6 from
Trucy to Philip Norcroses at 11
Back again at 3 my

at Husse
& Truey
& Norcros

12 *8
Birth
Truees
Jack &
Noros
Jack
*

my True I lived at 9th h morn of
a boy I went Back to Norcross
his wife delived ap. a y agt at 10
morn from thence to Cap
Porters to Caty Scott at 12th h
i way there all night

at Tru
Norcro
Cap
Porter

13 *9
Birth
Caty
Scotts
Jan
* *

at Cap porters Caty delived of a
fine Jan at 9th h m she declar
that Jeremiah Wakfield way
the Father of the same I came
home at 2 pm then went to
Esqr Husseys attinded by
Cap porter

at Cap
Port
recived
my fee
Cap Sop
& c

		April 27	(13)
111	3	at mrs Husseys & mr Gooding I pins & Cyrys stocking	at mrs Husseys & mr Gooding
14	4	at mrs Husseys	at mrs Husseys
5	5	at Ditos	at Ditos
6	6	at Ditos	at Ditos
8	7	Calld at ye 3d h morn to Georg Browns from mrs Husseys mrs Brown safe Bede of a fine Son at 12 o Clok the Child wd 11 lbs I returnd at 5 pm mrs of Hussey Gone to see her Husband	at mrs Husseys Georg Browns Son
19	1	at mrs Husseys I wrote Book Gone	at mrs Hussie
20	2	at Ditos the returnd all well	Ditos
1	3	I came from Ditos find that mr Learnd has been here receivd Letters from Hannah & sister Waters	came from mrs Husseys
2	4	Clear I went to see mrs Hamton her infant is much better mr Learnd sleep here	I was at mr Hamton
3	5	Clear & very pleas I sett out to Go to mr Bulbery stept out at ye Carne & funk in y mire came back & Changd my Cloath made a nother attempt & got safe there sett out for home Calld at Capt Cokes & mr Gooding was Calld on at mrs Hussey tarried all night a several of them before morn	I tarried at mrs Husseys the new milk at labe I was in past long turned by five

cross was in Travill. Her women were immediately Calld & Shee was Safe Delivrd at 5 hours 30 minutes Evening of a fine son." Then she added as a kind of aside: "Her Husband & Mrs Delino & her Childn went on board bound for Nantucket Early this morn." With some attention to context (and a quick search of family records), the characters in this little drama can be straightened out—Mrs. Norcross and Mrs. Delano were Mrs. Hussey's daughters.[44]

Now look at the sequence of events so casually described in the entry. The ship bound for Nantucket left "Early" in the morning; the midwife arrived at eleven; the baby was born at 5:30 that afternoon. What we don't know is whether Mrs. Norcross was already in labor when her husband and sister sailed down the river, having risen early to catch the northwest wind that would make for easy sailing to Long Reach.[45] Probably not. Earlier entries for the month suggest that Mr. Norcross had been waiting in port for almost two weeks anticipating the birth of his child. Martha first went to the Hussey house on April 9 and was still there two days later when "Captain Norcross came home" with the first ships of the season. She left on the eleventh, returned on the thirteenth, left again on the eighteenth, and was back the next day, remaining until April 20. When she was finally "called in" at the Hussey house on April 23, she had already spent a total of nine days waiting for a baby that would not arrive. It is doubtful she would have left Mrs. Norcross again for the Hewins delivery if there had been any sign of labor. That flat entry, "Her Husband & Mrs Delino & her Childn went on board bound for Nantucket Early this morn" was an ironic commentary on a month's frustration. The watched pot would not boil.

Here the more interesting point may not be the departure of the seafaring father (for men the conflict between work and family is an old and continuing one) but the presence of the distant sister. Betsy Delano, whose husband was also a mariner, lived in Nantucket. Did she sail up the river with Philip Norcross on April 11 hoping to attend her sister's delivery? Or had she spent the winter months in Hallowell with her mother while her own husband was at sea?

A second subplot is suggested by a clue so subtle that without long acquaintance with Martha Ballard's habits of deference, it is easily missed. She wrote of going to *Mrs* rather than to *Mr* Hussey's house, though in the same section she spoke of going to *Mr* Bullins, *Capt* Coxes, and *Mr* Goodins. In Martha Ballard's world, houses belonged to men. That in April of 1789 the Hussey house seemed to belong to a wife is significant. Obed Hussey was in Wiscasset jail, imprisoned for debt. She alluded to his situation on April 18, during one of her many visits to Mrs. Norcross. "Mrs Hussey Gone to see her Husband," she wrote, though with typical restraint she said nothing more. Obed Hussey was eighty years old that year. He never again saw his warehouses and fishing seines along the Kennebec. "Esquire Hussey expired in prison," Martha noted on June 17, 1790.[46]

A different kind of adversity is suggested in the dramatic journey across swollen streams and deep gullies to the Hewinses' delivery. That Ebenezer Hewins was trying to carve out a farm in the second mile of settlement suggests something about his own status. Earlier arrivals, like the Husseys and the Ballards, lived near the river. There is a kind of disorder as well as excitement suggested by Ebenezer Hewins's precipitous fetching of the midwife, a feeling compounded later by the entry regarding the burning of the cloak, and by the knowledge that Martha Ballard had delivered the Hewinses' first baby in 1787 just two months after the couple were married.[47]

The problem is not that the diary is trivial but that it introduces more stories than can easily be recovered and absorbed. It is one thing to describe Martha's journey across the Kennebec, another to assess the historical significance of Nancy Norcross's lingering labor, Obed Hussey's sojourn in jail, or Zilpha and Ebenezer Hewins's hasty marriage. Taken alone, such stories tell us too much and not enough, teasing us with glimpses of intimate life, repelling us with a reticence we cannot decode. Yet, read in the broader context of the diary and in relation to larger themes in eighteenth-century history, they can be extraordinarily revealing.

Each of the subplots in the April 1789 passage relates to a

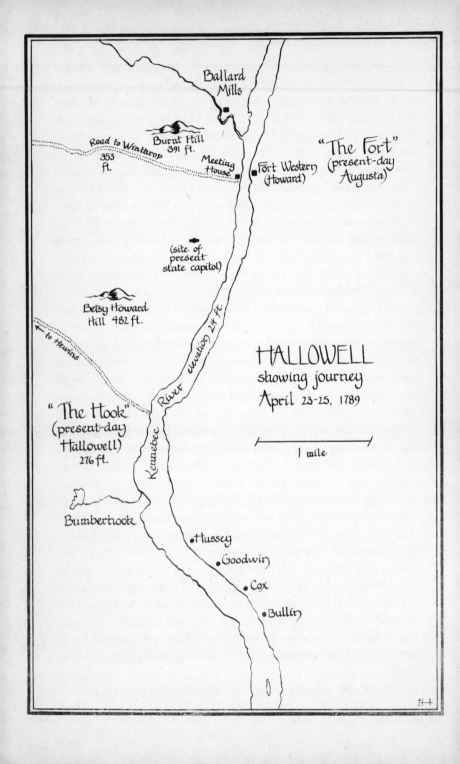

larger question in social history. Nancy Norcross suffered lingering labor in an era when old childbirth practices were being challenged in both England and America by a new "scientific" obstetrics promoted by male physicians. Obed Hussey languished in debtor's prison in an age when debtor petitions and even debtor insurrections were convulsing the nation and when some men were taking to the streets or the woods to preserve their property. Ebenezer and Zilpha Hewins married at a time of high premarital pregnancy rates in America, a period when political essayists as well as novelists were obsessed with the theme of seduction. The late eighteenth century was not only an era of political revolution but of medical, economic, and sexual transformation.[48] Not surprisingly, it was also a time when a new ideology of womanhood self-consciously connected domestic virtue to the survival of the state.[49] The nature of these phenomena is still being debated in the literature, yet few scholars would disagree that the period of Martha's diary, 1785–1812, was an era of profound change, or that in some still dimly understood way, the nation's political revolution and the social revolutions that accompanied it were related. It is not as easy as it once was to dismiss domestic concerns as "trivia."

Martha Ballard's diary connects to several prominent themes in the social history of the early Republic, yet it does more than reflect an era. By restoring a lost substructure of eighteenth-century life, it transforms the nature of the evidence upon which much of the history of the period has been written. The point can be illustrated by comparing evidence from her book with three documents left by prominent Hallowell men, Daniel Cony, William Howard, and Henry Sewall.

Daniel Cony was the Kennebec's best-known physician. He was studying medicine with his brother-in-law, Dr. Samuel Curtis of Marlborough, Massachusetts, at the time of the Lexington alarm. He marched with the Minutemen, served as adjutant of the regiment of infantry with General Horatio Gates at Saratoga, and according to the town historian "was at the surrender of Burgoyne, but not in any of the battles which preceded that event." He arrived in Hallowell in 1778, the same year as Martha, and became, in the words of a contemporary, a "faithful labourer in the medical field," and, we might add, an earnest promoter of medical organization. Though he practiced 150 miles into the hinterland, Cony was an early member of the Massachusetts Medical Society centered in Boston, and he continued that membership even after he became president of a new Kennebec Medical Society founded in 1797.[50]

Cony was one of a handful of Maine physicians mentioned in James Thacher's *American Medical Biography*, published in Boston in 1828.[51] He was, by all accounts, a leader in his profession, an associate if not a peer of New England's most progressive physicians, the very group of men who were promoting the new scientific obstetrics. Significantly, his only contribution to the literature of the Massachusetts Medical Society was an obstetrical paper, a one-page account of "a circumstance which I had never before met with" in a delivery he performed in August of 1787.[52] Since this brief paper makes no mention of a midwife, or of any woman other than the patient, it might seem that the obstetrical revolution was complete in Hallowell by that date, that doctors had supplanted midwives.

Martha's diary confirms that Cony delivered at least one woman in August 1787—his own wife—but it reduces his obstetrical career to its proper place in the medical history of the town. Several doctors, including some from neighboring towns, occasionally attended births in Hallowell, but their work was supplementary to that of the midwives. Martha herself attended 60 percent of the births in Hallowell in the year Cony presented his paper to the Massachusetts Medical Society, and she was not the only female practitioner active at the time. Martha and her peers were not only handling most of the deliveries, they were providing much of the medical care as well. In Martha's diary, it is doctors, not midwives, who seem marginal.

William Howard, the man who helped Martha Ballard across the river on April 26 when she was returning from the Hussey house, was the wealthiest man in the town. The son and son-in-law of Hallowell's earliest settlers, he lived and traded at Fort Western in partnership with his brother Samuel, a mariner.[53] A surviving account book listed under the names of William and Samuel Howard provides rich material for assessing the external economy of the Kennebec in the last decade of the eighteenth century. A standard merchant's ledger with debit and credit entries for each customer listed on opposite pages, it begins in 1788, though it carries some balances forward "from another Book," now lost.[54] Most entries date from 1788 through 1792, though a few go to 1800 or beyond. Almost all, including those for the Ballards, are listed under the name of a male head of household. Male products—lumber, fish, and furs—dominate the credit side of the ledger.

One might conclude from such a record that Kennebec women had no role in economic life beyond their own households. An intriguing page at the very end of the account book lists flaxseed sold by the Kennebec Agricultural Society, yet there is little evidence in the account book itself of any sort of textile production in the town. Martha's diary tells us what happened to the seed. It not only records when Ephraim Ballard planted the flax, but when she and her daughters weeded and harvested it. It not only identifies the male helpers who turned and broke it, but the many female neighbors who assisted her and her daughters with the combing, spinning, reeling, boiling, spooling, warping, quilling, weaving, bucking, and bleaching that transformed the ripe plant into finished cloth.[55] Martha's diary fills in the missing work—and trade—of women.

It also provides additional detail on the day-to-day operation of the male economy. Like most merchants, Howard served as a kind of banker, settling third-party debts with store goods or cash. Ephraim Ballard's accounts are typical, listing salt, rum, molasses, and nails on the debit side, several thousand feet of "clear" and "merchantable" boards among the credits, and on both sides of the ledger "notes" or "orders" on other men. On May 3, 1790, for example, the Howards debited Ephraim's account for "Willard Spoldings order dated 9 of June 1786" and "John Spoldings order dated 1 of July 1786." The diary shows where those orders came from. Early in April of 1786, Martha had noted, "Mr Ballard Been out to purchace Loggs." Twice in the next few weeks she wrote that "the Spolldings" had brought timber into the "Crik." She made no mention of the Spoldings on June 9 or on July 1, the dates given on the orders brought to William Howard, but she did note that Ephraim had gone to Pownalboro court on one of those days and to Vassalboro to "assist Brother Moore Rais his hous" on the other.[56] Together the account book and the diary tell us how Ephraim Ballard "purchaced" logs for his sawmill. Contracting with men like the Spoldings, he paid in credit at the local stores, settling debts at court days and house-raisings, eventually balancing his own accounts with sawn boards.

Martha had a part in all this, as she noted on April 25: "Thee Spolldings brot Loggs. We had 9 men dind beside our own famely." But she did far more than support Ephraim's efforts. During that same week, she noted that a hired hand had performed an errand for her at one of the stores at the Hook, bringing home "6 galn of Rhum, 2 lb Coffee, 5 lb sugar, & some Tobacco & 1 bushl ¼ of salt from Joseph Williams for me for assisting his wife in travil with her Last Child." A few days later, she reported sending twenty-one skeins of tow yarn to Mrs. Chamberlain to weave.[57] The Howard account book tells us a great deal about the male economy of eighteenth-century Hallowell. Martha's diary shows how women and men worked together to sustain this eighteenth-century town.

The comparisons with Henry Sewall are more direct, since he, too, kept a diary. Like Cony, Sewall was a veteran of the Continental Army. He had come to Hallowell from York, Maine, in 1784, shortly after experiencing an intense religious conversion. Appointed clerk of the U.S. District Court in 1789, he was also for thirty-two years the town clerk of Hallowell and Augusta and for seventeen years the registrar of deeds for Kennebec County.[58] His clear, almost mechanically even handwriting fills the pages of town and county records. The diary he kept from 1776 to 1842 is as remarkable in its own way as Martha's (though less steady).

In April of 1789, while she was fighting the spring freshet in Hallowell, he was far away in New York City attempting to establish himself in business. His diary entry for April 23, the day she sank in the mire while stepping out of her canoe, marks the distance between her world and his. He wrote:

About 2 o'clock P.M. Genl Washington, the illustrious President of the United States, arrived in this city. He approached in a barge which was built here for his use. On his passing the Battery, a federal salute was fired, which was followed by an instantaneous display of colors from all the shipping in the harbour. On his landing, the federal salute was repeated and all the bells in the city rang peals of joy upon the glad occasion.

For Sewall this was an especially joyous moment, for he had served under Washington. "I took a stand on the roof of Mr. Rob. Hunter's house," he continued, "where I had the satisfaction of seeing once more my quondam General; now advanced to the chief magistracy of the empire, which his valour & magnanimity (under providence) protected and established under the most trying circumstances."[59]

It is not easy to bring together the heroism of Sewall's "quondam General" with the heroism of Martha Ballard as she journeyed back and forth across the Kennebec that same week. The Revolution, the ratification of the Constitution, and the election of Washington certainly affected her life (if only in providing her with grandsons named George, Samuel Adams, and DeLafayette), but the political events that inhabit so much of the foreground in Sewall's diary are only a hazy background, if that, in hers.[60] Yet the converse is also true. In fact, we can learn far more about the world of war and politics from Martha's diary than we can about domestic life from Henry's. Eight times Martha Ballard crossed the river to deliver Tabitha Sewall. Not until the fourth delivery did Henry note her presence, and then only twice after that. Nor did he once mention the fees he paid her, nor the names of the other women present, nor the complications (social and medical) that attended the births. Sewall had little to say about the women of Hallowell, including his own wife. It is Martha's diary, not his, that tells us Tabitha was a bonnet-maker.[61]

Yet it is his diary rather than Martha's that describes the symbolic importance of women in the new republic. On February 22, 1800, he helped organize a parade to commemorate the death of his former commander, General Washington. At the head, following a military escort, were "16 Misses, clad in white, with black hats & cloaks, & white scarfs," representatives of the then sixteen states in the Union. (According to a later account, based on oral tradition, the white scarfs were "fastened on the right shoulder with a black and white rosette; tied under the left arm, with long ends falling to the bottom of the dress.") Led by the young women, the memorial procession passed into the meeting house, the militia companies followed by judges, lawyers, physicians, members of the fire society, and other dignitaries, "the music playing a dead march, & a detachment from Captain Bowman's artillery firing minute guns during the whole."[62] For the young Daughters of Columbia it must have been an impressive occasion, a ritual identification of their own lives with the survival of the new nation.

Martha attended the service at the meeting house "to commemorate the Death of General George Washington." Significantly, she said nothing at all about the parade of young women, though she noted the presence of "the Lodg of Hallowell, Captain Casts Company of militia, and a larg concoarce of people." Her life had been altered by the Revolution, but her identity was unrelated to the rituals of republicanism. In 1800, she was far more concerned with the death of Nabby Andros, a neighbor's daughter, than with the demise of General Washington. Her values had been formed in an older world, in which a woman's worth was measured by her service to God and her neighbors rather than to a nebulous and distant state. For Martha, politics was what men did at town meetings—necessary perhaps, but often troublesome and divisive. Though she lived through a Revolution, she was more a colonial goodwife than a Republican Mother. Her story allows us to see what was lost, as well as what was gained, in the political, economic, and social transformations of the eighteenth and early nineteenth centuries.

To understand Martha's world we must approach it on its own terms, neither as a golden age of household productivity nor as a political void from which a later feminist consciousness emerged. Martha's diary reaches to the marrow of eighteenth-century life. The trivia that so annoyed earlier readers provide a consistent, daily record of the operation of a female-managed economy. The scandals excised by local historians provide insight into sexual behavior, marital and extramarital, in a time of tumult and change. The remarkable birth records, 814 deliveries in all, allow the first full accounting of delivery practices and of obstetrical mortality in any early American town. The family squabbles that earlier readers (and abridgers) of the diary found almost as embarrassing as the sexual references show how closely related Martha's occupation was to the life cycle of her own family, and reveal the private politics behind public issues like imprisonment for debt. The somber record of her last years provides rare evidence on the nature of aging in the pre-industrial world, and shows the pull of traditional values in an era of economic and social turmoil.

The heroism is there, too. In the last decade of her life, when the world seemed to be falling apart around her—armed settlers attacking surveyors in the woods, husbands and fathers killing themselves, and, in the case of her neighbor Captain Purrinton, his wife and children as well—Martha found the courage to continue her work. On April 4, 1812, she rode "on horseback without a pillion" to a delivery. On April 26, 1812, just a month before her death, she attended her last birth.

The structure of the diary forces us to consider midwifery in the broadest possible context, as one specialty in a larger neighborhood economy, as the most visible feature of a comprehensive and little-known system of early health care, as a mechanism of social control, a strategy for family support, and a deeply personal calling. One might wish for more detail, for more open expressions of opinion, fuller accounts of medical remedies or obstetrical complications, more candor in describing physicians or judges, and less circumspection in recording scandal, yet for all its reticence, Martha's diary is an unparalleled document in early American history. It is powerful in part because it is so difficult to use, so unyielding in its dailiness.

Someday the diary may be published. What follows is in no sense a substitute for it; it is an interpretation, a kind of exegesis. Based upon a close reading of the manuscript and of supporting records, it attempts to open out Martha's book for the twentieth-century reader. The diary does not stand alone. A serious reading requires research in a wide range of sources, from Sewall's diary to Ephraim Ballard's maps. Wills, tax lists, deeds, court records, and town-meeting minutes provide additional documentation, as do medical treatises, novels, religious tracts, and the fragmentary papers of Maine physicians. But the diary itself is central. Because few readers will have seen the original, I have transcribed ten long passages, one for each chapter. These unabridged excerpts give a truer reflection of the original than the condensation published in Nash's *History of Augusta*. In each case, the "important" material, the passage or event highlighted in the accompanying discussion, is submerged in the dense dailiness of the complete excerpt. Juxtaposing the raw diary and the interpretive essay in this way, I have hoped to remind readers of the complexity and subjectivity of historical reconstruction, to give them some sense of both the affinity and the distance between history and source.

Martha Ballard rarely used punctuation. Like most eighteenth-century diarists, she capitalized randomly, abbreviated freely, and spelled even proper names as the spirit moved, sometimes giving more than one spelling of a name, including those of her own family, in a single entry. In the transcriptions that follow I have sought to preserve the flavor of the diary without creating undue hardship for the reader, by following these guidelines:

1. I have not attempted to standardize spelling, but I have spelled out many abbreviations, including those expressed as superscripts, as in "Williams" for "Will^{ms}" or "afternoon" for "aft^n." I have also routinely substituted "the" for "ye," "this" for "ys," and "their" for "yr."

2. I have added capitals at the beginning and periods at the end of sentences or what appeared to me to be sentences.

3. I have numbered the diary entries the way she did: in the left-hand margin, with the day of the month followed by the

day of the week. (Note that until 1799 she followed the practice of the old almanacs, assigning a "dominical letter" rather than a number to Sunday and numbering the remaining days of the week from 2 to 7.)

4. I have given all marginal entries in italics, those from the right-hand margin above and those from the left-hand below the regular entry for each day.

Opening a diary for the first time is like walking into a room full of strangers. The reader is advised to enjoy the company without trying to remember every name. It might help to know, however, that there are three familiar characters in the excerpt that opens Chapter One. We have already met the "Doctor Coney" who appeared at Mrs. Shaw's house on August 22. The "Colonel Howard" who offered white rum and sugar to Martha Ballard on August 4 was William Howard, the proprietor of Fort Western. The "Capt Sewall & Lady" who watched until 4:30 a.m. with James Howard on August 10 were Henry the diarist and his wife, Tabitha. Little James, whose illness is such an important part of this section, was not William Howard's son, however, but his half brother, a child of his father's old age. James and his widowed mother, the "Mrs. Howard" who summoned Martha Ballard, lived in one side of Fort Western, William and his family in the other.[63]

Knowing this much, the reader is prepared to open Martha Ballard's book. It is August 1787. The Kennebec flows calm and blue toward the sea.

CHAPTER ONE

AUGUST 1787

"Exceeding Dangerously ill"

3   6*   Clear & very hot. I have been pulling flax. Mr Ballard Been to Savages about some hay.

4   7   Clear morn. I pulld flax till noon. A very severe shower of hail with thunder and Litning began at half after one continud near 1 hour. I hear it broke 130 pains of glass in fort western. Colonel Howard made me a present of 1 gallon white Rhum & 2 lb sugar on acount of my atendance of his family in sickness. Peter Kenny has wounded his Legg & Bled Excesivily.

5   g   Clear morn. Mr Hamlin Breakfastd here. Had some pills. I was calld at 7 O Clok to Mrs Howards to see James he being very sick with the canker Rash. Tarried all night.

6   2   I am at Mrs Howards watching with her son. Went out about day, discovered our saw mill in flames. The men at the fort went over. Found it consumd together with some plank & Bords. I tarried till Evinng. Left James Exceeding Dangerously ill. My daughter Hannah is 18 years old this day. Mrs Williams

*The first number indicates the day of the month, the second number the day of the week. Letters indicate Sundays.

here when I came home. Hannah Cool gott Mrs Norths web out at the Loome. Mr Ballard complains of a soar throat this night. He has been to take Mr gardners hors home.

7   3   Clear. I was Calld to Mrs Howards this morning for to see her son. Find him very low. Went from Mrs Howards to see Mrs Williams. Find her very unwell. Hannah Cool is there. From thence to Joseph Fosters to see her sick Children. Find Saray & Daniel very ill. Came home went to the field & got some Cold water root. Then Calld to Mr Kenydays to see Polly. Very ill with the Canker. Gave her some of the root. I gargled her throat which gave her great Ease. Returned home after dark. Mr Ballard been to Cabesy. His throat is very soar. He gargled it with my tincture. Find relief & went to bed comfortably.

8   4   Clear. I have been to see Mary Kenida. Find her much as shee was yesterday. Was at Mr McMasters. Their Children two of them very ill. The other 2 recovering. At Mr Williams also. Shee is some better. Hear James Howard is mending. Hannah Cool came home.

9   5   Clear. I workd about house forenoon. Was Calld to Mrs Howards to see James. Found him seemingly Expireing. Mrs Pollard there. We sett up. He revivd.

10   6   At Mrs Howards. Her son very sick. Capt Sewall & Lady sett up till half after 4. Then I rose. The Child seems revivd.

11   7   Calld from Mrs Howard to Mr McMasters to see their son William who is very low. Tarried there this night.

12   g   Loury. At Mr McMasters. Their son very sick. I sett up all night. Mrs Patin with me. The Child very ill indeed.

13   2   William McMaster Expird at 3 O Clock this morn. Mrs Patin & I laid out the Child. Poor mother, how Distressing her

Case, near the hour of Labour and three Children more very sick. I sett out for home. Calld at Mrs Howards. I find her son very Low. At Mr Williams. Shee very ill indeed. Now at home. It is nine O Clok morn. I feel as if I must take some rest. I find Mr Ballard is going to Pittston on Business. Dolly is beginning to weave thee hankerchiefs. Ephraim & I went to see Mrs Williams at Evining. I find her some Better.
*death of Wm McMaster**

14   3   Clear & hott. I pikt the safron. Mrs Patten here. Mr Ballard & I & all the girls attended funeral of William McMaster. Their other Children are mending. James Howard very low. I drank Tea at Mr Pollards. Calld at Mr Porters.

15   4   Clear morn. I pulld flax the fornon. Rain afternoon. I am very much fatagud. Lay on the bed & rested. The two Hannahs washing. Dolly weaving. I was called to Mrs Claton in travil at 11 O Clok Evening.

16   5   At Mr Cowens. Put Mrs Claton to Bed with a son at 3 pm. Came to Mr Kenadays to see his wife who has a sweling under her arm. Polly is mending. I returnd as far as Mr Pollards by water. Calld from there to Winthrop to Jeremy Richards wife in Travil. Arivd about 9 o Clok Evin.
Birth Mrs Clatons son

17   6   At Mr Richards. His wife Delivered of a Daughter at 10 O Clok morn. Returned as far as Mr Pollards at 12. Walked from there. Mrs Coy buryd a dafter yesterday. Mr Stanley has a dafter Dangirous. William Wicher 2 Children also.
Birth Jeremy Richard dafter

18   7   I spun some shoe thread & went to see Mrs Williams. Shee has news her Mother is very sick. Geny Huston had a Child Born the night before last. I was Calld to James Hinkly

*Italics indicate marginal entries.

to see his wife at 11 & 30 Evening. Went as far as Mr Weston by land, from thence by water. Find Mrs Hinkly very unwell.

19   g   At Mr Hinkleys. Shee remain poorly till afternoon then by remedys & other means shee got Easyer. I tarried all night.

20   2   Clear. Mr Hinkly brot me to Mr Westons. I heard there that Mrs Clatons Child departed this life yesterday & that she was thot Expireing. I went back with Mr Hinkly as far as there. Shee departed this Life about 1 pm. I asisted to Lay her out. Her infant Laid in her arms. The first such instance I ever saw & the first woman that died in Child bed which I delivered. I Came home at dusk. Find my family all Comfortable. We hear that three Children Expird in Winthrop last Saterday night. Daniel Stayd at Mr Cowens.

21   3   A rainy day. I have been at home kniting.

22   4   I atended funeral of Mrs Claton & her infant. Am Enformd that Mrs Shaw has Doctor Coney with her. I calld to see James Howard find him low. Mrs North also is sick. A thunder Shower this Evinng.

23   5   I sett out to visit Joseph Fosters Children. Met Ephraim Cowen by Brooks' Barn. Calld me to see his Dafters Polly & Nabby who are sick with the rash. Find them very ill. Gave directions. Was then Calld to Mrs Shaw who has been ill some time. Put her safe to Bed with a daughter at 10 O Clok this Evinng. Shee is finely.
Birth Mr Shaws Dafter

24   6   Calld from Shaws to James Hinklys wife in travil. Put her safe to Bed with a son at 7 O Clok this morn. Left her as well as is usual for her. Came to Mr Shaws receivd 6/8. Receivd 6/8 of Mr Hinkly also. Came to Mr Cowens. Find his dafters & Jedy ill. Claton & David came inn from Sandy river. People

well there. Arivd at home at 5 afternoon. Doctor Coneys wife
delivrd of a dafter Last Evening at 10 O Clok.
Birth James Hinkleys son

Martha Ballard was a midwife—and more. Between August 3
and 24, 1787, she performed four deliveries, answered one obstetrical false alarm, made sixteen medical calls, prepared three
bodies for burial, dispensed pills to one neighbor, harvested and
prepared herbs for another, and doctored her own husband's
sore throat. In twentieth-century terms, she was simultaneously
a midwife, nurse, physician, mortician, pharmacist, and attentive
wife. Furthermore, in the very act of recording her work, she
became a keeper of vital records, a chronicler of the medical
history of her town.

"Doctor Coney here. Took acount of Births & Deaths the year
past from my minnits," Martha wrote on January 4, 1791. Surprisingly, it is her minutes, not his data, that have survived. The
account she kept differs markedly from other eighteenth-century
medical records. The most obvious difference, of course, is that
it is a woman's record. Equally important is the way it connects
birth and death with ordinary life. Few medical histories, even
today, do that.[1]

In June of 1787, as Martha's flax blossomed in the field beyond the mill pond, scarlet fever ripened in Hallowell. She
called it the "canker rash," a common name in the eighteenth
century for a disease that combined a brilliant skin eruption with
an intensely sore, often ulcerated throat. The "Putrid Malignant
Sore Throat," a New Hampshire physician called it. We know
it as "strep," scarlet fever being one of several forms of infection
from a particular type of streptococci. Although mild in comparison with the scourges of diphtheria that had swept through
towns like Oxford earlier in the century, scarlet fever was dangerous. Martha reported five deaths in the summer of 1787, 15
percent of the canker rash cases she treated.[2]

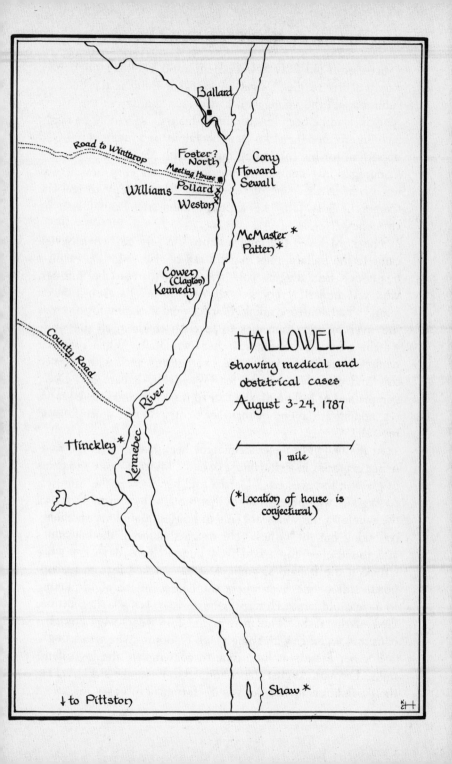

Ballard

Road to Winthrop

Foster?
North
Meeting House

Cony
Howard
Sewall

Williams
Pollard ×
Weston ×

McMaster *
Patten *

Cowen
(Clayton)
Kennedy

County Road

River

HALLOWELL
showing medical and
obstetrical cases

August 3-24, 1787

|———————————|
1 mile

Hinckley *

Kennebec

(*Location of house is
conjectural)

↓ to Pittston

Shaw *

Six-month-old Billy Sewall, Henry and Tabitha's only child, was the first to die. "What an excellent thing is the grace of submission!" the young father wrote on the day of the baby's funeral. Had he been less certain of his own salvation, he might have interpreted the sickness in his family as a judgment of God upon him for his continuing quarrel with Mr. Isaac Foster, the Congregational minister of the town. But Henry Sewall was not given to that sort of self-doubt. "How happy to feel the temper of holy Job," he wrote. "Whom the Lord loveth he chasteneth."[3]

The Lord loved the minister too. On July 28, when Sewall came to the Ballard mills to get a raft of slabs, Martha was in a neighbor's field digging cold water root to treat the minister, who was himself "very sick with the rash." By then a dozen families had someone ailing. Martha went back and forth across the river carrying remedies to feverish children, all the while watching for signs of illness in her own family. When a visiting nephew "seemed unwell," she swathed his neck with warmed tow and gave him hyssop tea. When Mr. Ballard and Dolly complained of feeling ill, she bathed their feet and brewed more tea, adding at the end of that day's entry, "I feel much fatagud my self."[4]

At the height of the epidemic, the heat that lay over the Kennebec exploded in a cloudburst of hail. "I hear it broke 130 pains of glass in fort western," Martha told her diary in the August 4 passage. Sewall noted smugly that though the storm "broke all the windows the windward side of houses, mine I saved, chiefly by taking out the sashes." He weighed some of the hailstones and found they topped half an ounce.[5] Two days later, fire struck at the Ballard sawmill. Martha watched it from the opposite side of the river where she had spent the night nursing four-year-old James Howard, whose sister, Isabella, had already died of the rash. "The men at the fort went over. Found it consumd together with some plank & Bords," she wrote.

For her there was little time to contemplate the loss of the mills. Through August she continued to nurse the sick, tracking their condition in her diary with formulaic phrases that went from "poorly" through "very ill," "very ill indeed," and "Exceeding Dangerously ill" to "seemingly Expireing" or in the opposite direction from "Dangirous" to "revived" or from "much as shee was yesterday" to "Easyer" and then "Comfortable." She recorded all the summer's events, her everyday work as well as the continuing evidence of God's chastening hand, in the same terse style. She "pulled flax," then bathed a child's cankered throat, "worked about house," then found a little boy "seemingly Expireing," picked saffron, then attended another child's funeral, drank tea, then laid out an infant in its mother's arms.

On August 11 she arrived at the McMaster house to find little William "very low." She sat with him all through the day on Sunday and into the night. At about three a.m. on Monday he died. With the help of Mrs. Patten she prepared the body for burial, then, as the neighborhood began to stir, started home, stopping in at the Howards', where James was still "very Low," and at the Williamses', where "shee" (presumably the mother) was "very ill indeed." Although Martha was exhausted by the time she reached her house, she sat down to write in her journal: "William McMaster Expird at 3 O Clock this morn. Mrs Patin & I laid out the Child. Poor mother, how Distressing her Case, near the hour of Labour and three Children more very sick."

"Poor mother." That entry contains the one burst of emotion to appear in the diary all summer. Although Mrs. McMaster was not the only woman in Hallowell to lose a child nor the only mother with two or three children suffering from the rash, something about her situation had pierced Martha's literary reserve. Perhaps the three-day vigil had brought back that summer of 1769 when she was herself "near the hour of Labour" and diphtheria flourished like witch grass in Oxford. Hannah, the daughter born in the epidemic, turned eighteen on August 6, the day the sawmill burned. Martha remembered the birthday, but for some reason, during this summer of illness, she neglected her usual remembrance of the Oxford deaths. Her daily activities were enough of a memorial.

Not all the illness in Hallowell in the summer of 1787 can be attributed to scarlet fever. There were the usual accidents on farms or in the woods; Martha poulticed a swollen foot for one of the Foster boys in early June and in August, though she wasn't called to administer aid, noted that "Peter Kenny has wounded his Legg & Bled Excesivily." There were also those "sudden strokes" that twentieth-century physicians would attribute to cardiovascular causes. On July 12, 1787, Martha reported that "a man fell down dead in the Coart hous at Pownalboro," a fate that had overcome old James Howard a few months before.[6]

Then there were the troubling deaths of Susanna Clayton and her infant. Martha had delivered the Clayton baby on August 16. The birth was uneventful, with no warning at all of the distressing news she would hear four days later as she was returning home from nursing Mrs. Hinkley, who lived in the southern part of the town opposite Bumberhook. James Hinkley had brought Martha upriver as far as Weston's landing, where she heard "that Mrs Clatons Child departed this life yesterday & that she was thot Expireing." Martha got back in the boat and went back down the river as far as the Cowen farm, where Susanna Clayton had given birth and was lying in.

She arrived in time to help with the last nursing and to lay out the baby in its mother's arms. These deaths brought no exclamation, no "Poor mother" (or "Poor husband"). The mere facts were enough to mark them as singular ("the first such instance I ever saw") and monumental ("the first woman that died in Child bed which I delivered"). Martha had seen newborn infants die, but in the more than 250 deliveries she had performed since coming to the Kennebec, no mother of hers had succumbed.[7] Susanna Clayton's death appears in the diary as an inexplicable stroke of Providence, an event as unrelated to the canker rash as fire or hail. Martha could not have known that puerperal fever and scarlet fever grew from the same invisible seed—Group A hemolytic streptococci.

No one in the eighteenth century could have related the two phenomena. Not until the 1930s did scientists unravel the mysterious epidemiology of scarlet fever. Depending upon prior exposure, the same toxin that produces a sore throat and a rash in one person may produce a sore throat, a wound infection, a mild and fleeting illness, or no symptoms at all in others. Yet all these persons can spread the infection. Scarlet fever can even be transmitted through the milk of infected cows.[8] It is not surprising, then, that Martha treated Isaac Hardin's son for an abscess as well as a rash, that Mrs. Kennedy had "a sweling under her arm" at the same time as her children were sick with the fever, or that puerperal infection and the canker rash both appeared at one house.[9] Susanna Clayton was the daughter of Ephraim Cowen, the man who summoned Martha on August 23 to treat his younger daughters, "who are sick with the rash." She had given birth on her father's farm just upriver from the Kennedys', where Martha had administered cold water tincture.[10] Susanna Clayton was the only one of Martha's obstetrical patients to die, yet other women and their babies may have been infected. Mrs. McMaster, the "poor mother" of the August 13 entry, gave birth on September 8. Her infant, whom Martha described as "very weak and low," lived only two days, and by September 23 the mother was herself so ill that Dr. Cony was summoned. He apparently recommended some sort of laxative. "Mrs Cowen & I administred remdys that Doct Coney prescribd," Martha wrote, adding that when the "physic began to operate," she left to care for another patient. Fortunately, Mrs. McMaster survived.

Focusing on the progress of an epidemic, as we have done here, obscures the fact that most of those infected eventually recovered. Billy McMaster and his newborn brother died, but his mother got better. Saray and Daniel Foster, Polly Kennedy, and the younger Cowen girls were soon up and about, and little James Howard, a child "Exceeding Dangerously ill" in August, was once again "mending" in September. At the end of one of her diary packets, Martha tallied births and deaths for the six years 1785 through 1790. In eighteenth-century terms, Hallowell was a healthy place. Its death rate averaged fifteen per thousand, about what one would find in parts of southern Asia today, but only half of that recorded for eighteenth-century seaports like Salem or Boston. Just as important, in almost every year the town had four times as many births as deaths.[11] Even in a sickly season, there was reason for hope as well as sorrow.

In western tradition, midwives have inspired fear, reverence, amusement, and disdain. They have been condemned for witchcraft, eulogized for Christian benevolence, and caricatured for bawdy humor and old wives' tales. The famous seventeenth-century English physician William Harvey dismissed the loquacious ignorance of midwives, "especially the younger and more meddlesome ones, who make a marvellous pother when they hear the woman cry out with her pains and implore assistance." Yet a popular obstetrical manual published in the same century dignified their work by arguing that Socrates's mother was a midwife and that "the Judges of old time did appoint a stipend for those women that did practice Physick well."[12]

In the early years of settlement, some American colonies did in fact provide free land, if not stipends, for midwives.[13] Yet the most famous midwife in early America is remembered for religious martyrdom rather than obstetrics. Boston ministers commended Anne Hutchinson for the "good discourse" she offered women in their "Childbirth-Travells," but when her teachings threatened to disrupt their authority, they condemned and banished her. The Puritans took their contradictions directly from the Bible. The Book of Exodus celebrates the courage of the Hebrew midwives who when told to destroy the male children of Israel "feared God, and did not as the king of Egypt commanded them." But the Apostle Paul, while acknowledging the good works of women who "relieved the afflicted," condemned those who wandered about from house to house, "speaking things which they ought not."[14]

English midwifery guides also warned against impiety and gossip. "I must tell you, it is too common a Complaint of the modest Part of Womankind, against the Women-Midwives, that they are bold, and indulge their Tongues in immodest and lascivious Speeches," warned one author who styled himself a surgeon. Another echoed the language of the Apostle in arguing that a good midwife "ought to be *Faithful* and *Silent*; always on her *Guard* to conceal those Things, which ought not to be spoken of."[15]

Samuel Richardson drew upon midwifery lore in creating the character of Mrs. Jewkes, the terrifying woman who holds the innocent Pamela captive in the novel that gave Martha Ballard's niece her name.[16] Charles Dickens exploited the same body of myth to different effect in his comic portrait of Sairey Gamp in *Martin Chuzzlewit*:

> She was a fat old woman, this Mrs. Gamp, with a husky voice and a moist eye.... She wore a very rusty black gown, rather the worse for snuff, and a shawl and bonnet to correspond.... Like most persons who have attained to great eminence in their profession, she took to hers very kindly; insomuch, that setting aside her natural predilections as a woman, she went to a lying-in or a laying-out with equal zest and relish.[17]

Martha Ballard had at least one thing in common with Sairey Gamp—she was very fond of snuff. Yet in eighteenth-century Maine, it was not necessary to set aside one's "predilections as a woman" in order to perform what Martha once called "the last ofice of friendship." Her diary tames the stereotypes and at the same time helps us to imagine the realities on which they were based. Midwives and nurses mediated the mysteries of birth, procreation, illness, and death. They touched the untouchable, handled excrement and vomit as well as milk, swaddled the dead as well as the newborn. They brewed medicines from plants and roots, and presided over neighborhood gatherings of women.

Two nineteenth-century novels by New England women focus on the homely mysteries of village healers, coming closer to Martha's diary than most English literature. Sarah Josepha Hale's *Northwood*, published in 1827, was said to have been based on her own memories of a late-eighteenth-century New

Hampshire town. Hale went out of her way to make clear that, though her gossipy healer Mrs. Watson was a fortune-teller, she was neither a witch nor a hag. No, she was "reputed one of the neatest women and best managers in the village. And many wondered how it happened that though she went abroad so much, she generally contrived to have her own work done in season, and quite as soon as her neighbors."[18]

The central character of Sarah Orne Jewett's *Country of the Pointed Firs* is also a good housewife. In the opening pages of the book, Jewett describes a "queer little garden," green with balm and southerwood, presided over by Mrs. Todd. Some of her plants "might have belonged to sacred and mystic rites . . . but now they pertained only to humble compounds brewed at intervals with molasses or vinegar or spirits." Stopping to visit Mrs. Todd at her garden fence, the local physician "would stand twirling a sweet-scented sprig in his fingers, and make suggestive jokes, perhaps about her faith in a too persistent course of thoroughwort elixir."[19]

Hale and Jewett idealized their New England villages—there is no diphtheria or canker rash in either book—yet they grounded their stories in a world Martha might have recognized. One of the central issues for her, as for Mrs. Watson, was how to get her work done at home while spending so much time with her neighbors. Her garden, though less romantic than Mrs. Todd's, also incorporated notions of healing handed down the centuries, and her diary reveals, as does Jewett's novel, the friendly distance between a "village doctor" and a "learned herbalist."

Later chapters will explore Martha Ballard's domestic economy. The remainder of this chapter will pursue Jewett's themes, reaching beneath the story of the August 1787 epidemic for clues to Martha's herbalism and to her relations with the town's other healers, male and female. Hallowell had several male physicians. In the last years of the eighteenth century, these included, in addition to Daniel Cony: Samuel Colman, who arrived at Fort Western in the 1780s; Benjamin Page, who set up practice at "the Hook" in 1791; and Benjamin Vaughan, an

Edinburgh-educated doctor and heir to the Plymouth Company claims, who settled on the Kennebec in 1796, offering himself not as a competitor but as a gentlemanly mentor to the local doctors. In addition, several physicians from neighboring towns—Obadiah Williams, James Parker, and John Hubbard—occasionally treated Hallowell patients. (Martha's brother-in-law, Stephen Barton, practiced in Vassalboro from 1775 to 1787, but spent the next decade in Oxford and died shortly after returning to Maine.)

Martha was respectful, even deferential, toward the men's work, but the world she described was sustained by women—Mrs. Woodward, Mrs. Savage, Mrs. Vose, Old Mrs. Ingraham, Sally Fletcher, Lady Cox, Hannah Cool, Merriam Pollard, and dozens of others, the midwives, nurses, afternurses, servants, watchers, housewives, sisters, and mothers of Hallowell. The diary even mentions an itinerant "Negro woman doctor," who briefly appeared in the town in 1793. Female practitioners specialized in obstetrics but also in the general care of women and children, in the treatment of minor illnesses, skin rashes, and burns, and in nursing.[20] Since more than two-thirds of the population of Hallowell was either female or under the age of ten, since most illnesses were "minor," at least at their onset, and since nurses were required even when doctors were consulted, Martha and her peers were in constant motion.

When Martha went to the field to dig cold water root on August 7, 1787, she was acting out the primary ritual of her practice, the gathering of remedies from the earth. Although she purchased imported laxatives and a few rare ingredients (myrrh, "dragon's blood," galbanum, spermaceta, and camphor) from Dr. Colman, she was fundamentally an herbalist. "Harvested saffron," "Cut the sage," "Gatherd seeds & Cammomile mint & hysop": such entries scattered throughout the diary tie her practice to English botanic medicine.[21] Three-quarters of the herbs in the diary appear in Nicholas Culpeper's *The Complete Herbal*, published in London in 1649 (and reprinted many times in America). Almost all can be found in E. Smith, *The Compleat Housewife: OR, Accomplish'd Gentlewoman's Companion*, an early eighteenth-century English compendium.[22] Martha administered herbs internally as teas, decoctions, syrups, pills, clisters, vapors, and smoke and externally in poultices, plasters, blisters, cataplasms, baths, ointments, and salves. "Find Dolly lame. Poultist her foot with sorril roasted," she wrote on October 11, 1787, and when Theophilus Hamlin came to the house feeling ill, she "made a bed by the fire & gave him some catnip tea." Presumably the warm drink and the fire would cure his cold by contraries. Sympathetic medicine also worked. When Martha used saffron to treat jaundice in newborn children, she was following the ancient doctrine of "signatures," the yellow plant being the obvious cure for yellow skin.[23]

There is no evidence in the diary of direct borrowing—she never mentions reading a medical book—yet Martha's remedies obviously rested on a long accumulation of English experience. When she used dock root to treat "the itch" or applied burdock leaves to an aching shoulder, she was following Culpeper's practice whether she knew it or not. More difficult to determine is her attitude toward the astrological concepts that informed his herbal. She may not have been aware, when she gave a newly delivered woman feverfew tea, that "Venus has commended this herb to succour her sisters."[24] But her quiet statement on July 26, 1788, "Dog Days begin this day," associates her with such ancient traditions. Since antiquity, the period in late summer when the Dog Star became visible in the heavens had been linked with illness. The almanacs, which had determined the very form of her diary, perpetuated such beliefs. In fact she had good reason for believing that dog days brought illness, for she consistently made more medical calls in late summer than at any other time of the year. Whether her neighbors were actually more sickly during August and September or simply more disposed to ask for help, we do not know.[25]

Her remedies are even closer to those in Smith's book. Like the English woman, she accepted the medicinal as well as the culinary virtues of common garden plants like green beans, onions, and currants and of household staples like vinegar, soap, and flour. On October 14, 1790, for example, she was "Calld in great hast to see Mrs Hamlin who was in a fitt. I walkt there, applyd Vinagar to her Lips, temples, & hands & onions to her feet & shee revivd." And on another day, "Mr Ballard is unwell Has taken some soap pills."[26] There is hardly an ingredient in Martha's diary that does not appear in Smith's compendium. Both women routinely used camomile, sage, and tansy. Both employed cantharides and Elixir Proprietas. Both concocted that most famous of all cures—chicken soup. Yet compared to Smith's receipts, Martha's medicines *are* "simples." The most elaborate remedies described in her diary employ at most three or four plants. In contrast, Smith's recipe for "Lady Hewet's water" contains seventy-five separate plants, seeds, roots, and powders. Nor is there any hint in Martha's diary of the zoological inventiveness that led Smith to recommend setting a bottle of newly made cordial "into a hill of ants for amonth," to combine goose dung, ground snails, and earthworms with saffron, or to wet bandages in the spawn of frogs.[27]

There is no indication that Martha used cow or sheep dung poultices, as did some New England healers, but she did believe in the curative powers of urine, as on September 23, 1786: "I was Calld Early this morn to see Lidia Savage who was very ill. Gave her some urin & honney & some Liquoris & put a plaster to her stomach. Went up afternoon. Find her Relievd."[28] She also accepted the pervasive notion that cat's blood had healing power. When a Mr. Davis came to the house suffering from shingles, she "bled a Catt & applid the Blood which gave him Relief."[29] She didn't say whether the cat she bled was pure black without a single white hair, as insisted on by some rural practitioners, but she did record one cure that clearly included the kind of detail which folklorists associate with magic. When her niece was suffering from consumption and all other remedies seemed to have failed, she tried a practice "recommended as very Beneficial by Mr Amos Page." The young woman rose from her sickbed "about an hour by sun in the morn went out & milkt the last milk from the cow into her mouth & swallowed it."[30]

Even within Martha's practice, however, such cures were exotic. Herbs, wild as well as cultivated, were the true foundation of her practice. She wilted fresh burdock leaves in alcohol to apply to sore muscles, crushed comfrey for a poultice, added melilot (a kind of sweet clover) to hog's grease for an ointment, boiled agrimony, plantain, and Solomon's-seal into a syrup, perhaps following an old method that called for reducing the liquid by half, straining this decoction through a woolen cloth, then adding sugar to simmer to the thickness of new honey.[31] Most of the wild plants she used had familiar English names, whether they were escapees from early gardens or New World varieties of Old World herbs. There are few distinctly American names in the diary.[32] She mentioned poulticing wounds with basswood, a plant not found in the English herbals, but when she and a grandchild "went to the field and got sennakle root," they may have been gathering a local variety of sanicle, a plant Culpeper credited with the power to "stay women's courses" rather than Seneca snakeroot, an American native. (A later entry does, however, refer to "a decoction of snake root & saffron.")[33]

The root Martha dug during the scarlet fever outbreak of 1787 was an indigenous plant, however.[34] According to a legend recorded in Rochester, Massachusetts (where Martha's brother, Jonathan Moore, was minister), a local man got cold water root from "an Indian named Nathan Hope" during an epidemic of diphtheria in 1754. Eventually it "developed into a wild herb common to all the region."[35] Martha may have heard about the root and its uses from Jonathan. Just as likely, the plant had always been "common to all the region," in Oxford as in Rochester, though Indians may well have taught the first settlers how to use it. Its association with diphtheria is suggestive. If Martha had learned about cold water root in Oxford, it is difficult to imagine her preparing her sore throat "tincture" in Hallowell in 1787 without thinking of her own children and the epidemic of 1769.

The eclecticism of English medicine encouraged the incorporation of Indian or African cures. An aura of mystery, if not magic, attached to persons who were otherwise stigmatized in colonial society. Smith's recipe book included "The Negro

Ceasars Cure for Poison" reprinted from *The Carolina Gazette*, and Hallowell patients sought out the "Negro doctoress" during her brief sojourn in the town. (Mrs. Parker even borrowed Martha's horse "to go and see the negro woman doctor.")[36] There is no evidence that Martha was curious about Indian or Afro-American medicine, however. She noted the presence of the black healer but did not bother to record—or perhaps even to learn—her name. Such attitudes help to explain why her remedies are closer to Culpeper's seventeenth-century herbal than to James Thacher's *The American New Dispensatory*, an early-nine-teenth-century pharmacopoeia that attempted to evaluate and incorporate Indian physic.[37]

In eighteenth-century terms, Martha was an "empiric," a person unconcerned with theory. Her own descriptions demonstrate that her most immediate concern was to make her patients feel better. "I gargled her throat which gave her great Ease," she wrote after preparing the cold water tincture for Polly Kennedy. The same remedy helped her own husband "find relief." The two phrases appear in the diary repeatedly. When one patient was suffering from dysentery, she "administerd a Clister which gave her Eas." When Hannah was ill, she gave her camomile and camphor and sent her "into a warm Bed. I hope it will relieve her." Beyond the physical comfort of hot tea or a soothing syrup was the comfort of an idea: Nature offered solutions to its own problems. Remedies for illness could be found in the earth, in the animal world, and in the human body itself. When Martha Ballard applied warmed tow to the neck of little Gideon Barton, she was doing more than assuaging pain, she was confirming the essential order of the universe.[38]

It would be a mistake, however, to describe her as a fringe practitioner preserving ancient English remedies lost to professional medicine. Most of the therapies we now associate with "folk" medicine were still a part of academic practice in her time. One of the Kennebec's best-educated physicians, Dr. Moses Appleton of Waterville, Maine, left a manuscript collection of recipes that included, in addition to erudite Latin formulas, a cure for dropsy compounded of parsley roots, horseradish, and mustard seed and a treatment for "the malignant sore throat" that called for applying carded black wool wet with vinegar and salt, ear to ear.[39] The most explicit reference to astrological (or, more precisely, lunar concepts) in Hallowell comes from Daniel Cony's family record. One Cony child, the doctor reported, was born on "the first day of the week, the first hour of the day and the first day of the moon," another on "the 5th day of the week, and the eleventh day of the moon."[40]

The technological simplicity of early medicine meant that male doctors offered little that wasn't also available to female practitioners. The stethoscope had not yet been invented. Watches with second hands were so rare that no one as yet counted the pulse (though in a general way most practitioners observed it). Nor did the clinical thermometer exist. Even the simple technique of percussion (tapping the chest and abdomen to discover fluid or masses) was yet to come.[41] A probate inventory taken after the death of Dr. Obadiah Williams included "A Quantity of Medicine & Bottles together with the Amputating Instruments." That brief sentence pretty well describes the medical arsenal available to an eighteenth-century physician—drugs and a few rudimentary surgical instruments. Williams *did* use his instruments. On March 5, 1789, Martha wrote, "There was a young man had his Legg Cutt off at Stirling by Doctor Williams. He brot it to Doctor Coneys & disected it." Martha didn't observe this dissection, but she did attend four autopsies in the course of her career, carefully recording the results in her diary (see Chapter Seven). That fact alone suggests that Hallowell's physicians considered midwives part of the broader medical community, a subordinate part no doubt (doctors dissected; midwives observed), but a part nonetheless.[42]

Midwives and doctors shared a common commitment to what Martha would have called "pukes" and "purges." Early medicine merged the two meanings of *physic* as "knowledge of the human body" and as "a cathartic or purge." Because all parts of the body were related, laxatives treated the entire organism, not simply the gastrointestinal system. "I was calld to see Lidia White who has had fitts this day, but had left her before I arivd.

Shee complaind of an opresion at her stomach and pain in her head, I left her a portion of senna and manna." Senna and manna were mild cathartics. When her daughter Dolly was ill, Martha noted that a combination of "Senna & manna with annis seed and Rhubarb . . . opperated kindly." She even used manna with infants.[43]

The emphasis on expulsion derived from the ancient theory of humors, the notion that health was achieved by a proper balance of the four bodily fluids—blood, phlegm, choler (or yellow bile), and melancholy (or black bile). When Martha wrote that Lidia Bisbe was "sick of a bilious disorder" or that Mr. Savage's daughter "puked up a considerable quantity of phlegm," she was expressing that world view, as was Moses Appleton when he recommended black wool "to keep back the humors."[44] The notion of humors had been greatly enlarged by the end of the eighteenth century, however. As one encyclopedist explained it, the term "HUMOUR, in medicine, is applied to any juice, or fluid part of the body, as the chyle, blood, milk, fat, serum." Writing of a "Child who had a bad humour on the head and feet," Martha was using the generic term.[45] Yet the importance of fluids, their condition, quantity, and means of expulsion, remained central.

When Martha noted that a lanced abscess "discharged a Large quantity," she may have been commenting positively on the effectiveness of the cure rather than negatively on the seriousness of the infection. Festering was also a method by which the body expelled troublesome humors. The application of "blisters," local irritants designed to raise a watery discharge, imitated another of nature's remedies. "Calld to see Mrs Weston. Shee being very unwell I aplyd a Blister, Batht her feet, put on a Back Plaster," she wrote on November 14, 1786.[46] Baths and plasters, like blisters, treated internal problems with external remedies. They cooled or heated, soothed or excited, according to temperature or contents.

Although theoretically a person might lose too much fluid, most remedies seem to have promoted expulsion. Constipation was dangerous, as was an unhealthy accumulation of bile. Menstruation, too, could prove troublesome if "obstructed," which is why Martha Ballard "prescribed the use of particullar herbs" for a young woman named Genny Cool. What those herbs were and whether they might also have been employed to induce abortion, we do not know. There is no mention in the diary of savine, the best-known English abortifacient, though Martha did gather tansy, a plant associated in some herbals with abortion. In her practice, however, tansy seems to have been employed as an *anthelmintic*, that is, an agent for expelling worms. (Intestinal parasites were common, as we shall see in Chapter Seven.)[47]

The most dramatic of the humoral therapies was bloodletting, a remedy Martha seldom mentioned and never employed. Along the Kennebec, the lancet was clearly a male implement. "Mr Stodard seemd to have more feavour," Martha wrote on February 16, 1795. "Doctor Page Bled him in the feet this morning. He has been bled, phisicked and Blistered before in his sickness." She noted that Dr. Colman bled one of her patients in the late stages of pregnancy, though it seems not to have been at her request. One home medical guide recommended bleeding "for pregnant women about the sixth, seventh or eighth month, who are plethoric and full of blood," but added that "children bear purging better than bleeding." Martha seems to have preferred purging for both groups. One of the few descriptions of bleeding in the diary involved a horse. "Mr Ballard went to Mr Browns for his mare," Martha wrote. "Had her Bled in the mouth. She bled all the way home & Continued to bleed an hour or two after coming home. We at length filld the incision with fur & it Ceast."[48]

That male physicians leaned toward dramatic therapies was only to be expected. Their status—and fees—required as much. Dr. Cony used rhubarb and senna, as Martha did, but he also prescribed calomel, the mercurial compound Benjamin Rush called the "Samson of medicine." One historian concludes that in large doses calomel "did indeed slay great numbers of Philistines." The impressive salivation that followed its violent purging was in fact one of the symptoms of mercury poisoning.[49] Hallowell's physicians also used laudanum (a liquid opiate), purple fox-glove (digitalis), and the bark (quinine), therapies associated with a newer "solidistic" overlay on humoral therapy.

Unlike humoral therapy, which concentrated on bodily juices, solidistic medicine loosely followed Newtonian physics in attempting to regulate the mechanical properties of "solids," usually defined as blood vessels and nerves. Doctors employed tonics to stimulate bodily force, sedatives to induce relaxation. In practical terms, humoral and solidistic approaches overlapped, since both tried to control respiration, perspiration, and excretion.[50] Thus, a physician might employ cathartics either to "flush out unbalanced humors" or "to relax the abnormal tensions which had constricted his patients' intestinal fibers." For the patient, the consequences were the same.[51]

Whether or not Martha understood solidistic theory, she rejected some of the remedies associated with it. (Here she departed from Smith, who added laudanum to cough syrup and recommended "jesuits bark" for ague and fever.) Martha was dismayed when Dr. Page attempted to use laudanum in childbirth (see Chapter Five). She was also convinced that the use of "the bark" contributed to the death of Mrs. Pillsbury during another outbreak of the canker rash. Martha had been nursing the woman ("The Lady was in a fine persperation the most of the night") when an urgent call from another family took her away. When she returned two days later, she discovered Mrs. Pillsbury "in a kind of delirium; her raising had ceast and her mouth very dry. They informed me shee had been much so through the night past. It is my opinion the use of the Bark was in some measure the Cause." Martha seems to have interpreted the "raising"—that is, the rash itself—as a useful phenomenon, an indication that the sweating had been successful in expelling the ill humor. She did not say who had suggested the bark, though it may have been one of Hallowell's physicians. A published pamphlet on the "Putrid Malignant Sore Throat" argued that "the tonic as well as antiseptic powers of the Bark must render it a medicine not only proper, but highly necessary in this disorder."[52] Martha disagreed. She seemed pleased when

"Old Mrs Kenny Came and advised to giv her a syrrip of vinegar & onions and a decoction of Gold thread and shumake Berries. It was done and shee seemd revivd." The revival was temporary. Mrs. Pillsbury died.[53]

Martha Ballard's dislike of the new remedies did not stem from a general mistrust of physicians—she was quite willing to call them to her own family in serious illness—but from an innate conservatism. She was most comfortable with the doctors when their ideas reinforced the old therapies and the long-standing social arrangements. When one of her own daughters fell ill, she walked to Dr. Colman's to get senna and manna, and when "shee soon became dilarious we sent for Doct Cony who approvd of what I had done—advised me to continue my medisin till it had opperation. She was siesd with a severe Puking soon."[54] In the world of eighteenth-century medicine, midwives and doctors sought—and generally achieved—similar results.

In twentieth-century terms, the ability to prescribe and dispense medicine made Martha a physician, while practical knowledge of gargles, bandages, poultices, and clisters, as well as a willingness to give extended care, defined her as a nurse. In her world, such distinctions made little sense. She sometimes acted under the direction of a doctor. More frequently she acted alone, or with the assistance of other women. It is no accident that Daniel Cony's name appears only at the end of the August entries you have read. When scarlet fever broke out in Hallowell in June, he was in Boston attending the General Court. He was back on July 19 to deliver his sister, Susanna Church, of a son, but was soon off to the interior settlements on business.[55] On July 26 Martha was summoned to *his* house to treat a servant, Peggy Cool, who was suffering from the rash.

Ironically, when the doctor did show up in the diary it was in the context of delivery. Martha's quiet entry for August 22, 1787—"Mrs Shaw has Doctor Coney with her"—suggests more than a casual interest in the doctor's whereabouts. Mrs.

Shaw was then nine months pregnant, and perhaps in labor, or at least experiencing some of the signs of imminent delivery, when the doctor was called. Why she called him we do not know. Perhaps she was worried about possible complications, perhaps frightened by the recent death of Susanna Clayton. As it turned out, Martha delivered the baby. "Put [Mrs. Shaw] safe to Bed with a daughter at 10 O Clok this Evinng," she wrote on August 23, and on the next day added drily, "Doctor Coneys wife delivrd of a dafter Last Evng at 10 O Clok"—that is, at exactly the same time as Mrs. Shaw. It would seem, then, that if his own child hadn't intervened, Cony might have delivered the Shaw baby. Still, whatever her original intent, Mrs. Shaw was apparently satisfied with her midwife: two years and one month later, she summoned Martha again.

Daniel Cony's presence at the bedside of Mrs. Shaw suggests that reverberations of the new scientific obstetrics had reached the Kennebec. Unlike the surgeons of an earlier era, who were called only in dire emergencies, usually to dismember and extract an irretrievably lost fetus, late-eighteenth-century physicians considered it appropriate to officiate at an ordinary delivery. Yet most of them limited their obstetrical practice to eight or ten cases a year, whatever they could conveniently fit into their practice. Significantly, Martha performed at least one delivery for Cony's sister Susanna Church and another for his sister-in-law Susanna Brooks.[56]

Kennebec doctors were not only part-time midwives, they were part-time physicians. Daniel Cony was a land proprietor and politician as well as a physician—perhaps a politician most of all. A Portland associate complained after a visit, "He had not been in the house half an hour before my head turned round like a top with politics. I would not live in the same house with . . . Daniel Coney for ten thousand pounds per annum."[57] Yet Cony knew how to use one specialty to reinforce another. In a letter to a Massachusetts congressman, he neatly dismissed his political opponents by offering a "chemical" analysis of their behavior. Such men, he wrote, "abound with 'vitriolic acid' with a certain proportion of 'aqua regia.' "[58] He became a fellow of the Massachusetts Medical Society not so much because of his medical skills, which by the standards of his own time were ordinary, but because his election to the legislature put him in frequent contact with the gentlemen who ran such associations. He was also a justice of the peace, as were fellow doctors Moses Appleton of Waterville and Obadiah Williams of Vassalboro.[59]

Samuel Colman, Hallowell's second physician, was less involved in public affairs, but almost as distracted. Still single when Martha's diary opened, he lived for a time at Fort Western, eventually opening a store where he sold scythes, hoes, and tobacco, as well as pharmaceuticals.[60] Waterville's Harvard-educated doctor, Moses Appleton, had similar interests: a single entry in his daybook lists debits for an almanac, a half-yard of calico, and a gallon of vinegar; prescriptions for senna, camphor, and an unguent; and fees for sewing and dressing a wound.[61] Dr. Page was more single-minded than the others (and the one most disposed to intrude on Martha's territory, as we shall see in Chapter Five), but he too doubled as a trader. In 1796 he advertised "a very handsome assortment of Drugs and Medicine, among which is a variety of patent articles," including "Andersons, Hoopers, and Lockyers Pills, Bateman's Drops, Turlington's Balsam of Life, and Daffy's Elixer." He also sold smelling bottles, nutmegs, British oil, and cephalic snuff.[62] That the region's most earnest prescriber of imported drugs was also its major supplier was a conflict of interest no one seems to have noticed—or at any rate been troubled by.

The most successful Kennebec physicians were Federalist gentlemen, organizers of agricultural societies, builders of bridges, incorporators of banks. Their involvement in medical organizations was part of this general commitment to voluntarism and civic betterment. (Colman, Appleton, and Page, like Cony, were members of the Massachusetts Medical Society, as well as promoters of regional organization.)[63] They were successful practitioners not only because of their acknowledged status as learned gentlemen but because the town's other healers chose to defer to them in hard cases. There were no laws to prevent Martha or her neighbors from administering calomel or drawing blood, yet they did not do so. By custom and training, bonesetting, tooth-pulling, bloodletting, and the administration of strong drugs were reserved for self-identified male doctors. When Martha "misplaced a Bone in the Great toe of my right foot," she was grateful for the help of Dr. Page, but most of the time she and her family got along quite well without him.[64] It was no doubt part of the men's strength that they supported neighborhood practitioners, offering chemical compounds and venesection only when tansy failed. Even their inaccessiblity was an advantage, a sign of their importance in the larger world.

Male physicians are easily identified in town records and, even in Martha's diary, by the title "Doctor." No local woman can be discovered in that way. Hallowell's female healers move in and out of sickrooms unannounced, as though their presence there were the most ordinary thing in the world—as it was. Historians have been dimly aware of this broad-based work, yet they have had difficulty defining it. Physicians who joined medical societies and adopted an occupational title can be recognized as professionals. But what shall we call the women? Persons who perambulated their neighborhoods hardly practiced *domestic medicine*, nor does *folk medicine* accurately describe the differences between them and male professionals. Other commonly employed categories are equally misleading. *Popular medicine* conveys the ferment of the nineteenth century, with its competing sects of herbalists, homeopaths, and hydropaths, but obscures the cooperative, if hierarchical, arrangements of eighteenth-century practice. *Lay medicine* connotes the lack of formal organization in female practice, but fails to suggest its complexity. A better label is *social medicine*, borrowing from the now familiar concept of social childbirth.[65]

Professionals sought to be distinguished from the community they served (hence the need for the title "Doctor"). Social healers, on the other hand, were so closely identified with their public we can hardly find them. Professionals cultivated regional or cosmopolitan networks, joining occupational associations. Social healers developed personal affiliations and built local reputations. Professional training, even if only in the form of apprenticeship, was institutional, fixed in place and time. Social learning was incremental, a slow build-up of seemingly casual experience.

Florence Nightingale's famous statement that "every woman is a nurse"[66] captures one element of social practice—its grounding in common duties—but it fails to convey the specialization that occurred even among female healers. Caring for the sick was a universal female role, yet several women in every community stood out from the others for the breadth and depth of their commitment. They went farther, stayed longer, and did more than their neighbors. It would be a serious mistake to see Martha Ballard as a singular character, an unusual woman who somehow transcended the domestic sphere to become an acknowledged specialist among her neighbors. She *was* an important healer, and without question the busiest midwife in Hallowell during the most active years of her practice, but she was one among many women with acknowledged medical skills. Furthermore, her strengths were sustained by a much larger group of casual helpers.

In the August 1787 passage, she named five persons who in some way shared the care of the sick during the canker rash epidemic. Hannah Cool was at the Williams house on August 7, Mrs. Pollard at Mrs. Howard's on August 9, "Capt Sewall & Lady" at the same house on August 10, and Mrs. Patten at the McMasters' on August 12. Although each person appears in the diary in much the same way, there were important differences between them.

Hannah Cool was living with Martha Ballard in the summer of 1787. She actually appears twice in the August segment: on August 6, when she "gott Mrs Norths web [of cloth] out at the Loome," and on August 7–8, when she was at Mrs. Williams's, where there was illness. Whether she was doing nursing or housework at the Williamses' we do not know, nor does it matter. In this period the occupations of nurse and maidservant overlapped. Hannah was probably a sister of Mrs. Williams, whose maiden name was Cool. Like most single women, she moved frequently between the homes of relatives and neighbors, performing whatever sort of work was needed. (Her sister Peggy died of the canker rash at Dr. Cony's, where she was also a servant.) Hannah was older and more skilled than most household helpers, however, capable of warping a loom as well as nursing. Living with Martha Ballard, she may have picked up some medical skills as well. In the spring of 1788, when Joseph Williams was critically ill and "went to Dr Williams to be Doctered," Martha noted that "Hannah Cool went to be his nurse."[67]

"Mrs Patin" and "Capt Sewall & Lady" were married folks fulfilling basic obligations of neighborliness. Sally Patten was the wife of Thomas Patten, the blacksmith. Martha Ballard had delivered their first child a year earlier. "Capt Sewall & Lady" were, of course, Henry and Tabitha, whom we have met before. In watching with little James Howard, they were returning the help they had received earlier that month when their own child was dying of the rash. Their obligation wasn't to Mrs. Howard in particular—she had been too busy nursing Isabella to have helped with the care of Billy—but to the common fund of neighborliness that sustained families in illness. Neither poverty nor wealth nor a recent bereavement excused one from helping where there was need. Henry's presence at the Howard house was somewhat unusual, however. Usually men sat with men, women with women or children. There is no entry in his diary for August 10, though he did note on August 14 that "Mr. McMaster buried a son, in his 4 year. It died of a canker rash."[68]

Merriam Pollard represents a different form of social healing. The wife of Amos Pollard, the tavern and ferry keeper, she was the mother of at least seven children, most of whom were grown. She represents a group of perhaps ten women who served as general care-givers to the town. A frequent watcher at bedsides and attendant at deliveries, she was particularly skilled in laying out the dead. She was not a midwife, at least not yet, though she did deliver one child when Martha was delayed.

Seeing Hannah Cool, Sally Patten, and Merriam Pollard at a single instant, an experienced observer could easily have distinguished between them. One was simply a servant, the second a helpful neighbor, the third a recognized healer. The tasks that they performed were also distinct. Given the dominant therapies, Hannah Cool must have spent her time brewing tea, spooning gruel, and emptying chamber pots. Sally Patten had the most passive role. As a watcher, her job was to sit beside the patient, offering comfort or conversation, noting alterations in breathing, color, or demeanor, summoning help when it was needed. Merriam Pollard had more specialized tasks to perform. Like Martha Ballard, she knew how to swab swollen tonsils, change dressings, apply plasters, and administer a clister. She was also prepared, when the time came, to wash and dress the dead, easing eyelids and limbs into sleeplike dignity.

Yet each of these women could, over the course of a lifetime, encompass all these roles—and others besides. The social construction of healing allowed the free flow of information from one level to another. Administering a doctor's or midwife's prescription, feeding the fire under a bubbling syrup, shifting and turning a sister in bed, helping with the stitching on a child's shroud, watching, listening, soaking in attitudes of hand and eye, susceptible helpers found their callings. Martha Ballard probably started out very much like Hannah Cool, doing nursing as well as housework for her relatives or neighbors. Once married, she would have had less freedom for general nursing but more scope for perfecting the gardening and cookery that were so closely associated with herbal medicine. As a young matron she no doubt watched with sick neighbors and assisted at births, until in midlife, with her own child-rearing responsibilities diminished, she became a more frequent helper and eventually a healer and midwife. Midwives were the best paid of all the female healers, not only because they officiated at births, but because they encompassed more skills, broader experience, longer memory. "Mrs Patin with me." The social base of female medicine is apparent in the very casualness of the entry. A midwife was the most visible and experienced person in a community of healers who shared her perspective, her obligations, her training, and her labor.

There is no need to sentimentalize this "female world of love and ritual," to use Carroll Smith-Rosenberg's now famous phrase,[69] to understand that birth, illness, and death wove Hallowell's female community together. Consider two bland sentences from the entry for August 14, the day of William McMaster's funeral: "Mrs Patten here," and then later, "I drank Tea at Mr Pollards." Both visits—Sally Patten to Martha Ballard and Martha Ballard to Merriam Pollard—were continuations of meetings at the bedsides of gravely ill children. Recall that Merriam Pollard had "sett up" with Martha at the Howards' two days earlier, and that Sally Patten, who had come to the McMasters' to watch with Billy, had helped Martha prepare his body for burial. Since Merriam and Martha were old friends, their tea party is easily explained, but what of Sally Patten's visit to Martha? What led her up the path toward the mills? Presumably she had crossed the river to attend Billy McMaster's funeral, but Martha's house was three-quarters of a mile beyond the meeting house. Her visit cannot have been a casual one. Was it a practical errand that brought her there, or a deeper need to consolidate the experience she had shared a few hours before? Even for Martha, the nightwatch had been profoundly disturbing. What must it have meant for a young mother still new to the circle of matrons?

Eighteenth-century physicians, like twentieth-century historians, had difficulty distinguishing one social healer from another, yet they understood the power of their presence. William Smellie, who wrote an important English obstetrical treatise, displayed an acute consciousness of the female audience for any medical intervention. Cautioning young physicians not to do anything to make "the gossips uneasy," he explained the importance of reassuring both the patient and her "friends."[70] The word "friends" appears repeatedly in doctors' writings from the mid-eighteenth to the mid-nineteenth century. The label is a telling one: female healers identified with the patients they served in ways that male physicians could not.

Little wonder that some physicians actively resented their presence. William Buchan, author of the immensely popular *Do-*

mestic Medicine, published in London in 1769 and reprinted at least fifteen times in America, deplored the social dimensions of traditional childbirth:

> We cannot help taking notice of that ridiculous custom which still prevails in some parts of the country, of collecting a number of women together on such occasions. These, instead of being useful serve only to crowd the house, and obstruct the necessary attendants. Besides they hurt the patient with their noise: and often, by their untimely and impertinent advice, do much mischief.[71]

Here, as elsewhere, Buchan distinguished between what was "necessary" and what was merely customary. Like other eighteenth-century reformers, he wanted to simplify as well as improve contemporary practice.[72] Groups of women cluttered a room with their ideas as well as their bodies.

In rural America, however, Buchan's ideas were just another strand in the dominant eclecticism.[73] Doctors might mistrust the ubiquitous friends, but they could not easily do without them. Female healers performed the messy, time-consuming tasks of healing and at the same time validated male practice. As long as both sets of practitioners shared the same basic assumptions, and as long as physicians were content with the income available from part-time practice, there could be little competition between them.

This chapter has approached the August 1787 passage (and individual entries within it) from several angles—as a case study of an epidemic, as an exemplar of Martha's therapies, and as a window into the broader system of social medicine. The same passage connects Martha's work with the most visible relic of Kennebec history—Fort Western, and its most prominent family—the Howards.

William Howard made his brief appearance in the August entries on August 4, the day of the hailstorm. "I hear it broke

130 pains of glass in fort western," Martha wrote, adding in the very next sentence, "Colonel Howard made me a present of 1 gallon white Rhum & 2 lb sugar on acount of my atendance of his family in sickness." Presumably, it was Howard who brought the news of the damage. The storm was impressive. So was the Fort. Breaking 130 panes was quite possible, since there may have been as many as twenty windows on the river side of the building alone, each containing from sixteen to twenty panes of glass.

The old Fort, because of its size, had been subdivided sometime after the end of the military era, creating two separate domestic spaces, its 100-foot front giving the appearance of two Georgian houses set end to end. When Martha's diary opened, Colonel William Howard lived in the north half of the Fort with his wife, their five children, and his wife's mother and unmarried sister (Martha's diary calls them "the Old Lady" and "Mrs Betsy"). The Colonel's father, Esquire James Howard, lived in the south side with his second wife, Susanna Cony, their two young children, and one or more of her children by her first marriage. John Howard, the judge's oldest son, may also have lived at the Fort, though Martha's diary does not mention him. As the town history explains it, John accidentally shot another soldier while on a military expedition to Canada in 1759, mistaking him for a bear. Although no one blamed him, he "sank into hopeless insanity," living out his life at the Fort, "gentle and inoffensive, but possessed of immense imaginary wealth." [74] That Dr. Samuel Colman lived at the Fort in the 1780s may have had something to do with John's condition, though we cannot know.

Even without the complications of mental illness, the old Fort rippled with tension. James Howard had astonished the town and dismayed his children by marrying, at the age of seventy-nine, a widow younger than his own youngest son. What was worse, the new Mrs. Howard had tangled the family inheritance by giving birth to a daughter, Isabella, and two years after that a son. The old man insulted his first family by naming the boy James, even though he already had a grandson of the same

name, one of William's children. In August of 1785 all three
James Howards lived at the Fort—the judge, his fourteen-year-
old grandson, and his two-year-old son.[75] Two years later only
the youngest James survived, and he lay "Exceeding Dangerously ill."

The Colonel's payment to Martha Ballard on August 4 ties
together the canker rash epidemic of 1787 with several earlier
episodes of illness at the Fort. Ironically, a citadel that never
faced an attack by French or Indians succumbed in the 1780s
to two invisible enemies, canker rash and the bilious fever.
Between September 11, 1785, and September 2, 1787, twenty-
one inhabitants of the Fort fell ill. Eight died.

The bilious fever was a severe gastrointestinal infection. As
one early medical guide explained, "When a continual, remit-
ting, or intermitting fever is accompanied with a frequent or
copious evacuation of bile, either by vomit or stool, the fever is
denominated bilious." Presumed to be most common toward the
end of the summer, the bilious fever might be accompanied by
the "bloody flux," or dysentery.[76] It first struck on the south
side of the Fort. On September 11, 1785, Martha "went to Esquire Howards to take care of two servants who were sick of a
feaver." One died, though Martha helped to nurse other members of the family back to health.

A month later, the fever (Henry Sewall identified it as "bilious") moved to the north half of the Fort. On October 11,
Martha was "calld in great haste to Colonel Howards. His wife
& five children very sick," Samuel was bleeding.

She "tarried all night" on October 11 and again on October
13, went home for a few hours, and returned for another vigil.
"Took a sleep forepart of the night," she wrote. "Sit up after
two in Mrs Howard's Chamber." She slept at home on October
15, but came back the next day. "Tarried all night & watcht.
Mrs Howard had a sever feaver fitt." After helping to "moove
the sick [and] dres their Blisters," she "returnd home at noone."
That ended her first period of intense nursing at the Fort. She
had spent parts of three days and nights with Esquire Howard's
family, seven with the Colonel's.

During the next few weeks Martha was busy with other matters. When she was unable to cross the river after returning from a delivery on October 22 during a heavy storm, she "tarried at Colonel Howards. Very kindly Entertaind. His famely very sick yet." Who did the entertaining we do not know—perhaps Mistress Betsy. There was no need for Martha to remain at the Fort, since another of Hallowell's nurses was by then attending the family. "Mrs Woodward went home from Colonel Howards accompanied by Mr Pollard," Martha wrote on October 26. Two days later she "was herself called back to the Colonel's" to asist Mrs Pollard & Bisby to Lay out the Corps of his wife just now Deceast. His Children yet very sick." One child died on November 6, but by then the rest of the family were "mending." The bilious fever had at last retreated.

Exactly one year later, canker rash reached the Fort. The assault was so sudden that the first hint of its presence is Martha's entry for December 14, 1786: "I went to meeting & was Calld to Colonel Howards to ascist Mrs Pollard to Lay out his son James. Mrs Betsy, Polly & Jack are very sick. I watcht. Doctor Colman unwel." By the time Martha returned home, she was ill herself, suffering from the "colick," but she took time to write in her diary: "I left Polly mending. Mrs Betsy & Jack very sick. Mrs Fairwel stays with them this night." Mrs. Farwell, like Mrs. Betsy, was an aunt to the children, a sister of their dead mother. Although Martha's own illness kept her away from the Fort for the next few days, she collected intelligence from her neighbors: "I hear that Esquire Howard had an ill turn last night," and later, "Georg Brown here this Evening. Enforms they are very sick at Colonel Howards. It is a sickly Time in this Town." Jack Howard died on December 17. Martha went to attend the funeral, "but by reason of Esquire Howards being taken very ill I was Calld in there & tarried with them till about 9 O Clok."

In a little more than a year, William Howard had lost his wife, a daughter, and two sons. His father would be next. The old man recovered from the December illness and seemed well on May 13 when Martha was called to the south side of the Fort to treat his wife. His death the next day was so surprising that

Martha turned her diary on edge, beginning her entry on the perpendicular: "A suden Change. He was well and dead in about three hours." A new siege of the Fort had begun. Martha stayed all night with Mrs. Howard, who "complaind of a soar throat," the first hint that the canker rash had returned. When Martha went to Henry Sewall's on June 10 to "see his Child sick with the rash," she also stopped at the Fort to see little Ibbee Howard. She found her "mending," but ten days later she was "siesd with a relaps of the rash." At about four a.m. on June 23, she succumbed. "I came home after Mrs Woodward, Savage & I had Laid out her Corps," Martha wrote. Six members of the Howard family had now died. Little wonder that the neighbors fluttered about young James when he too began to show symptoms of the rash.

All of this forms the background to that curious entry for August 4 describing the storm and the broken windows at Fort Western, then Colonel Howard's payment of white rum and sugar. It had been two years since Martha nursed the Colonel's family during the bilious fever, ten months since she had ministered to the canker rash victims. Now, in the midst of a sickness that had already taken one of his father's young heirs and was threatening another, and on the very day a storm assaulted the family bastion, William Howard thought to settle accounts with Martha Ballard.

Her description of the transaction is ambiguous. The Colonel's present was both a gift and a payment, an unsolicited offering and compensation for services performed. In other circumstances Martha was capable of recording her medical accounts with blunt exactness, as when "Isaac Hardin had 1 oz. of Burn Salv. Price 1/ which is not paid."[77] But she was also disposed to "forgive" accounts when she thought circumstances warranted. Perhaps the loss of a wife and three children was such a circumstance.[78] The Colonel's gift may have been a gracious acknowledgment of *her* gift. On both sides, the offering was generous. A gallon of rum and two pounds of sugar sold for ten to twelve shillings in 1787 (the equivalent of six visits by a physician), and this was only a partial payment. On September 2, a Sunday, Martha stopped in at the Colonel's. "The old Lady is unwell with a Cold," she wrote, adding, "Mrs Betsy made me a present of 2 Caps & a ribbon."

That same day Martha stopped at the south side of the Fort "to see Mrs Howards son. Find him mending." With that entry her account of the siege of Fort Western closed. James Howard survived the canker rash. He died at sea at the age of twenty-four, leaving a daughter, Isabella, whose heirs were still suing William's heirs forty years later.

Fort Western still stands. Now an Augusta city museum, it is a monument to the military ambitions of the Plymouth Company and the commercial achievements of the Howard family. Thanks to Martha's diary, it is also a reminder of the frailty of human life and the forgotten ministrations of Kennebec women.

In November 1787 Ephraim Ballard and his son Jonathan met with John Jones's agent and agreed to rebuild the mills that had burned on August 6. The actual work didn't begin until the following June. Martha was again weeding flax when the workmen came to begin the framing. On July 7, "We raised the saw mill Fraim. Mr. Marsh & Thomas were hurt. The Business otherways done with safety." She was relieved that though "there were a vast concorse of men and children, not many [were] disguised with Licquor. The young folks had a dance at evening, dispersed at midnight." The young folks in the Ballard family now included Martha's niece Parthenia Barton. Hannah Cool had left.

The men continued to work on the mill through the summer and fall, raising the "flume" on August 30, the "giers" on October 25, and "the slip" in late November. Meanwhile Martha nursed Mrs. Foster, the minister's wife, through a breast infection, harvested herbs, delivered babies, and helped Hannah and Dolly with the yarn. As the anniversary of the fire approached she was again pulling flax. Last year's crop, harvested in the epidemic and combed and spun into thread through the winter and spring, lay whitening in the sun.

CHAPTER TWO

SEPTEMBER 1788

"warpt a piece"

3   4   *I have been at home.*
Clear. I have been at home. Old Mr Smily here. Mrs Savage
warpt a piece here.

4   5   *I have been at home. Death of Mrs Springer & O Neall
Executed*
Clear. Mr Ballard gone to Mr James Pages on public business.
Jonathan & Taylor went to see the Execution of Oneal. I have
been at home. The Girls washt. Gilbreath sleeps here. The wife
of old Mr Springer Departed this Life this morn.

5   6   *Death of Doctor Colmans infant. I was there. Dolly finisht her
web 44 1/2 yds. Beriah Ingerham had a son born.*
Clear. I went to Doct Colmans at 1 hour pm. His Child Expird
at 4. I put on the grave Cloaths and tarried till 7. Colo North
and Lady there. I found Mrs Williams & Mrs Harris here at my
return. I sett up till very late to finish Hannahs stockins.

6   7   *Funeral of Mrs Springer & Doctor Colmans infant. I attended
the latter.*
Clear. I attended funeral of Doctor Colmans infant. Calld at Mrs

Williams. Find her very sick. The Doctor gave her a puke. I tarried all night.

7   E   *Hannah is gone to Son Towns with Sherebiah*
Clear. I came home. Left Mrs Williams very ill. I slept some & went there again at Evin. Mrs Pollard & others there. Charlotte & Polly Cool there. Parthena watches. The Reverend Mr Moore preacht.

8   2   *I was at Widow Williams*
Cloudy & Cool. I went to see Mrs Williams. Spent the afternoon. Left her more Comfortable. My girls washt. Mr Fillbrooks here this Eving. Mr Gill returnd from Winthrop.

9   3   *Town Meeting. I have been at home. Mrs Savage here.*
Clear day. Thee Town Mett to hear Reverend Mr Fosters Proposals but did not except them. Dolly & Parthena went to see Mrs Hamlin. Mrs Savage here. Shee has spun 40 double skeins for me since April 15th and had 2 Bushl of ashes & some phisic for James, & Dolly wove her 7 yds of Diaper. I let her have 1 skein of lining warp. The whole is 6/ X.

10   4   *I was at Wido Willimss. Voce here. Clarisa Barton is 18 years old this Day.*
Clear. Mr Voce & Parmer Laying Shingles on our house. We Brewed. I went to see wido Williams. Shee is Better. Dolly winding the warp for Check.

11   5   *I have been at home. Cyrus is 32 years old.*
Cloudy part of the day. Cyrus is gone to Gardners mill. He is 32 years old this day. I have been at home. Dolly warpt a piece for Mrs Pollard of 39 yards.

12   6   *At home.*
Clear. Dolly warpt & drawd in a piece for Check. Laid 45 yds. I have been at home knitting. Mrs Harris here at Eving.

13   7   *Mr Voce & son here shingleing the house. I have been at wido*
Williamss
Clear & pleasant. We spread the diaper out for whitening. I
was at wido Williamss. Shee is some Better. Dolly sleeps with
her.

14   E   *I was at meeting & at Wido Williams*
Clear & pleasant. I attended worship in public. Nathaniel Norcross desird prayers, he being sick with a feavor. Revd Mr Foster Delivered two Exelent Discoarses from Psalm 90 & 12 vers.

15   2   *At home. Receivd Letters from Brother Barton & Collins Moore*
of Sept 7th & 5th.
Clear. Mr Ballard gone to Mr Carrs on public business. I have
been at home. My girls washt. We receivd a Letter from Brother
Collins which informs that Sister Nabby was thought at the
point of death & our other Friends were well. Jonathan is gone
to Son Towns.

16   3   *At home. I was Calld to Eliab Shaws in the night.*
Cloudy. I have been at home. Am not so well as I could wish.
Mrs Savage, Wido Williams & Mrs Harris here at Evin. The
girls went to Mr Craggs. Jonathan is returned.

17   4   *At Shaws. Mr Learned Came here. Brogt me a Letter from*
Sister Waters of the 12th instant. David Fletcher a daughter Born
I was Calld between 12 & 1 hour morn to Eliab Shaws wife in
travil. Shee was safe delivd at the 11th [hour] of a fine Daughter.
I left them Cleverly & returnd at 4 pm. Mr Hains Learned Came
here. He left home Last wednesday. I receivd a Letter by him
from Sister Waters dated at Boston. Mr. Ballard is gone to the
hook. Taylor Came here this day.
Birth of Eliab Shaws Daughter. Receivd fee October 22, 1792 by
Ephraim.

Historians sometimes refer to the structure of relations in a community as a "social web." For eighteenth-century Hallowell, the metaphor is apt. In Martha's vocabulary a "web" was a quantity of thread woven—or about to be woven—in a single piece, as on September 5, 1788, when "Dolly finisht her web 44 1/2 yds."[1] Most textile entries in the diary document a personal relationship as well as a process:

"Polly [Savage] wound & warpt & I drawd in Mrs Williams webb"

"Hannah began to weave Cyrus' web"

"Dolly finisht Mrs Porters webb"

"Mrs Welch [or Hamlin or Child or Pollard or Densmore or Savage] here this day to warp a webb"[2]

In an economy characterized by family production, Martha not only employed her daughters, Hannah and Dolly, and her nieces, Pamela and Parthenia, but a succession of hired helpers like Hannah Cool and Polly Savage. She relied on married neighbors like Jane Welch or Hannah Hamlin to help her inexperienced girls warp the loom, the girls in turn weaving for other families in town. Though she grew her own flax, all the cotton she spun, and until 1790 the wool as well, was gotten in trade with neighbors. The production of cloth wove a social web.

The image can be extended. Imagine a breadth of checkered linen of the sort Dolly "warpt & drawd in" on September 12, 1788, half the threads of bleached linen, the other half "coloured Blue." If Dolly alternated bands of dyed and undyed yarn on the warp in a regular pattern, white stripe following blue stripe, then filled in the weft in the same way, alternately spooling both bleached yarn and blue, the resulting pattern would be a checkerboard of three distinct hues. Where white thread crossed white thread, the squares would be uncolored, where blue crossed blue the squares would be a deep indigo, where white crossed blue or blue crossed white the result would be a lighter, mixed tone, the whole forming the familiar pattern of plain woven "check" even today. Think of the white threads as women's activities, the blue as men's, then imagine the resulting social web. Clearly, some activities in an eighteenth-century town brought men and women together. Others defined their separateness.

September 4, 1787: "Mr Ballard gone to Mr James Pages on public business. . . . I have been at home. The Girls washt." Any account of gender definition in early America must begin with just such a contrast. Public business belonged to men, housework to women. In the past twenty years, that notion of "separate spheres" has shaped women's history. For many, the essential inquiry has been when and how women moved beyond the confining circle of domestic concerns into the larger world. Some have argued that the American Revolution connected women's private activities to the public sphere by publicizing their contributions to domestic manufacturing and stimulating a new appreciation of their roles as wives and mothers. Others believe it was women's activities in voluntary societies in the early nineteenth century that first gave them an identity within and beyond the household.[3]

Martha's diary complicates both arguments without challenging the evidence upon which they are based. There were no visible female organizations in Hallowell in the late eighteenth century, nor is there any evidence that Martha's identity was affected by republican ideology. The diary makes quite clear that men *did* monopolize public business, that households *were* formally patriarchal, and that women *did* uncritically assume that houses and even babies belonged to men and that the proper way to identify a married woman was by reference to her husband, as in "the wife of old Mr Springer Departed this Life this morn." Yet it also shows a complex web of social and economic exchange that engaged women beyond the household. Women in eighteenth-century Hallowell had no political life, but they did have a community life. The base of that community life was a gender division of labor that gave them responsibility for particular tasks, products, and forms of trade.

"Clear day. Thee Town Mett," Martha began her entry for September 9, 1788, adding in the margin, "I have been at home." There was no irony in the juxtaposition of those state-

ments. In political terms "thee Town" was an indigo square.
When Ephraim Ballard (who was serving as selectman and
town clerk in 1788) issued the warrant summoning the "free-
holders and other Inhabitants of the Town of Hallowell qualified
to vote" to the meeting house, he was addressing the adult male
population.[4] The men had much to talk about on September 9.
As Ephraim reported it in the official minutes, a "paper signed
by the Reverend Isaac Foster containing some terms which he
proposed for a dismission, had two several Readings."[5] That
Martha cared about that business is certain ("Thee Town Mett
to hear Revd Mr Fosters Proposals but did not except them,"
she wrote), but she had more to do than sit home waiting for
Ephraim to bring the news. Her full diary entry for September
9 restores women to a history that might otherwise bleach their
lives into anonymity:

> Dolly & Parthena went to see Mrs Hamlin. Mrs Savage
> here. Shee has spun 40 double skeins for me since April
> 15th and had 2 Bushl of ashes & some phisic for James, &
> Dolly wove her 7 yds of Diaper. I let her have 1 skein of
> lining [linen] warp. The whole is 6/ X.

While the men of Hallowell were at the meeting house con-
ducting public business, Martha and her neighbor were completing some private business of their own.

There was nothing new in such behavior. New England
women had long been engaged in barter and trade. The skein
of linen warp that Martha gave Mrs. Savage on September 9
symbolizes the household production that characterized pre-
industrial life, the neighborly trade that made such production
possible, and the gender division of labor that assured women
a place in economic life.[6] There is a striking congruence between
the Hallowell textile economy and the system of social medicine
described in Chapter One. Spinning, like nursing, was a universal female occupation, a "domestic" duty, integrated into a complex system of neighborly exchange. In both realms, training
was communal and cumulative, work was cooperative, even

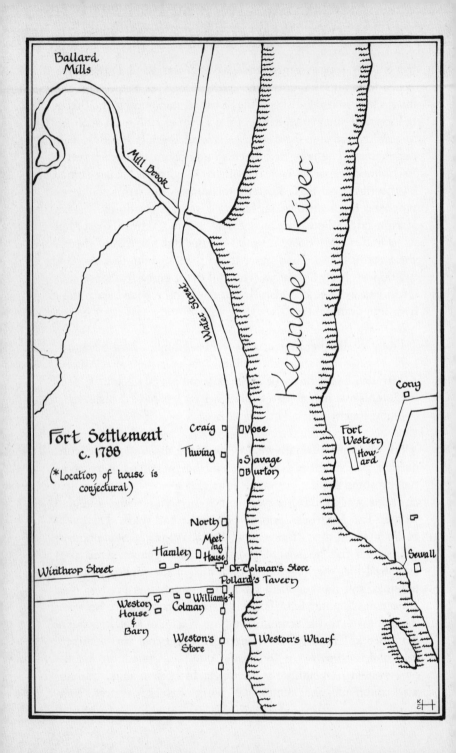

Ballard
Mills

Mill Brook

Kennebec River

Water Street

Fort Settlement
c. 1788

(*Location of house is
conjectural)

Craig   Vose

Thwing   Savage
          Burton

Cony

Fort
Western

How-
ard

North

Hamlen   Meet-
         ing
         House

Winthrop Street

Dr. Colman's Store

Pollard's Tavern

Sewall

Weston
House
&
Barn

Colman   Williams*

Weston's
Store

Weston's Wharf

though performed in private households, and the products remained in the local economy. The most experienced weavers, all of them women, extended the skills of their female neighbors in much the same way midwives extended the abilities of nurses and watchers. Men broke flax, sheared sheep, and performed other supportive services (just as they fetched and transported midwives and sat up with their male neighbors), but women had primary responsibility for the production of cloth. As in medicine, elite males connected the Kennebec with the Atlantic, importing finished cloth and raw cotton from Britain and the West Indies, commodities that women transformed into usable products.[7]

A closer look at textile production in the Ballard family helps us to see the complexity of this system. When Martha's diary opened in 1785, Hannah and Dolly already knew how to operate the great woolen wheel and the smaller flax wheel that the family owned. In the next two years they produced hundreds of skeins of cotton, wool, linen, and tow thread, most of which their mother carried to others to weave.[8] In May of 1787, the family began assembling the equipment needed for weaving. Cyrus brought home "the bars & other utensils for weaving" on May 19, 1787, and a few days later his father spent part of a day "fixing the loom." Martha did her part by combing flax, "doubling yarn for the harness," and "quilling," while her husband fetched a kettle from the Savage house for "boiling a Linning warp."[9] Dorcas Pollard warped the loom for the first time on May 25 and Hannah Cool "set the webb to work." These two young women helped to instruct Hannah Ballard, who was responsible for the web of forty yards that came out of the loom on July 4. On July 5, in preparation for the next round of weaving, Martha went to Mrs. Savage's to borrow a "sleigh" (an implement for controlling the pattern of a weave). Unfortunately, Mrs. Williams had already taken the one she wanted. Two weeks later she was successful in getting another from Merriam Pollard.[10]

Although Hannah and Dolly learned to weave check, diaper, huckaback, worsted, dimity, woolen "shurting," towels, blankets, "rag coverlids," and lawn handkerchiefs, as well as "plain cloth," the exchanges with neighbors continued. Merriam Pollard continued to "instruct Dolly about her weaving" until the girls were able to return some of her services in kind, as on September 11, 1788: "Dolly warpt a piece for Mrs Pollard of 39 yards." Trading fiber and yarn, borrowing tools and kettles, the Ballards contributed to their own self-sufficiency and strengthened their bonds with their neighbors. The intricacy of the textile network is suggested in a diary entry for April 20, 1790: "Cyrus borrowed a 40 sleigh of the widdow Coburn for Dolly to weav a piece for Benjamin Porter."[11]

That mother, father, daughters, and at least one son were all involved in setting up the weaving operation supports Ruth Schwartz Cowan's point that in early America "men and women had to work in tandem in order to undertake any single life-sustaining chore."[12] On closer examination, however, what is most striking about the Ballard economy is the independence of men's and women's labors, not only in production but in management and utilization of resources. "Mr Savage made the irons for our Loome," Martha wrote on May 21, 1787. "I paid him 4 shillings in cash." After all, Martha was willing to bake bread or mend packs for Ephraim's surveying journeys; that he was willing to sow flax and set up the loom for her is hardly surprising. This is the kind of cooperativeness one might expect of family members. That either activity was part of a fully integrated family economy seems far-fetched. There were really two family economies in the Ballard household, one managed by Martha, the other by Ephraim.

It is no accident that Martha's midwifery practice accelerated at exactly the same time as her daughters began to weave. Freedom from childbearing was one prerequisite for a midwife's work. A secure supply of household help was another. An entry for October 26, 1789, puts it succinctly: "My girls spun 23 double skeins & wove 27 1/2 yds last weak & did the houswork besides." By expanding textile production, Martha provided household help for herself and an occupation for her girls. She was not the sort of woman to turn her daughters into household drudges, even if she could afford to. Hannah and Dolly needed skills to sustain their future families as well as ways to contribute to their own support in the present. Weaving was the perfect solution: It could be accomplished at home. It could be coordinated with other chores. It produced many of the items —bedsheets, ticking, blankets, towels, and coverlets—the girls would need in their future homes.

An alternate solution would have been to keep the mother at home and send the daughters out. This was what Martha's younger sister Dorothy Barton was forced to do. Perhaps "forced" is too strong a word. Living for a while outside one's own family was a kind of education for young women in this period—Hannah Ballard, for example, spent eight months in Oxford in 1789 living with her "Aunt Waters" and other relatives. Still, economic necessity seems to have played some part in the Bartons' case. Dorothy gave birth to six daughters before a son survived, a fact that may account for the difficulty her husband had in establishing a farm in Maine.[13] Stephen and Dorothy Barton returned to Oxford in 1788, leaving their oldest daughters behind. Clarissa and Pamela had both spent some time with Martha Ballard, Pamela none too happily. "Pamela has spunn 5 skeins of Linning this weak & Been to Winthrop," Martha wrote drily in May of 1787. Pamela's sister Parthenia was a more satisfactory worker. She arrived on May 26, 1788, and, with occasional periods away working for other families, remained until her marriage in November of 1792. It was perhaps her presence that allowed Hannah to go to Oxford.[14]

We have already seen how a family mode of production encompassed wide-reaching exchanges with neighbors. Hallowell women exchanged daughters the way they exchanged kettles and sleighs, though as the girls grew older they themselves were responsible for negotiating their own terms and collecting their own wages. In slack times a woman might willingly part with her helpers, calling them home again when needed. Martha combined the long-term help of her daughters and niece with short-term help from other women. Married daughters were also integrated into this network of exchange. When Lucy

Towne suffered a "broken breast" after the birth of her fifth child, Martha dispatched Dolly to Winslow. Later Parthenia spent more than a month nursing Lucy during another postpartum crisis. Conversely, when Hannah had her first baby, Lucy sent her current helper (her sister-in-law Betsy Barton) to nurse her.[15]

In addition to family workers, Martha utilized the short-term help of neighbors. Between 1785 and 1800, thirty-nine young women lived and worked for some period in the Ballard house; almost all were the daughters of local men in the middle range of the town's tax lists. In contrast to other parts of America, there were no slaves in Hallowell in the late eighteenth century, and few indentured servants.[16] The vast majority of household helpers in Hallowell were single "girls" between the ages of fifteen and twenty-five, young women who fully expected to become mistresses of their own houses. Two of Martha's helpers, Polly Savage and Sarah Neal, had babies born out of wedlock, and two, Betsy Barton and Jane Welch, were widows, but these were the exceptions. The only married woman employed in Martha's house was Beulah Prince, a free black. The vast majority of Hallowell helpers were single women who alternated work at home with work "abroad," spending a week or two spinning at a neighbor's house, going home to help with the harvest, moving on to a sister's house where there was illness, going back to the first house or to another to spin or wash.

Such a shuffling and reshuffling of workers was part of the larger system of neighborly exchange that sustained male as well as female economies in this period. Cyrus went "to Gardners mill" to work on September 11, 1788, because the family mills were still silent; when the mills were restored he would work once more at home. But though the fire had temporarily disrupted the male side of the family economy, it had not disturbed the women's work. Understanding that helps to explain an event that would otherwise be puzzling: in the months following the burning of the sawmill, the Ballards remodeled and improved their house. Certainly Ephraim had a significant income as a surveyor and Martha's midwifery practice was growing, yet it seems incomprehensible that the Ballards would make capital improvements in the house at the very time they faced the task of rebuilding the mills. Incomprehensible, unless we realize that the house was every bit as much a workplace as the sawmill, and that plastering and closing in the upstairs chambers would provide more room for weaving. In earlier years the girls had moved their beds into the unfinished upstairs chambers in the spring, bringing them back down into the lower rooms in autumn. Now they would have bedrooms year round, and additional space to work.[17]

Theophilus Hamlin "Laid a floar" in the west chamber in October and in the east chamber in November. He also made improvements to the two lower rooms, finishing his carpentry work on December 22, when he "maid a Book Caise & put it up in the East room." Hamlin's work probably settled an unpaid debt for board. Three years before he had arrived at the Ballard house from Oxford, bringing letters from the Moore relatives and news of old acquaintances. He had spent at least a month there, helping Cyrus run the mill on one April night and on another getting out of bed with the other men to secure drifting logs. He was not an employee of the mills, however, but an independent tradesman eager to establish a place in the town. Boarding with the Ballards was a preliminary step to establishing his own household, which he did on July 16, 1788, when he brought his bride, Hannah Rockwood, from Oxford to set up housekeeping in the neighborhood near the meeting house.[18]

On September 9, 1788, the day of the town meeting, while Martha and Mrs. Savage were settling accounts, Dolly Ballard and her cousin Parthenia "went to see Mrs Hamlin." The girls had first gone calling on July 27. Their September visit may also have been a social call, though Hannah Hamlin, like her husband, was soon participating in the neighborhood economy. "Mrs. Hamlin wound and warpt a piece here," Martha wrote on November 4, and again on December 8 and December 15. The precise nature of these exchanges is not clear. Hannah may have been setting up the loom for the Ballard girls, or she may have been borrowing the Ballards' equipment to do her own work.

Perhaps both factors were involved. As a young housewife, she
had neither space nor resources to fully employ a loom; warping
one web for the Ballards allowed her to warp another for herself.

Medicine and textiles are but two strands of a broad and
largely invisible local economy managed by women. Housewives traded goods and labor, employed their own and their
neighbors' daughters, and reckoned accounts independently of
their husbands. Although men owned houses ("I went to *Mr*
Densmores to have a gown tried on"), women collected their
own rewards ("I gave *Mrs* Densmore 1/6 for doing my
gown").[19] Once in a while an entry documents the integration
of male and female accounts, as when Martha went to the Hussey house on September 30, 1789, and "had 6 lb of sheeps wool
of the old Lady which is to go towards what they owe Mr
Ballard."[20] Such entries are rare, however. Most of the time,
Martha's and Ephraim's accounts were harmoniously separate,
he trading lumber with landowners and merchants, she bartering
cabbages and textiles with their wives or settling store or midwifery accounts with the men themselves. On November 10,
1789, she wrote: "Borrowed 6 lb & 13 oz of muttun of Mr
Andrews & receivd Candles I Lent him; I have since paid for
the muttun in Baking." And on January 16, 1787: "Mrs Weston
& I setled all Between Shee & I, viz for 3 quarts of Brandy I
had the 9th instant, for ginger spice pepper & Butter on her
part, 2 Days work of Dolly 2/, & 2 pr Due to me before & 12
Cabbage heads @ 4/ which shee had 9th inst." (Nathaniel Weston was a local merchant who ran a sloop in the coastal trade.
Since he was frequently away, his wife probably kept store as
well as household accounts.)

Brandy, ginger, spice, and pepper were of course part of the
mercantile trade, but the cabbages Martha gave Mrs. Weston
and the candles she "lent" Mr. Andrews were also a part of the
Kennebec economy. Female trade was interwoven with the mercantile economy and with the "family economies" of particular
households, but it was not subsumed by either. The two and a
half pumpkins Mrs. Woodward brought to Martha's house on

September 24, 1789, represented economic interdependence as well as friendship. A month later, Mrs. Woodward would comb seven pounds of wool for Martha, wool Martha had gotten from Mrs. Cummings in August or from Old Lady Hussey in September or from Cyrus, who had bought 14 1/2 pounds of wool "on Board Danes vesel" on September 29.[21] In a young and growing town, there were few resources that couldn't be turned to advantage, Martha's oven, for example. The house the Ballards rented from John Jones may have been cramped and unfinished, but it did have a bake oven, something many chimneys in the neighborhood lacked. Mrs. Forbes, Mrs. Savage, Mrs. Williams, and Mrs. Vose all baked in it from time to time.

Female exchanges weave in and out of the diary almost imperceptibly:

"A piece of Check for an apron" from Mrs. Fletcher; "3 lb of flax" to Mrs. Densmore.

"5 lb of Poark" from Mrs. Pollard; "1 1/2 bushel ashes" to Mrs. Brown.

The spinning of "16 skein of Linnen yarn" from Mrs. Savage; a "back plaster" to Mrs. Weston.

"7 lb of Butter" from Mrs. Cummings; "1 lb of hoggs lard" to Mrs. Bolton.

"1/2 peck potatoes to plant" from Mrs. Woodward; "soap pills" to Mrs. Hamlin.

Yarn "coloured Blue" from Mrs. Porter; "1 ounce salve" to Mrs. Edson.

"400 plants" from Mrs. Bolton; "2 lb Tow" to Mrs. Welch.[22]

Such entries represent a minimal record of Martha's economic exchanges with her neighbors. Most transactions never made it into the diary. On June 21, 1787, for example, she reported that Merriam Pollard had "sent home 5 lb of poark which shee Borrowed 12 of April 1786," but the entry for April 12 says simply, "I went to Mr Williams. Mrs Pollard came home with me." Much of the diary can be reduced to just such a simple grammar of coming and going:

"I went to Mr Westons" (or "Pollards" or "Howards" or "Husseys" or "Fosters").

"Mrs Savage [or Densmore or Burton or Hamlin or Woodward] came here."

Such entries are a kind of outline describing *where* and with *whom* but not always *what* Martha Ballard did. In the September 9 reckoning with Mrs. Savage, for example, she listed five different commodities or services that had apparently been exchanged in the past six months, yet only one of those products, some yarn "Brot home" on May 9, appears in any of the diary references to the Savage family during that period. The typical entry reads: "Mrs. Savage here" or "Mr Savage his wife & Polly drank tea." When and how the ashes, the medicine, the diaper, or the linen warp changed hands we do not know. Nor do the five items indicated in this reckoning represent all the transactions with the Savages that summer. Separate entries imply additional exchanges of products or services.[23]

Some of the missing transactions may have been recorded on fugitive scraps of paper or in chalk on a wall. Many were probably never written down at all. At the local level, and particularly among women, New England was still primarily a memory economy. Even among merchants as sophisticated as the Howards, written accounts were sometimes incomplete. Sometime after 1799, for instance, William Howard and his sister-in-law Margaret added a marginal note to a Kennebec deed saying they believed that when Back Lot #1 changed hands in 1779 the purchaser had offered notes of hand payable in corn even though no compensation had been mentioned in writing.[24]

Evidence of female trade seldom appears in official records, and when it does the incongruity between the legal language and the actual events is almost comic. In September of 1781, for example, Ephraim Ballard, who was then serving as a constable, was sent to attach the "goods or person" of Susanna Howard (James and Ibbee's mother) to ensure her appearance at a Lincoln County court. Her neighbor Nathaniel Hersey was suing her, claiming that "on divers days & times" she did "with force & arms milk one Hundred and fifty Quarts of . . . milk (of the value of Forty Shilling) from a certain Cow the Property of the said Nathaniel."[25] From the language of the summons one might imagine Mistress Howard climbing over the fence at night, armed with a dagger or pistol, to extract the contraband milk. Clearly what was at stake here was an unsettled debt accumulated over a very long period. Mr. (or Mrs.) Hersey had been supplying the milk itself or the use of a cow (a not uncommon arrangement). Apparently the debits had grown too heavy on Mrs. Howard's side of the fence or a squabble of some sort had broken the chain of trust. Such occurrences were rare, however. Most of the time pumpkins, ashes, flax, and quarts of milk changed hands silently. We do not know why Martha Ballard recorded two settlements in one year with Mrs. Savage and none with Mrs. Woodward, whose exchanges seem just as steady and almost as substantial. Perhaps some neighbors had shorter memories—or tempers—than others.

Martha reckoned with her household helpers as well as her neighbors, although only a few detailed accounts survive. One, dated March 31, 1791, appears on a blank page in the middle of January 1790. It begins: "Due to Ephraim Ballard on settlement with Parthena Barton," though it is clearly in Martha's handwriting. Martha also recorded her final accounting with Pamela Barton on July 21, 1787. It opens with the ominous statement, "Shee has lost 1 months time or rather workt for her self since shee came here & had 10 yards Cloth at 2/8 per yard." After subtracting lawn for an apron and leather and the making of a pair of shoes, Pamela was debtor to her aunt for one shilling seven pence.

Pamela probably learned some of her most useful skills in Martha's household. Late in the nineteenth century, her daughter recalled that though her mother "never went to school only six weeks after her father moved from Oxford," she was "very good at figures—could reckon up a web to weave in her head when I should be obliged to take a slate and cipher it.[26] For Pamela, as for most women born in the eighteenth century, spinning, weaving, and trading were the best education available. Martha went further than most in keeping written accounts.

Bound into the diary at the end of 1795 are two slim pieces

of paper giving amounts "paid out" in 1795 and 1796. Whether she kept similar lists in other years we do not know. Yet the 1795–1796 accounts are no more complete than the diary itself. Even when taken together, the two sources leave much unexplained. The account for November 10, 1795, for example, reads: "To Mr Dickman for spirit and sugar, 8 [shillings]." The diary entry for the same day says, "I went to see Mrs Dickman. Find her and infant Cleverly. Receivd 12/." Was the eight shillings debited in the first account part of or in addition to the twelve shillings credited in the diary? And did Martha settle with *Mr.* or *Mrs.* Dickman?

The 1795–1796 lists record some but not all of Martha's purchases at the stores. An account for September 7, 1795, fills in the diary entry for that day ("I went to the stores at the Hook") by recording explicit purchases of ribbon, muslin, pins, lace, tape, and silk from Timothy Page and Moses Sewall. But there is no account for April 22, 1795, when the diary tells us she "calld at the most of the stores" at the Hook and "bot 28 lb rice and an ounce turnip seed of Captain Fillebrown, Cost 8/3."

Scattered entries suggest that the lists were an effort to get some measure of control over cash expenditures. Under June 19, 1795, for example, Martha wrote: "Suky Kenady Cash 2/8." In the diary, she explained, "Sucy Keneda brot home 8 skeins Lining yarn for which I paid by 1 peck flax seed 1/6, Cash 2/8." A November 14 account lists a payment of six shillings to another servant, Sarah Neal. Presumably this, too, was in cash. Although the diary entry for the same day makes no mention of Neal, it does suggest where the six shillings may have come from: "Mr Greely here at night with his oxen. He has paid me for him self and oxen Cash 9/ and brot me 1 gallon molasses and 1 lb Coffee." Why Martha recorded one transaction in the diary and the other on a separate sheet, we do not know.

Even for her, it was probably difficult to balance such accounts. Yet she made the effort. Following the 1795–1796 lists is a summary of amounts "received" and "paid" in the years 1794, 1795, 1796, and 1797. These totals, however, don't represent all of her exchanges, but only those reflected in the separate accounts. On the average, she took in twenty pounds annually and expended eighteen. Her expenses varied more than her receipts, going from a low of just over fourteen pounds in 1795 to over twenty pounds in 1797, the one year in which she did not show a substantial surplus. Her attempt to rationalize accounts for these years may represent a new effort during a time of unusual stress (see Chapter Six) or an ongoing practice for which no other evidence survives.

Martha's record-keeping seems disordered and inconsistent because her economic life encompassed such a wide range of behaviors. She "bought," "borrowed," and "traded" goods; received "gifts," "presents," "rewards," "payments," and "fees"; dealt in flax, bread, and molasses as well as in cash; "reckoned" and "made settlement" with her neighbors and sometimes "forgave" (or forgot) their debts. Within this jacquardian weave, her midwifery accounts stand out for their consistency and completeness. Although it is not always clear *when* and *what* Martha was paid, *that* she was paid can easily be discovered. This may have been a consequence of the cultural significance of midwifery as well as the importance of such income to her own economy. In 1782, Jacob Bailey, a Tory refugee from the Kennebec, characterized the classical Yankee farmer as a person "able with his own industry to make a comfortable living, besides discharging his tax-bill, paying the midwife, and providing a plentiful and greasy dinner on Thanksgiving sufficient to feast an hundred ploughmen."[27] Midwifery bills were not quite equivalent to tax bills, but Martha's diary suggests there was a code of honor that required full, if not always prompt, payment.

Consider the entry for September 17, 1788, in the diary segment that begins this chapter. On that day, Martha delivered Eliab Shaw's wife of a daughter. "Receivd fee October 22, 1792 by Ephraim," she wrote in the margin. Although the transaction took four years to complete, the account is straightforward, a clear record of duty performed and compensation received. Such clarity is typical of the midwifery entries. Even when she failed to record the form and date of the payment, she noted the settlement of the account with a firm X X. (For more on this process, see Chapter Five.)

In comparison, most other transactions are difficult to unravel. Look again at the entry for September 17. Hidden in the account of Mrs. Shaw's delivery is another economic relationship: "Mr Hains Learned Came here." Learned was Martha's cousin. He had been at the Ballards' for a few days in May en route to Livermore, Maine, where he was about to settle. This time he would stay, on and off, for more than a month. Almost three years later, on July 29, 1791, Martha wrote, "Went to Mr Burtuns. Left four Dollars and an order on Mr Cogsill of Boston for 3,000 of shingles left by Hains Larned in Oct 88, which he is to purchase articles with for me in Boston." That comment leads back to an oblique entry for October 22, 1788: "I went to Mr Westons. His Lady lent me 6/. To Doctor Colmans. Had one thousand of shingles. A number of young Ladys here at Evining. Mr. Learned sleeps here." Although the form of the entry suggests the shingles came from Mrs. Weston or from Dr. Colman, they had obviously come from Learned, who may have been paying Martha for the meals he had eaten on September 17 and on other days, and perhaps for washing, sewing, or provisions. What Martha "had" on October 22 was not the shingles themselves, but a note on Mr. Cogsill of Boston, who had received part of Learned's lumber that year.

With the help of Mr. Weston—and Dolly Ballard and Lydia Densmore—Learned's shingles became a new dress. As we have seen, Martha left Learned's order with Weston on July 29, 1791. On September 14, "Dolly wrode to Mr Burtuns. Brot home 8 yards Chintz, which Mr Burtun Bot for me at Boston. It Cost 3/10 pr yard." On September 16, Lydia Densmore and three of her children came to Martha's house. "Shee cutt out my gown," Martha wrote. Six days later, Martha balanced accounts with the dressmaker by attending her in childbirth.

Lumber went down the Kennebec, English chintz came up, but the exchange of one for the other often involved an astonishing number of transactions—men with men, women with men, and women with women.

Trade entries, like work entries, are among the random notations in Martha's diary. In fact, there are only three items in her daily entries that appear to be totally systematic: births, the weather, and her own whereabouts. If there is a fourth consistent category, it is names of visitors or of persons visited. Those "trivial" entries that so annoyed earlier readers are often composed of little more than the names of persons leaving or arriving, as on September 3, 1788, "I have been at home. Old Mr Smily here. Mrs Savage warpt a piece here." Or on September 16, 1788: "Am not so well as I could wish. Mrs Savage, Wido Williams & Mrs Harris here at Evin. The girls went to Mr Craggs. Jonathan is returned." Names and locations—social connections—form the fabric of Martha's diary.

Forty-three names crowd the fifteen entries that begin this chapter. Martha mentioned six members of her own household, acknowledged news from four relatives to the westward, reported hearsay information about eleven persons, noted visits by her husband or children to six households, recorded twelve visitors to her own house, documented her own repeated visits to three others, and listed five of the persons she met there. The tumble of names is enough to discourage any casual reader, yet Martha surely left out some. At the Colman funeral on September 6, for example, she must have encountered several neighbors, though she didn't record their names. At the Williamses' house on September 7, she documented her omissions by writing, "Mrs Pollard *& others* there" (emphasis added).

The September entries also show that Martha considered other people's movements as important as her own. Though she was "at home" on seven of the fifteen days, her diary still recorded connections to the world beyond. There were only two days in the entire passage when she neither visited nor received visitors, and on those days other members of her family left the house. Nineteenth-century writers were puzzled by such running about. One Maine historian, remembering his mother's many journeys on horseback, concluded, "Men and women in the last century were different from the race of the present." The same theme appears in a midnineteenth-century history of Winthrop, Maine, a neighboring town to Hallowell. "The first settlers in a new country cultivate the social affections," the author wrote, telling a story about a woman who, when invited to visit her neighbor on baking day, carried her dough along with her. "What a spectacle it would now present to see a horse, saddled and pillioned, carrying a gentleman and lady on his back, the gentleman having before him a kneading trough, in which was dough for a batch of bread!" He didn't seem to recognize that necessity as well as "social affections" motivated such behavior, nor did he understand that women and their kneading troughs could get to their neighbors' houses with or without the help of their spouses.[28]

In her novel *Northwood*, Sarah Josepha Hale described the eighteenth-century healer Mrs. Watson as a charitable soul, always ready to nurse the sick or watch with the dying, though she warned that "those women who have neither her sleight to work, nor constitution to endure fatigue, must not imitate the worst part of her example—gadding." [29] Martha Ballard was a "gadder." So were most of her neighbors. In fact, too great a concentration on one's own household was probably somewhat suspect. During the year Henry was in New York, Tabitha Sewall and her baby boarded with cousins. "I have not been out since Christmas," she wrote at the beginning of March, "except a few minutes to Brookses. I have had a number of invitations to ride in slays, but did not accept; for I cannot carry Abby and I cannot enjoy myself to leave her at home." [30] Tabby's behavior was unusual, even for a young mother. Perhaps her reclusiveness was a foreshadowing of the mental illness she would suffer later in life.

In 1790 Martha recorded 642 encounters, at home or abroad, with 299 persons outside her family. Interestingly, the ratio of males to females on this list (157 males, 142 females) is exactly the same as in the Federal Census for that year, which counted 622 white males in Hallowell and 565 white females (the 12 free blacks were not differentiated by sex).[31] Martha's web included both kinds of thread, indigo and white. In contrast, Henry Sewall reported 184 encounters with 115 persons, only thirteen of whom were women. All the 1790 accounts in William Howard's book are under male names.[32] Surprisingly, even when households rather than individuals are the measure, Martha's diary is more comprehensive than the men's. According to the census, Hallowell had 184 households in 1790. Martha recorded some sort of contact with 89, the Howards 59, Sewall's diary 35.

We are not talking here about intense and sentimental relations with a few persons, but about intermittent and seemingly casual encounters with many. Of the five names most frequently mentioned in the 1790 entries, Mrs. Savage, Mrs. Woodward, Mrs. Hamlin, Mrs. Pollard, and Mrs. Burton, none appeared more than a dozen times. Of course, quick visits by near neighbors may not have reached the diary. Still, the steadiness of the listing suggests that Martha did keep a rather thorough record of visits and that extensive rather than intensive relations were the norm.

William and Samuel Howard's account book, though kept for a very different purpose, confirms this pattern. Among his Hallowell accounts for 1790, few debits amount to more than one or two pounds. The exceptions are intriguing—Dr. Colman (who once lived at the Fort), Nathaniel Hersey (the man who sued William's young stepmother, Susanna Howard), and Peter Parker, a blacksmith closely associated with the Howards in another lawsuit. That is, despite the eminence of the Howards, few Hallowell families were willing to become totally dependent on them. Like Martha, most people spread their debt among the dozen or so traders in the town, going to the Fort settlement on one excursion, to the Hook on another, trading with neighbors in between. Martha's diary suggests that this was not just an economic strategy but a deeply ingrained social habit.

The diary also shows that patterns of visiting were as gender-linked as work. Husbands and wives seldom went calling together. Martha recorded thirteen visits by couples in 1790, as on September 5, when "Mr Hamlin and Burtun and their wives here," but hundreds of occasions when women came alone or in company with other women or girls. The entry for September 16, 1788, "Mrs Savage, Wido Williams & Mrs Harris here at Evin," is typical of the 1790 entries as well. In the same way, men usually traveled with men, even for pleasure, as Jonathan Ballard did on September 4, 1788, when he and the hired hand,

Taylor, went downriver to Pownalboro to see the execution. Much of the visiting in Hallowell, like trade, fell into unmixed squares.

Women occasionally left town, as Hannah Ballard did on September 7, 1788, when she went with Sherebiah Towne to see her sister Lucy in Winslow. But it was more common for men than women to travel long distances. The Howard account book is in fact a regional rather than a purely local document, reflecting the reach of the family's trade into upriver towns like Vassalboro or Winslow. Sewall's diary records journeys in the opposite direction as he attended federal district court in Wiscasset and Portland. Vertical connections were also important for small operators like Ephraim Ballard. The sawmill in part accounts for the fact that in 1790 Martha provided sixty-eight overnight accommodations and ninety-five meals to persons outside her family; only six of the overnight guests and twenty-nine of the mealtime visitors were women. Tabitha Sewall must have had similar opportunities. "Took in our housefull of Boarders; & among the rest, a Mr Wight from Medfield, a young ministerial candidate," Henry wrote during the annual court week at Hallowell in January 1790.

Women did, of course, stay away from their homes overnight, in their own neighborhoods, when a delivery or serious illness demanded their services. In her accounts of births and watchings for 1790, Martha mentioned by name 17 percent of the adult women of the town, a remarkable figure given the fact that she often just wrote "calld the women" or "the neighbors came" in describing such events. One of the deliveries Martha performed in 1790 was at Henry Sewall's house. As Henry described it, "Mrs Sewall sent out early in the morning for Mrs Ballard and about 3 o clock in the morning for her women—and was delivered of a son about 3 in the afternoon. Very pleasant. Killed a Cow."[33] Martha's account includes a list of the helpers. It also shows how a meeting at a delivery helped to activate the town's female medical—and charitable—network:

Mrs Sewall was ill till 3 hour pm when shee was through divine asistance made the Living Mother of a Living Son,

her 3d Child. Mrs Brooks, Belcher, Colman, Pollard &
Voce assisted us. I went to Colonel Howard at Evening to
ask assistance for Polly Taylor. Colonel Sewall gave me
6/8 as a reward. Conducted me over the river. I Calld at
Mr Craggs. Was informd that Hannah North was thot to
be Expiring this morn, but is revived. Mrs Colman informed me that the Doctor her Husband, gave Hannah a
dose of Calomel for worms which gave relief. She went
next day to see Mrs Goodin and took Cold which has brot
her into the sittuation shee now is . . .[34]

Attending the delivery of one woman, Martha watched over the
welfare of two others. Polly Taylor was very much on her mind
when she arrived at the delivery. The day before she had borrowed a neighbor's horse to go and see her, finding her "very
low." Obviously she talked about Polly's condition with the
other women at the delivery. On the way home, she "went to
Colonel Howard" to ask for help. It was not the Colonel, however, but "Mrs Betsy Howard & Mrs Colman" who the next
day "sent some things here for Polly Taylor, wine, sugar, apples, Bread, and fine linning raggs." Martha was also concerned
about Hannah North, having been informed on November 11
that she was "very sick." At the delivery, Dr. Colman's wife
filled in some of the details, and on the way home, calling to
see Hannah's cousin Mrs. Craig, she learned more.

The references to Polly Taylor are particularly interesting because there are frequent entries in Hallowell's poor relief accounts for the 1790s for payments to "Ebenezer Taylor poor
man."[35] Perhaps he was Polly's father. The official records
make no mention, however, of the assistance Martha and her
neighbors were providing, apparently spontaneously. On November 22, 1790, Martha went to Weston's store. "Bot for Polly
Taylor with money which Mr Jackson gave for her 1 lb rasons,
1 quart moloses and 2 S Bisquit."

Martha's entry for November 13 mentions three of the town's
four wealthiest families, five of the middle sort, and one of the
poorest. According to a tax list for 1790, the four richest men in
Hallowell were William Howard, Charles Vaughan, William

Brooks, and Joseph North.[36] Martha called at Howard's house, noted the illness of North's daughter, and acknowledged the presence at the delivery of Susanna Cony Howard Brooks (the "Mrs Howard" of Chapter One). Only the Vaughans are missing from her description. In fact, they seldom appear in the diary. Ephraim Ballard did surveying for "Mr Vahn," but Martha apparently had no contact with the family. She never mentions Dr. Benjamin Vaughan, Charles's brother, or any of the women. She may never have met them. Latecomers to the region, the Vaughans remained somewhat aloof from their Kennebec neighbors, though the doctor, at least (as we shall see in Chapter Seven), fancied himself a benefactor of the town.[37]

Beneath the eminence of the Howards, Brookses, Norths, and Vaughans, Hallowell's wealth distribution was remarkably even. As in many New England towns, wealth was a matter of age more than of class. Sixty-five percent of the men on the list, many of them very young, paid less than three shillings tax. Supply Belcher and Jesse Vose, the husbands of two of the other attendants at the birth, were in that group, as was Henry Sewall, the father. Ephraim Ballard, assessed at four shillings two pence, was among the top 20 percent of the town's taxpayers, as were Amos Pollard and Samuel Colman, the spouses of Tabitha Sewall's other attendants. The poorest (or youngest) men in the town were assessed only a poll tax. These included Anderson Taylor, probably a relative of Polly.[38] (Anderson may have been the "Taylor" who went with Jonathan Ballard to Pownalboro on September 4, 1788, to see the execution.) Thus, in a single brief entry in the diary, Martha covered the full spectrum of affluence in the town.

Such a description gives deeper meaning to the metaphor of the web. Economic and social differences might divide a community; the unseen acts of women wove it together. From the Book of Proverbs ("She stretcheth out her hand to the poor") to countless sermons in New England churches from the seventeenth through the nineteenth century, women were praised for their ability to reach out to others in need, regardless of wealth or social position. Four years after Martha's birth, the

Reverend Mr. Jared Eliot of Killingsworth, Connecticut, eulog-
ized a local midwife in such terms: "Her Ear was open to the
Complaints of the Afflicted, and her Hand was open for the
Supply of the Needy." She was also above dissension: "If others
were so Unhappy as to divide into Parties, and to burn with
Contention, yet she remain'd a Common Friend to all." [39]

Martha's diary reflects the same ethic. As a midwife she was
bound to serve anyone who needed her, regardless of their social position. She was not a democrat, but she was benevolent.
In the same month when "Edmond Fortes of the State of Virginia, a Negro man, with his wife and children," was warned
out of the town, she delivered "Black Edmund's" wife, "Lydia,"
of a son. [40] Her charitableness showed itself not only in physical caring but in a reluctance to pass judgment on her neighbors' behavior. "Mrs McNight sleeps here. Her Husband hastened her out a Dores as shee says," she wrote on December
14, 1787, offering no additional detail on the family fight. Martha would not turn the woman away, but neither would she
record without qualification the story of the abusive husband.
She was perhaps restrained by the stereotype of the gossipy
midwife as much as by her own deeply held Christian values.
There is very little of what might be considered gossip in Martha's diary, though after seeing Calvin Edson lying in the road
drunk, she offered a special prayer for his newborn daughter:
"May God Almighty bless her and help her to shun her father's
wicked example."

While other Hallowell folks were busy suing one another,
Martha self-consciously excised contention from her diary. In a
rare admission of trouble, she noted, "I went to Mrs Westons
afternoon. Mr Brooks there. Shew dislike at my informing Mrs
Weston of some afairs which hapned in the school." [41] Yet even
here she masked the details of the offense with that vague label
"some afairs." She seldom went even that far in mentioning
disagreement, or potential disagreements, with neighbors.

The Eliot sermon, like many published in the early eighteenth
century, played on the disparity between the value of women's
contributions and their seeming invisibility. "To denominate a

person Eminently Useful, it is not necessary that they are Advanced to the highest Dignity, either in Church or State," he wrote. Ten years before, Cotton Mather had elaborated on the same theme, describing the pious women of New England as "the Hidden Ones." In real life, of course, women weren't hidden at all. They fed travelers, bargained with their neighbors, and moved about their towns at will, on horseback, in canoes, or afoot. Yet in one sense they were hidden, even in Martha's diary. Women, to use a Biblical metaphor, performed their works under a bushel; men's candles burned on the hill.

There is a consistent leveling in Martha's references to her female neighbors, a blurring of social rank, that contrasts with her usual manner of describing men. Once in a while she used the term "Lady" or its variant "old Lady" in describing other women, and occasionally she referred to a single woman of rank as "Mistress," preserving the earlier, honorific meaning of the word, but most of the time she referred to single women by their first names, to married women, unless they were black, simply as "Mrs," and to widows as either "Mrs" or "wido." Men, on the other hand, might be addressed as "Mr.," "Doctor," "Captain," "Esquire," "Reverend," "Lieutenant," "Colonel," or "Judge," the most distinguished men in the town usually having more than one title to choose from, "Esquire" as well as "Doctor" Cony, "Judge" as well as "Colonel" North. And of course there were two kinds of "Captain," as in Captain Brown, who called the militia company together, and Captain Howard, who commanded the family sloop.

Titles reflected the hierarchical and formal structure of public affairs. Militia titles were especially important. Whatever else the Revolution had done, it had helped to reinforce that old distinction. Massachusetts legislation published in 1786 arranged the men of each town and county into companies, regiments, brigades, and divisions, each headed by an appropriate set of officers. Captain Brown was required to call his train-band together four days in a year "for the purpose of examining their arms and equipment, and instructing them in military exercises." Colonel North was required to assemble all the train-bands in his regiment for an annual muster. In time, Hallowell would have a major general in the person of Henry Sewall, who for thirty years commanded the Eighth Division of the Massachusetts Militia, comprising the Maine counties of Lincoln, Kennebec, and Somerset.

On court days, Colonel North became Judge North. The Massachusetts judicial system had three tiers. The lowest courts, responsible for enforcing laws against Sabbath-breaking, profanity, and fornication, and for judging small claims, were conducted by a single justice of the peace. At the next level were the Courts of Common Pleas and General Sessions presided over by all the justices of the peace in a given county. In Lincoln County, after 1786, these courts met twice each year, alternately in Pownalboro and Hallowell. Pownalboro had an impressive courthouse and jail, but until 1790 the Hallowell court met at Pollard's Tavern. Capital trials and appeals from the Pleas and Sessions were heard by the Supreme Judicial Court, presided over by circuit judges who traveled from county to county. To ratify their authority and the dignity of their calling, these men appeared on the bench in robes and wigs, wearing black silk in summer and scarlet in winter. Jonathan Ballard observed one result of this court's labors when he went to Pownalboro on September 4, 1788, to see the execution of an Irishman named John O'Neil for the murder of Michael Cleary of Pemaquid Falls. Like militia musters, courts offered dignity to ordinary men, who served as grand jurors, petit jurors, constables, clerks, and referees, if not as judges. Women participated in court proceedings only as witnesses.

At the local level, the town meeting also offered offices, if not titles, to most men, at least during some period of their lives. Of the twelve adult males mentioned in the diary segment for September 3–17, 1788, seven can be found on the list of town officers for that year. James Page and James Carr, like Ephraim Ballard, were selectmen. Beriah Ingerham (or Ingraham) was on the Committee to Inspect the Fishery; Mr. Palmer (or Parmer) was both a Packer of Fish and a Culler of Hoops & Staves. Colonel North was the town's Sealer of Weights & Measures.

Dr. Colman was a Field Driver, and Elias Craig ("Mr. Cragg") was a Surveyor of Lumber.[46] Town offices reflected the major commercial products of the town, the commodities men shipped down the river into the streams of international trade. They also reflected male ownership of land, buildings, and cattle, some officers being responsible for the maintenance of public buildings and roads, others for surveying the fences that presumably made good neighbors or for managing the capture of stray animals belonging to bad ones.

There were no Committees to Inspect the Kitchens and Gardens of Hallowell, no Packers of Candles or Cullers of Linen Thread, nor was there a Sealer of Reels and Sleighs. Women's invisibility in town records reflected the patriarchal organization of society as well as the perishable and invisible nature of their work. Land endured from generation to generation, its boundaries defined in closely written documents entered into leatherbound volumes by conscientous clerks like Henry Sewall. Butter, ashes, and "fine linning rags" simply disappeared. Consider the differing obligations of Merriam Pollard, who so frequently laid out the dead, and of her husband, Amos, who was town sexton as well as a tavern keeper. A sexton in early New England was not only responsible for tolling the meeting-house bell, something Hallowell did not have in 1788, but for supervising burial, that is for allotting a discrete piece of ground to the dead. In comparison, Merriam Pollard's concern was for the perishable body itself. The clothing as well as the flesh it covered would soon decay; the ceremonial significance of the careful washing and dressing presumably would not. Day by day women negotiated the fragile threads of ordinary need that bound families together.

If women had a collective consciousness, it was surely developed in such work. There is a telling symmetry in a set of entries for September 20–21, 1789. While "Mrs Cleark, Medcalf, Ney, Hollowell, & Mrs Sewall" watched with Martha Ballard at Mrs. Sherburne's delivery, "Captain Brown called his Company together." A delivery in Hallowell was a kind of muster, and Martha Ballard was both captain and clerk. Yet she had little patience with the noise and combativeness of male politics. "Mr Ballard Cyrus & Silva at Town meeting," she wrote on one March day. "There was but little done Except contend (a great evil)."[47] She also had reason to question the manly exercises of the militia. During one muster she reported, "the field piece was fird the most of the night which interrupted my patient much." The next day after the birth of a "fine son," when "Every Circumstance seemd agreeable," she was hastened from the house to treat three of the young troopers. "Alas what Changing seins take place," she wrote, "at 8 in the Eving as a number were Collected & *diverting themselves*, if I may use the Expression, by fireing the field pieces, three men ... were wounded by an unexpected discharg by reason of its not being properly swabed. The two were thought to be mortally wounded ... I went & Bathed their wounds."[48] At such times a woman might well question the wisdom of her town's rulers and protectors.

CHAPTER THREE

OCTOBER 1789

"Mrs Foster has sworn a Rape on a number of men"

SEPTEMBER

30 4 *I was at Mrs Husseys*
Clear Except a lite shower afternoon. I went to Captain Herseys, Mr Whites & Esquire Husseys. Had 6 lbs of sheeps wool of the old Lady which is to go towards what they owe Mr Ballard. I was Called to Mr Fosters door & askt some questions. *Colonel North interogated me Concerning what conversation Mrs Foster had with me Concerning his Conduct.*

OCTOBER

1 5 *I have been at home.*
Clear Except some showers. We had Company this afternoon. Mrs Hannah North, Mrs Chever & a Mrs Weston from Cohors. Mr Savage here. Informs that Mrs Foster has sworn a Rape on a number of men among whom is Judge North. Shocking indeed.

*This last sentence begins in the right margin but spills over into the space below the regular entry and is separated from it by a line. The sentence appears to have been added later.

2   6   *At Mr Goffs*
A rainy morn. I was called at 4th hour morn to Mrs Goff who
was in travil. I walkt to Daviss Store, crost the river & went by
land on hors back. Arivd at the 6th hour. Old Mrs Goff returned
from Boston at 1 hour pm. I tarried there this night.

3   7   *At Mr Goffs. His first grand child Born.*
Clear. Mrs. Jackson & Mrs. Stickney went home. I slept an hour
this morning. Mrss. Goffs illness increast & shee was safe delivrd at 11 hour & 30 minute morn of a daughter. Her marm,
Mrs Bullin, Mrs Ney were my asistants. Mrs Jacson Came back
at 1 h p.m. I returnd home at 6 afternoon. Find Mr Ballard
returnd from his tower of surveying yesterday. Mr Bullin from
the westward informs me Colo Thomson of Bilrick has Buried
his only Child. Mr Burtun & wife here.
Birth John Goffs daughter. First child. X X

4   D   *I have been at home.*
Cloudy. Wind South East. I have been at home. Pikt green peas
in our gardin. Josh Sinclear brot us a barril of herrin smokt. My
girls went to Mr Hamlins at Evening. Hannah tarries there. A
rainy night.

5   2   *I have been at home. Receivd 1/2 Bushel of rie of Captain
Hersey as reward for asisting his Lady.*
A rainy day. I combd 7 lb of flax for myself & 4 for Cyrus. Mr
Ballard went to Captain Coxes. Hannah is at Mr Hamlins. Polly
Savage here. Drank Tea. Mr Savage returnd Jonathans hors
which he rode to Green. I am informd there was a man Drownd
in Jones Eddy who Came passage from Boston with Captain
Howard.

6   3   *I have been at home.*
A very rainy day. I Combd flax. Mr Ballard went to Esquir
Coneys & to Town meeting. Thee sweap of one of the mills
got off thee crank so neither of them were tended this night.

7   4   *I have been at home. It is 12 years since I left Oxford.*
Clear. Mitty Devenpord dind. Joshua Sinclare & Mr Richardson
drank tea. I finisht combing my flax. Had 10 lb Tear. My girls
washt.

8   5   *At Mr Daws. There was a muster of the troops & regiment*
Clear & pleasant. I was Calld at the 8th hour morn to Mr Daws
at the hook to his wife in travil. The rigament & troop Con-
vened there on Mr Shuball Hinkleys Land. I tarried with Mrs
Daw till Evn when shee had her women. She remained ill
through the night.

9   6   *At ditoes. His wife is the 32d woman I have put to Bed since
February 5th.*
Clear forenoon. Cloudy afternoon. Mrs Daw was safe delivered
at the 6th hour this morn of a fine son which weighd 11 lb. I
tarried with her till 4 pm then Came to Mr Densmores. Tarried
all night.
Birth Mr Daws son, the 4th, X X

10   7   *At Mr Densmores & Trues. Mr Hatch went from here.*
Clear & very pleasant. I went to Mr Trues to see Genny Coy.
Find her more Comfortable, then returnd home. Mr Hatch &
wife & Rufus Ballard here. Son Town Been here. Informs his
famely are well & that Mrs Barton was delivrd of a son the 8th
instant. The Reverend Mr Isaac Foster removd to Varsalboro
this day. Mr Ballard is gone to the hook.

11   D   *At home*
Clear. We had Chickens for dinner. This day is the Aneversary
of the Ordination of the Reverend Isaac Foster over the Church
& flock in this Town three years since.

The town historians have had much to say about the Reverend
Mr. Isaac Foster, about his calling and ordination, his encounters

with Henry Sewall, and his eventual dismissal by the town. They have had nothing at all to say about his wife, Rebecca. Except for a few cryptic documents in the records of the Supreme Judicial Court and a tantalizing set of entries in Martha's diary, her story is lost. "Mrs Foster has sworn a Rape on a number of men among whom is Judge North," Martha wrote on October 1, 1789, without further explanation. It is tempting to superimpose the controversies that dominate Isaac's story— the theological argument between Calvinists and liberals, or the practical problem of sustaining a tax-supported church in a religiously divided town—on Rebecca's, but that approach does nothing to explain her troubles. If anything, Joseph North had been a supporter and ally of her husband. Her accusation is an ugly tear in local history, an unexplained rent in the social web.

Still, Isaac's story is a necessary prelude to Rebecca's. Tracing it out through Martha's diary and through parallel entries in Henry Sewall's gives us some insight into the religious complexities of the town, into Martha's own religious temper, and ultimately into her response to the trial for rape.

Isaac Foster arrived in Hallowell in April of 1786, preached on probation for the next few weeks, accepted a call from the town in August, was ordained in October, and almost immediately began to tangle with disaffected evangelicals. This is the story that is told so compellingly in Henry Sewall's diary, the story that the town historians have preserved. It is a narrative drearily familiar to anyone who knows the ecclesiastical history of eighteenth-century New England. In fact Martha's own brother, Jonathan Moore, would go through the same process in Rochester, Massachusetts, four years later, and for much the same reasons —he was too liberal in theology and too illiberal in his dealings with his neighbors.[1]

Henry Sewall had himself experienced a profound religious conversion a short while after coming to the Kennebec in 1783. In an unbroken stretch of woods somewhere between Pownalboro and Hallowell, "light and peace broke in upon his mind."

In describing the experience later, he used the language of Psalm 132: "We heard of it at Ephratah: we found it in the fields of the wood."[2] Henry might have applied for admission to the newly organized Congregational church in Hallowell. Instead, he sought out a smaller, more intimate private meeting of like-minded Christians. "Met for reading, prayer, & singing at Esqr. Pettengill's—some power in the morning," he wrote on one Sabbath, and, on another, "Had a gracious & remarkable manifestation of God's power in my soul."[3]

At the time, Hallowell's new church had no minister. Preaching, in early New England, was both an ecclesiastical and a civil responsibility. A prospective minister had to please the town as a whole, at least the adult male part of it, as well as the tiny minority who made up the membership of the covenanted church. Until a minister was called, services were read by laymen or conducted by visiting clergy. Both Ephraim Ballard, who was a church member, and Colonel Joseph North, who was not, were on the committee appointed by the town meeting to "procure a Gospel minister." Henry Sewall and his friends tested each candidate according to the standards of their own private society. "He is an Arminian; &, I believe an Arian," Sewall wrote after hearing one prospective pastor preach, adding, "From such doctrine I turned away—and met with a few brethren in the afternoon, at Esq. Pettingills, where the presence of the Lord was experienced in a sensible manner."[4]

The town meeting had already turned down two candidates when Isaac Foster arrived in the spring of 1786. "Mr Foster a yong Gentleman from Stafford in the state of Connecticut performed," Martha wrote on April 16. On May 8, the town voted to give him a call, 57 for and 4 against.[5] There is no indication that Henry Sewall was among the dissenters, though by the middle of July he was clearly worried about the young gentleman's preaching. On July 28, when Martha noted, "Mr Foster Deliverd a discoarce from Math 25/41 verse," he groused, "Mr Foster preached—poor Doctrine." The next week he labeled the sermon "Arminian Doctrine" and the following week "rank Arminianism." (In comparison, the sermons of Mr. Emerson of Georgetown were "food indeed!")[6]

Sewall's discomfort with the minister was awkward, since Rebecca and Isaac Foster were living in a house owned by his cousin Thomas Sewall. He made a few gestures of neighborliness, lending his horse for a journey to the "westward," Foster in turn carrying letters to Henry's family in York. But there were also tensions. On August 8, 1786: "Had a conference with Mr Foster—could not convince him of the impropriety of his doctrine." On August 12: "Conversed with Mr. Foster respecting experience." On August 15: "Had a close, plain, & Solemn interview with Mr. Foster respecting his (as I call them) heretical doctrines."

Had Sewall known more about Foster's background, he would have been even more alarmed. The young pastor's father, the Reverend Mr. Isaac Foster of Stafford, Connecticut, had been dismissed from his pulpit in 1783 for "heretical doctrines," though he had managed to keep a fragment of his congregation together in a separate church. Isaac's brother John, also a minister, was eventually licensed by the Universalists, an outcome Henry Sewall could have predicted after hearing the man preach in Hallowell on October 8. Martha reported, "Attended divine servis afternoon. Was agreeably Entertaind with a discoarse delivered By Revd John Foster of Paxton." Sewall fumed, "Mr John Foster (brother to Isaac) preached—flagrant free-will doctrine."

That Martha enjoyed the very sermons Henry found objectionable had as much to do with temperament as with theology. There were self-conscious liberals in her family; her brother, Collins Moore, would be involved in the establishment of a Universalist society in Oxford in 1791, and certainly Jonathan Moore's dismissal from his pulpit would have something to do with his arguments with ardent Calvinists in Rochester. But it would be a mistake to read the religious controversies that rent New England in this period solely in terms of abstract doctrine. Martha Ballard's and Henry Sewall's diaries help us to see the web of human connections and personal commitments that often underlay abstract arguments about "Arminianism" or "free will."

If Martha's diary is at all a reflection of her personality, we must assume that she valued deeds more than ideas. A woman

who measured life in "doing for others" might be expected to
enjoy a sermon on Matthew 25, the chapter in which Jesus distinguished those on his right and his left hand, the sheep and
the goats, according to whether they had fed the hungry,
clothed the naked, or comforted the afflicted. For her, theological speculations about the nature of the final judgment probably
mattered less than Christ's remembering who had "performed"
well in daily life, who had offered service to "the least of these."

For Martha, attending church was a pleasant duty, especially
if the sermon was well delivered. "Public worship," as she
termed it, was not a calling out from ordinary life but a valida-
tion of it. Seeing her friends and neighbors gathered in orderly
rows in the meeting house confirmed her place in the universe
and in the town. She was pleased to see a "yong Gentleman"
in the pulpit. Henry Sewall, on the other hand, went to church
to be awakened, not to be "agreeably entertained." For him
there *was* a radical disjunction between worship and ordinary
life. He expected the heavens to open.

As the ordination drew near, Sewall fasted and prayed with
the brethren at Esquire Pettingill's, then composed a list of
seven objections, which he presented to the ordination council
gathered in Hallowell on October 11. He was not successful in
blocking the nomination. Though his presentation "took up the
forenoon" and the delegates debated the matter "till near sunset," they then "proceeded to the meeting house, & laid hands
on the Candidate." Sewall had made enough of an impression,
however, that the next day two members of the council visited
him to give "the reason of their laying hands on Mr. Foster—
viz that he did in the most solemn manner before the council,
profess to hold fully to all the cardinal points in the calvinistic
scheme of divinity—& also gave a full account of a work of
saving grace on his own soul!!!!! If he *speaks truth*," Sewall concluded with apparent irony, "he is a christian!"

For the rest of Foster's ministry, Sewall boycotted public
worship, preferring the purity—and perhaps the intimacy—of
the private meetings. "Met with a few brethren at Esquire Pettingill's," he had written after one such gathering. "Had meat

to eat which the world knows not of."[7] For her part, Martha was more interested in the common kind of meat. "Mr. Foster here," she wrote on February 7, 1787. "Mr. Ballard carried him some meet from Cyrus and sause from our selves."

The Fosters had recently moved from Thomas Sewall's house to the Ballards' neighborhood. Ephraim brought in a load of firewood and found a man to help make "a kirb" for the minister's well. On February 21 Martha "began a Linnen Stockin for Lady Foster"; on March 3 she "finisht Mrs Fosters hoes," and on March 6 she joined Mrs. Weston and Mrs. Pollard for an afternoon's visit. The next day "Mr. Foster & Lady" dined at the Ballards'. Small courtesies, petty exchanges, casual visits incorporated the minister's wife into the female community.

Rebecca Foster was twenty-seven years old when she arrived in Hallowell, exactly the same age as Martha's oldest daughter, Lucy Towne, though she probably seemed younger, having been married only a short time. Her first child, named Isaac for his father and grandfather, was still an infant.[8] She was born in Lebanon, Connecticut, a town with a rather exotic history. Not only was it the home of Hannah Brewster, one of the few published female poets in New England, it was the site of an Indian Charity School established by Eleazar Wheelock, who later founded Dartmouth College. (Rebecca's father, James Newcomb, had contributed financially to the school.)[9] Whether the example of Hannah Brewster and other outspoken sisters in the Congregational church of Lebanon had affected her, we do not know; but there is a terse entry in Martha Ballard's diary which suggests that some part of her Lebanon heritage had followed her to Hallowell. "I was at Mrs Fosters," Martha wrote on August 22, 1787. "Indians there."

These may have been local Indians. Probably they were Christianized Indians, perhaps missionaries associated with Wheelock's movement. Samson Occom is the most famous of these. Occom's missionary companion in England in the 1760s, Nathaniel Whitaker, had been pastor in Canaan (now Skowhegan), Maine, since 1784. A physician as well as a minister, Whitaker was an occasional visitor to the Ballard house: "Doctor

Whitaker & son slept here. His hors fell down Bank. Our men helpt him up again."[10] (Whitaker, too, would soon face expulsion and, in a curious reversal of the Foster case, a trial for rape.)

Martha treated "Lady Foster" with deference but also with maternal solicitude, spending three extra days caring for her when her second baby was born in September of 1787, something she seldom did even for Lucy. A week after the birth, she noted, "Mr Foster made me a present of a silk handkerchief."[11] Perhaps her concern for the Fosters was in part motivated by her dismay at the way they had been treated by certain other townspeople. Early that year, on January 25, 1787, Ephraim had gone "to see Thomas Sewall to Converse with him concerning ills he is accused of spreading of the Revd Mr Foster," returning "with out any Satisfaction." Had Isaac Foster been the sort of man to turn the other cheek, his tenure in Hallowell might have been longer. Instead, he swore out a complaint before Judge North accusing Henry and Thomas Sewall of slander.

A few days later, on January 29, Martha "went with Mrs Brown to hear the trial of Capt Sewall & Thomas Sewall for defameing the Revd Mr Isaac Foster." The court was a simple hearing before a single justice of the peace, the lowest level of the Massachusetts judicial system. For Martha, who usually ignored such matters, it must have been both distressing and satisfying. "They were found gilty & find & Laid under Bonds," she reported, adding, "I went to see Mrs Foster after cort was over." Henry Sewall saw it differently. "I was charged with reporting that Mr Foster was a liar and that I could prove it— which facts I did not pretend to deny," he wrote. "Produced evidence to prove my assertion which I thought I did—though Mr. North was pleased to think otherwise."

Neither diary describes the "evidence" presented in court that day, though later events show that one of the witnesses was Rebecca's servant, Margaret Fox. Apparently, one of the accusations was that Foster was guilty of Sabbath-breaking. On this occasion the servant supported her master and mistress. Later, however, at a church council, "Margarett Fox gave a very contrary evidence concerning her working on the Sabath from what shee did when called in the cause of Capt. Sewall's defameing the Rev'd Mr Foster."

Sewall refused to accept the verdict, but in June, when his appeal was entered at the Court of General Sessions in Pownalboro, he asked for a continuance, his lawyers pleading "the absence of one of my material witnesses, together with the great inconvenience of the attendance of several others *who were women etc.*" Since the continuance was denied and Sewall, "reduced to the dilemma—either to come to trial without my evidences, or settle the matter by paying up the costs," decided to pay, the trial was never held and the women never testified. Who they were we do not know. If Martha was aware of this second trial, she did not mention it in her diary. A hearing at Judge North's house was one thing; a trip to Pownalboro, another. For most women, attending court was more than "inconvenient." It was a venture into an alien world.

Henry Sewall inhabited a world of opposites—of litigation and Grace, of courts and prayer circles, of precise penmanship and religious rapture. The two institutions that dominated his thinking, the court and the church, had one thing in common, however: they were both ritualized structures set apart from everyday life. And in both he was among the Elect. Henry's world was ostensibly larger than Martha's. He traveled farther, read more, wrote more, and by any account left a larger imprint on the affairs of state and town. Yet when her diary is used as the measure, his life seems small. He leaped from indigo square to indigo square, from courtroom to town meeting to the gatherings of saints, with little awareness of the finespun fibers between. Despite his conflicts and his losses, his was a remarkably safe world, a world in which most questions had answers, events had beginnings and ends, and problems could be categorized if not resolved.

Martha's world was a web without a selvage, a shuttle perpetually in motion. She nursed Isaac Foster through scarlet fever in July 1787 and attended Rebecca in childbirth in September. On October 20, when Peggy Fox came to the house to say her mistress had "took Cold" and that her breast was painful, Martha rushed to her aid. By the time the breast infection was cleared up, the minister was again in bed. Martha sat up with him all through the night on November 4. By November 18, he was back in the pulpit, though still able to "perform . . . but one Exercise by reason of his weakness." The following spring, it was little Isaac who was ill. Martha diagnosed "the salt rhume."[12]

On April 2, 1788, though Henry's diary took no notice, Martha walked over the still frozen river to deliver Tabitha. Henry was still boycotting public worship, the private meetings now being held most Sundays in his own house. On March 9, he had invited a visiting pastor to dinner. "Mr. Smith attended Mr. Foster's meeting for his own satisfaction; which he amply obtained," he wrote.[13] On May 1, Henry Sewall and Ephraim Ballard were both present for a justice's court in which Thomas Sewall won three shillings plus costs from Isaac Foster for "house hire."[14] By June, the battle had moved back to Pownalboro. Foster was once again suing Henry for defamation. That case was continued to the following term, but in a separate action the minister successfully defended himself against a Boston creditor. The stakes had moved from shillings to pounds. "Met at my house," Henry reported the next day. "Had a full meeting in the afternoon—Mr. Foster not having returned."[15] The following Sabbath Isaac Foster preached from Micah 6:8: "He hath shewed thee, O man, what *is* good; and what doth the Lord require of thee, but to do justly, and to love mercy, and to walk humbly with thy God."[16]

Henry left Hallowell in July 1788 for an eighteen-month stay in New York City. The war continued without him. As Isaac Foster's creditors initiated an appeal, Rebecca again struggled with illness. Though she had earlier called Dr. Colman to attend her, on August 1, early in the morning, she summoned Martha, who found her "very unwell. Her Breast is Likely to Break." Martha "aplyd a poltis of Sorril & returnd home," but two days later the patient was still "very distrest." On August 4, after spending most of the day nursing her, Martha gave in to the inevitable. "I opend her breast. It discharged a Larg quantity. I left her much more comfortable." Rebecca's youngest child was eleven months old.

On September 14, Martha "attended worship in public" and heard Isaac Foster deliver "two Exelent Discoarses from Psalm 90 & 12 vers." The text, "So teach *us* to number our days, that we may apply *our* hearts unto wisdom," was too pointed to have been accidental. Foster's days were indeed numbered. Five days before, the town had met to consider his dismissal. They canceled his contract on October 30, called a church council in early November, and formally dismissed him on December 18. Perhaps the disaffection was mutual. In a letter to the town dated December 18, 1788, he said, "I have long been desirous a dismission should take place." Certainly theological issues had something to do with the pastor's troubles, but his habit of suing his enemies may have had more. His financial difficulties may have been a concern on both sides; certainly the key issue in negotiating the dismissal was how much money the town would have to pay. Foster asked for two hundred pounds and eventually got a hundred, not a bad sum after two years' service.

Martha attended the Church Council held November 20–21 at Pollard's Tavern in Hallowell. If this council was like most others, it considered a broad range of issues, doctrinal and personal. In Jonathan Moore's case, for example, there were at least nine different articles ranging from accusations of lying to insinuations that the minister had "abused" his wife by failing to provide necessities in season. In Rochester, a single-minded parishioner with the militia rank of major had pursued Jonathan Moore as doggedly as Colonel Sewall had pursued Isaac Foster in Hallowell.[17] Yet Foster's troubles had as much to do with general structural problems in New England's religious establishment as with anything he or his opponents did or did not do. The old system of town-supported churches could not accommodate the religious diversity that now existed. In fact, two of the five ministers who participated in Foster's ordination were themselves deposed within five years. When a ministerial association was formed in Lincoln County in 1790, eight of the twelve participating churches were without pastors.[18]

The Rochester council had "bewailed" and "deprecated" the "strife and bitter contention" in their town, urging Jonathan Moore and his opponents to "lay aside all wrath, anger, malice & revenge & put on bowels of Compassion one towards another" for the sake of the church and of the "rising generation." That was no more likely to happen in Rochester than in Hallowell as long as the state tolerated dissent while clinging to the notion of a single tax-supported church. A hundred years earlier, a group like Henry Sewall's would have been fined for repeated absence from church. That a rival society could flourish outside the meeting house shows how far religious pluralism had already come. The next step, of course, was to ask for exemption from taxes, and in fact the dissenting brethren did just that in the town meeting that considered Isaac Foster's dismissal.

When their petition was denied, they and the neighboring ministers came up with an ingenious solution. With Isaac Foster out of the pulpit, they tried to organize a church. Since the town already had a legitimately constituted Congregational church, this was legally impossible. The council debated the matter and concluded that since several members of Sewall's society, including Henry's brother Jotham, actually lived in Chester, thirty miles away, they could establish a Chester church—though it would continue to meet in Hallowell. So it was that Hallowell acquired two Congregational churches in 1790, organized along doctrinal lines.

Although the town formally barred Isaac Foster from the pulpit on December 18, 1788, he remained in Hallowell for most of the following year, haggling with the town over the terms of his dismissal and attempting to settle the debts that rapidly accumulated. "Mr Ballard & I were Seited to give our deposition concerning what we heard Judg Howard & his widdow say about some Beef he gave the reverend Mr Foster," Martha wrote on June 24, 1789. By the middle of October she could note that Charles Webber was "ataitching peoples Efects on acount of what Mr Foster ows him." Within a town debts and counterdebts might accumulate for years without anyone asking for a reckoning, but once the social web was broken neighbors rushed to get their due. It was during this difficult period, when the Fosters were neither in nor out of the town, that the alleged rape occurred.

"Mr Savage here. Informs that Mrs Foster has sworn a Rape on a number of men among whom is Judge North. Shocking indeed." The news that Mr. Savage brought was shocking, but not as unexpected in real life as in the diary. Martha had known something of Rebecca Foster's complaints for more than six weeks, though she carefully avoided describing them in her diary. The entry for August 19, 1789, the day Rebecca first confided her troubles, is as bland as any in the diary: "Calld at Mr Westons, Pollards, Mrs Fosters & Mr Savages. Came home at 1 h pm feel fatagud." Nothing more. Again on August 25 a bare report: "I went to see Mrs Foster. Burtun & wife and Mrs Cooskin here." If Martha and Ephraim had not been summoned to Vassalboro on December 23 to give evidence "in the Cause between this Commonwealth & Joseph North Esquire," we would know no more. Perhaps concerned that she would have to repeat her testimony later before a full court, she sat and wrote all she could remember of what Rebecca had told her during those August visits. This account is the only surviving testimony in the Foster case. All that remains in the official court records is the formal indictment, an expense account, and the verdict.

My testimony was that Mrs Foster on the 19 of August Complaind to me that shee had received great abuses from people unknown to her, such as throwing stones at her house, strieveing to get in & Lodg with her. After relating those abuses [she] said that was not the worst shee had met with since Mr Fosters absence, but shee hoped they would not quite kill her, that they Could do nothing wors than they had unless they killed her. She also said that said North had abused her wors than any other person in the world had, but shee believed it was best for her to keep her troubles to her Selfe as mutch as shee Could till her Husband returnd which shee hopt would be soon.

The diary entry continued, filling a full page and parts of two others:

Shee also Complaind on the 25 (if I remember the day aright) of said Norths treating her wors than any other person had & said he did go after an other woman besides his own wife & that his wife was jealous of him. Shee seemd Exceedingly troubled when she related her tryals but not being askt any question for information did not descend to particulars relating to the Charges she now Lais at that time, which was the last time I Converst with her while her Husband was absent.

Quiet listening. No questions. Martha was unwilling to invite any more information than she was given unbidden. No gossip, the bare facts were all anyone was going to get from her. There would be no speculation, no judgment, either before the court or in her diary. "I also testified that said North said to me Last weak (which I find by this diarey to be on the 18th instant) that he really believd Mrs Foster was treated as she Complains but he Should Deny the Charg Exhibited against him. He also said he never had the least reason to suspect her virtue or modesty." The diary entry for "the 18th instant"—that is, December 18, 1790—reads, "Colonel North was here. Examined me what conversation Mrs. Foster had with me Concerning his Conduct towards her last August. Mr Carr here. Capt. Nichols & Levy & Rhubin Moore dind here. . . ." Again the hearing caused her to write down details she had recorded only in her memory.

Three days after the Vassalboro court, Martha turned the diary on its side and wrote in the margins this addition to her testimony:

The 26 instant I called to mind Mrs Foster saying Colonel North had positively had unlawful concors with a woman which was not his wife and I Begd her never to mentin it to any other person. I told her shee would Expose & perhaps ruin her self if shee did. I told her I supposed it was an Enemy of his who was her informer & that the informer might have miss receivd a story relative to Jack. Shee replyd no it is his Father. I mean he is guilty.

The addendum is much more forceful than the initial testimony. The vague assertion that North "did go after an other woman besides his own wife" became a direct accusation: the judge "had *positively* had *unlawful concors* with a woman which was not his wife." Martha's description of her own response changed from the passive "not being askt any question for information" to the active "I Begd her never to mentin it to any other person." The effect, if not the intent, of the addendum was to heighten the intensity of Rebecca's early revelations. They appear much less tenuous than in the original description, and Martha's own intervention more significant. There is no reason to suspect conscious reshaping of the testimony here, though it seems obvious that the hearing had affected Martha's memory of the early conversations. Even the stark phrase "he is guilty" has heavier meaning in light of the formal process then underway.

The addendum, taken with her description of the hearing itself, suggests she had been deeply impressed by Rebecca's testimony. "The Charg was said North Broke into the house of Isaac Foster in the night time," she wrote, "& Ravisht the wife of said Foster. On trial Mrs Foster apeard very Calm sedate & unmovd notwithstanding the strong atempts there were made to throw aspersions on her Carrectir. She on oath affirmd that said North Broke open the Door of her house & parpetrated the Crime of ravishment notwithstanding her Exerting her self as much as her strength would admit of." She had first written "Rape," then crossed it out and written "ravishment" in the margin. Was there a distinction in her mind, or was she simply striving for the language she remembered from court? The statute defines the crime as to "*ravish* and carnally know any woman, committing carnal copulation with her by force against her will." The prescribed penalty was death.[19]

Martha was in a difficult position. Judge North was not only one of the most powerful men in Lincoln County, he was her near neighbor and, as an agent for the Kennebec Proprietors, her husband's employer. The Mistress Hannah North who came calling on October 1 was his daughter. When Ephraim returned from his "tower of surveying" on October 3, it was Joseph North who would authorize his accounts. "I Begd her never to mentin it to any other person," Martha had written. "I told her shee would Expose & perhaps ruin her self if shee did." Would her advice have been different if she had known the full story, if she had pressed Rebecca for details on August 19, asked the questions that might have brought out all of the facts? The reticence was on both sides. Rebecca talked around the problem, starting with vague accusations of "abuse." As far as we can tell she did not use the word "rape," though she surely alluded to it when she said "they Could do nothing wors than they had unless they killed her."

When Joseph North came to trial, the actual indictment charged assault "*with an intent* . . . to ravish and carnally know." Since rape was a capital crime, justices and grand juries frequently reduced the charge in order to get a conviction. Only ten men were tried for rape in Massachusetts in the entire eighteenth century, none after 1780. Between 1780 and 1797 there were sixteen indictments and ten convictions for attempted rape, still a small number considering that the population of the state approached 400,000.[20] The women's reticence is hardly surprising, given the rarity of the accusation and the severity of the penalty. Rebecca could not say what she needed to say. Martha could not hear her. Martha was willing to entertain stories about young Jack North, but not his father. Her concern that a woman might "Expose & perhaps ruin her self" by accusing a high-status male suggests the difficulties in prosecuting such a crime.

Rebecca's anguished allusion to the "abuses" she had "met

with since Mr Fosters absence" takes on an almost gothic quality in the light of the accusations she eventually made. According to the indictments Elijah Davis committed his assault "with
an intent to ravish" on August 3, Joshua Burgess on August 6,
and Joseph North on August 9. Her cryptic comments to Martha
about people throwing stones at her house and striving to get
in and lodge with her are transformed in the formal accusation
into a week of terror. Alone in her house, disconnected from
the community her husband had once served, her vulnerability
was complete. Martha said nothing about the other men, except
to note on December 4 that "Elijah Davis was carried to Varsalboro" and "Captain Biges apprehended."

Henry Sewall returned to Hallowell in November of 1789,
about a month after Rebecca Foster's accusation became public.
He says nothing at all about the case in his diary, yet it is surely
the "affair" he alludes to in a letter to George Thatcher dated
January 27, 1790. Characteristically, it was the legal procedure,
rather than the accusation itself, that interested him.

Nothing of consequence has transpired in this quarter, except Colo. North's affair; and this has made considerable
noise. His examination, as you have doubtless heard, was
had before Esq. Wood at Vassalboro the 22 December, and
the matter referred thence to the Sessions at Hallowell term
for advice. The Sessions were of opinion that the matter
could not come legally before them; but consented to hear
the statement of the evidence produced before Esq. Wood;
whereupon they proceeded to give their opinions as individual Justices (and not as Sessions) which were six to two
for acquiting Colo. North. Esq. Wood, however, notwithstanding this advice, concluded the evening before the
Court rose to order Colo. North committed. But Colo.
North having made his escape, he arrested the officer for
neglect of duty. Upon further consideration, however, he
thought proper to release the officer, who has since sued
Esq. Wood for false imprisonment. However this dispute
between the Justice and the Officer may terminate, it is

pretty clear it cannot materially affect the original process. Colo. North has not been seen here since the evening the attempt was made to apprehend him. It is said, he is gone to Boston upon business.[21]

One of the magistrates present at this hearing may have been Dr. Obadiah Williams of Vassalboro. In the collection of books the doctor left at his death was a small pamphlet entitled *The Trial of Atticus Before Justice Beau For a Rape*. This little work, a satirical drama, sets the argument over "Colo. North's affair" in the larger context of Anglo-American legal reform. If it had been published in Hallowell in 1791 instead of Boston in 1771, one might consider it a comment on the Foster-North case. The hero of the drama, Atticus, is a sober and learned man spitefully accused by a country bumpkin named Ezekiel Chuckle and his silly wife, Sarah. Judge Beau, Lawyer Rattle, and a host of witnesses with names like Deacon Scant, William Froth, and Mrs. Prim play their expected roles. When Prim accuses Atticus of generally lewd behavior with young women, the Justice asks, "Do you know this to be true?"

MRS. PRIM. Yes, Sir, as well as I know I am alive.
JUSTICE. Did you see it yourself?
MRS. PRIM. No, Sir, but brother Sam's wife told me that Cousin Eunice see Miss Sally Faddle, and her own sister was there, and told her of it. I could tell a thousand such things, I suppose, if I tried, but I won't now; so that's all.

While Atticus upholds the formality of the law, the country folk accept the informal power of reputation. Any effort to get them to be specific, to distinguish hearsay from fact, to weigh reasoned commentary against gossip, is futile. One scene even parodies the traditional use of testimony taken from unwed mothers in delivery, a practice still followed in the Kennebec, as we shall see in Chapter Four. Interestingly, it is not a midwife who takes the testimony, however, but a quack named Dr. Pip. *The Trial of Atticus* is an ephemeral document in a much larger argument over the roles of community standards in the enforcement of justice. *Atticus* presents a legalist argument, that abstract laws, interpreted and upheld by specialists, are the surest protectors of justice. Its butt was a judicial system that gave immense power to untrained justices of the peace, men who were as likely to be merchants, land speculators, or physicians as lawyers. It was the lay nature of New England law, its reliance on gossipy witnesses and rustic juries, that disturbed the author. The conflict between judicial and lay standards of evidence was an old one, of course, evident even in seventeenth-century witch trials, where judges seldom accepted the evidentiary standards of village accusers.[22] But the growth of the legal profession in the eighteenth century had made such issues more acute.

The Trial of Atticus was a satire on law, but it was also a story about rape. The attitudes it reveals suggest why it was so difficult for women to press charges for sexual assault. The stricter the rules of evidence, the more difficult it was to win a case that required juries to accept the word of a woman against the word of a man, unless he happened to belong to a stigmatized group. The assumption of *Atticus* is that women were silly creatures, easily influenced by the rivalries of the men around them, and given to spite. A trial for rape, then, was really a contest between the men involved—the husband or father, the accused, the judges, and jury—rather than a judgment of the events themselves. This was, of course, exactly the position taken by Henry Sewall in his letter to George Thatcher. He was far more concerned with the conflict between Joseph North and Obadiah Wood than with what happened between Rebecca Foster and the men she accused. This is surprising, given Sewall's general concern with moral behavior, yet he was already prejudiced against the Fosters, while his experience as clerk of the U.S. District Court gave him plenty of opportunity to associate with lawyers and to adopt their point of view. His letter, like the play, is essentially comic, a satirical dismissal of rural pettiness masquerading as law.[23]

Martha was unaware of legal issues or of squabbles between the judges. Her only comment on Esquire Wood's attempted arrest of Joseph North is a single sentence in her entry for January 18, 1790: "Colonel North flew from judgment."

North escaped the ignominy of being arrested by his own officer, but he did not escape trial. On July 10, 1790, he was "set to the bar" in Pownalboro Court House before the honorable justices of the Supreme Judicial Court, Francis Dana, Robert Treat Paine, Increase Sumner, and Nathan Cushing. The judges had sailed upriver from Boston as they did twice each year, bringing their white wigs and their black silk robes. Martha came downriver from Hallowell in the dress Lydia Densmore had made her. It was the first time she had been below Pittston since her arrival in the Kennebec twelve years before.

July 6, 1790. "I left home Early Bound for Pownalboro. Mr Ballard allso. We went on Board Leut. Pollards Boat. Stopt at Pittstown. Got to Mr Hatchs where we took Lodgings during the Courts setting. Went into coart afternoon." Characteristically, Martha said more about the journey than about the events that transpired once she got there. Her entries for the next few days, probably written retrospectively, are extraordinarily terse, eventually degenerating into mere etceteras. Fortunately, the minutes of the Supreme Judicial Court fill in some details about the general operation of the court, though they tell us little about the Foster case. There were thirty-nine cases listed on the docket; fewer than half were actually heard. Most were routine procedures—suits over the settlement of estates, appeals from lower court cases involving debt, breach of contract, or trespass, actions against towns for failing to maintain roads. There were two divorces and one petition for citizenship. But three of the thirty-nine cases, in addition to Judge North's, involved sexual offenses. These included a sensational slander suit, a trial for incest and infanticide, and Nathaniel Whitaker's appeal from an assault conviction.[24]

July 7, 1790. "Pownalboro. Attended coart." On the second day, the court sat in judgment on Hannah Barker, who had appealed her conviction from a lower court for slandering Polly Noble, daughter of a Newcastle justice of the peace. Barker had apparently said to one neighbor, "God of Heaven! What do you think has happened to Noble's family? Polly has been up to Boston & had a Negro Bastard," and had told another that "Poll" had been repeatedly guilty of fornication and that her father had "catched her at it under the counter." The court sustained the earlier conviction, fining the defendant the whopping sum of seventy-five pounds. Martha had been right: telling tales about a justice of the peace, or his family, might "Expose & perhaps ruin" a person.

July 8, 1790. "At ditto. Attended etc etc." Martha was present, though she gave no details when the jury heard the case of Thomas Meloney, charged with cohabiting with his sister Joannah and murdering an infant born of her body. Their father deposed that the two were indeed brother and sister, that "they have Lived in one house together Ever Since Johannah had her first Child," that she now had three children, but that "I don't know who was the father of them children." The old man signed his testimony with a mark.

July 9 1790. "At ditto. Attended etc etc." On the fourth day the court reversed a lower court conviction of Nathaniel Whitaker for the attempted rape of Milly Lambard. This was a curious case, in some ways the opposite of Rebecca Foster's. Whitaker had been installed as pastor in Canaan in 1784 and dismissed in 1789. Either immediately before or after his dismissal, Milly Lambard initiated the assault action. The crime had allegedly occurred four years before "in a field in Canaan."[25] Since Whitaker had been in Martha's house several times, it is surprising that she said nothing about the case. Perhaps the acquittal settled it in her mind, and she had no desire to expose the man further.

July 10, 1790. "At ditto. Attended. The Caus between this Commonwelth & Joseph North Esquire was tried & given to the jury." Whether Martha Ballard gave oral testimony in the upper room of the Pownalboro Court House or only affirmed her written deposition we do not know. The indictment, the verdict, and an expense account are all that have survived of the official court papers, though a brief statement sworn to by Elijah Davis suggests one direction the defense might have taken. Davis said he was in Winslow, eighteen miles away, at the time of the alleged assault and that "Major Henry Warren of Plimouth in the county of Plimouth" could attest to the same if he were called. He also claimed that "Messrs Lummus, Hunt, and Martin of Lebanon in the State of Connecticut, can testify that the General Character of the said Rebeckah as a woman of truth is notoriously bad." Unfortunately, he produced none of these witnesses—"the Reason why he has not procured the testimony of all the above mentioned witnesses, is because he has not had sufficient time for that purpose." (His case was continued to the next session and then dropped, the Fosters having left the area.)

Perhaps Joseph North also attacked Rebecca Foster's reputation. In the initial hearing in Vassalboro, as Martha observed, "strong atempts . . . were made to throw aspersions on her Carrectir," yet Martha also wrote that Judge North told her "he really believd Mrs Foster was treated as she Complains but he should Deny the Charg Exhibited against him." This is a puzzling statement. Was North saying that the woman had mistaken him for someone else? If the crime had occurred on a very dark night, that defense might have been possible. Perhaps he was distinguishing between the treatment of which she complained and the crime for which he was charged, saying that what happened happened but it was hardly an assault. He could not have been pleading compliance, however, since he had also told Martha "he never had the least reason to suspect her virtue or modesty." Since there were no witnesses to the crime, he may simply have insisted he was somewhere else at the time.

The alleged rapes in Hallowell, like most in eighteenth-century New England, were what twentieth-century analysts would call "acquaintance rape." As we have seen, there was a great deal of coming and going among neighbors. Any of the men named might have stopped in at Isaac Foster's house, to convey goods or news, to check on the family's welfare, or drink tea, to inquire about the pastor's affairs or to ask for lodging. Suppose a solicitous friend like Joseph North were to show up too late some night, perhaps a bit the worse for drink, throw stones at the window, and insist on coming in? Would that constitute breaking open "the Door of her house"? And if he begged a kiss, was that more than a pretty lady might expect?

Increase Sumner, one of the judges at Colonel North's trial, kept notes on an assault trial held in another county two years later. The pattern of testimony demonstrates the difficulty in reconciling contradictory testimony and conflicting assessments of character. The young woman in this action claimed her assailant had enticed her into the bushes when she carried water to the field, "ask'd me to lay down," and when she refused "pushed me down . . . & tried to be concerned with me." The witnesses for the defense claimed that the maid was the one who had enticed the man, that she "play'd about" and refused to go back to the house after delivering the water, that she herself went to the bushes for "slippery Elm bark," and that he refused to follow. One witness testified that "her Character is better than common," another that she "is called a liar in the neighborhood."

In Rebecca Foster's case, however, the mystery took on a deeper character. On April 20, three months before the trial, and eight months and seventeen days after the first of the alleged assaults, she had given birth to a daughter. Because the Fosters had moved from Hallowell to Vassalboro, Martha was not on hand for the delivery. She had written, "Neighbor Savage informed me that the Reverend Isaac Fosters lady was safe delivered of a daughter last evening and is cleverly." Unfortunately, we don't know exactly when Isaac Foster left home, but even if it had only been a few days before the presumed assaults, the timing was ambiguous enough to create a problem. Perhaps it was the pregnancy that finally forced Rebecca to tell her story. Neighbors—or her own husband—may have asked questions she could not answer.

That is why Martha's testimony was so crucial. She could affirm that Mrs. Foster had mentioned "abuses" by Joseph North just ten days after the alleged assault occurred and before any pregnancy could have been confirmed. Rebecca Foster may have remained silent, as Martha advised, until she was forced to speak. If her pregnancy was ill timed, then her accusations may

well have been intended to affirm her innocence (or to cover up
the guilt of an extramarital alliance). North's peculiar statement
that he believed Mrs. Foster had been treated as she complained
and that he never had any reason to doubt her modesty takes
on a new meaning in this context.

Any effort to solve the mystery only deepens it. Barring the
discovery of other documents, the case must rest with Martha
Ballard. When the court recessed for the Sabbath on July 11,
she and Ephraim had left their lodgings and gone to Eastern
River to visit friends. The next day, Ephraim returned to court
without her.

*July 12, 1790. "At Mr Kiders. Mr Ballard attended Coart. North
acquited to the great surprise of all that I heard speak of it."* Her
reference to "the great surprise" suggests that the evidence
against North had been damning. Certainly many of the people
she "heard speak of it" were other women, though of course
they were not on the jury. This brief entry is the closest she
ever came to asserting the judge's guilt. Given her usual habits,
the omission of a title before his name is telling.

*July 13, 1790. "Clear & hott. We Came to thee Coart house—saw
Melona receive the punishment which the Coart inflicted at 8 hours morn
then returnd to Mr Hatches, Paid our reckoning & sett out for home. I
wrode Mr Pollards hors. We dind at Magr Smiths. Calld at Mrs.
Poullins & Mr Jacksons. Arivd home near sunsett. Find Alice Ballard
here. Gillbreath helping Cyrus."*

Martha had taken her one and only trip to Pownalboro. The
day after she returned, she wrote simply, "Clear. Mr Foster
here. Took Breakfast." The rest of the month she hoed cabbages
and visited with her neighbors. The short sojourn of Isaac and
Rebecca Foster in the town was now history. William Howard
dropped his action for debt against the minister, the Walker case
was settled, and when the Supreme Judicial Court met again in
Pownalboro, the indictments against Elijah Davis and Joshua
Burgess were dropped. By then Isaac, Rebecca, and their children were far away from the Kennebec. They had joined Rebecca's parents, who had earlier emigrated to New York State.

In September of 1792, the Reverend Mr. Ezra Stiles, touring

in Westchester County, New York, reported, "Isaac Foster still at Bedford in the Parsonage House, but don't preach—drinks a Quart Rum a day. Wife handsome but mentis inops. Poor. Works for Colonel Sacket. A Devil incarnate—an abandoned Minister!"[26] Perhaps Stiles was passing on malicious gossip, perhaps not. If Rebecca was indeed mentally unstable, her credibility in the rape trial would be undermined, but even assuming that Stiles's information was correct, Isaac's intemperance and Rebecca's disability could have been consequences rather than causes of their nightmare in Hallowell. A nineteenth-century history of Bedford reports only that Isaac Foster preached two years in Bedford, leaving, "as tradition reports, with his name and that of his wife in bad repute." [27]

The Fosters went next to Rehobeth, Maryland, a town that took its name from the ancient site of Isaac's well. Here they could say with the patriarch, "the Lord hath made room for us" (Genesis 26:22). Isaac was pastor of an Episcopal church in Coventry Parish from 1795 until his death in 1800. Sometime thereafter, a family tradition reports, Rebecca and her youngest son went off to Peru hunting for gold. They were never heard from again.[28]

There is little more to add, except that for almost four years after Isaac Foster's dismissal Martha neglected "Public Worship." She attended church three times in 1789, the year after Foster was dismissed, eight in 1790 and in 1791. There were weekly meetings held in the meeting house, at the Hook, and in Henry Sewall's office. She ignored most of them. Not until 1794, when the town was formally divided into parishes, the remnants of the Chester church taking over the South Parish, the moderates in the old Hallowell church taking over the Middle Parish, did she regularly "worship in Public." [29]

The spring of 1791 brought an important change in the Ballard family. "Mr Ballard and Cyrus gave up their possession here to Peter Jones," Martha wrote on April 12. Peter Jones was a brother of the exiled John Jones, who would himself arrive in

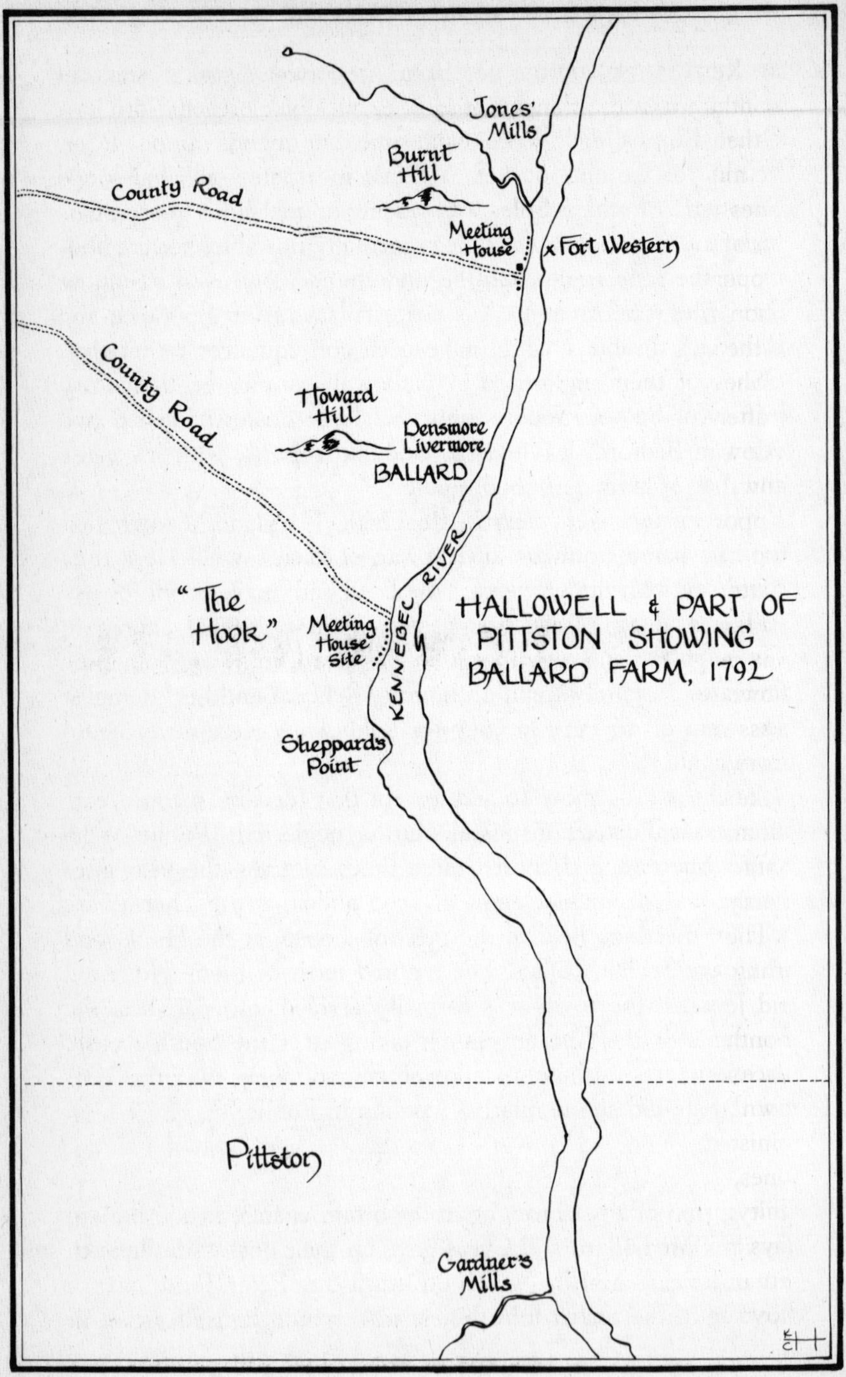

Jones' Mills

County Road

Burnt Hill

Meeting House

x Fort Western

County Road

Howard Hill

Densmore
Livermore

BALLARD

KENNEBEC RIVER

"The Hook"

Meeting House Site

HALLOWELL & PART OF
PITTSTON SHOWING
BALLARD FARM, 1792

Sheppard's Point

Pittston

Gardner's Mills

the Kennebec a few months later. After twelve years and four months as Jones's tenants, the Ballards had given up—or lost —their lease. On April 21, as Martha told it, "We removd from the mills to the house which was Old Leut Howards, and Peter Jones went to the mills with his family." She wrote in the margin of the next day's entry, as though nothing in particular had happened, "At home. Began my gardin." Her story of the transition from one house to another is told almost inadvertantly, in the course of a quiet chronicle of daily work.

She was relieved when the "old cow" delivered safely on May 3 after the two Ephraims drove it from the mills, though the following Sunday, when the boys went looking for "the young Cow," they found its calf dead. The poultry also suffered a temporary setback. When young Ephraim went to fetch a hen that had been left sitting on its eggs, he found it surrounded by shattered shells and a few pecking chicks. "She hatcht 16," Martha lamented. "Eleven of them perisht for want of proper care." [30] The new garden, too, offered problems. After her husband plowed it, Martha struggled with the neglected ground, "digging grass roots [and] raking them off" before she could plant. Still, the two cows gave enough milk that Martha was able to churn and make cheese. By the middle of May, beans, corn, and peas were up, and there were beet greens for dinner. On August 23, 1791, just four months after she first turned the soil at the Howard farm, Martha gathered "a ripe water mellion." [31]

The men continued their old work in new settings, the father riding outward from the Howard farm to do surveying, Cyrus and Jonathan working at other men's mills. In the first seven months after the move, Ephraim Sr. helped "Lay out a Burying place & meeting house spot given by Mr Charles Vahn to this town" (the Hook would soon have its own meeting house and minister), surveyed land for half a dozen men, including John Jones, spent three days making plans for the "Proprietors of Unity," four days surveying at "7-mile Brook," and fourteen days running lines for the State of Massachusetts. "Mr Ballard sett out for to Explore the Country Back of fort Hallifax imployd by this Commonwealth," Martha wrote on November 9,

1791. He also spent several days surveying a plot of unimproved land "at the North End of this town" that would eventually become the Ballard farm.[32]

Meanwhile, Cyrus and his father were fitting out a mill they had leased somewhere in Pittston.[33] Cyrus lived at home for the first few months after the move, shearing sheep, helping with the haying, and going occasionally to Winslow or to Vassalboro. In September he carried his bed and chest downriver to the new mill, perhaps one built by Ephraim's old patron Silvester Gardiner.[34] Cyrus typically worked in Pittston during the week, returning home on the Sabbath. "He tended his mill all last night," Martha wrote on October 16, a Sunday.

Jonathan lived away from home during the first few months, stopping in once in a while for breakfast or dinner, in June bringing his mother "part of a smoked salmon." Perhaps he was employed upriver somewhere, though probably he was working with or for Peter Jones. Suddenly at the end of July, Martha announced "Cyrus Brot Jonathans things down here" and then "Cyrus led Jonathans sow home."[35] On November 22 she reported stiffly, "The Gentlemen who were Chosen as referees in the Cause between Peter Jones & my son Jonathan sett this day. They gave Jones to 8 [shillings] damages & the Cost of Coart was 2 pound. I would wish my son might learn to govern his temper for the futer."[36]

(Peter Jones's temper was the subject of a later entry in Martha's diary. The source of the information was Jonathan, who had reason enough to exaggerate the man's deficiencies. His mother obviously believed him. "Jonathan here," she wrote on June 21, 1792. "Informed me Mrs Jones is very unwell ocationed by her Husband's ill usage & keeping her in the seller Barefoot. O the wretch. He Deserves severe punishment." There is no evidence Jones ever was punished, at least by any earthly court. On May 9, 1796, Martha reported the "mallancoly news" that "Peter Jones was Drowned this afternoon in the mill stream.")

In contrast to the disruptions in the men's work, textile production was easily restored. On June 15, 1791, Hannah put the first web into the loom. Spinning, weaving, and sewing continued almost uninterrupted for the next two years. "Hannah Beemed the woollin shurting," Martha wrote on a Monday, and on Wednesday of the same week, "Hannah got the shurting out, 20 yards & put another web in."[37] Martha and her girls even turned worn clothes into coverlets, cutting narrow strips of cloth from old petticoats or breeches, joining the pieces end to end in continuous strings of filler for the loom. These coverlets were an earlier version of the rag carpets that nineteenth-century housewives tacked down on their wooden floors, strong linen threads, widely spaced across the loom, interwoven with the rags, to form a durable—and heavy—covering. Preparing the rags was as much trouble as weaving them ("Cutting & sewing rags for a coverlid," Martha Ballard would say), though it took a good deal less time than spinning an equal weight of yarn. The girls wove the coverlets in series, filling in the appropriate length for a bed, leaving a foot or so of unfilled warp for a fringe and beginning again without cutting the threads, one patch of weaving following another until the end of the web was reached. "Hannah got the Coverluds out 4 of them," Martha wrote.[38]

Parthenia Barton still lived with the Ballards, and a new set of neighbors was integrated into the production system. Mrs. Welch and Mrs. Livermore now warped in the place of Mrs. Savage and Mrs. Hamlin, and when the girls needed to borrow a reed, they went to the Chamberlains as well as to the Pollards.[39] They "washt & Bleacht yarn at Mr Densmores Brook" rather than at the mill pond. Young Ephraim, now thirteen, also participated in the neighborhood economy: "Ephraim got in our Pees & helpt Mr Waid get his Oats in," and on another day, "Cyrus & Ephraim helpt Mr Livermore about his hay."[40]

For the first time, however, Martha had a conflict with a neighbor. On September 1, 1792, she spent part of the day gathering corn that "swine had broke down in our field." No mention of the identity of those swine, but the next day, she reported, "Mr. Livermore's swine in our field a number of time. I went my self & informd him." This mild encounter seems to have led to a major altercation the next summer. On July 26,

1793, Mr. Livermore came to the house and "threatened giting a warrent for me because I had my Turkeys put up. [Hogs and fowl both ran wild, until "put up," or penned, prior to slaughtering.] He Claimed them as his, accused me with stealing one of his last year. His wife Came here afterwards & Declard shee saw some of my famely drive her Turkey from here, which I find was a mistake or falshood as Every one of us say we did not. Shee Came into our house & had a Long Conversation, two much to write." Too much—and perhaps too upsetting—to write. Martha disliked controversy. Only the most outrageous violations of neighborliness made it into her diary.

In contrast, the relationship with the Densmores was uniformly cordial. The Densmores lived just upriver from the Ballards, on land owned by Daniel Cony.[41] "Mr Ballard at Esquire Coneys this morng. Helpt Mr Densmore fraiming & raisng his House Fraim," Martha wrote on July 4, 1791. (A new house was one of the "improvements" settlers made on land they hoped to buy.) The Densmores moved in on September 15 even though the chimney was not yet up to the ridgepole. Thomas Densmore was a tailor as well as a farmer. He was also a slaughterer, if the frequency with which he killed cows or pigs for the Ballards is any guide. His wife, Lydia, as we have seen, was a dressmaker. Neither pregnancy nor an unfinished house nor a houseful of children prevented her from pursuing her trade. On September 14, the day before she moved into the new house and just a week before she started in labor with her ninth (or tenth?) child, she brought her three youngest children to the Ballard house to fit a dress for Martha.

On November 15, 1791, Martha wrote: "Dolly went to Mr Densmores to Learn the Taylors art. I wish her Sucscess & happiness." Although Martha used Mr. Densmore's name in both of the entries referring to Dolly's apprenticeship, it was Lydia Densmore's skills—dressmaking and weaving—that Dolly perfected. Dolly had suffered from a recurring illness during the first months at the Howard farm, a malaise serious enough to have brought Dr. Cony, who recommended port wine, but she now seemed recovered.[42] She stayed with the

Densmores a year. Her brothers carried her bed and bedding to the new house, where she slept during the week, coming home on Sundays—or when needed. "Dolly and Sally Densmore here," her mother would write, or "Dolly came home to instruct the girls how to draw their piece of Dimmity."[43]

With Hannah and Parthenia minding the kitchen and the loom, Martha was free to practice midwifery, tend her garden and herbs, and care for her animals. She doctored her animals the way she did her neighbors' children. When a sheep came from the field "wounded in the neck," she "drest it with Tarr," and when a lamb was born "with the Entrales all out," she "put them in to the boddy again [and] sewd up the breatch," noting with satisfaction that the animal "suckt & walkt afterwards."[44] In 1792 turkeys were a compelling interest. Martha found the first turkey on its nest on April 7. From then until the end of May she was busy "setting" the big birds. "Put 17 eggs under a turkey," she wrote on May 4 . . . and on May 6 . . . and on May 28. By the end of the month she had put seventy-two eggs under her birds. On May 26 "the black turkey brought out 14 chicks." By June 2 there were forty-three fledglings in the yard. Another fourteen hatched in mid-August, not long before the first of the spring brood was ready for the table.

Meanwhile, Martha's midwifery practice grew. The Howard farm stood midway between the Fort and the Hook and near the road to Winthrop. Messengers fetched her from all directions. "I have spent but one whole Day at home since October 23," she wrote on November 11, 1791. Her practice continued to expand until she was attending more than fifty deliveries a year. It was a perfect system, the girls washing and cooking and gathering skills and goods, the mother moving gracefully between her garden and her neighbors' needs. But families, too, have their seasons of planting and harvest. The productivity in the Ballard household was not directed toward enriching the parents but toward launching the young folks in households of their own.

CHAPTER FOUR

NOVEMBER 1792

"Matrimonial writes"

OCTOBER

28 G *At home. A Marriag in my Family.*
Cloudy fornoon, a little rain & Thunder, Clear before night.
Cyrus was not at home. Thee Matrimonial writes were cellibrated between Mr Moses Pollard off this Town and my
daughter Hannah this Evening. Esquire Cony performed the
ceremony. My son & his wife & son tarry here.

29 2 *At home. We killd three young Turkeys.*
Cloudy. Dolly went to Mr Densmores, Mr Ballard to the hook.
I have been at home. Sally here helping the girls. Mr Pollard &
Savage supt here.

30 3 *At home. Roasted a Turkey.*
Clear & pleasant. Mr Ballard been to Colonel Sewalls & the
Hook. I have been at home. Sally & the girls put a Bed quilt in
to the fraim for Parthenia. Sarah Densmore & Dolly here the
Evng.

31 4 *At home.*
Clear. Mr Ballard went to Pittston. Polly Pollard, Mrs Damrin,

& my daughter Dolly quilted all day. Mrs Livermore afternoon. I have been at home. Mr Town sleeps here.

NOVEMBER

1 5 *At Mr Hodges Birth 38th. Son Town went home.*
Cloudy & some rain. Mr Town left here after breakfast. The girls had the Ladies to help them quillt. I was Calld to see Mrs Hodges at 4 h pm. Shee was safe delivered at 11 h Evening off a very fine son her sixth child. Mr Ballard came home.
Birth Ezra Hodges Son X X

2 6 *At dittoes & Mr Burtuns & Magr Stickneys. Birth 39. Bizer Benjamins wife delivered of 2 sons Both dead.**
Clear forenoon, Cloudy afternoon, rain at Evening. I receivd 6/ of Mr Hodges & returnd home at noon. Left my patient cleverly. Calld at Mr Burtuns. His Lady is cleverly. I Bot off him 2 iron kettles which cost 7/, 1 spider at 3/6, 2 pepper boxes & 2 dippirs at /6 each, 2/, 1 yd binding /1, ginn 2/6, total 15/1.† I went to Magr Stickneys at 9 h Evn. His wife delivered at 11 h 5 m off a daughter. I tarried all night.
Birth Benjamin Stickneys daughter X X

3 7 *At Mr Stickneys & Mr Devenports.*
Rainy forenoon. I tarried at the Magrs till after dineing. Recevd 6/ as a reward. Mrs Conry came with me to Mr Devenports where we spent the remainder of the afternoon. Returned home at dusk. I left my patients Cleverly.

4 G *At home*
Clear. I have been at home. Dolly here. Dolly not [sentence incomplete]

---

*Here Martha is reporting a delivery she did not attend.
†In eighteenth-century accounting, a virgule (/) divided shillings and pence. "7/" therefore means 7 shillings, "/6" means 6 pence.

5   2   *At home. J Jones here.*
Clear. Mr Ballard at Pittston. Mr John Jones & a Mr Dutten
here. My girls washt. I at home.

6   3   *At Mr Burtuns.*
Clear. I went to see Mrs Burtun who has had an ill turn & is
Better. Dolly sleeps here.

7   4   *At home. Ephraim was Banking the house.*
Clear. Cyrus Came here. I have been at home. Helpt quillt on
Hannahs Bed quilt. We got it out late in the Evening.

8   5   *At home. Mr Jones here, Son Cyrus allso.*
Foggy morn. Sun shone at 10 h. Cyrus went to his Brothers.
Mr J Jones here. I have been at home. Mrs Edson here to warp
a web of Mrs Densmores. Mr Pollard & Pitt here the night.

9   6   *At home. Cyrus went to Pitston. Mrs Parker returned home.*
Cloudy morn. Cyrus went to Pittston afternoon. It raind before
night. A sever N E Storm in the night. I have been at home.
Mrs Bradbury & Betsy Champny here.

10 7   *At home*
Cloudy & some rain. I have been at home. Stript Turkey
feathers.

11 G   *At home. Mr Pages & Jones here.*
Clear part the day. Mr Ballard returnd from Pitston. Mr J Jones
& Mr Page & son Jonathan dind here. Mr Pollard & Pitt supt.
I have been at home. Mr Ballard paid John Jones 21 dollars in
part of a note he had against him.

12 2   *At home. Cyrus came up here.*
Clear part of the day. Mr Ballard at the hook & to Joness mill.
Cyrus came here at 6 hour pm. I have been at home.

13   3   *At home. Cyrus sleeps here.*
The sun rose clear. Cloudy some part the day. Mr Ballard is gone to Varsalboro. Cyrus up to Mr Savages 2 hour pm Clearing a wood road.

14   4   *At Savage Boltons & others*
Cloudy & a very Chilly air. I went up as far as Savage Boltons. He paid me 8/ at Mr Burtuns for attending his wife the 19th of January last. I Bot 2 puter dishes weight 5 lb at 2/, 1 coffee pot 3/6, six table spoons 1/8, total 15/2. I paid 7/2 cash. Mr Bolton answers 8/ of it.

15   5   *At home. Cyrus & Dolly returned home.*
Clear. Mr Ballard workt at the Bridg over the gully. I have been at home. Mrs Densmore dind & took Tea. Mr Seth Williams & his wife here. Cyrus came home. Has quit thee grist mill he has tended. Dolly returnd from her apprentiship with Mr Densmore. Cyrus tended Mr Hollowells mill 14 months. Capt Nichols has hired it now.

16   6   *At home. Finisht a pair of hos for Dolly.*
Snowd the most off the day. I have been at home. We killd 2 Turkeys. Mr Ballard went to Mr Pollards. Bot 5 1/2 lb flax at /9, 5 lb Butter at /10.

17   7   *At home*
Clear. Mr Ballard been up to Jonathans & to the hook. Cyrus went to Pittston and brot his chest & things home. I have been at home. Have not been so well as I could wish.

18   G   *At home. Mr Shubal Pitt and Parthenia Barton joind in Mariage.*
Rainy. Mr Pollard & Pitt dind here. Thee latter was joind in the Bands of wedlock with Parthenia Barton. The ceremony performd by Samuel Duttun Esq. I have been at home. We had no Company Except our famely attend. Thee Justice gave the fee to the Bride.

There were three marriages in the Ballard family in 1792, two of them described in the diary segment that opens this chapter. The other occurred in February, when Jonathan reluctantly married Sally Pierce, who had initiated a paternity suit against him. Martha's descriptions of the three weddings and the events surrounding them—one so dramatic, the others so placidly domestic—illuminate little-known marriage customs in rural New England.

Some historians see the mid-eighteenth century as a transitional time in the history of the family, an era when young people began to exercise greater freedom in choosing marriage partners, when romantic and sexual attraction between couples became more important than economic negotiations between parents. Others argue that romantic love and economic calculation had long coexisted in the English-speaking world, that well before the eighteenth century, marriages were primarily contracts between individuals rather than alliances of families.[1] Martha's diary supports the notion that children chose their own spouses; there is no evidence of parental negotiation, and little hint of parental supervision in any of the courtships she describes. The diary also confirms the prevalence of premarital sex. Yet there is little evidence of romance and much to suggest that economic concerns remained central. The weddings in the Ballard family were distinctly unglamorous affairs, almost nonevents. For the women, they were surrounded by an intense productivity, a gathering of resources that defined their meaning and purpose.

"Thee Matrimonial writes were cellibrated between Mr Moses Pollard off this Town and my daughter Hannah this Evening," Martha wrote on October 28. The misspelling of "writes" for "rites" is a charming accident. Most of what we know about patterns of marriage in eighteenth-century New England comes from official records, the scanty "writes," of men like Henry Sewall, who was serving as town clerk in 1792 and who entered marriage intentions and sometimes marriage dates in the town book. Martha imitated the starched formality of such records in describing the groom as "*Mr* Moses Pollard *off this town*," as if he were some newly arrived gentleman rather than the grown-up son of her old friends Amos and Merriam Pollard.

Marriages were regulated under Massachusetts law according to "An Act for the Orderly Solemnization of Marriages" passed on June 22, 1786. This new legislation reflected the old colonial faith in community surveillance. A justice of the peace or minister could perform marriages only when the bride or the groom or both belonged to his town. Furthermore, the couple had to present a certificate signed by the town clerk indicating that their intent of marriage had been appropriately "published" either at three "publick religious meetings, on different days, at three days distance exclusively" or by posting for "the space of fourteen days, in some publick place."[2]

In 1792 Henry Sewall entered twenty-one intentions of marriage in the town book, noting that one engagement "fell through" before a certificate was issued and that another "broke off." In the case of John Chamberlain and Mary Brown, he wrote, the certificate was "barred by a written objection filed by his Father." That was in May. In December Sewall added: "Certificate issued by consent of the Father who filed the objections aforesaid." Martha's entry on December 16 fills in the details in this domestic drama: "John Chamberlain was marid the 10 instant, removed his wife to Sidney the 11th; Shee was delivered of a daughter the 12th and it Expired before night."[3] As we shall see, John Chamberlain's story was not unique.

Conscientious town clerks, and Henry Sewall was one, not only kept orderly lists of intentions filed and certificates issued but also tried to compile and enter into the official record lists of marriages actually performed. In April of 1793 three Hallowell justices "returned" their marriage lists to Henry Sewall. Samuel Dutton officiated at his only ceremony of the year when he joined Parthenia Barton and Shubael Pitts "in the bands of wedlock." Daniel Cony married only one other couple in 1792 in addition to Hannah and Moses Pollard. Parthenia and Hannah seem to have gone out of their way to avoid the most popular (or available) of Hallowell's justices, Joseph North.[4]

"Thee Matrimonial writes were *cellibrated* between Mr Moses Pollard off this Town and my daughter Hannah." Despite the verb there is little evidence of celebration in Martha's scanty description. Here was no gathering of far-flung (or even immediate) family and friends. Cyrus wasn't there, though it was a Sunday, his usual day at home, nor did Lucy and Ezra Towne ride down from Winslow. Except for Jonathan and his family, there seem to have been no other guests, not even the groom's parents, who were, after all, good friends of the Ballards. If anyone baked pies or cakes, Martha Ballard didn't say so, nor did the roast turkey appear until Tuesday, two days *after* the wedding. There is no more sign of special festivity in the entry for November 18: "Mr Pollard & Pitt dind here. Thee latter was joind in the Bands off wedlock with Parthenia Barton." In Martha's description, the wedding appears almost as an afterthought to the young men's presence at dinner.[5]

What is even more puzzling is the apparent failure of the brides to leave home. Through the month of November, Hannah and Parthenia continued to act like Martha's "girls," quilting, washing, and helping with the housework. Moses and Shubael came and went. "Mr Pollard & Pitt here the night." "Mr Pollard & Pitt supt." "Mr Pollard and Pitt waited on their wives & Dolly to Mr Pollards."[6] The entry for the day of Parthenia's wedding, "Mr Pollard & Pitt dind here," was part, then, of a larger pattern. What is especially striking is Martha's pairing of the two names. On November 8, when Martha noted that the two were "here the night," Moses was a husband, Shubael still a husband-to-be. Again on November 30, both men "took breakfast," apparently having spent the night. If they had been sleeping and taking meals there consistently, it would not have been necessary to note their presence.

Twentieth-century readers puzzle over such behavior because

we think of a wedding as a discrete event, a brief and festive occurrence. The guests gather, the music plays, the proper words are said, and the celebration begins. It is difficult to imagine a "wedding" that meanders through six weeks of housework and family suppers, to comprehend a world in which brides sleep at home (with or without their grooms) for more than a month after they have been "joind in the Bands of wedlock." But that, in fact, is what happened at the Ballards' and in many New England households in the late eighteenth century. The rituals of marriage began with "publication" (in Hannah's and Parthenia's case six weeks before the ceremony) and ended when the young couples finally "went to housekeeping" at about the same interval after.

The phrase "went to housekeeping" had perhaps an even greater resonance than the words "joind in Mariage." Until Hannah and Parthenia actually left the house, they remained "the girls." Once they had gone, they were forever after "Daughter Pollard" and "Mrs Pitts." Martha later recalled that she had gone to housekeeping the same day as she was married, but in Hallowell that practice was unusual. All the marriages recorded in the diary followed the same leisurely pattern. Hannah, Parthenia, and Jonathan all went to housekeeping more than a month after marriage, as did Dolly and her cousin Betsy Barton three years later, and Ephraim, Jr., in 1804. (During the interval between Betsy Barton's marriage and her departure from the house, Martha noted that she and the other "girls" had "Closd an opperation for the itch and washt hoping they are Cured.")[7]

Henry Sewall's diary confirms the pattern. He was married in Georgetown on February 9, 1786, spent a few weeks with his wife's family, then returned to Hallowell, leaving Tabitha behind. Not until July 7, when Tabby arrived from Georgetown with "Miss Esther," presumably a cousin or sister, did the young couple "go to housekeeping." What is similar about all these cases is the coming and going of the groom—almost as in courtship—the bride remaining in her parents' house. When "Mr Pollard and Pitt waited on their wives & Dolly to Mr Pollards" (while the Ballards roasted a turkey at home), Hannah was making her first formal visit to her husband's family. Significantly, she and Moses were accompanied by other people, just as Tabby Sewall had been when she finally came from Georgetown to Hallowell.

According to Ellen Rothman, even in the early nineteenth century wedding rituals affirmed ties of community. A week of neighborly visiting following the wedding was more common than a journey, and when couples did take a trip, other people often went along. This practice began to change in the second half of the nineteenth century. "Beginning in the 1870s, etiquette books advocated that the couple leave the church—where middle-class weddings increasingly took place—together and alone, and that instead of the 'harassing bridal tour,' they enjoy 'a honeymoon of repose, exempted from claims of society,'" By the 1880s, "honeymoon trips to 'romantic' locations were expected to follow weddings."[8]

In the late eighteenth century, romance was still subordinate to the larger process of establishing a new economic relationship. The issue for Hannah and Moses was not where they would spend their wedding night but when and how they would begin housekeeping. Providing household goods seems to have been a joint responsibility of mother, father, and daughter. On October 20, eight days before Hannah's wedding, Martha bought a case of knives and forks, some small spoons, sewing silk, and 28 3/4 yards of a fabric she called "Camblesteen" from one store at the Hook and a dozen plates from another. Three days later, Ephraim returned to the second store to purchase six bowls (whether on his own credit or Martha's we do not know). For both of them the coming wedding was an excuse for collecting debts. On October 17 he brought home "9 1/2 yd. Camblet teen, 5 yds Linning, & 3 lb Tea and a handkf which he had off Mr Bridg for our attendance at Supreme Cort." A month later, Martha used a note of credit she had collected from Savage Bolton to help buy pewter dishes, a coffee pot, and six tablespoons at Burton's.

Earlier Mr. Burton had given Martha a looking glass, "which I bestowed on my Daughter Hannah."[9] Whether Hannah was the recipient of all the goods assembled that month we do not know.

The mention of two iron kettles, two pepper boxes, and two dippers in the entry for November 2 is suggestive. While one might certainly use two kettles, two pepper boxes were hardly necessary. Was Martha helping to supply Parthenia as well as her daughter? Even taken together these purchases seem few, yet household inventories from Hallowell suggest that the goods assembled in October and November of 1792 were in fact representative of what a young couple might have—a few plates and bowls, some pewter spoons, knives and forks, a coffee pot, a couple of kettles, and a frying pan, or "spider." Even well-established households in the town had little more.[10]

While Martha circled from Mr. Burton's to the Hook collecting crockery and tinware, Hannah and Parthenia intensified their own work. "The girls had the Ladies to help them quillt," Martha wrote on November 1, four days after Hannah's wedding. Quilting was the most insistent of the matrimonial preparations. The first round brought the neighbors, the women coming by turns, Sally Cox and Sarah Densmore on October 30, Polly Pollard, Mrs. Damrin, and Mrs. Livermore on October 31, and the unnamed group of "Ladies" on November 1. Whether Parthenia's was the first or the only quilt to go into the frame during that three-day period we do not know.

A different kind of stitching, less social, more intense, consuming the total attention of the two brides for a full day or more, began later that month. Hannah had begun "piecing a Bedquilt" on November 20 (two days after Parthenia's wedding), but had interrupted her work to weave a tow and woolen blanket. On November 26, she put the quilt "into the Fraim" and with the help of Parthenia and Dolly "quilted it out before shee slept." Parthenia's "Callico Bed quilt" came next. This time Martha as well as the girls helped with the quilting. Parthenia finished it the next day.

These quilts probably combined a top made of imported fabric, a filler of combed wool, and a homespun lining, the three layers being stretched tightly on a wooden frame, marked with chalk, then quilted together.[11] (In the fanciest quilts, the stitching formed an intricate maze of feathers, fans, and scrolls.) One of the oldest pieced quilts known to have been made in America is a Maine coverlet, long identified as a "wedding quilt" because of the appliquéd hearts in the center.[12] Hearts or no hearts, the quilts made in the Ballard house in November of 1792 were clearly associated with the transition from girlhood to marriage. In this sense, quilting, too, was one of the rites of marriage.

Marriage customs are more easily discovered in Martha's diary than the rituals of courting. "Moses Pollard waited on my daughters & Parthenia to his dads this Evening," she wrote on December 19, 1791, adding, "This day is the Anavarsary of my marriage. I went to housekeeping the same day." Whether the juxtaposition of the two entries was coincidental or prophetic, "Mr. Pollard's" name appears only four times more before the notice of his marriage to Hannah. In fact, there are no explicit references to Hannah and Moses "keeping company" in the year before their marriage. On March 15, 1792, Hannah returned from the Burtons' house, where she had been caring for their children. "Mr Hamlin, Burtun, Pollard, Pattridge, Esquire Hales Lady, 2 Mrs Bisbes, Rockwood, & Sally Hamlin with her," her mother wrote, adding, "The Ladies dine & drank coffee here. Mr Haywood, Pollard, & Patridge waited on them & my daughters at Evening to Mr Pollards." Without the knowledge that "Mr Pollard" was about to become Hannah's husband, there would be no way to separate him out from the crowd of visitors.

The mixture of sisters and friends, married and unmarried people, and uneven numbers of males and females is typical of the gatherings of young folks described in the diary. It was also common for such groups to gather at "Mr Pollard's" or "Mr Thomas's"—that is, at the two taverns in the town. On October 11, 1793, for example, a year after Hannah's and Parthenia's weddings, "Esquire Ebenezor Hail & Lady & Mrs Strattne, Daughter Pollard & Mrs Pitts dind here. Dolly & Sally went to Mr Pollards with them." Dolly was then twenty-one years old, though Sally Cox, the new helper in the Ballard family, was just eighteen. There seems to have been no taboo against young ladies participating in mixed gatherings at taverns or elsewhere, accompanied or alone. "Dolly & Sally at Mr. Thomas's at Evening," Martha wrote on October 30. Her description for December 23, 1794—"Dolly & Sally went to a Daunce at Mr Capins. Were attended by a Mr Lambart and White"—is a rare example of what we would think of as courting or dating.[13] (That Martha referred to Barnabas Lambard as "a Mr Lambart" suggests her future son-in-law was still a relative stranger.)

Dolly's courtship lasted four months, but resulted in only three entries in the diary. "Mr Lambart and White spent Evening," Martha wrote on February 11, 1795. On March 1, when Charles Gill and Betsy Barton were married at the Ballard house, Lambard was among the persons present. On March 15, during the period before the Gills went to housekeeping, Martha wrote, "Mr Gill & Lambart & D. Livermore here at Evening," combining the newly married husband, the suitor, and a casual visitor in a single stroke. Then on April 19, "Mr Barnabas Lambart auskt our Consent that he might Marrie our daughter Dolly." The two were published the next day and married on May 14, Esquire Brooks officiating.

In Martha's diary the passionate intensity we associate with romantic love appears only as an aberration. "Enformed that Mr Smith was gone away & is feared he Desirs to Deprive himself of Life on acount of Polly Hamlin's refuseing to wed with him," she wrote on February 27, 1786. For a time the woes of the abandoned suitor created anxiety—and entertainment—in Hallowell. "Smith & Polly Hamlin are in all Conversation at present," Martha wrote after taking tea at a neighbor's. By March 5 she could report a rumor that Smith had hanged himself, though ten days later he was back in town, apparently resigned to his fate.[14] In contrast, Martha described her own children's courtships as casually as she noted the black turkey sitting on its nest.

If Hannah or Dolly had been keeping the diary, there might have been more evidence of romance. It is a mistake, however, to draw too sharp a distinction between traditional notions of marriage as an economic (and sometimes spiritual) partnership and supposedly newer ideas that emphasized sexual attraction and romance. There is plenty of evidence from northern New England to suggest that sexual attraction played a central role in courtship, but there was no inherent conflict between that motive and the need to find a hardworking and productive spouse capable of bearing his or her full share of the work of a farm or business. Group work parties, often referred to in New England as "frolics," reinforced the connection.

In each of the two autumns before Hannah's marriage, there were quiltings at the Ballard house, each involving several days of individual and group work before the men arrived for a dance. On November 8, 1790, "The girls quilted a Bed quillt & went to Mr Craggs spent Evng." The next day, "The girls quilted two quilts. Hannah Rockwood & Mrs Benjamin helpt the Evening. We Bakt mins and pumpkin pies. Mrs Porter here." Then on November 10, "My girls had some neighbours to help them quilt a bed quilt, 15 ladies. They began to quilt at 3 hour pm. Finisht and took it out at 7 evening. There were 12 gentlemen took tea. They danced a little while after supper. Behaved exceeding cleverly . . . Were all returned home before the 11th hour."

The next year, on September 19, Martha wrote that her girls had spent part of the day "peecing Bed quillts." This can hardly have been the intricate patchwork common to the next century, however, for they also managed to do the family wash that day and then to go to a neighbor's house with Moses Pollard at night. The next day they "put a Bed quillt into the fraim" and "Bakt cakes & pies." On September 21, they "had a quilting, got out one & partly quilted another," before the gentlemen arrived for refreshments and a dance.

Young men helped to celebrate the completion of quilts just as young women celebrated a house- or barn-raising by gathering for a dance. Huskings, too, brought young folks together for labor and fun—and sometimes, too, for abandoned drinking and sexual liaisons.[15] Martha was clearly relieved when at the raising of the sawmill there were only a few persons among the "vast concorse of men and children" who were "disguised with Licquor." Her comment after a quilting that the young folks "were all returned home before the 11th hour" contrasts with her report of a later husking and quilting at the Densmores', "my young folks there came home late," or of a winter frolic, "Jonathan and girls go sleigh riding, get home at half past 12 at night."[16]

On one of her rare visits to church, Martha heard a visiting pastor (a "good old Gentleman") give a discourse "adapted to the youth." "His Exortations were Excelent," she wrote. "May they be deeply impresst on their minds for their future good."[17] As a parent—and a midwife—she knew too well the dangers facing the youth of her town. Yet the freedom and abandon of group "frolics" was limited. Barn-raisings and husking bees encouraged hard work and responsibility to the group even as they gave opportunities for sexual experimentation and carousing. Taverns, too, were never purely recreational, since they were the sites of political meetings, patriotic celebrations, and in some years town meetings and courts, as well as dances and drinking parties. The courting patterns and matrimonial customs of eighteenth-century Hallowell wove couples into the larger community, reinforcing gender roles, celebrating group identity, and, though it may not be so obvious, maintaining the boundaries within which sexuality might be expressed.

It snowed on October 23, 1791, the day Martha was summoned to Sally Pierce. Because this was going to be an illegitimate birth, she knew what she had to ask. She also knew what Sally would say.

> Shee was safe delivered at 1 hour pm of a fine son, her illness very severe but I left her cleverly & returnd ... about sun sett. Sally declard that my son Jonathan was the father of her child.

In the margin Martha wrote simply, "Sally Pierce's son. Birth 27th."

Before we can understand the full import of that entry, we need to know something about the legal position of unwed mothers in eighteenth-century New England. Massachusetts law

TABLE I   LINCOLN COUNTY COURT OF GENERAL SESSIONS
FORNICATION AND PATERNITY ACTIONS, 1761–1799

Date	Women	Men: "Unknown"	Presented	Convicted
1761–1765	9	2	1	1
1766–1770	20	3	3	2
1771–1775	11	2	0	0
1776–1780	12	1	2	1
1781–1785	21	0	4	4
1786–1790	0	0	3	2
1791–1795	0	0	6	6
1796–1799	0	0	0	0

NOTE: Kennebec County was separated from Lincoln in 1799. There are no fornication or maintenance cases in the first General Sessions Record Books for the new county. Unfortunately, court papers for the early nineteenth century have not survived.

had always defined sexual intercourse between unmarried persons as a crime. In the seventeenth and early eighteenth centuries, courts had punished men who fathered children out of wedlock as rigorously as the women concerned, often relying on testimony taken from mothers during delivery to establish the fathers' identity, but by the middle of the eighteenth century, most historians argue, fornication had become a woman's crime.

William Nelson has shown that while fornication prosecutions still accounted for more than a third of criminal actions in Massachusetts between 1760 and 1774, in only one case was the *father* of an illegitimate child prosecuted—a black man suspected of cohabiting with a white woman. By the end of the century, actions against women had also disappeared from court dockets. Prosecutions dropped from seventy-two per year in the years 1760–1774 to fifty-eight during the revolutionary years and finally to fewer than five after 1786. Nelson found only four prosecutions after 1790 in the entire Commonwealth. Lincoln County records show the same decline. Between 1761 and 1785, seventy-three women but only ten men were presented for fornication or related crimes. No women were presented after 1785.[18]

Historians are still debating the significance of such changes. Some stress liberalization, arguing that as courts became more concerned with mediating property disputes than enforcing Puritan standards of moral behavior, sex became a private affair. Others perceive the decline in fornication prosecutions as reflecting generational tensions in a society that had given up the legalism of the Puritans but had not yet developed the repressive individualism of the Victorians. More recent studies have emphasized gender issues, arguing that changes in fornication proceedings reflected a larger argument over female sexuality, an argument vividly displayed in eighteenth-century novels of seduction, some of which openly challenged the prevailing double standard.[19]

Against such evidence, Sally Pierce's declaration appears a quaint and inexplicable throwback to an earlier era. It was not. Evidence from Martha's diary and from supporting legal documents casts doubt on the notion that sexual behavior had in fact become a private concern. The diary suggests that even in a newly settled lumbering town like Hallowell, sexual norms (though neither Puritan nor Victorian) were clearly defined and communally enforced, that courts seldom prosecuted sexual deviance because informal mechanisms of control were so powerful. It also casts doubt on the use of General Sessions records or elite literature to define the double standard. There were certainly inequities in the way male and female culpability was defined in this period, yet there is no evidence that in rural communities women who bore children out of wedlock were either ruined or abandoned as early novels would suggest.

The prosecutorial double standard originated in a 1668 Massachusetts law that introduced the English practice of asking unwed mothers to name the father of their child during delivery. At first glance, questioning a woman in labor seems a form of harassment. In practice, it was a formality allowing the woman, her relatives, or in some cases the selectmen of her town to claim child support. The man she accused could not be convicted of fornication (confession or witnesses were needed for that), but unless there was overwhelming evidence to the contrary, he would be judged the "reputed father" of her child and required to pay for its support. The assumption was that a woman asked to testify at the height of travail would not lie.

In fact, early courts showed a remarkable reluctance to question such testimony. Although Alice Metherell of Kittery, Maine, had been convicted of a false oath in an earlier case of bastardy (she had delivered a black child after accusing a white man), she was able in 1695 to get maintenance from John Thompson and even to defend herself against a slander suit from him. As late as 1724 Bathsheba Lyston's accusation of Daniel Paul stood, even though a witness testified that the summer before, "she was a telling what a great Liberty a Young woman has to what a young man hath for, said She, I will Let any Young man get me with child and then, Said She, I can lay it to who I please because a woman has that Liberty granted to them."[20] Courts were obviously less concerned about the possibility of a false accusation than about the problem of having to provide public support for fatherless children. Yet one need not interpret the law cynically. It formalized a common assumption in English society, evident in the Chesapeake as well as in New England, that women were guardians of the sexual values of the community. In this regard, the witnesses in the procedure were as important as the mother herself.[21]

Other than Nelson's general overview, there has been little scholarship on changes in fornication procedures in Massachusetts in the middle decades of the eighteenth century.[22] We know that courts gradually abandoned the practice of fining married couples whose first child was born too soon, but we know almost nothing about the single women whose cases began to dominate the dockets by midcentury. Unfortunately, earlier studies have made it difficult to trace the direction of change by failing to relate paternity suits to fornication procedures. They have also given too little attention to the documentary impact of changes in legal procedures.

A 1786 "Act for the Punishment of Fornication, and for the Maintenance of Bastard Children" confirmed the old laws, but made one important change. A new clause made it possible for women to avoid appearing at the Court of General Sessions to answer a fornication charge by voluntarily confessing to the crime before a single justice of the peace and paying a fine (six shillings for the first offense and twelve shillings for any later ones). William Nelson has assumed this was a first step in the decriminalization of sexual behavior. Possibly—though he fails to notice that the procedure made it easier for a woman to initiate a paternity action. If a woman named a man at the time of her initial confession, and then "being put upon the discovery of the truth respecting the same accusation in the time of her travail, shall thereupon accuse the same person," *he* would be tried before the Sessions and, if convicted, be required to provide for the child.[23] In fact, the two actions were typically combined on one form, suggesting that confessing to fornication was simply a preliminary step to suing for the maintenance of one's child.

This was the procedure Sally Pierce followed. On July 19, 1791, Martha wrote that Mrs. Savage had come to the house to inform her "that Sally Peirce swore a Child on my son Jonathan & he was taken with a warrent. Mr Abisha Cowen is his Bondsman for appearance at Coart." In October, just as the law required, Sally confirmed her accusation before Martha Ballard. She was not the only unwed mother to do so. For thirteen of the twenty out-of-wedlock births in the diary, Martha recorded the name of the father, using stylized language that suggests she had indeed "taken testimony" as the law instructed. Lucy Shaw, for example, "declared that David Edwards was the True Father of the Child."[24] In five of the cases in which Martha made no record of the father's name, there were unusual circumstances. Two babies were stillborn, one of the mothers being in convulsions at delivery. In another case, Martha wrote, "Called at the riseing of the sun to Sarah White, she being in travil with her forth Child, & is yet unmarried."[25]

The remaining two were to a free black woman, Mehitable Slocum, whom Martha always referred to in the diary as "Black Hitty." In the first of Hitty's deliveries, Martha mentioned no father. In the other, she identified him in the margin but not in the main entry as "Nicholas," adding, "This man is a Portugues who was Brot here by Mrs Hussey from Nantucket." The form of the entry suggests she was conveying casual information rather than the solemn testimony assumed in the other cases. If

TABLE II   MARTHA MOORE BALLARD DIARY, 1785–1812
PATERNITY RECORD

Total Number of Deliveries	814	
Deliveries to single women	20	(2.4%)
Women giving father's name	13	
Women not giving father's name	7	
Stillborn child	2	
"Black Hitty"	2	
Sarah White's fourth child	1	
Unexplained	2	
Total First Births (1785–1797)	106	
Conceived out of wedlock	40	(38%)
Premarital pregnancy	31	(29%)
Illegitimacy	9	(8%)

Hitty held an anomalous place in her midwife's diary, she nevertheless succeeded in contracting a marriage. Six months after the baby's birth, the town clerk recorded the marriage of "Nicholas Hilson to Hitty Slocum (Negroes)."[26]

All of this argues that the mothers, rather than Martha, initiated the confession at delivery, and that it was part of a process of suing for maintenance. A black servant or the mother of several bastards was unlikely to sue. A stillbirth rendered the question moot. In the two remaining cases in which Martha failed to record the name of the father, there is no obvious explanation. Perhaps these two young women simply chose not to confront the father. Significantly, Sarah White, the mother of four, is the only one of Martha's patients to appear in the quarterly court records for Lincoln County, and she appeared only once, in 1782, when she was fined four shillings after a presentation by the grand jury.

Fragmentary documents in the loose file papers of the court relate to two other cases mentioned in the diary. These suggest the process that must have been followed in the others. Abigail ("Nabby") Tower accused Moses Palmer before Nathaniel Dummer on April 19, 1794, when she was just three months pregnant. Judge Dummer asked her about the time and place of conception. She answered that it had occurred on January 5, 1794. "How do you know?" he continued. "I know it was that time," she answered simply. Where did the conception occur? "In Mr Zenith Lathrop's chamber." Did she keep company with any other person about that time? "No, I did not." There is no evidence that he questioned her judgment or sought other witnesses. Noting that the child "if born alive will be a bastard," Dummer issued a warrant for Palmer's arrest, then bound him through a recognizance to appear in court once the child was born. Nabby confirmed her accusation before Martha during her delivery on October 11, but when the next court met in January, Moses had been discharged, probably because he had come to an agreement with the mother.

We know about the other case from a rare bit of gossip in Martha's diary. On November 6, 1788, she noted that her daughters had returned from a neighbor's house with the news that "Hannah Fletcher has sworn shee is with child by Joseph Fuller." A loose piece of paper in the Lincoln County court files, signed by Ebenezer Farwell, J.P., notes that Hannah Fletcher had voluntarily appeared on November 3 and that a warrant had been issued for a Joseph *Fellows*. That the Ballard girls carried the news home to their mother three days after the examination before Esquire Farwell suggests that a voluntary appearance before a justice of the peace was in some sense public. Since Martha did not attend Hannah's delivery, we do not know whether she held firm in her accusation, or if in fact she carried the baby to term.

Fornication actions in the county courts were the apex of a broad, community-based system of enforcement. Since the procedure began with individual judges and midwives, very few of whom left records, formal court documents provide at best a glimpse of the process. That women are overrepresented on county court dockets may have less to do with a decline of interest in prosecuting men for fornication than with the voluntary nature of paternity proceedings. The very structure of the process required an admission of fornication on a woman's part in order to establish an action for paternity against a man. At the initial stages—the examination before the justice of the peace, the testimony in travail—both parties were visible, but if the man chose to settle out of court rather than to contest the

TABLE III   FORNICATION ACTIONS IN NATHANIEL THWING
"CRIMINAL RECORD," 1773–1803

Total Number of Actions	10
Female alone	4
Male alone	5
Both female and male	1
Persons appearing in both Thwing's and Sessions records	
Women	3
Men	1
Partners appearing in Sessions records but not in Thwing's	
Women	2
Men	0

accusation or if the woman for some reason decided to drop charges, the man's name disappeared, though her conviction for fornication would remain.

Scattered file papers for the period after 1786 show four incomplete actions of paternity for every one that reached the Sessions. A record book kept by Nathaniel Thwing, a justice of the peace in Woolwich, Maine, suggests that the same pattern was present earlier. His book also shows the diffuse—almost hit or miss—nature of surviving records. Because a paternity action usually took months to complete, more than one judge might be involved. Even for the cases Thwing dealt with, the record is seldom complete. Between 1773 and 1798 he recorded confessions, warrants, or recognizances in ten cases of fornication or paternity. Potentially, of course, this meant that twenty persons—ten men and ten women—were subject to court action. Actions against five of the women and six of the men appear in his book. Three of these women, but only one of the men, also appear in the file papers or dockets of the Court of General Sessions. Two of the women who do *not* appear in Thwing's records, but none of the men, turn up in Sessions documents. Using Thwing's record as our model, we can conclude that half of all women but only 10 percent of men accused at the local level ever appeared in county court records.

It is important to emphasize that the charges were dropped,

not that the men were acquitted. Conviction was certainly possible if a woman wanted to persist in her accusation and if she followed the prescribed procedure: there were only three acquittals in the nineteen maintenance actions that went to trial in Lincoln County between 1761 and 1799. It is impossible at this distance to know why so many women were ready to settle out of court even though their chances for a conviction were good. The phenomenon of dropped charges is of course a familiar one to those who deal with personal behavior suits even today. In some cases, the couple were reconciled. The Lincoln County files for January 1794 contain a scrap of paper with the barely legible signature of Mary Crawford of Bath, who certified "that Samuel Todd of said Bath hath agreed to make me satisfaction for getting me with child by promising to marry me, therefore, I wish that the prosecution I commenced against him for so doing may be squashed."

The negotiations between Joanna Trott and John Wright of Woolwich were less productive. In May of 1788, Nathaniel Thwing convicted Joanna of slander after her lover's father complained that when his son offered to take the child and have it brought up in his house, she had answered, "No, you shall not have it to carry there, for they, meaning your complainant & his wife will murder it, for they have murdered two or three already." To say that paternity cases were often settled out of court does not mean that they were settled easily or pleasantly. It is merely to argue that the threat of a lawsuit was sometimes as effective as an actual prosecution.

So it was in the case of Sally Pierce. In official documents there is no evidence whatsoever that she sued Jonathan Ballard for the maintenance of her child, though the diary tells us that she did. The record of Sally's action disappeared because it was successful: Jonathan married her in February, four months after the child was born and a month before his scheduled trial at the Sessions.

Though trials for fornication were unusual, fornication was not. Between 1785 and 1797 Martha delivered 106 women of their first babies. Of these infants, forty, or 38 percent, were conceived out of wedlock. (See Table II.) The great majority of the women concerned (thirty-one of the forty) had already married the fathers of their children. For these mothers, the average interval between marriage and delivery was 5.6 months, though there were enough "near-misses" to blur the distinction between legitimacy and illegitimacy. "Was calld by Mr Young to go and see the wife of John Dunn who was in Labour," Martha wrote on August 25, 1799, a Sunday. "She was safe delivered at 7 hour 30 Evening of a fine son. . . . Mr. Dunn was married last Thursday. He was 20 years old last July."

Did the women who conceived out of wedlock differ in some fundamental way from those who did not? Probably not. Unwed mothers, pregnant and nonpregnant brides often came from the same families. Even in the families of town leaders, premarital pregnancy was common. Martha delivered the children or grandchildren of seventeen of the men who served as Hallowell selectmen between 1778 and 1800. One man was himself accused of fathering an illegitimate child (before marriage), two had premarital pregnancies in their families, and five had both premarital pregnancies and out-of-wedlock births. Ephraim Ballard belonged to the last group. He was without question a solid citizen, serving four terms as selectman, on committees to hire a minister and build a church, and as a moderator of town meetings. Of the five Ballard children who married, three (Lucy, Jonathan, and Ephraim Jr.) conceived their first child before marriage. Lucy and her youngest brother both managed to marry before their babies were born; Jonathan, as we have seen, did not.

Daniel Savage, another of Hallowell's perennial town leaders, had three daughters whose first births are recorded in the diary. Martha Savage was pregnant at marriage, Hannah was not, and Rachel gave birth out of wedlock to a stillborn child, then married a few months later. Sarah White, the woman who delivered her fourth child though "yet unmarried," was also the daughter of a town selectman. One of her sisters gave birth out of wedlock, another delivered a month after marriage.

Why did some women deliver out of wedlock when their sisters did not? One difference may be in the choice of suitors. Eighty-seven percent of the men who married their pregnant lovers were sons of established families in the town or remained to become householders on the censuses of 1790 and 1800. This was true for only 39 percent of those who failed to marry. It would be tempting to believe these men fled before the vengeance of irate women and their fathers. More likely, they were already less committed to the town and to the women in it, being part of the transient population of mariners and lumbermen. (In the same way some Hallowell men, married and unmarried, had casual sexual alliances with women in other port cities.)

In the case of Sally Pierce's sister, Hitty, social differences were an issue (we shall return to her story in a later chapter). For other women, it may have been a simple matter of irresolvable differences during the period of engagement. Becky White was published to Seth Partridge in January of 1787, but they did not marry; she gave birth to his child eleven months later. Polly Savage, the young woman who did so much spinning for the Ballards when they lived at the mills, gave birth in November of 1788, more than a year after she was published to Elihu Getchell, who married someone else. Polly kept her little daughter at her parents' house until she married Abiezer Benjamin in 1790. (She was three months pregnant at the time.) Single mothers typically remained in their families of origin and eventually married.

None of this was confined to Maine. Premarital pregnancy was common throughout New England, in old towns as well as new, Oxford as well as Hallowell, and it had been so for at least a generation. Although Martha and Ephraim were married almost two years before their first child was born, several of their siblings, including Ephraim's sister Hannah Towne, had early babies. As we have seen, Hannah's son and Ephraim's daughter continued the tradition in the next generation. Martha's sister, Dorothy Barton, was almost five months pregnant at marriage. Her story is especially interesting considering the names she and Stephen gave their daughters. Samuel Richardson's novel *Pamela* tells the story of a maidservant who marries her employer's son by heroically resisting his sexual advances. The heroine of *Clarissa Harlowe* is less fortunate: thrown into the arms of the fiendish Lovelace by her parents' insistence on an arranged marriage, she is raped and left to die. Pamela Barton was not pregnant at marriage. Clarissa Harlowe Barton was.

It was their sister Hannah, however, who lived a life worthy of a novel. Returning to Oxford with her parents, she gave birth to two children said to have been fathered by her employer, whose wife was an invalid. When the man's wife died twenty years later, he married Hannah, but not in time to prevent the suicide of their youngest son, who killed himself out of humiliation while a student at Brown. The oldest child, however, became a prominent citizen of Worcester County. In the words of a family historian, Hannah's descendants "have little cause to be ashamed of her for she has given them a remarkable and splendid heritage." [27]

There were surely differences in attitudes toward sexuality in Hallowell just as there were differences over politics or theology. Some families probably condoned premarital sex. Others encouraged formal and decorous behavior. Yet nearly everyone in the town agreed with certain fundamental propositions. One was that marriage should certainly follow, if it did not always precede, conception. Another was that fathers as well as mothers were responsible for children born out of wedlock. In courtship, sexual activity was connected with a comprehensive transition to adulthood, to good citizenship and economic productivity. The communal rituals of birth marked women as well as men as sexual beings, and affirmed the obligations as well as rights of fatherhood.

All of this contrasts sharply with the seduction literature of the eighteenth century, which describes innocent young women strangely disconnected from their communities by the machinations of unprincipled lovers who abandon them in foreign countries, imprison them in mysterious villas, or leave them to die in strange taverns.[28,] As Susan Staves has argued, such a construction of seduction belongs to a particular historical moment. Some young women in all periods of history have engaged in illicit intercourse, she writes, yet "such girls need not be seen as sweetly pathetic. Instead, they may be seen as loathsome temptresses, damned sinners, sordid criminals, pioneers of sexual freedom, boring fools, or simply as normal." Readers in the eighteenth century shed tears over such maidens not simply because they were powerless but because "those qualities that made them vulnerable to seducers—beauty, simplicity, and the capacity for affection—were precisely those qualities the culture found desirable in women."[29]

Such values had been heard of in the Kennebec. In 1795 a Lincoln County woman sued a man in county court claiming that for three years he had begged her to marry him. Finally, "by his assiduity, assertion, protestations, and assurances of his feeling" (one suspects the presence of a lawyer here), he "so endeared himself to her" that she agreed. "Wanting craftily, subtilly and cruelly to deceive, seduce and despoil her of her innocence and happy virgin situation," he "obtained his cruel purpose." Pregnant and abandoned by her seducer, she was "rendered Miserable and her good Name Forever lost."[30] What is remarkable about the case is that the woman avoided the old system of justice by initiating a civil suit before the Court of Common Pleas rather than an action of paternity before the local justice of the peace. Perhaps she found it impossible to simultaneously defend her "innocence" and pay a voluntary fine for fornication. The seducer was acquitted.

This story might have come from the pages of a novel. In sentimental literature, of course, the heroine would never have attempted any sort of suit at all, yet the language of her plea echoes the argument of contemporary fiction, most of which turns on a belief in female innocence and to a large extent female passivity. In contrast, the old system of justice asked young women to cooperate with old women in witnessing to male culpability. It also required an acceptance of female sexuality and an acknowledgment of fleshly sin. Such a system had difficulty comprehending rape, let alone seduction; its working assumption was that if a woman became pregnant, she had somehow acquiesced. Still, on its own terms it did hold men responsible for their behavior. It is difficult to imagine a sentimental heroine naming her seducer at the height of travail or describing the day and place of conception for the local J.P. Sentimental heroines died rather than confront their betrayers.

In Hallowell, betrayed women collected cash payments, then went on to marry other men. For a sentimental heroine, a forced marriage to her seducer could never have been an acceptable solution as it was for Sally Pierce.

If one did not know about Sally's confession to Martha in October, it would be easy to miss the suppressed anxiety, the suspense, the tension of the entries regarding Jonathan through the early winter of 1792. "Jonathan stayed from home last night," Martha wrote on December 29, and on January 6, "Jonathan has not been at home since yesterday." The same entry reappeared on January 11, January 29, and in slightly different form on February 20: "Jonathan has not been here this day till morning." He was missing again on February 26, but three days later his mother wrote, "My son Jonathan Brot his wife & little son here."

Henry Sewall's records show that Jonathan and Sally had been published on February 11, which means they could have been legally married on February 24 or sometime thereafter. Like the Pollards, the Ballards were not present at their son's wedding, though Martha made the new bride welcome as soon as she could.[31] "Helpt Sally nurs her Babe," she wrote on March 2. Soon she was referring to the "Babe" as "Jack." Jonathan and Sally stayed alternately at the Ballards' and at the Pierces' for the next four weeks, and on April 4, 1792, "went to housekeeping."

For Jonathan, only one wedding ritual remained. At the Hallowell town meeting in June he, along with six other newly married men, was elected a "hog reeve," a humorous acknowledgment by the town fathers that another roving stag had been yoked.[32]

In one year, then, the Ballard family had been touched by most of the matrimonial rites (and several of the "writes") common to an eighteenth-century town. The town clerk recorded the marriage intentions of the three couples and the justices of the peace said the vows. While Jonathan passed under the watchful eye of the law—and his own mother—into the ranks of respectable householders, Hannah and Parthenia amassed the goods essential to housekeeping.

Martha's diary entries continued in December 1792 as they had begun in October with the young brides hard at work, now weaving rag coverlets rather than cloth, while the mother continued to make purchases at the stores. On December 12, she wrote, "Clear but very cold. Mr Pollard came and Conducted my daughter, & his spouse, home to Houskeeping." Ephraim drove the team, Dolly went along to help unpack. "Cyrus went & Bot 2 pails," perhaps his contribution to the new household. The next day the new Mrs. Pitts "made her Candles & some for me." Parthenia washed on December 14, went to visit Hannah on December 16, and on December 20, she and Shubael also went to housekeeping. "Shubael Pitts came and removed his wife from here," Martha wrote. "May they prospir in this life & be happy in the future."

For a time the young couples did prosper. "Mr Ballard to son Pollards," Martha wrote on May 9, 1793. "Brot the haslett of a Veal home from them." As Parthenia and Shubael's first anniversary approached, Martha could report that "the Ship which Pitt Built was Lanched this forenoon."[33] Martha now dignified Hannah and Parthenia with the titles "Daughter Pollard" and "Mrs. Pitts." "Daughter Pollard & Mrs Pitts took Tea here," she would write, or "Mr Pollard & Pitts & their wives took Tea."[34]

For the first few months after the brides "went to housekeeping," Betsy Barton came to help Martha with her work. A more permanent helper, Sally Cox, arrived in the spring, soon taking Parthenia's place as a member of the family. Dolly continued to work at home, going to neighbors' houses for short stints of dressmaking. With a new set of helpers in place, Martha was free to serve her neighbors.

CHAPTER FIVE

DECEMBER 1793

"Birth 50. Birth 51"

NOVEMBER

15   6   *At Mr Parkers. Mrs Holdman here.*
Cloudy & Cold. Mrs Holdman here to have a gown made. Mrs
Benjamin to have a Cloak Cut. Polly Rust after work. I was
Calld to Mr Parkers aftern. Mr Ballard is better.

16   7   *At ditoes. Mrs Holdman left here.*
Cloudy. I was at Mr Parkers and Colonel Sewalls. Mrs Parker
unwell. Colman Bled her at Evening.

17   F   *At ditoes & Mr Poores. Birth 47th a daughter. At Capt*
Meloys allso
Rainy. I was Calld from Mr Parkers at 2 hour morn to Mr
Poores. Doct Page was Calld before my arival. I Extracted the
Child, a dagt. He Chose to Close the Loin. I returnd home at 8
hour morning. Receivd 6/ as a reward. Mr Ballard & Ephm
attend worship, Dolly & Sally aftern. Charls and John Coks
supt here. I was calld to Capt meloys at 11 hour Evening. Raind.
Birth Mr Poores daughter X X

18   2   *At Capt Meloys. Birth 48th. I receivd 24/.*
At Capt Meloys. His Lady in Labour. Her women Calld (it was

a sever storm of rain Cleard of with snow). My patient deliverd at 8 hour 5 minute Evening of a fine daughter. Her attendants Mrss Cleark, Duttun, Sewall, & myself. We had an Elligant supper and I tarried all night.
Birth Capt Meloys dagt X X

19   3   *At ditoes & Mr Parkers. Mr Turner here.*
Clear. I returnd home after dineing. Revd Mr Turner and Esq Cony supt here. I was Calld to Mr Parkers at 11 Evening.

20   4   *At Mr Parkers*
Cloudy. I was at Mr Parkers.

21   5   *At ditoes*
Cloudy morn. Clear of at night. I was at Mr Parkers. Mrs Cowen there. Hannah North allso.

22   6   *At ditoes*
Cloudy morn. Clear at noone. I came home. Find my famely well. Mr Ballard gone to Winslow.

23   7   *At Capt Meloys*
Cloudy. Mr James Page here. Mr Ballard paid him 6/ towards his Tax. I went to see Mrs Meloy. Find her Tolerable Comfortable. Old Lady Coutch there.

24   F   *At home. Doct Cony here*
A very heavy rain foren. Sun shone at 12. Mr Ballard went to meeting. Dolly is unwell pukeing in the night. Esquire Coney Calld here. He has been to Join Mr Smith & Mrs Nancy Cleark in Marriage.

25   2   *At Esquire Matthew Howards [Haywards]. Birth 49th.*
Clear & pleast. Dolly went to her Brothers. Polly Pollard Came home with her to have a gown made. Esquire M Howard Calld

me to see his Lady who was delivd of a daughter at 8 hour 10 minutes Evening. I tarried all night.
Birth Esquire Howards daughter X X

26   3   *At Ditoes.*
Clear. I left my patients very well at 7. Arivd at home at 9 hour morn. Receivd 7/6 as a reward. Mr Ballard & sons bringing brick from the hook. Dolly & Polly Pollard are gone to the shops this afternoon.

27   4   *At Mr Poors. Mrs Greely there.*
Clear. Son Pollard brot my daughter here to warp a web. Polly went home with him. Mr Poor Calld me to see his wife who is not so well as Could be wisht. Find Mr Livermores sons Laying a hearth in our kitchen. The Bridg acrost the gully was Coverd this day.

28   5   *at the hook*
Clear. Mr Ballard gone to survey for Esquire Petingail. Daughter Pollard went home. I went to the hook. Mrs Poor is yet low. Mr Lathrop paid me my fee for attending his wife the 19th of March last.

29   6   *at Mr Parkers*
Clear. I was Calld to Mr Parkers.

30   7   *at ditoes*
at ditoes

DECEMBER

1, 2, 3, 4, 5   *At Mr Parkers 5 Days*
At Mr Parkers. His Lady is about house. The river is difucult to pass. I knitt while gone from home 2 pair gloves and 5 pair & 1/2 mitts. The river was past on the ice this day.

6 6 *At Mr Whites*
Clear. I was Calld to Benn Whites at 2 hour morning. Wrode in a sleigh.

7 7 *At Whites & Parkers. Birth 50. Birth 51.*
At Whites. His wife was deliverd at 12 O Clok of a daughter and I was Calld back to Mr Parkers. His Lady was deliverd at 9 hour 30 minutes of a daughter. I am some fatagud. Son Town here.
Births Mr Whites and Mr Parkers daughters.

8 F *At Mr Parkers. Returnd home*
Snow hail & rain. Mr Parker went for his Nurs. I left his Lady at 4 pm as well as Could be Expected & walkt over the river. Wrode Mr Ballards hors home. I had a wrestless night by fataug & weting my feet.

9 2 *At Mr Finnys & the hook*
Clear. Mr Ballard Surveying for Mr Pollard & Page. I went to Mr Finnys & Benjamins. Brot my wollen web yarn home & went to Mr Peter Clearks. They ingagd to weav it. I Calld at Capt Meloys Store. Bot a Shall [shawl?] at 5/6. He made me a present of a muslin apron. I bot at Capt Fillebrowns 5 2/1 pints Brandy, 2/9; 3 puter poringers, 4/6; paper pins, /10. Total 8/1.

The fifty-three deliveries Martha performed in 1793 took her along the length of the town and beyond, from Henry Mc-Causland's mill at Cobbossee Great Pond as far north as Winslow, where Lucy Towne gave birth to her ninth child. The year's deliveries encompassed the town socially as well as geographically. She delivered *Captain* Molloy's and *Esquire* Hayward's *ladies* as well as Mr. Cummings's servant "Bulah" and "Black Hitty."[1] Her patients in 1793 included the wives of Samuel Norcross, lime-burner and potter; Jeremiah Dummer, mer-

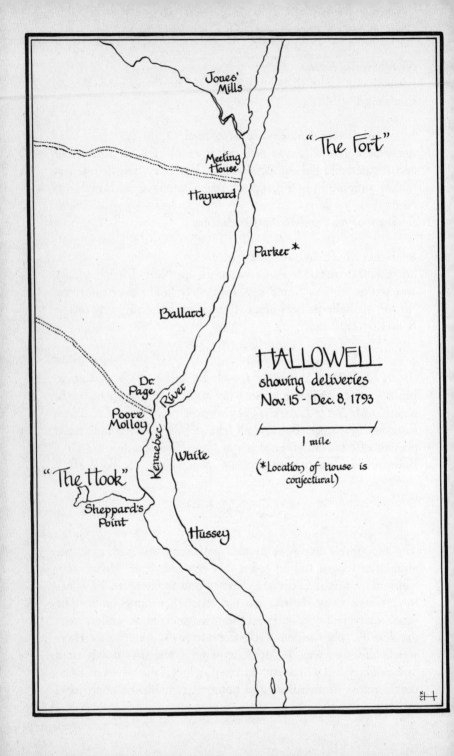

Jones' Mills

"The Fort"

Meeting House

Hayward

Parker *

Ballard

HALLOWELL
showing deliveries
Nov. 15 – Dec. 8, 1793

Dr. Page

Poore
Molloy

Kennebec River

White

|————————|
1 mile

(*Location of house is
conjectural)

"The Hook"

Sheppard's
Point

Hussey

chant and potash manufacturer; and Theophilus Hamlin, housewright, as well as common woodsmen and farmers in the outlying precincts of the town.[2] She found it "very bad wriding" to Asa Mason's house, though this year she didn't complain, as she had in another, of encountering a plague of fleas. She delivered the wife of William Pitt, who had a house, shop, and capital in trade worth 810 pounds, as well as the wife of John LeLejunee (she spelled it Lashnee), who had a bakehouse valued at thirty-one pounds. Each family had a story. Thomas Hinkley's son ("his 9th by two wives") was Birth 22. Stephen Hinkley's child ("by Judy Busell out of wedlock") was Birth 39.[3]

"Birth 50. Birth 51." Two entries crowded into the margin for December 7 provide visual evidence not only of the irregular rhythm of Martha's work but of the expansion of her practice. The fifty-three babies she delivered in 1793 represent an increase of 29 percent over the year before. Old neighbors, new residents, and her own children were contributing to a population expansion that would double the town by the end of the decade.[4] Jonathan and Sally's second child, a boy given the patriotic name of DeLafayette, was "Birth 7th" for the year. Peter Jones's baby, born at the mills, was "Birth 15th." The Ballards' new neighbor and dressmaker, Lydia Densmore, produced "Birth 20th."

Fifty-three deliveries a year seems like a comfortable load, even for a part-time practitioner, an average of one case per week. Yet Maine weather and the unpredictability of labor made nonsense of averages. Martha might sit at home for weeks, then do a month's work in forty-eight hours, speeding between one laboring woman and another. She also had to deal, inevitably, with cases of so-called "false labor." One winter day, she hastened downriver to Sheppard's Wharf in a wilderness of snow, taking refuge in the trader's house until Samuel Hussey came to take her across the river to his wife, who was—or had been or at least thought she was—in labor. Martha was patient in such circumstances. Experience had taught her that intermittent labor was a normal part of pregnancy. She sat at the Husseys' for seven days until a summons from another woman took her back upriver to her own neighborhood. By the time the Hussey delivery began in earnest, the river had thawed, broken up, then frozen again. "Walkt to the Loading place," Martha wrote. "From there Crosst the mountains of ice. Arivd allmost fatagud to death."[5]

A woman caught between the premonitory tightening in her belly and the feel of snow in the air was suspended between two uncertainties. If she called her midwife, labor might stop; if she did not, she might give birth unattended. In the segment of the diary that opens this chapter, Martha recorded four trips to the Parker house before that reluctant baby—Birth 51 for the year—arrived. "His Lady is about house," she wrote on the fourth day of her third visit. The condition of the river compounded the risk of going home. Martha settled into her knitting, producing two pairs of gloves and five and a half pairs of mittens before being called away, at two in the morning, by Mrs. White, who lived two miles away by sleigh. That was the signal for the Parker baby. Martha performed two deliveries in twenty-four hours, without sleep, walking home across the river the next day in snow, hail, and rain. "I had a wrestless night by fataug & weting my feet," she wrote. A third of the year's deliveries came in such strenuous clusters of two or three.

Martha numbered births the way she weighed candles or counted cabbages or mittens, but with even more intensity and seriousness. Numbers were a measure of productivity, though in the moral sense of diligence, of mastery of a chosen task, rather than in the mercantile sense of income or outgo. She didn't isolate births from the other activities in the diary, but she did give them precedence. Despite their ragged appearance, the birth entries were carefully structured and remarkably consistent. The left margin invariably included the father's surname, the sex of the child, and an XX for fee paid; the right gave the location of the birth and its number. The body of each entry offered additional detail, usually the exact time of delivery ("9 hour 30 minutes"), the hour of her summons or departure ("I left his Lady at 4 pm"), the condition of the mother and child ("as well as Could be Expected"), and the method of travel ("walkt over the river"). In addition some entries included the form or amount of payment ("Receivd 7/6 as a reward"), the names of the attendants ("Mrss Cleark, Duttun, Sewall & myself"), and comments on unusual occurrences at birth ("Doct Page was Calld before my arival").

Individual entries may seem flat and unrevealing. Taken together, they provide an unparalleled record of an eighteenth-century practice. Even the most routine and formulaic pieces of information are useful. Rare comments on obstetrical complications mean more when seen in relation to hundreds of bland notations that say simply "delivered" or "safe delivered"; a twenty-four-shilling fee acquires new significance when framed with all those other entries recording six shillings or a plain XX, while the appearance of a doctor at a delivery becomes more noteworthy when the hundreds of other deliveries in which no one thought to call a physician are considered. In midwifery as in so many other aspects of Martha Ballard's diary, it is the combination of boredom and heroism, of the usual and the unusual, that tells the story.

In medical terms the success of Martha Ballard's practice is conveyed in what she didn't write. For 768 of the 814 delivery entries in the diary she included no medical detail at all, simply noting "delivered" or "safe delivered," sometimes with an additional reassurance such as "left My patients very well." In only forty-six deliveries, 5.6 percent of all the births in the diary, did she give any hint of complications. Even then she seldom elaborated. A woman was "safe delivered tho very ill indeed" or "Her case was some alarming but shee revivd and seems comfortable." In a particularly difficult case she might add a special thanks: "She had a Laborious illness but Blessed be God it terminated in safety. May shee and I ascribe the prais to the Great parent of the universe."[6]

Such a record is exactly what one might expect of a skilled practitioner. One medical historian has estimated that 96 percent of all births occur naturally and spontaneously. The remaining 4 percent involve obstructions of some kind and require intervention. In addition, 1 percent may result in accessory complications, fainting, vomiting, tearing of the perineum, or life-threatening hemorrhages or convulsions. The eighteenth-century English physician Charles White was not far wrong when he said that a healthy young woman might deliver unattended in the middle of the town common and still do well.[7] As twentieth-century reformers insist, birth is a natural process, not a medical event.

Yet, as Martha would be quick to add, a natural process might still be uncomfortable and frightening, and when mismanaged even a normal birth could be dangerous. Like most of her contemporaries, she feared unattended birth.[8] She fretted when a missing horse delayed her response to a call. "My anxiety was great for the woman but I found her Safe," she wrote after one such event. On other occasions she was not so positive. Unattended women were "in a deplorable condition" or "suffering for want of help."[9] To her mind, those frenzied journeys and patient watchings mattered.

Her results attest to her skill. Her comment on August 20, 1787, that the death of Susanna Clayton and her infant was the "first such instance I ever saw & the first woman that died in Child bed which I delivered" allows us to add the 177 prediary deliveries to the total: in almost 1,000 births Martha did not lose a single mother at delivery, and only five of her patients (including Mrs. Clayton) died in the lying-in period. Infant deaths were also rare. The diary records fourteen stillbirths in 814 deliveries and an additional five infant deaths within an hour or two of delivery.

By our standards, mortality was high. Martha saw one maternal death for every 198 living births. Today that rate is one per 10,000. But as late as 1930, there was one maternal death for every 150 births in the United States; the major gains in obstetrical safety have come in the past fifty years. In fact, many historians believe that the routine employment of physicians in the nineteenth century probably increased rather than decreased

TABLE IV   SUMMARY OF DELIVERY DATA FROM TWO MANUSCRIPT SOURCES

	Martha Ballard 1785–1812	James Farrington 1824–1859
Deliveries		
Total Recorded	814	1233
Average per year	33	35
"Difficult" Births		
number	46	246*
percent of total	5.6%	20%
Stillbirths		
number	14	36
ratio to live births	1.8/100	3.0/100
Neonatal Deaths		
number	20	?
ratio to live births	2.5/100	
Maternal Deaths		
total	5	5
at delivery	0	4
within two weeks	5	1
ratio to live births	5/1000	4/1000

*James Farrington categorized the 20% of births listed as something other than "natural" labor, as follows: "tedious" (102); "premature" (41); "preternatural" (39); "complicated" (33); and [after 1838] "instrumental" (31).

SOURCES: Martha Moore Ballard Diary, 1785–1812, MS, Maine State Library, Augusta, Maine; and James Farrington Medical Record Books, 1824–1859, MS, Special Collections, Dimond Library, University of New Hampshire, Durham, N.H.

mortality. Records of an early-nineteenth-century New Hampshire physician, whose case load was almost identical to Martha Ballard's, shows higher stillbirth ratios and four maternal deaths at delivery, though only one during the lying-in period (see Table IV). What is even more striking is the large number of complications recorded in his records: 20 percent of his deliveries (as opposed to 5.6 percent for her). The difference was partly in perception—as a physician he was attuned to biological anomalies in a way that she was not—yet there is good evidence that birth *had* become a more complex process in the nineteenth century, as physicians began to employ ergot, opiates, and forceps in what Martha Ballard would have considered routine deliveries. Those dangers did not decrease as hospital delivery became more common. A study of a Portsmouth, New Hampshire, hospital found stillbirth rates in the second decade of the twentieth century five times as high as Martha's.[10]

The more appropriate comparison, of course, is with her own contemporaries. Estimates based on parish registers for seventeenth- and eighteenth-century English villages range from ten to twenty-nine maternal deaths per thousand births. In some eighteenth-century London and Dublin hospitals, maternal mortality ranged from 30 to 200(!) per thousand births, compared with 5 per 1,000 for Martha (see Table V).[11] There are few comparable New England records, though such as there are suggest that maternal mortality, like other forms, was lower in rural America. Lydia Baldwin, an eighteenth-century Vermont midwife, claimed only one maternal death in 926 deliveries, though the lack of detail in her records makes it impossible to determine whether she included deaths in the lying-in period as well as deaths at delivery. Hall Jackson, a Portsmouth, New Hampshire, physician claimed no maternal deaths in 511 births, though again his records are sketchy. Martha's stillbirth ratios are comparable to (though slightly lower than) both Baldwin's and Jackson's[12] (see Table VI).

Martha's obstetrical entries were routine and predictable because most deliveries were routine and predictable. The terseness of her records also reflects a traditional reticence about the details of sex and birth. Martha's patients were not anonymous bodies but friends and neighbors. She was no prude, yet she was probably unaccustomed to saying, let alone writing, all she knew and saw. Even among publishing physicians a certain reserve was expected. The author of one English midwifery manual defended the lack of anatomical detail in his text on the grounds that his work was designed not to "give the least Offence to the most modest Reader."[13]

Beyond that, the lack of detail reinforces what we already

TABLE V   COMPARATIVE MATERNAL MORTALITY RATES

Place	Total Births	Maternal Deaths	Deaths per 1000 Births
London A			
1767–1772	653	18	27.5
1770	63	14	222.2
London B			
1749–1770	9108	196	21.5
1770	890	35	39.3
London C			
1747–"present"	4758	93	19.5
1771	282	10	35.4
London D	790	6	7.5
Dublin A			
1745–1754	3206	29	9.0
Dublin B			
1757–1775	10726	152	14.1
1768	633	17	26.8
1770	616	5	8.1
Martha Ballard			
1777–1812	998	5	5.0
1785–1812	814	5	6.1
United States			
1930			6.7
1935			5.8
1940			3.8
1945			2.1

SOURCES: Charles White, *A Treatise on the Management of Pregnant and Lying-in Women*, Worcester, Mass., 1793); Martha Moore Ballard Diary, 2 vols., MS, Maine State Library, Augusta, Maine; *Maternal and Child Health Practices: Problems, Resources and Methods of Delivery*, ed. Helen M. Wallace, Edwin M. Gold, and Edward F. Lis (Springfield, Ill.: Charles C. Thomas, 1973), p. 285.

know about her craft, that it was traditional rather than experimental. Unlike the publishing physicians of the period, some of whom kept obstetrical case notes, she had no interest in instructing others (at least through the written word) or in testing

TABLE VI   COMPARATIVE STILLBIRTH RATES

	Total Births	*Total Stillbirths*	*Stillbirths per 100 Live Births*
Martha Ballard 1785–1812	814	14	1.8
Hall Jackson 1775–1794	511	12	2.4
James Farrington 1824–1859	1233	36	3.0
Portsmouth, N.H. 1809–1810	541	14	2.7
Marblehead, Mass. 1808	222	7	3.3
Exeter, N.H. 1809	53	1	1.9
United States* 1942			2.0

*Fetal death ratio, defined as fetal deaths of 28 weeks or more gestation per 1,000 live births.

SOURCES: Martha Moore Ballard Diary, 2 vols., MS, Maine State Library, Augusta, Maine; J. Worth Estes, *Hall Jackson and the Purple Foxglove: Medical Practice and Research in Revolutionary America, 1760–1820* (Hanover, N.H.: University Press of New England, 1979), p. 120; James Farrington Medical Record Books, 1824–1859, MS, Special Collections, Dimond Library, University of New Hampshire, Durham, N.H.; Lyman Spalding, *Bill of Mortality for Portsmouth*, broadside [Portsmouth: 1809, 1810]); John Drury, *Bill of Mortality for Marblehead, 1808*, broadside (Marblehead, 1809); Joseph Tilton, M.D., *Bill of Mortality for Exeter, New Hampshire*, broadside ([Exeter: 1809]); Helen M. Wallace, "Factors Associated with Perinatal Mortality and Morbidity," in *Maternal and Child Health Practices: Problems, Resources and Methods of Delivery*, ed. Helen M. Wallace, Edwin M. Gold, and Edward F. Lis (Springfield, Ill.: Charles C. Thomas, 1973), p. 507.

and promoting new methods. Her training was manual rather than literary. Having mastered her craft she had no need to explain it. Although the outcome of each delivery mattered (it was important to note whether a woman who had been "very

ill" was now "comfortable"), the process was of little consequence. Furthermore, the cultural setting of the work discouraged a technical presentation of the result.

Excessive bleeding was "flooding" in her diary as in the obstetrical literature, but she did not use Latinisms like *matrix* and
vagina or technical terms like *Os Pubis* and *Os Tincae*. In fact,
what is most striking is the absence of any reference to the
explicit processes of birth. Her women are seldom even in "travail." They are simply "unwell," and as the delivery proceeds it
is their "illness" rather than their "bearing pains" or even their
"labor" that increases. Where an English midwife might
"touch" a woman (a euphemism for an internal examination),
Martha "inquired into her case." Once in a while she refers to
a presentation as *preternatural* as a physician might, but her des-
ignation of one woman's labor as *supernatural* was surely a slip
of the pen.[14]

Her reference to the encounter with Dr. Page at Mrs. Poor's
delivery in the November 17 passage is a case in point. In the
context of the larger history of obstetrics, it is also extraordinarily interesting. "I Extracted the Child," she wrote. "He
Chose to Close the Loin." The language is almost Biblical in its
circumlocution. Presumably she meant that Dr. Page had delivered the placenta or afterbirth and then applied the traditional
bandages around the abdomen and thighs. Because the delivery
of the placenta was a source of some controversy in the period,
the incident is worth examining in detail.

Early-eighteenth-century advice books urged the immediate
extraction of the placenta, even if it meant reaching into the
womb. "With my left hand I was oblig'd to keep her Belly
down," wrote one English midwife, "whilst with my right hand
I peel'd off and loosen'd the *secundines* from the *Matrix*." Many
physicians promoted similar methods, arguing that if there was
room for a baby in the womb there was certainly room for a
hand. No one advised rough pulling on the umbilicus, however,
a method usually attributed to "ignorant midwives." By the
last quarter of the eighteenth century a few physicians claimed
that doing nothing was the best approach of all. "Nature does

more of this work than art can do, both for the Mother and child," wrote William Hunter, "and therefore no art should be used."[15]

Martha Ballard's silence on the subject suggests that she was quite comfortable with Dr. Page's method, whatever it was, yet his insistence on "Clos[ing] the Loin" may suggest his own mistrust of her skill. The word "Close" is itself suggestive, since in the form of a noun it denoted the wrapper or binding applied to the abdomen and thighs after birth. William Hunter described the process this way: "As [the placenta] comes away I know it will be followed by a suction of air. On this account as it comes out I close the Vulva, and keep my hands on the parts below. Then I call for a bason, and give it [the placenta] away and apply a dry warm cloth to the Vulva. . . . After this I apply several cloths & then ask for what is called the close. I keep the parts close with my hands, and then take out one cloth and apply it over them dry. I take another and put it about her thighs etc. I give her another to put over her stomach and belly."[16]

Hunter recommended plain dry cloths, apparently rather loosely applied. Older writers suggested tying the knees together after applying a large, soft, dry double clout "very warm to the *Labia Pudendi.*" Regardless of method, the phrase "Close the Loin" suggests a kind of intimacy, a physical caring that was more often associated with midwifery and nursing than with medicine in this period. It was not simply a matter of guiding an attending nurse in the application of the "clouts." The extraction of the placenta and the "closing" of the vulva were parts of one operation, the "suction of air" to be followed by a kind of capping of the parts. There was a strong belief in the period that allowing an ingress of air into the birth canal after delivery would cause afterpains and inflammation of the womb.[17]

According to the diary, Dr. Page "*Chose* to Close the Loin." The implication of intent is suggestive. Martha used the verb "to choose" in describing a similar encounter in Pittston the year before. She had been called to see the wife of Peter Grant, but the family "had called Doctor Parker before I arived and he *seemed to chuse* to perform the opperation which took place at 1 hour 11 am."[18] The language is not accidental. There was something strangely officious about the behavior of Drs. Page and Parker. Older physicians were content with emergency work or with delivering their near relatives. These men were different. Rather than deferring to the midwife, as would have been proper with one of her age and experience, perhaps remaining in an outer room with the husband in case of emergency, they *chose* to participate in the routine work of birthing. For Martha Ballard the behavior of Dr. Page was particularly troubling. The young man was not yet twenty-four years old and still unmarried, yet he seemed bent on making midwifery a part of the full-time practice of medicine.[19]

Her second encounter with Ben Page was more dramatic. She had been sitting up all night with Hannah Sewall, a young bride who had recently arrived in Hallowell from the coastal town of York. (Her husband was another of Henry's cousins.) "They were intimidated," Martha wrote, "& Calld Dr Page who gave my patient 20 drops of Laudanum which put her into such a stupor her pains (which were regular & promising) in a manner stopt till near night when she pukt & they returned & shee delivered at 7 hour Evening of a son her first Born."[20] The "intimidation" may have had something to do with the fact that Hannah had grown up in an elite family in a coastal town and was already familiar with medical delivery. Dr. Page's behavior, however, can only be attributed to inexperience. English obstetrical literature recommended the use of opiates for *false* pains but not for genuine labor; he was apparently having difficulty telling one from the other. Martha's characterization of the pains as "regular" suggests she may have been using her timepiece to monitor the contractions. That she pronounced them "promising" suggests she had conducted an internal examination (or "touch") to check the dilation, though we cannot be sure. Perhaps her measurement of the pains was merely impressionistic; she had sat through enough "lingering" labors to know productive pains from spurious ones.

Thereafter she was unmerciful in reporting Dr. Page's mistakes. "Sally Cocks went to see Mrs Kimball," she wrote. "Shee was delivered of a dead daughter on the morning of the 9th instant, the operation performed by Ben Page. The infants limbs were much dislocated as I am informed." She even questioned his judgment on nonobstetrical matters. Called to examine an infant's rupture, she recommended the application of brandy. "They inform me that Dr Page says it must be opined, which I should think improper from present appearance," she wrote. Dr. Page must have had some success or patients would not have been willing to call him, yet some part of his ability to enter the practice was due to the high birth rate in the town, to Martha's own heavy schedule, and to Dr. Cony's frequent absences. Henry Sewall even called him once "in Mrs. Ballard's absence," but fortunately it was a false alarm and Martha was able to perform the delivery. In June of 1798, while Martha was engaged with another case, Page again delivered a stillborn child. Her report was blunt: "The wife of James Bridg was delivered this morn at 1 hour of a son. It was Born dead and is to be interd this Evening. Doctor Page was operator. Poor unfortunate man in the practice." Perhaps this misadventure induced some humility. A month later Martha again found "a patient in the hands of Doctor Page," but this time "he gave the Case up to me and she was (after I removd obstructions) safe delivered."[21]

Benjamin Page was unfortunate, but he was also ill prepared and overly confident. Martha's reference to his dislocation of an infant's limbs suggests lack of familiarity with the difficult manual operation required in breech births. The English midwife Sarah Stone warned against such "boyish Pretenders," who, having attended a few dissections and read the major treatises, pretended to understand the manipulative arts so important to midwifery. Even Henry Bracken, an English *accoucheur* who insisted that midwives call in a doctor in difficult births, cautioned, "I would never advise any one to employ a *young* physician."[22]

Still, Ben Page had certain advantages: a gentlemanly bearing, a successfully completed apprenticeship, and credit with certain younger members of the Kennebec elite. His list of patients is impressive. Benjamin Poor was a printer and eventually the publisher of Hallowell's first newspaper, his wife a school-teacher. David Sewall was a merchant, his wife the daughter of one of York's first families, and the sister of Sally Keating Wood, Maine's first novelist. James Bridge was a Harvard grad-uate, attorney, and eventual Judge of Probate for Kennebec County. Significantly, his wife was Hannah North, the judge's daughter. All three husbands were, like Benjamin Page, ambi-tious, educated, and new to the town. Furthermore, they could afford a physician's fee. (In the early 1800s, when Martha Bal-lard was charging under $2 for a delivery, Page was collecting $6.)[23]

We should not conclude, however, that Hallowell's elite fam-ilies were abandoning traditional delivery en masse. Whether status is determined by position on the tax list, by education, or by election to public office, Hallowell's "elite" were as likely as ordinary families to employ Martha Ballard. To the end of the century she performed two-thirds of the deliveries in the town, whether the babies were the children or grandchildren of public officials and merchants or of ordinary timbermen and farmers. Ten of the twelve wealthiest men on the tax list for 1790 are known to have had children or grandchildren born before 1800. Martha performed deliveries for eight. Of twenty-five men who held town, county, or state office between 1785 and 1796, nine-teen are known to have had children or grandchildren born be-fore 1800. She performed deliveries for fourteen. The exceptions are predictable. In addition to Colonel North and his son-in-law James Bridges, they include Daniel Cony, who delivered his own children, and Beriah Ingraham, whose wife or mother ("Old Lady Ingraham") was a midwife.[24]

Several of the more prominent Hallowell families employed Martha Ballard. She delivered two of Supply Belcher's children before his removal to Farmington in 1794. Known to contem-poraries as the "Handel of Maine," he published a collection of compositions in 1794. Sarah Sheppard, whose husband was Charles Vaughan's agent at the Hook, was also one of Martha's patients. (Mrs. Sheppard had the distinction of owning a piano.)[25] There were others. About ten days after Martha's encounter with Dr. Page at the delivery of Hannah Sewall, she was called to the home of Chandler Robbins, a Harvard graduate and new resident of the town. "Mrs Robbins Linguerd till 4 hour pm when her illness came on," she wrote, adding, "Doctor Parker was Calld but shee did not wish to see him when he Came & he returned home." In childbirth, the ultimate decision still rested with the mother. Martha noted, without comment, that Mr. Robbins had given her eighteen shillings, three times her usual fee.[26]

In the diary, the transition to medical obstetrics is a far more complex process that it appears in secondary literature. Historians have attributed the rise of "male-midwifery" in England and America to two factors, fashion and forceps. Forceps capable of delivering a living child were a humane alternative to the crude techniques of barber surgeons called in to save a mother's life by dismembering her child. Midwives and physicians both assailed the frequent use of "the *Hook* and the *Knife*," describing "Infants born crying, with their Brains working out of their Heads" and mothers dying "under the Hands of the *Operator* after some of the *Limbs* and *Ribs* of the Child were brought away."[27] In fact Benjamin Page's mentor, Dr. Thomas Kittredge of Andover, Massachusetts, owned forceps and the medical treatises that promoted their use.[28]

Yet instruments can hardly explain the introduction of male-midwifery in a town with so few emergency births. Martha Ballard summoned a physician twice in twenty-seven years, once in the first year of the diary, when she arrived late to a delivery and found the patient "greatly ingered by some mishap" by an inexperienced midwife, though the woman did "not allow that shee was sencible of it." Significantly, she sent for Dr. Colman, a doctor who did not perform deliveries, to deal with what was by then a *medical* emergency. Although Colman was unavailable, "Dr. Williams fortunately Come in & prescribed remidies which aford some relief." The mother apparently survived.[29]

The description of the second case is more expansive. "My patients illness Came on at 8 hour morning," Martha wrote.

Her women were Calld, her Case was Lingering till 7 pm
I removd difuculties & waited for Natures opperations till
then, when shee was more severly attackt with obstructions
which alarmed me much. I desird Doctor Hubard might be
sent for which request was Complid with, but by Divine
assistance I performed the oppration, which was blisst with
the preservation of the lives off mother and infant. The life
of the latter I dispard off for some time.

In the margin of that day's entry she wrote, "The most perelous
sien I Ever past thro in the Course of my practice. Blessed be
God for his goodness."[30]

Martha was frightened by this "perelous sien," but her ability
to negotiate it alone may have increased her confidence. Never
again did she feel it necessary to summon a physician. She certainly encountered her share of breech births, obstructions, and
fainting mothers, but she knew what to do. "The foets [fetus]
was in an unnatural posetion but I Brot it into a proper direction
and shee was safe delivered," she reported calmly after one difficult birth, and following another she wrote, "There were some
obstructions to remove. When performd the patient was safe
delivered." Her nondescript entries are a quiet corrective to
eighteenth-century obstetrical manuals, which are filled with the
horrors of birth, babies lodged in the birth canal or stuck crosswise in the pelvis, mothers bleeding to death or succumbing
from putrefying tissue left in the womb. "[She] was Exercised
with pain & fainting after delivery," Martha summarized. "I
made use of Camphor & other remedies. Shee revivd & I left
her & Child Cleverly."[31]

The construction of the last sentence is pleasingly ambiguous.
In some English dialects to leave a person "Cleverly" meant to
leave them in health. That was certainly the intended meaning
of Martha's statement. Yet leaving a mother and child "Cleverly" also meant applying one's own adroitness and dexterity.
A midwife's skill was mirrored in her patients' well-being. Typically, Martha gave God the credit for her success, but she knew
that He had worked His will through her hands.

Without seeming to do so she compared her own record with

those of her peers, working into the diary hearsay evidence of difficult births that occurred outside her practice. "Mr George Brown informd me that Capt Smiths wife had 2 Children Born Last night. They are dead," she wrote. In this case the practitioner may have been Mrs. Hinkley, who is known to have delivered another of Captain Smith's children. Sometime later Martha noted that Mrs. Hartford had been "delivered of two Dead Babes by Esquire Cony this morning, one of each sex."[32] Behind these statements is her own quiet awareness that she herself had never lost a pair of twins. She reported multiple births as though they were as ordinary as any others: "I was calld in haste at 11 hour Eveing to Mr Isaac Clearks Lady in travil. Shee was safe delivered of a fine son & a daughter before 12. All likely to do well."[33]

A statistical comparison between Martha Ballard and her competitors is something of an anachronism, however, as is an effort to isolate and categorize her delivery techniques. She simply did not see her work in that way. In fact, the most descriptive account of the birth of twins in her diary says almost as much about her own journey as the delivery itself. Mrs. Byrnes

was seizd with her illness very severe about noon, calld her women a little before sun sett and shee was safe delivered of Two Daughters before 8 hour Evening. There was but a short space between the Births. They are fine Children. May God long preserv them. I sett up with my Patients, Mrs Conry and Benn White's wife allso. It was a very Cold night. I was Calld to Mrs Byrns yesterday. Mr Ballard & Dingley broke thro the ice and got me over the river. I was fatagud in Climbing the bank on the other side. Mr Dingley & Graves assisted me.[34]

Characteristically, the one obstetrical comment in the entry ("There was but a short space between the Births") is embedded in seemingly extraneous references to the weather, her journey, the names of the men who assisted her across the river and of the women who sat up with her through the night. The biological event fades into the clutter of social detail. Where is the center of the picture? Is it Martha Ballard scrambling up the icy bank, Mr. Dingley grasping one arm, Mr. Graves reaching toward her from above, while Ephraim slowly turns his boat in the ice-rimmed river below? Is it Mrs. Byrnes, exhausted from her eight-hour labor, bearing down for the second delivery? Is it Mrs. Conry easing two perfect babies into the cradle, or the three drowsy women leaning toward the kitchen fire, the midnight cold at their backs, small clouds of mist above their whispers?

There is no center, only a kind of grid, faint trails of experience converging and deflecting across a single day.

A description of childbirth taken from Martha Ballard's diary could not include anything so precise as the dilation of the cervix or the extraction of the afterbirth. Nor would it focus on the three stages of labor easily recognizable to twentieth-century women in the eighteenth-century distinction between "grinding or preparing pains," "forcing pains," and "grumbling pains." The diary description would have three stages, but they would be defined in social rather than biological terms, each marked by the summons and arrival of attendants—first the midwife, then the neighborhood circle of women, finally the afternurse. Parturition ended when the mother returned to her kitchen.

The first stage of delivery lasted from several hours to several days and at first might not even be accompanied by genuine labor. The *expectation* of labor was enough. "I helpt Mrs Lithgow make Cake & Pies & knit on my Stockin," Martha wrote two days after her arrival at Esquire Lithgow's in Winslow. The long distance necessitated the early summons, but Mrs. Lithgow was not far wrong in her estimation, as the next day's entry attests: "I finisht my stockin. My patient was unwell all day." She was delivered at ten the following night of a "fine son."[35] Whether she was actually in labor the whole time or only uncomfortable and anxious, we do not know. The important thing is that her midwife was there and willing to stay.

Most women stayed on their feet as long as they could during this stage of delivery, working as able, resting as necessary. Mrs. Thwing "Capt [kept] Chamber all day" before her third delivery." Mrs. Walker "was sprigh about house till 11, was safe delivered at 12 hour & 15 minutes of a fine Son." (Martha had arrived early that morning.) "By turns" Mrs. Lathrop was "able to work till near sunset when she was more unwell." Martha measured the intensity of labor by her own ability to work or sleep. "Find the patient some what ill but I had op[portunity] to take rest by sleep," she wrote, and during another labor, "I sett up the most of the night. Shee seemd very Comfortable towards day and I took sleep." She was patient but watchful during this period, sometimes even sharing a bed with her patient.[36]

Martha probably administered herbal remedies and perhaps even mixtures laced with wine or rum, though the only explicit references to alcohol during labor suggest dismay at the women's capacity for drink. At William Chamberlain's house: "My patient is not very well. We find shee has an inclination to drink rhum. She drank about one quart. Her illness increast ... was delivered at 3 hour morn of a son her first child." And a week later at another house: "At Mr Catons yet. His wife is not fitt to be left. He went to the river. Shee wisht to Drink wine and Eat Bisquit. He procured it and shee Drank Eleven glasses this day and Eat Bisquit and wine at Evening 3 times." The next day she was delivered "of a son at 2 hours 30 minutes pm and of a daughter at 3 hour pm ... I could not sleep for flees."[37] In both cases Martha attributed the inclination to drink to the mother herself, though she may have approved an effort to relax and partially sedate a patient who was experiencing lackadaisical and not very productive labor.

The transition from the first to the second stage of delivery was marked by the calling of "the women." Here too there were occasional disappointments—"the women went home Except her Sister Blanchard"—but generally the arrival of the women signaled the imminence of birth. The calling of the women may have marked a biological transition. In normal labor the full dilation of the cervix brings the onset of what eighteenth-century practitioners called "forcing" or "bearing" pains, the active stage of labor in which the mother, coached by her midwife, assisted in expelling the child. Martha Ballard explicitly linked a new intensity of labor with the summoning of the neighbors, writing that one woman's "illness Came on so great that her women were Calld" or that another "was not so ill as to call in other assistance this day."[38]

There were practical reasons for delaying the call, there being no good reason why five or six women should share the passive watching and waiting that accompanied the early hours of labor. Once the second stage of labor began, however, additional women were needed. Most early American women literally gave birth in the arms or on the laps of their neighbors. The physical equipment for delivery was very simple. As Henry Bracken explained it, "Some Midwives use a particular Kind of Stool, and others a Pallet-Bed with only a double Quilt upon it, placed near the Fire, if the Season require," though with "a little Alteration of the Clothes" a mother's own bed "or a Woman's Knee" would do.[39] Though a Vermont midwife who practiced during this period is said to have owned a birthing stool, there is no evidence that Martha Ballard had one. The diary alludes to a "time piece," "medicines," and "specktakles," all in connection with midwifery journeys, but never once does it mention a stool, a piece of equipment that surely would have added complexity to her scrambles up the ice-covered banks of the Kennebec. "The women" are the most obvious piece of equipment in the diary.

Whether her patients reclined, crouched, knelt, or delivered upright, Martha required at least two assistants.[40] "Find his mother and Ben Churches wife there. We calld the McCausland wives after Sunsett."[41] Eighty percent of the entries that offer names mention between two and four women. One entry (perhaps incomplete) lists a single assistant; the remainder, five or more. "My company were Old Lady Cox, Pitts, Sister Barton, Moody, Soal, & Witherel," Martha wrote, omitting the usual formality of "Mrs" in her tumble of names. Listing the ten assistants at Jeremiah White's house was equally confusing: "Mrs White sent for her women. They were with her all night, Viz. old Mrs White, Norcross, Moses & Benn Whites wives, Jackson, Stickney, Coburn, & Lydia his sister."[42]

Although a few women, like Merriam Pollard, seem to have been drawn beyond the circle of their own neighborhoods, most birth attendants, except for relatives, lived nearby. Some young mothers delivered at their parents' houses, others summoned their "marm" or sisters from afar; but nearly everyone relied on neighbors. There is a striking correspondence between the names on Martha's lists and known residence patterns in the town. The Mrs. Sewall who appeared at Martha Molloy's delivery on November 18, 1793, was probably not Tabitha, who lived a considerable distance away, but Ruth, the wife of Henry's cousin Moses. She and Mrs. Dutton lived near the Molloys at the Hook. Tabitha Sewall may well have been present a few weeks later, at the delivery of her neighbor, Mrs. Parker (though a little later there would be an estrangement that would prevent that kind of intimacy). When Tabitha Sewall delivered her fourth child, the attendants included Mrs. Parker, Mrs. Vose, and another near neighbor, Susanna Cony Howard Brooks.[43]

The attending women offered emotional as well as physical support. After two days of intermittent labor, "Mrs Coin [Cowen] was Lingering and very much deprist in Spirits. We called Mrs Fletcher. Mrs Soal Called there. Mrs Savage & Fletcher tarried all night." The patient was delivered a few hours later "with 5 pains after my inquiring into her Case."[44] The women helped to dress the infant and to lift the mother in (or out) of bed. Performing their simple duties, they no doubt traded stories, measuring one woman's pains—or the size of her child—against another's. George Thomas's son "weighed more than the lite side of Mr Densmore's stilyards would weigh"; Captain Ney's baby "measured round the Breast (after being drest in thin Cloaths) 18 1/2 inches." In contrast, Hannah Getchel's illegitimate child was "the smallist I ever saw alive." (It died the next day.)[45]

In one birth out of twenty-four, the child died. Of these, forty percent were stillborn; the rest died in the first day of life. When the delivery was abnormal, Martha searched for causes: "Shee had a fall not long since which probably was the cause," or "I know not what to ascribe the death of the infant to but the cough the Mother had." One infant "survivd about an hour and Expird without any aparant distress. It seemd to be struck with a mortification," Martha wrote.[46] In such circumstances it was comforting to have the women with her; they could witness her efforts to ensure a safe delivery and they could assist with the sorrowful task of preparing the infant for burial.

The presence of the women was even more important in cases of illegitimacy. "At Benjamin White's with his Sister Rebeckah who is in Travel tho unmarried," she wrote on December 2, 1787, noting that Becky's women were with her when she declared Seth Partridge to be the father of her child. In the most sensational case of her career, Martha was especially careful about noting the presence—or absence—of witnesses. Sally Ballard's sister Mehettable Pierce declared that her child "was begoten by John Varsal Davis, Esquire. This shee positively affirm[ed] in the presence of the wife of Jonathan Ballard who with Hosea Houland were my assistants in the case. The latter was stept in to an other room when I Examined my Patient," Martha explained, adding that they had also summoned Mrs. Titcomb, who "did not arive till after the Birth." Davis came to see the mother and child that afternoon, whether on a cordial visit or to determine whether Hitty had remained true to her accusation, we do not know. Davis, a Plymouth Company heir and clerk of the country court, was not disposed to marry the mother, but he seems to have paid child support until the baby died at the age of three (see Chapter 7).[47]

Martha was not summoned, however, to what may have been an even more sensational delivery. On August 29, 1795, Henry Sewall reported in his diary that "last night Charlotte Cool, who lives in character of Household Servant, gave birth to a second *bastard child* at Peter Parkers, said to be by Colo. Wm. H——d." For Sewall, there must have been great satisfaction in the event. Mrs. Parker, the woman whom Martha delivered in December of 1793, had earlier sued him before Judge North for slander. Sewall had apparently spread, though not originated, rumors about her (or her maid's?) alliance with Colonel Howard.[48] As usual, the details are missing, but the underlying issue—the Colonel's behavior—seems clear. It was one thing for young couples to have a child born too soon after marriage, another for public officials like Howard and Davis to flout local norms. But what was one to do unless the women themselves were willing to confront the men? Hitty Pierce sued John Davis, but as far as we know, Charlotte Cool made no effort to prosecute Howard.[49]

Traditionally, the attending women at a delivery joined in a celebration afterward ("the Ladies who assisted took supper after all our matters were completed"), sometimes staying the night if there was room in the house or the weather was bad ("took a nap by the fire after midnight. Her women all tarried"). There would be a clutter of beds in the kitchen and chambers as the women fitted into the niches of an already crowded household. "There were 22 in number slept under that roof the night," Martha reported after one delivery, including in her count the children and hired helpers and visiting relatives as well as the attending neighbors. Some women could afford an "elligant dinner" for their women; others sent their midwife home searching her clothes for fleas. There was piety in some households ("We all took some repose . . . took Breakfast and afterwards attended prayers"), confusion in others ("his mother had fitts after [the] delivery. I attended in Each room and left all cleverly"). At the house of Scip Moody, one of Hallowell's free blacks, there was more neighborly concern than space. "I tarried all night, Mrs Cain & Ben White's wife allso," Martha wrote. "We had no where to sleep so we sett up."[50]

During another all-night vigil, Martha herself became the patient. "I had a severe Cramp in my Limbs in the night . . . the Ladies who were there used me with great kindness."[51] Perhaps there was a kind of pleasure in nursing the friend who had so often cared for them.

The third stage of birth—the lying-in period—began with

the arrival of the afternurse and the departure of the midwife. In her entry for December 8, 1793, Martha made the connection explicit: "Mr Parker went for his Nurs. I left his Lady at 4 pm." Barring unforeseen complications, she would not return. Mrs. Parker made an uneventful recovery, though six weeks later she called Martha back to see her infant, who seemed unwell. Her husband used this occasion to pay Martha. A few days later, when she was in the neighborhood delivering another baby, she again "Calld at Mr Parkers," noting that "her infant is better."[52] Postpartum checkups, like prenatal care, were unusual. Return visits occurred if the mother or infant was unwell or if Martha Ballard happened to be in the neighborhood and made a courtesy call.

For this reason the diary tells us less about the postpartum period than about delivery itself. The few descriptions that survive suggest that the term "lying-in" was a misnomer. Most women spent very little time in bed. Even in the first hours after delivery, mothers were not allowed to languish. "Got my patient up, Changd her lining [linen] and came home," Martha wrote, in this case twelve hours after delivery, or "help[ed] Mrs William up & maid her Bed and returned home." Commenting on a casual visit to another patient, Martha described what must have been the normal process of recovery. Six days after delivery Martha found Mrs. Joy "down in her kitchen. Shee Came out of her Chamber yesterday. Shee informs me that shee has made her Bed this three days. Her infant is finely."[53] It wasn't the size and position of the woman's uterus but her ability to make her own bed that signified recovery. Mrs. Joy may have been a day or two ahead of schedule. Under normal circumstances a woman "kept chamber" for a week, gradually assuming responsibility for the care of her infant and her own surroundings until she was able to "return to the kitchen," a ubiquitous and apt description for the end of lying-in.

The length of convalescence depended upon the economic circumstances as well as the physical condition of the mother. As the birth entries make clear, the range of resources and of housekeeping skills among Martha's patients varied widely.

Elite women could obviously afford a more leisured and orderly lying-in. Henry Sewall reported that Tabitha "got below" three weeks after the delivery of her seventh child. With a toddler and three other children to care for as well as the infant, she was probably happy to delay her emergence as long as possible. This time she had been fortunate in engaging Mrs. Conner, the most sought-after of the local afternurses. In comparison, Isaac Hardin's wife hardly paused after delivery to catch her breath. "I am informd that Mrs Hardin wove 1 1/2 yards this day & 3 the next," Martha wrote in the margin of her entry for March 12, 1794. The baby had arrived three days before.

For many Maine women, as for their English counterparts, alcoholic drinks were a part of lying-in. A store manager in another part of Maine wrote his employer, "The women in these parts have been very fruitfull this winter and had I not assisted many of them with tea, sugar, rum &c in their lyings in I do not know what would have become of them, for they seem destitute, of all comforts, and their husbands are to repay in labour." Two days after her niece Pamela Porter was delivered, Martha sent her the same list of commodities, minus the tea. The continuous caution of the prescriptive literature against the use of "strong spiritous liquors" during lying-in reinforces the evidence. The concern of some authors was that strong beverages would induce fevers by adding heat to the body. Thin-water gruel was much better, they insisted, than caudle or thick gruel mixed with liquors.[54] Maine women did not agree. Rum, sugar, and tea were necessary comforts for a lying-in.

The scarcest commodity in Hallowell households was not rum, however, but help. As we have seen, the same young women who warped looms and swept kitchens in Hallowell occasionally did nursing ("Parthena gone to nurse Mrs Foot"; "Philip Bullin conducted Becky Fought to his brothers as nurse after birth"). Few of these young nurses could stay long, most having other obligations to their families or employers. After one of her own daughters delivered, Martha noted that Debby Low had come and gone in a day and that the mother had no help except for her sister, who had brought her two young children with her and another baby as well. Under such circumstances, getting well was a woman's best defense.[55]

There were a few older women who specialized in nursing, and those who could afford them were fortunate. Martha Ballard and Henry Sewall both mentioned Mrs. Conry or Conner. Since neither surname appeared on either the 1790 or 1800 census for Hallowell, Augusta, or other nearby towns, she may have been a widow living as a dependent in a daughter's or sister's house. Mrs. Vose, probably the wife or mother of one of the men by that name in the town, also did nursing, as did Mrs. Stone. Nurses were probably paid less than midwives, though in some families, at least, they inherited the traditional place of honor at an infant's baptism. At the baptism of one of the Reverend Mr. Foster's children, "Mrs Vose carried it." Henry Sewall gave Mrs. Conner the same honor when his daughter Mary was baptized.[56]

A successful delivery did not assure the survival of the child, nor did all women pass through the lying-in period without incident. Experienced afternurses could handle the usual complications, though occasionally Martha was called back to administer remedies two or three days after delivery. "Shee had an ill turn. Her milk is Cuming," was the common explanation. There were more exotic complications, of course. Two weeks after a birth, Martha went back to the Norcrosses and "Cleard her infants breasts of milk." Women then as now suffered from afterpains, hemorrhoids, and phlebitis. In thirty-eight of the 481 births between 1785 and 1796, Martha returned to her patients to treat some sort of complication. In thirty-four of these cases, at least one specific symptom is mentioned. Seven women had sore breasts, three experienced fever, two had taken cold, another had contracted a sore throat, five had an "ill turn" when their milk came in, another a severe headache, two experienced unusual weakness, and one had cramp pains a month after delivery. Six days after delivery, Moses Sewall's wife was "Exercisd with a swelling in her Left Legg & Severe pain." In the final case, Martha attributed the postpartum crisis to the misbehavior of a husband.[57]

"I was called in hast to Mrs. Williams," she wrote, "shee

being in a Deliriam by reason of a mistep of her Husband tho not desiring to injure her. I tarried till 3/O Clok morn. Left her rationall tho Exercisd with some pain." It is hard to imagine what the young husband had done. Had he administered the wrong medicine? Let the fire go out? Crawled in bed with his wife—or the afternurse? The suddenness of the crisis suggests that an emotional upset rather than a fever had induced the "Deliriam," though we cannot be sure.[58]

As we have seen, five of Martha's patients died during the lying-in period. One woman was seriously ill with the measles when she gave birth. Another was in convulsions when she delivered a stillborn daughter and was still experiencing "fitts" four days later when she died. She was no doubt a victim of eclampsia, the most severe stage of an acute toxemia of pregnancy, a condition that is still considered one of the gravest complications of childbirth today. The other women may have died of puerperal infection, historically the major cause of deaths in childbed. The infectious quality of puerperal fever was first suggested in the 1840s by Dr. Oliver Wendell Holmes in the United States and Dr. Ignaz Semmelweis in Austria, but the bacteriological nature of the disease was not settled until the 1880s, when Louis Pasteur demonstrated the presence of what is now known as streptococcus in patients suffering from the affliction. Puerperal fever is a wound infection caused by the invasion of the uterine cavity by a number of bacteria, alone or in combination. The patient may feel normal in the first few days after delivery, but then an elevation in temperature, headache, malaise, and pelvic pain signal infection. (With certain strains of bacteria there is a profuse discharge characterized by a peculiarly foul odor.)[59]

The description of Mrs. Craig's death fits the pattern. She was "safe Delivered of a very fine Daughter" on March 31, 1790. Five days later Martha reported finding her "not so well as I could wish." The midwife returned the next day and administered a "Clister [enema] of milk, water, & salt" and applied an "ointment & a Bath of Tansy, mugwort, Cammomile & Hysop which gave Mrs. Cragg great relief." A week later she was called back because her patient was "Exceeding ill." Mrs. Craig had taken rhubarb and the bark on her own but had not improved. When a physician was called the next day, he "plainly told the famely Mrs Cragg must die." She expired that evening. Martha helped "put on the grave Cloaths," then stayed with the family the night. "The Corps were Coffined & sett in the west room," she wrote. "Purge & smell very ofensive." Meanwhile, the neighbors came by turns to "give the infant suck."[60]

Martha attempted no diagnosis in this or in the remaining cases, though infection seems the likely cause. As we have seen, Mrs. Caton died four days after delivery during the scarlet fever epidemic of 1787. The remaining women fell ill a few days after delivery and died two weeks later. What is significant about these five deaths, of course, is their rarity. A woman might experience acute discomfort during lying-in—afterpains, sore nipples, swollen legs, and even "Deliriam"—but few died.

Most women went through delivery every other year, summoning a midwife, calling their women, welcoming the afternurse, returning to their kitchens. For the next year they would breast-feed the newest baby while caring for the older siblings, fitting in work at the loom or in the barn and garden as they could. Some historians have discerned an effort in New England toward the end of the eighteenth century to control family size. There is little evidence of that in Hallowell. Even with incomplete registration, there are more than seven children per family in the town clerk's records. Martha delivered four women of a twelfth, one of a thirteenth, two of a fifteenth, and one of a sixteenth child.

For most women, breast-feeding retarded conception, creating birth intervals that averaged twenty-four months, in Martha Ballard's practice as in most of the western world. Martha was impressed enough to note it when Ezra Hodge's wife delivered her fifth baby just two months after her oldest child turned five, but such feats of fertility were rare.[61] The rhythm of childbearing kept the traditional beat. If there was any effort at family limitation, it came toward the end of the childbearing years. In some families, birth intervals grew further apart; in a few, deliveries stopped abruptly. Tabitha Sewall had eight children in fourteen years and then quit bearing. But the effect on the town's fertility was slight. Not even widowhood could retard Susanna Cony Howard Brooks. She produced eight children in sixteen years of marriage to three different husbands. Nor is there any evidence that women choosing medical delivery were opting for small families. After her adventure with laudanum, Hannah Sewall gave birth to ten more children. Hannah Bridges had an additional seven, including another set of twins, after that first pair of stillborn infants. In Martha's own family, fertility was unchanged from generation to generation. Her mother had had ten children, she nine, her sister Dorothy Barton thirteen. Her own daughters and daughters-in-law were equally prolific. Lucy and Dolly had eleven children each, Sally twelve, and although Hannah's completed family size is unknown, she had given birth to eight children before the diary closed.

Since a family labor force was the basis of the New England economy, parents were understandably concerned about producing the proper balance of boys and girls. In about a quarter of her delivery entries, Martha noted the birth order of the child, and often the sex ratio as well. "Her 8th Child; the number of sex are Equal," she wrote, or "7th Child of which 4 are daughters."[62] (These descriptions give no indication of a gender bias; Hallowell women gave birth to "*fine* daughters" as well as "*fine* sons," though the adjective "lusty" may have been reserved for boys.) Martha was pleased when Mrs. James Hinkley "was safe dilivrd at sun set of a daughter," explaining that the woman had seven sons and until then only one daughter, then "in her 15th year." Martha's neighbor Lydia Densmore had the opposite problem. In 1797, she gave birth to her twelfth child and ninth daughter. Fortunately, the family business—tailoring and dressmaking—was well adapted to girls.[63]

What was expected, then, was a heroic commitment to childbearing, an outlook reflected in Martha Ballard's own willingness to spend herself in delivering others. She was compassionate, gentle, concerned for her neighbors' welfare, but though she assumed that a certain amount of suffering was the common lot of womanhood, she was impatient with whining. Mrs. Baxter, for example, really seemed to enjoy illness. "Find her better but insensible of the favour," Martha reported after one visit, and a few days later added, "went to see Mrs Baxter who I think is better tho shee is not of that mind." When the woman suffered "a turn of hysterics," Martha sat with her through the night and into the next afternoon, though a week later she was dismayed to hear that "Mrs Baxter is no Better or shee is insensable shee is."[64]

More distressing was the behavior of her old friend and neighbor Elizabeth Weston, who was overwhelmed by her last pregnancy, an unexpected and probably unwelcome event. She was forty-five years old, her youngest child already six. Furthermore, since her daughter Betsy had recently married Thomas Fillebrown, she was more disposed to welcome grandchildren than another child of her own.[65] Her anxiety grew more intense during the last weeks of pregnancy. Though her previous delivery had been uneventful, she grew fearful that this one would not go well. There were as yet no physical signs of labor, but she wanted her midwife with her.

Martha spent almost two weeks in and out of the Weston house, leaving when necessary to deliver other women. "Mrs Wesson remains much as shee has been," Martha wrote on October 28, after four days of sleeping and waiting with no sign of labor. "[She] Consented that I should go home & see how my famely were." If there had been a half-frozen river between them, the long vigil might have been justified, but the Westons and the Ballards were still relatively near neighbors despite the Ballards' removal from the mills.

Still, Martha returned the next day, listening, watching, and apparently growing increasingly annoyed. "Mr Wesson brot me some work," she wrote on November 4. By November 6 she had had enough. "I Came home," she wrote. "Mrs Wesson as well as she has been." The woman presumably got the point. When she called again she meant it. The summons came on November 9 at 3:00 a.m., and "Shee was safe delivered at 4 hour 30 minutes of a fine son." A safe delivery did not relieve the problem. A week later Martha wrote, "I began to make candles & was calld to see Mrs Weston. I find her as well as Could be Expected but of the mind Shee Cannot take care of hir infant at home. A stupid afair I think, but Shee must do as shee pleases."[66]

A harsh judgment from an old friend. When Martha returned a month later, Mrs. Weston was as determined on illness as ever. "She is weak," Martha reported, adding by way of explanation, "Shee has not walked her room any since shee was put to bed. Her infant is at Mr Hewins."[67] Perhaps one of the town's physicians took over the management of her case. Martha had nothing more to say about it. She delivered Elizabeth Weston's daughter Betsy Fillebrown of her first child on February 2, making no reference to the presence or absence of the grandmother. (Mrs. Weston was, however, clearly present when her daughter gave birth to a second child two years later.) Perhaps there was a brief estrangement between the two women, though if so the old patterns of neighborliness had clearly been restored by the end of the summer.[68]

In sending out her infant to be nursed, Elizabeth Weston violated a particularly strong taboo. Only a severe and intractable illness could justify separating a mother and child. When Lucy Towne fell ill of a fever a week after delivery, she struggled to continue nursing her child. Not until ten days later, when the baby itself seemed to be suffering, was a neighbor summoned to give "the poor Babe suck," Martha explaining that "its mammy has not but very little for it." Even then, steps were taken to preserve lactation against the time when Lucy would once again feed her child. "Lucy is a little mending," her mother wrote. "Parthena drew her Breasts got a small matter of milk." During this period two different neighbors nursed the baby.[69]

A considerable part of Martha's medical practice involved treating infants for "sore mouths" and their mothers for "painful breasts." Women could develop abscesses at any time during lactation. Martha had various remedies. In one case, after a poultice of sorrel proved ineffective, she "opened" (lanced) the breast. When one of her own daughters developed an abscess she was concerned enough to call Dr. Howard, who "recommended a wheat bread poltis." When that failed, she tried applying yellow lily roots, but that only seemed to increase the pain. Meanwhile the infant grew "restless for want of the Breast . . . we could not git any milk from my daughter's breast." This time, she was reluctant for some reason to lance the sore herself. When Dr. Howard did not think "it fit to open," she sent for Dr. Colman, who performed the operation: "It had a Copeous discharg," she reported, adding with satisfaction, "Shee seems more comfortable; the infant is cleverly."[70]

For Martha the final stage of any delivery was collecting her fee. In the margin of her diary entry for December 17, 1793, she wrote, "Receivd 12/ March 5th 1794 of Mr Hamlin." That Theophilus Hamlin paid twelve shillings for his daughter's delivery was unusual; that it took him three months to do so was not. Martha's standard charge in the 1790s was six shillings, paid in cash, in kind, or in credit at one of the local stores.[71] Perhaps more payments were in kind than the cash values recorded in the diary would indicate. On November 28, for example, in the diary excerpt that opens this chapter, she wrote, "Mr Lathrop paid me my fee for attending his wife the 19th of March last." In the margin of the March 19 entry, she wrote, "receivd sugar Nov 28."

Midwifery payments reflected the economy of the town. In the course of her career Martha received everything from "1m shingles" to "a pair flat irons." Most payments were in food, textiles, or household necessities: cheese, butter, wheat, rye, corn, baby pigs and turkeys, candles, a great wheel, unwashed wool, checked cloth, 1/2 quintal of cod, teapots, thimbles, a looking glass, handkerchiefs, and snuff. Martha rarely commented on a payment unless it was unusually generous or notably meager. "Received 2 lb coffee, 1 yd ribbon, & a cap border as Extraordinary for waiting on her," she wrote after one delivery. In contrast, Savage Bolton gave her "1 1/2 Bushl of apples in the fall not very good."[72]

She occasionally "forgave" a family the fee. When she delivered Charles Clark's fourth child, she noted "her 3d is destitute of reason by reason of fitts." She had come to that delivery expecting to collect the unpaid fee for the third baby as well as the new charge for the fourth, but seeing the family's sorrow she wrote off the earlier debt. "I gave this fee Sept 5th on acount off the infirmity off their Child," she wrote in the margin of the first entry.[73] Martha was also capable of seeing to the physical as well as the medical needs of her patients. As we have seen, a day after delivering Mrs. Welch of a stillborn child, she sent Mr. Ballard "to see that she had wood, made her a shovel etc." But after a later delivery to the same woman, who was now conspicuously without a husband, she felt less charitable. "Called by Mr Garish to see Mrs Welch who was ... delivered ... of a daughter which shee declared said Gerish was the father of," she wrote. Whether the woman was successful in getting child support from Gerish we do not know. She paid for this delivery herself "by weaving 14 & 1/2 yds all wool Cloath."[74]

Fees exceeding six shillings usually meant additional expenses. "I receivd 9/ as fee & hors hire & medisin," she wrote after an arduous journey on muddy roads to the Buzel delivery. Probably most husbands avoided the cost of "horse hire" by fetching the midwife themselves or by relying on a neighbor. That fewer than a fifth of Martha Ballard's patients in 1793 paid more than six shillings suggests that she used medicine sparingly. The length of labor did not affect the fee. She spent a day and a half with Mrs. Hinkley and only five hours with Mrs. Coutch, though she received exactly the same fee, six shillings, from each.

Payments larger than nine shillings were very rare during any part of her career. In fact, the conclusion is inescapable that it was the generosity or affluence of the father rather than extra services by the midwife that accounted for very large fees. Certain men among the Kennebec gentry—William and John Brooks, Theophilus Hamlin, Chandler Robbins, Samuel Colman—almost always paid twelve shillings or more. Henry Sewall stayed closer to the six-shilling standard, though in October of 1799, when Tabitha delivered her eighth child, a daughter, he gave Martha Ballard twelve shillings. Perhaps he was especially grateful for the outcome of the delivery. Though he didn't mention it in his diary, Martha Ballard noted that "Mrs Sewall . . . was viry ill a little while but is cleverly now." [75]

Peter Parker's payment didn't make it into the margin of his daughter's birth entry in 1793, but he eventually paid, and paid generously. "Mr Parker gave me 18/ for attending his Lady in her illness with her Last Child," Martha wrote on January 27, 1794. A few days later, after another trip to the Parker house, she added, "his Lady made me a present of 1 1/2 yards ribbin." After crossing the river eight times and spending nine full days at the Parker house, off and on, she deserved the extra payment. Not all her patients had the wherewithal or the inclination to act accordingly. She received only six shillings from Mrs. Norcross after that famous April delivery (described in the Introduction), even though she had made four trips downriver and had spent nine days waiting for a "lingering labor." The Norcross case was by no means an isolated one. One year Martha spent two days each with Mrs. Hersey, Mrs. Pierce, Mrs. Cocks, and Mrs. Plaisted, four days with Mrs. Savage, and made three trips to the Sewalls', spending a total of seven days with Tabitha. Two husbands paid six shillings, one seven, one nine, and another apparently nothing at all. Henry Sewall gave Martha eight shillings and three pence.[76] The length of labor was clearly one of the acts of God over which neither the midwife nor her patients had any control.

Martha's standard fee—six shillings—is comparable to what Ephraim could claim for a day spent "writing plans" or appraising an estate. Of course, the time involved in a delivery was more variable (and the hours less appealing). Still, midwifery paid better than most female occupations. For example, a weaver working full-time at her loom could earn at most four shillings a day. Because most men seem to have taken pride in paying for their wives' deliveries, midwifery also gave Martha greater access to cash or store credits than women whose trade was entirely within the female economy.[77] Perhaps most of the cash values listed in the diary really were a form of credit. When Martha stopped in at Captain Molloy's store on December 9,

1793, to buy a shawl, she was probably collecting part of the twenty-four-shilling fee he had given her three weeks before. It is not surprising that the really big fees in the diary, those double, triple, and even quadruple fees offered in about 15 percent of cases, were offered by storekeepers and merchants. They could afford that kind of extravagance since, with the markup, twenty-four shillings at the store cost them considerably less. John Sheppard was the most consistently generous of the merchants, probably because as agent for the Vaughans he could afford it.

The "Elligant supper" served after Mrs. Molloy's delivery reinforces the notion that John Molloy was showing off a bit in multiplying the midwife's fee. Prosperity did not ensure domestic tranquillity, however. Martha Molloy gave birth to a second child two years later and then disappeared from Martha's midwifery records, presumably because she and her husband had moved to Portland or some other coastal town, though his shipping business occasionally brought him back to Hallowell. (On June 13, 1796, Martha noted: "Capt. Molloy sleeps here this night.") In 1801 Martha Molloy sued for divorce in the Supreme Judicial Court, charging her husband with desertion and adultery. Supporting testimony came from Mary Wyman of Salem, Massachusetts, who admitted that John Molloy was the father of her illegitimate child. Her deposition did not spare details:

> She affirmed that John Molloy, mariner, Did at Salem . . . Lodge in the same Bed with me the deponent thro' the Nights of the thirteenth, fourteenth, fifteenth, sixteenth and seventeenth days of January, in the Year of our Lord One thousand and Eight hundred, in my Chamber, in the House of Mr. Ashley in said Salem, and both of us being undressed without any Cloths on except our Linen, and that He the said John Molloy had carnal knowledge of my Body, during those Nights aforesaid . . . and then and there did Beget me with a Female Child, which was born on the thirteenth day of October last past, and I further declare that he solemnly declared that he was a Widower, at the

same time, but afterwards I heard that he had a Wife and two Children at Portland and that his wifes father had taken his Daughter Home to his own House.[78]

Martha Molloy was one of two Hallowell women to get divorces that year. Nabby Sylvester (another of Martha's patients) also charged her husband with infidelity, claiming he had "committed divers act of Adultery" in Boston and in the West Indies.[79] Martha never mentioned these divorces or any others in the diary. Still, her quiet entries suggest the realities of maritime marriage. After a delivery at Nathan Burges's house, she wrote drily, "Her husband is at Sea if living."[80]

Novelists and filmmakers have long exploited the drama of birth, the agony of labor, the shadowy threat to the mother's life, the anxious pacing of the father. Martha Ballard's diary shifts the focus of adventure from the labor itself to the midwife's journey. If spring breakup brought high adventure, winter offered a numbing course in endurance. One day, called at daybreak during a heavy snow, she trudged across the river and "as far as the plain beyond Esquire Howards Bridge," when she "mett a mesage Enforming the woman was got safe to Bed." (No delivery, and hence no fee.) "I had two falls, one on my way there, the other on my Return. The Storm continues yet. The snow is Levil with the top of the lower pain of glass of our north window. I travild some Rods in the snow where it was almost as high as my waist."[81]

Some weeks she barely thawed from one journey before she began another. Setting out in a "doleful storm," she went by horseback as far as Pollard's tavern, then took a sleigh upriver to the Boltons', Mrs. Savage with her. "We were once over sett," she wrote, carefully accounting each mishap. "Once I got out & helpt push behind the carriage. We arivd safe at sun sett." The baby was born at eight; at six the next morning ("clear but very high wind") Martha was on her way through the brilliant cold to a house five miles downriver. "Men shoveled through drifts & we arivd at 9," she wrote. She was called back upriver the following day, this baby arriving "in the middle of the night," stopped home the next morning ("clear, calm, and cold,") to take a nap before leaving again ("clear and *excessive* cold") to officiate at yet another delivery.[82]

The Kennebec country offered adventures for every season. Even in good weather there was a certain thrill in crossing a modest stream "on the string piece of the bridge." Given the rough country beyond the river, riding was also unpredictable. "My hors mird in a swamp and I fell off," Martha reported after one delivery. The mire "by the Bridg between here and Dens-mores" was also a pitfall, though ordinary ruts and ridges could be just as troublesome. "The hors Blunderd & I fell & hurt me," Martha would write, usually without further comment or explanation. The family horse was a stumbler, but he was at least familiar. Mounting Captain Springer's horse after another delivery, she found herself thrown to the ground as the beast ran under a shed. "Broak my specktakles and allmost my limbs," she reported drily.[83] Since she generally rode sidesaddle, falling off a horse was easier, but perhaps less dangerous, than it would have been if she had ridden astride. At least she was well padded with petticoats and skirts. She certainly preferred sidesaddle. "I wrote a mans saddle which fatagud me very much," she complained after one journey home.[84]

A cloudy night could transform any journey into a pilgrim's progress, as on the April night when she and Woodward Allin "carried a candle to the top of Burnt Hill." Lacking light, she resorted to wilderness savvy. "Calld in hast to go to Mr. Whites," she wrote. "The Boys Landed me at Jackson Landing. I took of[f] my shoes & walkt in my stockins. Steerd as strait a Coars as I Could and reacht Mr Whites very soon but was much fatagued."[85]

Martha was proud enough of her adventures to write about them, though she was also pleased to note when more com-modious transportation was available. "Was conducted home in a carriage by Mr Pitt," she wrote after delivering Jonathan and Sally's second baby. But there was little danger of her growing soft. In 1798, after another delivery in the Hussey neighborhood, she crossed the river to the Sheppards', walked from there to the Parmers', and then rode "a Colt home on which woman never was before."[86] She was sixty-two years old.

What took Martha Ballard out of bed in the cold of night? Why was she willing to risk frozen feet and broken bones to practice her trade? Certainly midwifery paid well, at least by the standards usually assigned women's work. Martha cared about her "rewards," and she kept her midwifery accounts carefully. Yet money alone cannot account for her commitment. Nor is it enough to say that serving others was her way of serving God. She interpreted her work, as all of life, in religious terms: God rescued her from the spring flood, sustained her through difficult deliveries, preserved the lives of mothers and children, and gave her the strength to continue her work. (Even such a prosaic end-of-the-year summary as "I have Lost 42 nights sleep the year past" was a kind of spiritual accounting.) Yet religious faith is also an inadequate explanation. Midwifery was a form of service and a source of material rewards, but even more than that it was an inner calling, an assertion of being. Martha Ballard's specialty brought together the gentle and giving side of her nature with her capacity for risk and her need for autonomy.

The fathers who fetched her in the black of night leaned on her skill, offering her the command of their horses and bedchambers, bestowing lumber credits and teapots for her service. The women who circled around her at the height of travail respected her caring and sustained her strength. The women who reached for her in the anguish of travail extended her motherhood in their own. Martha Ballard needed her patients as much as they needed her.

CHAPTER SIX

JANUARY 1796

"find my house up in arms"

1   6   *At Capt Moses Springers. Mr Swetlands Child Expird*
Clear and Pleasant. I washt and washt my kitchen. Was Calld at 9 hour Evening to see the wife of Capt Moses Springer who is not so well as Shee Could wish. Her husband is gone a trip to Boston. I tarried there all night. Slept some after 1 o Clock.

2   7   *At ditoes*
Cloudy. I was at Capt Springers this day. His Lady is more Comfortable. I began to knitt me a pair of socks.

3   D   *At Ditoes and at Eliab Shaws. Birth 1st for the year. Recd 6/ of Dickman in snuff on Shaws account X.*
Rainy afternoon. I returnd from Capt Springers. Left her about house. Shee made me a present of 1/2 lb Souchong Tea. I Came home at 11 hour. Bakt and Cleand my hous and did other matters. Was Calld at 7 hour Evening to see the wife of Eliab Shaw who was very ill when I arivd and was Delivered at 9 of a dead son. It appeared to have been dead for some time. The skin allmost all Came off. The mother is as Comfortable as Can be Expected.
Birth Eliab Shaws son. Dead born X X

4   2   *At ditoes and other Neighbors.*
Clear and remarkable pleasant. I returnd home Early this morn.
Was Calld in at Mr Kimballs to see a sick Child. It has the rash
and Canker. I took Breakfast at Son Pollards. They are well.
Calld at Mr. Lambarts. All well there. At Mr Densmores. Polly
is more Comfortable than when I saw her last tho feeble yet.

5   3   *At home. Sally Cocks here.*
Clear and very pleasant. Mr Ballard and Bullin surveying for Mr
Bridg. Cyrus went to Winthrop. Carried 21 yards all wool
Cloath to Mr Allin to dress for mens Cloaths. I have done my
house work & washt the west room. Sally Cocks was here.
Informs me her Sister Pages infant is very sick.

6   4   *At home. Had Company.*
Cloudy. I have been washing. Son Jonathan dind here. Mr Livermore, his wife and Cousin, & Mrs Holdman took Tea. I feel
some fatagud this Evening. I laid my Washing aside when my
Company Came and finisht it after they went away Except
rinsing.

7   5   *At Mr Gills.*
Snowd. I was Calld Early to Mr Gills. Find his wife unwell. I
did her housework. Feel very unwell. Have a pain in my head.
We Calld Esquire Brooks Lady at Evening. Shee tarried all
night.

8   6   *At ditoes. Sally Cocks Came there*
Clear Except some squalls of Snow. Very Cold at Evening.
Mr Gill Brot Sally Cocks and I Came home. Feel very much
fattagud.

9   7   *At Ditoes. Birth 2nt. Received 12/ and 4 lb Sugar*
Clear and Cold. I was Calld at 3 hour this morning to See Mrs.
Gill again. Shee was safe delivered at 5 of a son (her first Child
by Mr Gill) and is very Comfortable. Mr Gill bestowed 12/ as
a reward for my service and I returnd home. We brot Harnon

Barton with us. Calld at Mr Pollards and Lambarts. They are all well. I finisht my washing and did my other work. Mrs Dingley sent home a shirt which shee made for Mr Ballard.

10   D   *At home. Am not so well as I Could wish*
Clear and cold. Cyrus went to meeting. Harnon Barton went to Mr Pollards. Came here again before Cyrus returnd from meeting. I have felt very unwell. Mr. Burtun sent for me but I Could not go. Her youngest Child is Burnt. Phillip Bullin returnd here.

11   2   *At home. Mary Densmore wrode here in a sleigh*
Clear. Cyrus & Bullin gone to the Meddow. Mr Densmore brot his daughter Mary to my Door in a sleigh but did not Come in. Hannah Goodin & Fanny Cocks, Nancy Hilton and Sally Smith here.

12   3   *At home*
Clear and pleasant. Mr Finny here giting wood 1/2 the day. Ezra Town went to see his Unkle and Aunt Gill. Laban Princes wife & Child sleep here. Mr Ballard returnd from surveying at Mr. Tabors. I have done my housework. Feel fatagud.

13   4   *At home. Mr Town here*
Clear. I have been at home. Bulah has washt for me. I paid her 1/6 for her Service. Mr Town Sleeps here.

14   5   *At William Mathews*
Snowd. I was Calld at 7 hour Evening to see Mrs Mathews who is in Labour. I tarried all night. Slept none.

15   6   *At ditoes. Birth 4th. This is the 612th Birth I have attended at Since the year 1777. The first I assisted was the wife of Petton Warrin in July 1778*
Cloudy. I was at Mr Mathews. His wife was delivered at 6 hour morning of a fine daughter after a severe illness. Her first Child. I received 9/. Made a present of 1/6 to the infant. I returnd home and find my house up in arms. How long God will preserve my strength to perform as I have done of late he only knows. May

I trust in him at all times and do good and hee will fullfill his promis according to my Day. May he giv me strength and may I Conduct accordingly.
Birth William Mathews dagt. X X

16   7   *At home*
Cloudy. Snowd some. I have done my house work and ironed my Cloaths. Mr Ballard been at Coart.

17   D   *At Mr Peter Clearks. Death of Timothy Page's infant.*
Clear day. Snowd at night. Mr. Densmore, his wife and Daughter Mary, Son & Daughter Lambard, Ephraim & Phillip dind here on roast Chickins. I have not been to Meeting. I was Calld at 6 hour Evn to Mr Peter Clearks to see the wife of William Moore who was in Labour. Mr Eads Came there for me. Shee would not dismis me. I had no sleep.

18   2   *At Mr Clearks & Stephen Hinkleys. Births 5th and 6th. Received of William Moore 7/ 10 1/2 as a reward.*
Clear and pleasant. I was Calld from Mrs Moore to Steven Hinkleys wife at 10 hour morning. Shee was delivered at 11 of a son. I part drest the infant and was Calld to return to Mrs Moore. Find her more unwell. Shee was delivered at 4 hour 30 minutes of a son. The Children were the first Born of thier mamys. I returnd home at 8 hour Evening. Brother Ebenezer Moore sleeps here. I made Bids, washt dishes, swept house, and got supper. I feel some fatagud.
Birth Stephen Hinkleys son. Birth William Moores son. X X.

Twenty years after settling in Maine, Martha and Ephraim were still pioneering, she riding through driving rain to deliver babies in flea-infested cabins in the second and third miles of settlement, he swatting mosquitoes and black flies on uncharted swamps and streams from Damariscotta Pond to the Penobscot.

|"How long God will preserve my strength to perform as I have done of late he only knows," Martha wrote on January 15, 1796. She had begun the new year still exhausted from the old. |

For both of them, 1795 had been a strenuous year. In February, while she was climbing "mountains of ice" at the Husseys' landing ("allmost fatagud to death"), Ephraim was inching his way through crusted snow along the river between Hallowell and Vassalboro. In late April, when she was falling from her horse on a muddy road to the Hook, he was in East Andover hacking his way from beech tree to elm. In June, while she was weeding beans and cucumbers and bleaching cloth and nursing the sick, he was leading a gang of men "Laying out a road to New Sharon on Sandy river."[1] Ephraim spent a total of fifty-nine nights in the woods in 1795, not quite as many as Martha passed sitting with laboring women or coiled in wakefulness in unfamiliar beds, yet for a man who had seen his seventieth birthday it was a notable record. Endurance was a theme of his life as of hers.

"Mr Ballard went to Captain Cocks to have a glass put in his compass," Martha wrote on January 27, 1795. "He allso sett out to survey the Town of Varsalborough this afternoon. Expects to be gone the remainder of thee weak." By the time her husband returned, Martha had delivered three babies, including a new grandchild, a daughter born to Sally and Jonathan in a rented house at the mouth of Bond Brook. When the baby was four days old, the ice in the river broke, undamming a winter flood that sent the young family flying into the night. Martha found Sally and the baby at the Burtons' house, "Comfortable to admiration . . . do not find that she has taken Cold notwithstanding shee was out three or four hours on her bed in a Sleigh. They did but just Escape before their house was startd from the foundation and the Chimney thrown down." While the men busied themselves retrieving whatever of the family's "affects" they could, Martha nursed the mother and infant, giving thanks for their preservation. "May they and all Concerned give praise to his great name, to him who is kind to the Evle and unthankfull, whose tender mercies are over all his works," she wrote.[2] Though she no doubt included all of humankind, even herself, among the "evil and unthankful," the prayer may have been weighted toward Jonathan, whose behavior still gave her concern.

Jonathan wasn't the only one of the Ballard children to add to her worries in 1795. When Dolly recovered from the mumps to marry Barnabas Lambard in May, Martha prayed that her daughter's health might be up to the new responsibilities. Imploring "the author of Mercie to Bless them by restoreing her impared health and granting them long to liv in lov and harmony," Martha may have been thinking of the pregnancies that would inevitably follow. Both of Dolly's sisters had babies in 1795. Lucy Towne gave birth to her tenth child in September, a frail little girl who died two hours after delivery ("it had an obstruction of breath at the Nostrils"). Hannah Pollard was so ill after the birth of her second child in October that she became delirious; not for six weeks was she well enough to sit at the table.

In November, new and unexpected troubles struck the family. Returning from a delivery on November 15, Martha was surprised to find Ephraim at home—he had left five days before on what was to have been an extended surveying tour. Her explanation was brief and breathless: "They were assaulted when a sleep last Thursday night in the wilderness by men they knew not, who robd him of his papers and instruments. They demanded them of him with a muskit presented at his breast. May we Ever praise God for his goodness in preserving him and his assistants from hurt in person." In the margin of the day's entry she noted her latest delivery, summarized the story of the assault, then added: "This is the 600th Birth at which I have attended Since I Came to this Eastern Clime."

That she reached her 600 milestone on the same day as Ephraim returned with his alarming news was a coincidence, yet for both of them the demands of life in an "Eastern Clime" were accelerating. At midnight on November 26, two weeks after the attack on her husband, Martha sat down to summarize the day's events in her diary. It had been an ordinary day. In most respects her account was just as ordinary. Weather. Comments on her own work and that of her husband and sons. References to Derius, the male helper who was then living with them, and to her own hired girl, Sarah Neal. And then, just the briefest glimpse of her own discouragement:

> Clear and Cool. I have been doing my housework and Nursing my Cow. Her Bag is amazeingly Sweld. Derias went from here. Mr Ballard and Ephraim got wood home. Cyrus Cleand wheat and went to the fort. Sarah went to watch with Mary Densmore. Doctor Williams came there. Shee returnd and Sarah Densmore with her at 11 hour Evening. I have been picking wool till then. A womans work is never Done as the Song says and happy shee whos strength holds out to the End of the rais. It is now near the middle of the night and Mr Densmore Calls me to his house. I sett up till day.

"A womans work is never done." The words dropped gently onto the page. The song Martha was thinking of was probably an American version of an English ballad first published in London in the middle of the seventeenth century. She could easily identify with the harassed housewife of that song:

> *There's never a day, from morn to night,*
> *But I with work am tired quite;*
> *For when the game with me is at the best,*
> *I hardly in a day take one hour's rest:*

Even without the demands of midwifery and nursing, there was work enough to do:

> *Sometimes I knit, and sometimes I spin,*
> *Sometimes I wash, and sometimes I do wring,*
> *Sometimes I sit, and Sowe by my selfe alone,*
> *And thus a woman's work is never done.*

Unlike the woman in the ballad, however, Martha had no young children at home. There were no toddlers to take "from their naked beds,/To put on their clothes and comb their heads." Nor was there a sucking infant, "that at my breast/Doth knaw and bite, and sorely me molest." She had surmounted the early trials of motherhood. Yet there were still three and sometimes four men in the house to cook and wash for, poultry and pigs to feed, and a cow to tend to; and for the first time in years she had no daughters at home. Since Dolly's marriage in May, she had endured a succession of temporary workers—Patty Easty, Sarah Neal, Nabby Jewell—never certain whether they would be there when she returned from a delivery.³ "Maids may sit still, go, or run,/But a Woman's work is never done." Martha sat up all night at the Densmore house on November 26, then rushed off to a delivery the following day ("I had a Severe turn of Cramp in my Limbs in the night). She went from that delivery to another, suffering a second fit of cramp, then came home in a rain storm to her unfinished chores: "I have done my housework and Boild brine. Took down pumpkin which was Dried." Unlike the religious sentiments with which she usually framed her experience, the old song made gender the defining reality in a woman's life. Behind the song was the even older proverb, "*A man works from sun to sun*, but a woman's work is never done."

"This is the 600th Birth at which I have attended Since I Came to this Eastern Clime," Martha wrote on November 15, the day she learned of the attack on Ephraim. On December 31, she updated the tally: "Birth 608th Since I Came to this Town." Two weeks later, after coming home from another delivery to find her house "up in arms," she again recorded her total: "This is the 612th Birth I have attended at Since the year 1777." Although counting deliveries was a traditional habit among midwives, it was unusual for Martha to give so much attention to numbers. Three times in eight weeks she computed her lifetime total, the tally creeping forward painfully from 600 to 608 to 612. She had begun to doubt her ability to hold out "to the End of the rais." Yet how could she grow weary when her husband, ten years her senior, was still setting his compass by the stars?

*   *   *

The archives of the states of Massachusetts and Maine contain more than a dozen maps drawn by Ephraim Ballard, from a 1757 Oxford plan to surveys completed in Maine in 1802, when he was seventy-seven years old. The papers of the Plymouth Company and of the Massachusetts Committee on Eastern Lands also yield documents with his name, commissions signed by Daniel Cony instructing him to find "judicious & disinterested chainmen," to search for ponds, streams, and mill seats, to assay the quality of the soil, the "groth of Timber," and "the most prominent mountains," and to provide the committee with duplicate plans "with a list of the Names of all the settlers . . . and the time Each settled thereon." There are also reports from Ephraim detailing the length of each tour, the conditions encountered, and the expenses incurred. Into his eighties Ephraim was giving land depositions to the Kennebec County Court.

As a surveyor, Ephraim thrived or suffered according to the fortunes of the great proprietors, men like Charles Vaughan, Joseph North, or Daniel Cony, who prospered by exploiting the timber on their lands as well as by selling settlers lots. Unfortunately, squatters had long been settled on some of this unsurveyed land, for which many of them were ill disposed to pay, given the sometimes questionable deeds absentee proprietors could offer. Because the land claims of the Plymouth Company and their nearest rivals overlapped, settlers could never be certain where their interest lay. Hence the need for a Committee for the Sale of Eastern Lands. Beginning in the mid-1780s, the state became involved in negotiating boundaries, contracting with surveyors like Ephraim Ballard to run the disputed lines. Daniel Cony of Hallowell was both a Kennebec Proprietor and a member of the committee on Eastern Lands. (Between those duties and his service as representative to the General Court, he also found a little time to practice medicine.)

Martha's diary gives a good sense of the rhythm of Ephraim's work (in 1795 he made six journeys of from six to fifteen days each) and the state papers of its larger context, but a brief diary

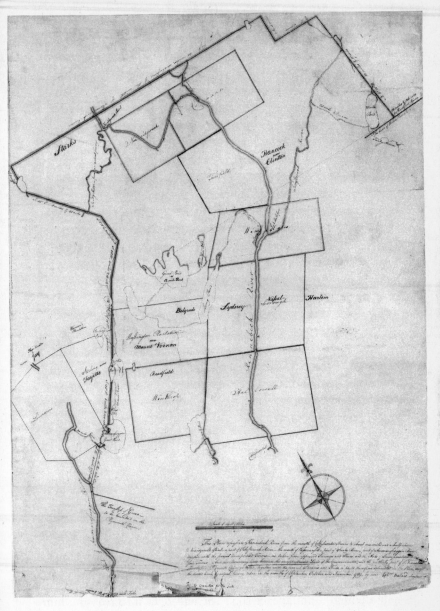

EPHRAIM BALLARD PLAN OF KENNEBEC RIVER, 1789.

Ephraim's signature is in the lower right-hand corner of the text.

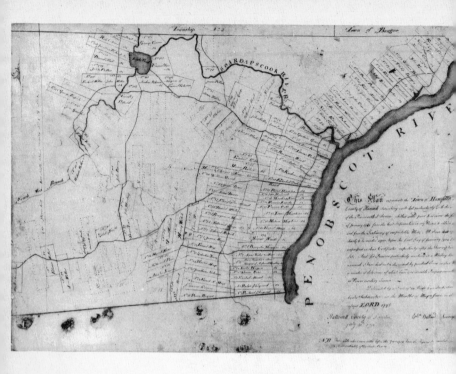

EPHRAIM BALLARD PLAN OF HAMPDEN, 1795.

kept by his fellow surveyor and Oxford neighbor Thomas Fish gives a better idea of its mundane realities. During surveys in Livermore in the 1770s, Fish's men breakfasted on bear, dined on partridge, and fed raw porcupine meat to their dogs. But the wildlife that really impressed them couldn't be dropped with a gun. "Thar come a Scout of Gnats Down upon us this Day, the first we have Sean and we expect thousands Directly," Fish wrote. "The Black flyes Seam to abate, but the muscatoes are Vary Numer's among us and a grait many of them will weigh half a pound—not apeace tho'," he added, as if to reassure himself. As for food, there was a limit to what a single crew could carry with them—or shoot. Without supportive neighbors, surveying was an adventure in survival. One hungry Sabbath, having made a breakfast of chocolate and cheese without bread, Fish and his men sat in camp wondering what they were going to find for dinner. Hearing a crackling in the brush, Fish grabbed his gun, thinking it was a moose, "but as sone as it came in Sight Who Should it be but our Nabour Foster with half a bushel of meal to his Back, which Rejoyst us as much as the Sight of a moose." This was a Sabbath worth remembering. Neighbor Foster "thot mercy was before Sacrifise. Tho it was Sunday, he new we had Noe bread and Soe come out to us."[4]

In the 1790s, Ephraim still found such conditions. Surveyors contracted by the job, providing their own crews, equipment, and supplies. In a letter to Cony in June of 1792, Ephraim apologized for failing to complete a recent tour "by reason of my being lame & the flys so intolerable," though he assured his employers that he would return to finish the job "as soon as the flys abate." He had not been able to find any mast timber on the tract in question, though he hastened to assure the honored gentlemen that he might be wrong: "I have often observed when traveling through the wilderness . . . there has been a vast quantity of very valuable timber within the space of a mile when there was no Discovery to be made of it at a very small distance in the woods."[5] He knew that proprietors, like settlers, survived on hope.

The uncertainties of weather, terrain, and local support made surveying a risky business. Ephraim frequently found himself begging his employers for more money. On January 12, 1795, he wrote the Committee on Eastern Lands a long account of his troubles during the year before. On his first journey he had hired a second surveyor and enough men for two gangs but had encountered "considerable snow . . . 5 1/2 feet on the high land and quite impractictible to proceed." Because the other man "did not incline to be dismissed," he had to pay him and some of his men for more than two weeks' work. In August, when he attempted to go out again, he found that "it was wheat harvest" in the nearby towns and that he "had to give extravegant wages for Carrying out provissions" to the surveying crews. Fortunately, the committee allowed him his expense.[6]

The wheat harvest may or may not explain the difficulty he had in getting men to carry provisions. As we have seen, surveyors not only had to contend with snow, flies, and long weeks in the woods but with the noncooperation and sometimes the hostility of nearby settlers. In the autumn of 1795, Ephraim was surveying land downriver from Hallowell under a joint commission from the Commonwealth, the proprietors of Kennebec Purchase, and Henry Knox, the representative of the rival Waldo claim. Things went well enough at first. He made two journeys of a week or more in September and early October, leaving for a longer tour on November 10. On November 15, he was back with the alarming news of the attack.

Martha's brief telling of the story captured the essential elements—Ephraim's surveying instruments and papers were gone, he had been awakened with "a muskit presented at his breast." Ephraim filled in the details in his report to the Committee on Eastern Lands.

Being laid down to rest in the Woods, with my Assistants, nearly in the line between land belonging to the Commonwealth & the Plymouth company about five miles Northwardly of Damariscotta great Pond & about one o'Clock at night I was awaked by the firing of guns around my head, & one gun presented to my breast. Four armed men coming, or pressing towards me, & my Assistant & uttering the most horrid Oaths, & demanding of me to 'deliver up, to deliver up all, God damn you, deliver the Compass, deliver up the papers, deliver up the Cannisters, God damn you take nothing out, if you do you are a dead man' and after robbing me of my plan & papers & breaking my Compass & uttering much profane & abusive language they left me. I continued at this place with much anxiety till day light, when to my great joy I was relieved by the friendly aid & assistance of three of the Sons of Mr. Jonathan Jones. . . . they conducted us into the Settlement to the house of Mr. Phineas Ames, a Son in law to Mr Jones, where we were treated with civility & hospitality.[7]

Mr. Jones paid for the "civility" of his sons and son-in-law. On November 9, one of his sons came to the Ballard house with Philip Bullin to report that "the unruly gang" had burned two of his barns, destroying fifty-nine tons of hay, a horse, and two swine. "That they may be detected and brot to Justice is my real wish," Martha wrote. Toward the end of the month she reported that another man had been "robd by those rufans who robbed Mr Ballard."[8]

To Martha and Ephraim, there was no question about who was right. Mr. Jones was a "yong gentleman." His father's assailants were "rufans." Ephraim had been a reluctant participant in the revolution against the British. He was unlikely now to sympathize with a group of rough-talking farmers who had taken arms against his genteel employers. The "horrid Oaths" that burst through the woods that November night epitomized disorder of the worst sort. Only the "civility & hospitality" of men like Jonathan Jones could restore it.

The angry settlers saw things differently, of course. The intimidation of Ephraim was part of a larger struggle to save their own land from "the avaricious appetite of men who are striveing to be independent Lords in a glorious Republic." No man had the right to a million acres. Those with the muscle and will to clear and cultivate the wilderness were the true owners of it. In their view, the fight against the proprietors was nothing less than an attempt to save the Revolution. They did not mean to harm Ephraim, only to intimidate him, and through him the land-hungry proprietors. They vowed that no surveyor should run any line, "for the Plymouth Company was endeavoring to take their land from them." They had "fought for it once and were determined to fight for it again."[9]

They did fight. Sporadic demonstrations in the back country culminated in the so-called Malta War of 1809, a year in which Martha's own nephew, Elijah Barton, was tried for murder in company with other resisters. For the moment, however, it was easy to divide the good from the bad: Ephraim had been attacked by ruffians.

* * *

In the months after Ephraim was forced at the point of a musket to give up his surveying instruments to an army of squatters, Martha devoted the emotional center of her diary to laundry. On January 4, 1796, as you have read, she was washing clothes, alone, when her neighbors the Livermores and two other friends came to call. "I laid my Washing aside when my Company Came," she wrote, "and finisht it after they went except for rinsing." Such an interruption might have been a minor irritation (or a welcome pleasure) had she not been called away early the next morning to a woman in labor. Not until three days later was she able to finish her wash. The next week, "Bulah" (Beulah Prince), a black woman, came with her child to spend the night and to do the laundry, but she could not stay, nor was washing the only insistent chore for a lone woman in a house full of men.[10]

On January 15, Martha returned from a delivery to compose a diary entry that for the third time that winter summarized the course of her career, a diary entry that was simultaneously a celebration, a lament, and a prayer. "Birth 4th," she wrote in the margin, even though this was only the third delivery of the year. "This is the 612th Birth I have attended at Since the year 1777. The first I assisted was the wife of Petton Warrin, July 1778." She crowded this last bit of history into the margin, the handwriting getting smaller and smaller as it moved down the page. In the main entry she had written: "I returnd home and find my house up in arms. How long God will preserve my strength to perform as I have done of late he only knows. May I trust in him at all times and do good and hee will fullfill his promis according to my Day. May he giv me strength and may I Conduct accordingly."

Martha prayed not for ease or for release from her burdens, but for *strength*, for the physical ability to continue the work she had done for so long. It was strength to endure to the end of the race she had asked for in November. It was strength that she now called for, twice in a single entry. She was only a few weeks short of her sixty-first birthday. Her body ached. The attacks of colic were coming more frequently. She had no one to preserve order at home when she walked out under the stars to serve her neighbors: "find my house up in arms." The image is a curious one, as though the floorboards, pothooks, and bedsteads had risen against her. It was not her husband and sons who were disturbed. If they had been home at all, they had gotten their supper and breakfast themselves, leaving their platters and mugs, unmade beds, and stiffening socks behind them. It was no human enemy but Martha's *house* that had taken up arms against her.

The phrase "in arms" recurs in the entry for April 27, 1798, when she was again without a servant yet obliged to spend five days away performing deliveries. "I returned home at 10 hour morn," she wrote, "find my house alone and Everything in arms. Did not find time to sit down till 2 pm." The phrase is idiomatic, of course, yet it suggests an attitude. A house could be an adversary. Turn your back, and it rippled into disorder. Chairs tipped. Candles slumped. Egg yolks hardened in cold skillets. Dust settled like snow. Only by constant effort could a woman conquer her possessions. Mustering grease and ashes, shaking feather beds and pillows to attention, scrubbing floors and linens into subjection, she restored a fragile order to a fallen world.

This instrumental, near-adversarial relationship to her house is obliquely confirmed by the dearth of positive references. She celebrated the growth of lambs and parsley in her diary, but never the arrangement of her furniture or rooms. There is only one entry that suggests anything like an effort at decorating, and Dolly was responsible for that. "Dolly put new Trimming on my Case Draws. We movd it into her Bedroom," Martha wrote on a November day when she was still recovering from attending two deliveries in twenty-four hours. In the same entry she noted that Sally had done the washing and helped Dolly dress nine chickens for cooking. "I have not done much work," she explained. "Have not got over my fatague."[11] That was no doubt true, yet it is also clear that she preferred it that way. Whenever possible, she delegated routine housework to others.

In her universe, "Girls washt" was an important statement,

something on the order of "got across the river safely." She didn't mind doing heavy work in the garden or barn, but there were certain perennial tasks of housekeeping she avoided when she could. "I have washt the first washing I have done without help this several years," she had written on January 4, 1793, a few weeks after Hannah and Parthena had "gone to housekeeping."[12] Fortunately, Dolly and Sally Cox had soon replaced them. There is little difference between a diary entry for 1790, "The girls washt & scour the East and bedroom floors," and one for 1795, "My Girls have made me 2 Barrils of Soap this weak," except that the identities of the "girls" had changed. Hannah and Parthenia had done the washing and scrubbing in 1790; five years later it was Dolly and Sally who made the soap.[13]

Martha's curious focus on washing in the autumn and winter of 1795–1796 relates to much broader themes in her own life and in the history of women's work. She had defined herself as a "gadder," as a woman who left home, frequently, to care for her neighbors. Yet she was also a housewife, a dutiful and productive housewife, who had more than enough work to accomplish at home. Those two impulses were resolved in the first ten years of the diary by the presence of her daughters. The trials she faced after 1795 not only demonstrate the importance in her own life of her career as a midwife, but they show what it meant to regulate one's work to the rhythms of mothering.

Historians have distinguished three general systems of labor in early America: chattel slavery in the South, indentured servitude in the mid-Atlantic region, and family labor in New England. Scholars have perhaps given too little attention to the complexities and contradictions of that system of "family" labor. For one thing, a family labor system was inherently cyclical. A couple spent their first years of marriage raising workers and their last bereft of help. The middle years were the harvest time of family life: a man who was unable to clear his land or fence his fields when he had grown sons at home would not have a second chance, nor would there ever be a period in a woman's life when her productive power was greater. What Martha was experiencing, then, was the inevitable passing of a stage in the life cycle of her family.

Yet the circular progression in the development of any family from hired help to family help and back to hired help was never just that. Martha's diary suggests that the presence of daughters in the home actually attracted other workers. She had been fortunate in her daughters, and even more so in being able to keep other long-term helpers who worked beside them. When Dolly's dressmaking business called her away from home, Sally filled the void. "Dolly went to Colonel Sewalls, Sally washt," Martha wrote, or on a day when both girls were home, "Dolly and Sally have washt, scourd my puter & washt the kitchen."[14] It is no accident that Martha's midwifery practice and her textile production grew together during the years her girls were in their teens and early twenties. Summoned in the middle of the night or caught with a "lingering" labor, she could count on "the girls" to do the ordinary chores as well as the spinning and weaving. Nor should we conclude that the advantages were all on her side. Midwifery credits brought calico and ribbon into the household and helped to provide teapots and crockery for brides.

The particular mix of boys and girls in a family, and their order, also helped to shape a family's destiny. One wonders how Martha's and Ephraim's lives might have differed had their youngest child been a girl or their oldest son better fitted for adulthood. As it was, Cyrus and Ephraim Jr. were still living at home in 1795 when the last of the girls had gone. Had Cyrus married or the three older girls survived diphtheria or had Lucy remained in Hallowell, Martha might have had granddaughters old enough or near enough to help her into old age. Instead, she struggled to help Hannah and Sally (and eventually Dolly) with their babies, all the while managing her own household and carrying on her midwifery practice.

There had been a time in early New England, and perhaps in some parts of the region there still was, when aging fathers could dominate their sons through the power to dispose of land. Ephraim had experienced such a system. He was thirty-eight years old and the father of four children before his own father's death gave him secure possession of the Oxford mills he had long been promised. Ironically, one of the consequences of the method of land disposition in Maine, a system in which a few wealthy proprietors claimed vast acres, was a loosening of paternal power. In Maine, the "Ballard" mills belonged to John Jones, and the farm they cultivated for almost ten years was part of the Howard domain. Ephraim might have traded his patrimony in Oxford for some sort of land in Maine, eventually hacking out a farm in a back-country settlement. Instead, he tied his fate to the great proprietors, renting, working, and watching for his children to thrive. In 1800, he finally built a house of his own on land that seems always to have been in Jonathan's name.

So it was that "Old Man" and "Old Lady Ballard," as they must by then have been called, continued to work at their arduous callings. Still, their circumstances were not identical. The old song had it right—a man's work had boundaries; a woman's work did not. When Ephraim had trouble hiring assistants or provisioning chainmen, he could carry his burdens to the proprietors or home to Martha. Her problems were different. Some part of her duty was sustaining him, yet there seemed no one left to care about her. Her spirits rose and fell with the presence of a maid.

"I am very sick but under nesescity of getting breakfast for Mr Ballard and Cyrus. God grant I may have some one to assist me in my business," Martha complained on one January morning. But when Cyrus went to the Hook later in the day and brought Nabby Jewell, she suddenly felt better. "Nabby and I have made chicken, minc, apple and pumpkin pies," she wrote. "Bulah Calld here. We made some flower bread allso."[15] In 1796 eight girls entered—and left—the household. It was the uncertainty as well as the extra work that distressed her. She might plunge herself into her domestic duties only to be interrupted by a delivery. On June 4, for example, she was busy cleaning the head and feet of a newly slaughtered calf when Joseph Young called to say his wife was in labor. From Mrs. Young she went to Mrs. Carter and then to Mrs. Straton. Having managed three deliveries in twenty-four hours, she was ready for a rest. "I came home at Evening and do feel much fatgud," she wrote, "but was oblidged to sett up and cook the orful of my veal."

In the autumn of 1796, Ephraim was again preparing for a "surveying Tour," this time to lay out two ranges of townships between the New Hampshire line and the million-acre Bingham purchase.[16] On September 1, he tied up two birch canoes on the shore near the house. During the next few days the entire household was mobilized. Young Ephraim "brot his dady a box for Chocolate," Ebenezer Moore went to Winthrop for a compass, and Martha set herself to "mending things & makeing Baggs for Mr Ballards Tour into the woods." On September 5, the party left, Captain Abraham Page and Philip Bullin pushing off in the loaded canoes, Ephraim riding Jonathan's horse by land to Fort Halifax. Returning from an all-night delivery on October 14, Martha was delighted to "find that Mr Ballard Came home yesterday and Blessed be the author of all our mercys he appears to be in Tolerable good health."

It took her three days to wash the clothes, bags, and blankets he brought with him, "a dirtyer parsil of Cloaths I never saw," she wrote.[17] Meanwhile, she had been having a new kind of trouble with servants. "I had 13 Dollars and one Crown restord with an acknowledgment that it was taken unjustly out of my husbands desk," she wrote on September 5, the day Ephraim had left for the woods. "The persons name I forbear to mention here." Perhaps Ephraim convinced her she had been too lenient, or perhaps they had discovered other money missing. On October 29, she wrote, "Patty Easty Came here this afternoon and subscribed her name to an acknowledgment that shee took a quantity of silver money out of Mr Ballards desk unjustly last August and promist to restore the same. Phillip Bullin and Polly Wall were the witness."

The formality of the process—the written confession, the use of witnesses—suggests a turn of mind quite foreign to Martha Ballard's kitchen. One wonders who wrote the "acknowledgment" to which Patty "subscribed her name." Since Ephraim had both written and witnessed hundreds of legal documents, one suspects his involvement. Yet the penetration of legal language, and legal attitudes, into the household, came from the young women as well as their employers. Even Sally Cox, toward the end of her term, "showed great anxiety about her wages." Sally Fletcher simply walked out, returning to collect her "duds," as Martha wrote, and threatening to "sue us in a weak from this time if we did not pai her what was her due." Martha huffed, "She looks thin fased to what shee did when shee left us."[18] The crimes of these young ladies remain obscure; their attitude was familiar. Like the armed men who burst from the woods to attack Ephraim or the traders whose lawsuits filled the Court of Common Pleas, they were determined to get what they thought was their due. At such moments there must have been a comforting congruence between Ephraim's troubles and Martha's, a shared sense that the world had indeed slipped from its familiar orbit, that the axis of the universe was changing.

Perhaps it was so. In recent years, historians have connected the political revolution against English authority with a wider revolution against hierarchical relations of all sorts. John Adams alluded to that argument in his famous answer to Abigail's request to "remember the ladies": "We have been told that our Struggle has loosened the bands of Government every where. That Children and Apprentices were disobedient—that schools and Colledges were grown turbulent—that Indians slighted their Guardians and Negroes grew insolent to their Masters."[19] English visitors to post-Revolutionary America were astonished at the lack of deference shown by household workers. "To call persons of this description servants or to speak of their master or mistress is a grievous affront," one English observer wrote. He told of approaching the house of a gentleman and asking the young woman who answered the door whether her master was home. "I have no master," she replied. "Don't you live here?" he asked. "I stay here," she answered. "And who are you, then?" "Why, I am Mr———'s *help*. I'd have you to know, *man*, that I am no *sarvant*; none but *negers* are *sarvants*."[20] By that definition, Beulah Prince, who helped Martha with the washing on January 13, was one of the few *servants* in Hallowell. Yet Beulah too came and went. There had been slaves in the Moore family when Martha was a girl in Oxford. Hallowell's non-whites were free.

Such changes should not be exaggerated, however. Saucy servants also appear in New England records in the seventeenth and early eighteenth century. Keeping a maid was a fundamental problem in an economy that relied on family labor. Martha's trials had less to do with the Revolution than with the inevitable transitions in her maturing family. The problem was not that she had a harder time attracting neighbors' daughters in 1796 than in the earlier years, or that girls like Sarah Neal stayed for shorter periods, it was that she no longer had her daughters and Parthenia or Sally Cox to maintain the stability her household regimen required.

As 1795 drew to a close, Martha affected a kind of bravado, blithely dismissing Elizabeth Taylor in December ("I am determined not to pay girls any more for ill manners"). But by the middle of January she was desperate. She was horrified by Elizabeth Taylor's bad manners, by Patty Easty's theft, and by Sally Fletcher's "thin fased" behavior, but most of the time she seemed grateful to have any help at all.

Diary entries for the spring and summer of 1798 are typical. On May 8, Martha sent her husband to Winthrop to see if he could get Hepsy Brown to come and work for her. He was unsuccessful. Polly Barbareck came on May 10 but left again the next week, Martha giving her four shillings for her service and a small looking glass. On May 30, Ephraim went to Sidney to "seek a girl" but couldn't find one. Nabby Smith came on June 1 and stayed about six weeks. Happy days: "Nabby and I went into the field and gathered strawberes after we finisht our washing." That was on June 25, but on July 17 there was another crisis: "Nabby left me." The effect on Martha's morale—and on her diary—was marked. Crisp and confident entries gave way to long laments, and in a few places even developed into vignettes of woman's oppression. The day after Polly Barbareck left, Martha scrubbed the bedroom and kitchen even though she had a funeral to attend that day. During the next few days she was ill. Her sense of abandonment may account for the length of the diary entry for May 22 and 23 and for its tone:

> I have been very unwell. I Eat a little cold puding and Cold milk twice in the coars of the day and perform part of my washing. I Laid myself on the bed in the bedroom was not able to rise from there. My Husband went to bed and not come to see me so I lay there in my Cloaths till 5 hours morn when I made shift to rise. I got the men Break-fast but was not able to Eat a morsel my self till after 3 pm but I finisht my washing. How many times I have been necasatated to rest my self on the bed I am not able to say. God grant me patience to go thro the fatages of this life with fortitude looking forward to a more happy state.

The old virtues—duty, hard work, service to others—had turned against her. If Ephraim noticed her little demonstration of despair, he made no response. God was her only ally; her only defense was to serve until her strength failed, then wait for somebody as self-sacrificing and as dutiful as herself to respond. "My daughter Pollard and Mrs Dingley here, helpt me do my work, washt my kitchen," she wrote after one illness, and again, "I have done a larg wash and am fatigued. I brewed also. Daughter Lambert came before I had finisht. She assistd me."[21]

Despite her domestic trials, Martha delivered more babies in each of the two years after Dolly's marriage than in any other year in her career. Although deliveries declined in 1798 when she was truly ill for a time, and when the illness and death of her daughter Lucy Towne took some of her attention, they rose again in 1799. Commitment to her neighbors only partly accounts for her struggle to keep moving. In the fifteen years since her fiftieth birthday, she had come to identify with her calling as a midwife. She had no wish to abandon it.

* * *

The last three years of the eighteenth century were important ones for Hallowell. In February 1797, the Massachusetts legislature separated the three parishes, creating two towns. The southern parish remained Hallowell. By June the middle and northern parishes, Martha's part of the town, had become Augusta. Separation didn't diminish commercial rivalry between the two sections. The presence of Daniel Cony in the state legislature soon assured two decided victories for Augusta. "The midle pier of the Kenebec Bridg was finisht and there were 7 discharges of the field piece and 3 cheirs," Martha wrote on September 9, 1797. On November 21, she continued, "The Kennebeck Bridg was dedicated. Mr. Ballard and son Cyrus attended. David Wall, James Savage & Asa Fletcher were burnt some by the Catradges takeing fire thro Carelessness." Augusta acquired additional luster in February 1799, when it became the shiretown of a new Kennebec County.[22]

During this period of expansion, the town voted to build a new road "to Sidney in the route to Belgrade," a small decision that had more effect on the Ballard family than any of the others. The new road would cut across the farm that Jonathan had purchased from Savage Bolton, creating a fork that would become known in the nineteenth century as Ballard's Corner. In December 1799, Martha and Ephraim moved to a new house on the road to Sidney. During construction, Martha always referred to it as "Mr Ballard's house" or "his house," perhaps from long habit, perhaps because consciously or unconsciously she felt excluded from the decision. She could hardly have opposed a move that would at last give the family a homestead, yet the consequences, as we shall see, were far more fateful for her than for Ephraim.

Ephraim had always been a steady but quiet presence in Martha's diary. In 1800, he moved to the forefront of her struggles with her girls. "I workt very hard in my gardin, then had my evning work to do by reason of Hepsy's going to walk streat with Lydia Nudd," she wrote on a spring day in 1800, continuing the same theme the following day: "I have had my house work to do and more than all my hard work to bear frowns (from one who Calls himself my friend) and taunts from Hepsy for takeing proper Care of my house. May God forgive their Erer and enable me to perform the trust reposed in me as the head of a family as he dictates to me is right."[23]

This entry tells us a great deal about how Martha saw her marriage. A husband and wife were to be friends, sustaining one another in time of trouble. They were also to be autonomous partners, each respecting the authority of the other in their God-ordained domains. As "the head of a family," Martha was responsible for the management of a house and the workers in it. Yet as she faced her saucy servant, Ephraim offered only frowns. Was there a subtle sexual rivalry here, the young girl winning the approval of the old man against the increasing demands of the overburdened and exhausted wife?

Martha's martyrdom continued for more than a week. Wednesday she was so unwell she could not sit up until two or three in the afternoon, when Jonathan's wife came in and got water for her, bathed her feet, and made her a dish of tea. "I had not had so much as a drop of water given me to wet my mouth," she wrote, "till my husband Came to dine when he gave me a little which had been in the house 2 days." The next day, and the next, and the next, she asked God for patience "to sufer what he is pleased to inflict upon me." She managed to do her baking as well as her housework on Saturday. On Sunday there was another falling out with Ephraim: "My husband went to meeting but finds time to keep up the fair of Hepsy and torment me. I had no sleep this night. He lay before the kitchen fire. He compared me to Everdon. O God pardon his sin in this Cruel conduct towards me." The reference to "Everdon" is mysterious. Perhaps Ephraim had compared her with someone whose behavior he disliked. The name "Everdon" appears in early Oxford records, and in 1801 Martha mentioned a visit from a "Mr Benjamin Everendon." Another explanation is just as likely. In some English dialects the adjective "everdon" was used to describe an incessant downpour, as in an "everdon rain."[24]

What actually happened in the Ballard house is perhaps less

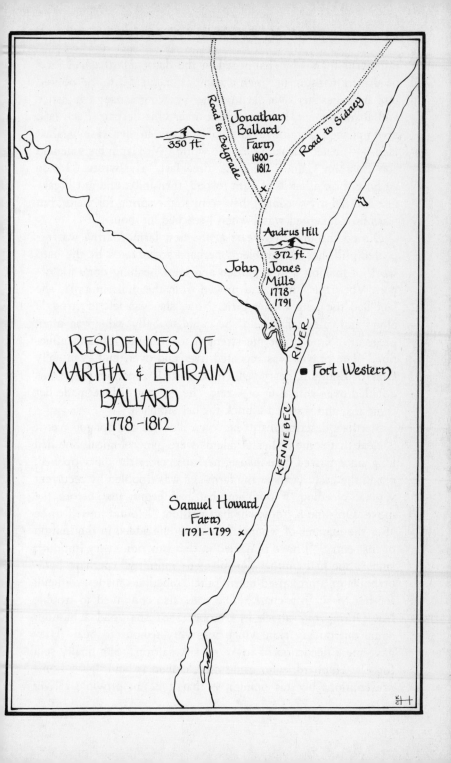

RESIDENCES OF
MARTHA & EPHRAIM
BALLARD
1778-1812

350 ft.

Road to Belgrade

Jonathan
Ballard
Farm
1800-
1812

Road to Sidney

Andrus Hill
372 ft.

John Jones
Mills
1778-
1791

KENNEBEC RIVER

Fort Western

Samuel Howard
Farm
1791-1799 ×

important than what happened in the diary. Martha had long used it to measure her own accomplishments. Now she poured into its pages her own feelings, her growing sense of injustice and abandonment, her struggle to overcome despair. Each task accomplished became a kind of witness in her case against Hepsy—or her husband—or the world. "Mr Capin his wife and son Ephraim Came here, took Breakfast," she wrote. "I rose early, put on a kettle of yarn to boil, then milkt and got breakfast and did my washing, then went to the spring for water, but alass how fatagued was I when I reached my house."[25]

During the first two years at the new farm, Martha was repeatedly ill, her old problems perhaps accentuated by the hard work of making a new garden and reestablishing domestic order. When the family had moved from the mills in 1791, she had had the help of her girls. Now, she was left to struggle alone and offer what help she could to Sally, who was often pregnant. "God grant me strength to bear my toil and affliction." The prayer was repeated over and over, and eventually God, or Ephraim, heard. On November 28, 1800, when she was doubled over with a fit of "colic," he got out of bed, made her some tea, and warmed a brick for her stomach.

Martha's descriptions of her own illnesses are opaque, yet it is clear that some of her problems were gynecological. She had long since passed menopause, perhaps before the diary opened, but in the early years at the farm she was troubled by recurrent vaginal bleeding, a problem that had begun just before the move. On June 8, 1799, she had written, "I found myself to be after the manner of woman." In 1806, she added in the margin of that entry, "I have remained in that situation every [month?] since." She had another unexplained "infirmity" (perhaps hemorrhoids or a prolapsed uterus) that sometimes made it difficult for her to sit in a chair.[26] The colic also continued to trouble her. During one attack in October 1801 she "had a humour come out on my skin which was very tedious to bear. They gave me a decoction of snake root & saffron." She finally sent for Dr. Hubbard, who came on October 15 and "gave some prescriptions but his opinion is that it is not provible I Ever shall injoy a good state of health again." She pondered the prognosis for the next few days, keeping to her bed most of the time. On October 20, she was up picking wool, gathering hollyhock seed, and cutting broomcorn. On November 8, she stayed up all night attending a woman in labor.

Her midwifery practice had passed its peak, however. Deliveries dropped from fifty-one in 1799, the last year at the Howard farm, to twenty-six in 1800. By 1802, she was down to eleven deliveries a year. Poor health was one problem. (She recorded twenty-one days of illness in 1800, seventy-five by 1802.) The location of the new house was another. Jonathan's farm stood on a broad plateau in an isolated neighborhood high above the river. The road from the meeting house was breathtakingly steep, enough to keep Martha away from church and the stores except when the weather was especially pleasant and her health good.

One of her brief pleasures during this period was the arrival of Dorothy and Stephen Barton, who had returned to Maine after ten years in Oxford. They lived for a while in the center of Augusta before moving to a farm in Malta (now Windsor, Maine). "I have not been able to sett on a Chair this day by reason of my infirmaty," Martha wrote on September 1, 1801.

> I swept my Chambers, lower rooms and seller, then left home to be free from work. Walkt down to Mr Moodys. There rested a little and went on to Brother Bartons. Laid down on the Bed a little while then Sister and I went to Shuball Pitts. I tarrie there all night.

The visit seemed to do her good. She felt well enough the next day to call on several friends and to deliver Betsy Gill's baby on September 3. The next day she attended a lecture at the meeting house, meeting her husband there. There was still tension between them. Perhaps he was annoyed at her abrupt departure. Though he had a horse, he "went on and left me to walk." Fortunately, he stopped at Thomas Bond's, who now lived at Jones's mills, where Martha "overtook him and wrode

TABLE VII   MARTHA BALLARD'S OBSTETRICAL PRACTICE, 1785–1812

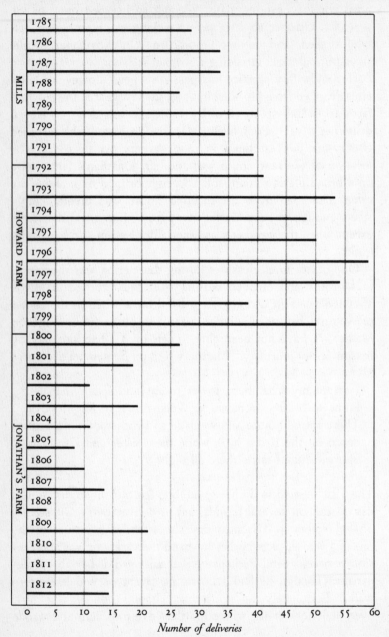

Number of deliveries

home. I do feel very ill indeed." It wasn't the walk that had overcome her, however, but the seeming indifference of her husband. "I have not been able to sett up but very little this day," she wrote on September 5, "but have reproaches from those who I think ought to use me with more kindness. I really pray that God will pardon the sins of us all." On Sunday, Ephraim went to church without her, leaving her home, "very unwell" and with "no one to help me."

In August 1802, Ephraim made a third attempt to run the southern line of the Kennebec Purchase. His second try in June of 1798 had been thwarted by rumors that settlers were mustered to prevent it. This time he faced more than rumors. Somewhere in the woods in Balltown he was turned back by a party of armed settlers. According to the official account, "On his quitting the ground, fifteen guns at least were discharged within his hearing with intent to terrify and deter him from a similar attempt."[27]

Martha reported his departure for Balltown on August 26 and his return two days later but nothing at all about the attack. Perhaps he did not tell her. That he was profoundly disturbed is obvious from the account which she left. It begins with a comment on her own health and ends with a prayer. In between is another small chronicle of duty and despair.

My Lott is Singular but with patience I wish to Conform to it. My husband returned at Evening from Ballstown much fatagued with his Journey. Had a fitt of shakeing. I heat a Blankett and put it about him at about 3 hour morning. He being relaxed dirtied the Bed. I rose, shirted him and removed the dirty lining. Went to Bed again but was so Cold that I Could not sleep. I rose again before the sun rose. Washt the things which were unclean but felt so unfitt to attend worship that I tarried at home. My famely all attended. O my God when will the Time be when I may have it in my power to go to thy house to worship again?[28]

Once again, washing symbolized Martha's self-denial and her feeling of oppression. She had risen at three to heat a blanket,

had gotten up again a few minutes later to remove her husband's dirty linen, had risen at dawn to build a fire, heat water,
and wash away the embarrassing evidence of his illness, and
now watched him, miraculously recovered, ride off to church.

At one level her entry can be read as an elaborate apology
for her own absence from meeting. She may well have been
thinking of the rebuke given to the Biblical Martha, Mary's sister, a story told in the Book of Luke. While Mary "sat at Jesus'
feet, and heard his word," Martha was left with the practical
duties of providing for their guest. "Lord, dost thou not care
that my sister hath left me to serve alone?" she asked.

> Jesus answered and said unto her, Martha, Martha, thou art
> careful and troubled about many things: But one thing is
> needful: and Mary hath chosen that good part, which shall
> not be taken away from her.

Martha's diary was a witness, on this bitter Sabbath, that she
had not willfully chosen a lesser part.

CHAPTER SEVEN

FEBRUARY 1801

"A Desection Performd"

1   1   *At My Sons to see John who we were aprehensive was near the Close of life.*
Clear and pleasant. I was Calld to see John Davis at my sons. He apears to have the symtoms of the near aproach of Death. Doctor Cony & Colman were Calld. His Constitucion seemd so far spent that he was not able to take medisin. He had severe spasms which were relievd by salt and water only he revivd a little. Reverend Mr Stone was invited to see him after meeting. He made a well adapted prayer on the ocation. I tarried thro the night with the Child. Doctor Colman allso.

2   2   *At my sons. Tarried again this night. I am informd that Daughter Pollard has had trouble with one of her Breasts.*
Clear and very pleasant. I left my sons forenoon. Came home. Took care of my business. Was Calld again afternoon to my sons. Find John apparently near the Close of life. Doctor Colman there administring a decoction of the pink beet without affect. I tarried all night, the Father and Doctor Colman allso. Mrs Saunders Calld to watch. I laid down by the fire at 11. Was Calld on at midnight when an alteration in the patients breathing took place. It was not able to swallow after that nor had it any great struggle. Its life went out as a Candle.

3   3   *At my sons. John Expired at 1 h 10 m this morning. AE 2 years, 7 months & 13 days. He was a promising Child. How oft are our Expectations Cut off.*
Cloudy and some snow. John the son of J. V. Davis Expired this morning at 1 hour 10 minutes. Mrs Saunders, Oliv Fletcher and myself put on the Grave Cloaths. Finisht the performance at 3. Doctor Colman Conducted me home at 6. I went on the bed and slept. Mr Ballard went to Colonel Duttuns for hay. Bill Cypher went with the Team.

4   4   *At my Sons. A Desection Performd on the boddy of John Davis junior. At S J Fosters, Birth 3d. July 13th receivd as a reward 10/10.*
Clear. I was Calld to my sons to see the Desection of the Son of Esquire Davis which was performd very Closly. The left lobe of the lights were found to be much inflamed, the intestines allso in which were 4 intersections, an inflamation of the kidneys and Blather. There were not a single worm Contained in the boddy but a small quantity of what the operators supposed to be the bed in which they had resided. The gaull blather was larg and very full. The opperation was performd by Doctors Colman and Page. Judg North, Son Jonathan & myself were attendants. I was Calld from there to see the wife of S J Foster who was in Labour and was safe Delivered at 7 hour Evening of her second son & 5th Child. I tarried all night. The patient as well as Could be Expected.
X X Birth S. Juet Fosters 2nd Son X X

5   5   *At Mr Fosters and at the interment of Esquire Daviss son. Reverend Mr Bowers attended. Mr Stone allso*
Snowd. I Came home from Mr Fosters. Find Son and Daughter Lambard & Ephraim were Come down. They and Mrs Conry dind here. We then attended Funeral of the son of John V Davis. The procession was from Doctor Colmans and interd in the grave yard by Colonel Howards. We Came to my sons and supt then Came home. My Children sleep here.

6   6   *At home. Part of my Children here.*
Clear. Sons Lambard & Ephraim went to Pittston. Jonathan, his

wife and 3 Children dind and took tea. Esquire Davis here. Mr
Lambard, his wife and Ephraim went home at Evening. Betsy
has a pain in her head. I gave her sage Tea. She Bathed her
feet. I het Bricks & put to her feet.

7   7   *At home.*
Snowed. Son Pollard here. Informs me his wife is very unwell.
Her Breast is in danger of Breaking. I have been at home. We
bakt and Churnd 7 lb 14 oz. butter. Doctor Cony here. Mr Ballard & Cyrus signed a petition to send to General Coart.

8   1   *At home. Unwell.*
Clear and cold. Windy. I have been unwell. Mr Ballard to meeting. Was informd that Daughter Pollard is some better.

9   2   *At John Pages. Birth 4th. Receivd 6/ as a reward.*
Snowd. I was Calld by Alpheus Lion to go and see the wife of
John Page. We past by Mr Hamlins 20 minutes before 7 this
morning. The patient was Delivered at 11 of her second son
and 3d Child. I left all as well as could be Expected. Past Mr
Hamlins 20 minutes before 5 hour pm. Reacht home before
dark. Was Cold and fatagued.
Birth. John Pages 2nd Son.

10   3   *At home. Esquire Davis here at Evening.*
Clear. I have been at home. Mended Mr Ballard's mitts & knit
some. Esquire Davis here at Evening. He gave Mr Ballard 8 1/2
Dollars on acount of the trouble we had with his son.

Martha's account of the death of little John Davis brings together a collection of seemingly unrelated themes. It is the last
episode in a real-life seduction story, a missing piece in a political argument over the behavior of the Kennebec judiciary, an
episode in Ballard family history, and a rare document in early
medicine. We first met John Davis in Chapter Five, when Mar-

tha took testimony from his mother at delivery. He was the child of Mehettable Pierce, Sally Ballard's younger sister. His father, as we have seen, was John Vassall Davis, a Kennebec County justice of the peace. Witnessing both the beginning and the ending of the child's life, Martha provided a rare document in social as well as medical history.

February 5 . . . *at the interment of Esquire Daviss son.* Martha's casual use of the term "Esquire Daviss son" obscures the controversy surrounding his existence. The child was living evidence of his parents' crime and his father's status. Legally a bastard, he nevertheless bore the illustrious name John Vassall Davis. It is hard to know which fact was most disturbing to sober citizens of the county, that the judge had fathered a child out of wedlock or that he had so openly and flagrantly acknowledged it.

In January of 1799, an anonymous Lincoln County resident wrote an impassioned letter to Governor Increase Sumner of Massachusetts. Since the county was about to be divided, he thought this was a good time to reform the judiciary. He was convinced that in the past many magistrates had been appointed "who were not exemplary in their lives either as Citizens or Christians." They were guilty of drunkenness, profanity, gambling, Sabbath-breaking, and dueling. Furthermore, "Female chastity has fallen a prey to the seducing arts of a Justice."[1]

Although the letter went on for sixteen pages, the man refused to sign it, asserting that his name would add nothing to the contents and would only incur the ill will of men with whom he now lived in peace. Yet he urged Sumner to take his allegations seriously. Before the Governor appointed any man to the new Kennebec County court he should ask:

Is he not a prophaner of the sabbath, and disregarder of revelation? Does he not spend even holy time in gambling, or in taverns, or with his mistress? Does he not exhibit his bastard son with apparent pride glorying in his shame? . . . Does he not advocate the horrid practice of dueling?[2]

Governor Sumner was familiar with the sexual scandals of the region. Ten years before, as a member of the Supreme Judicial Court, he had presided over the rape trial of Joseph North. He had probably also heard, through the epistolary circuits that linked Boston with Maine, about William Howard's supposed alliance with Charlotte Cool. Yet he no doubt knew that the man who most fully exemplified his anonymous correspondent's charges was John Vassall Davis, Esquire.

The nineteenth-century *History of Augusta*, written by James W. North, Judge North's grandson, includes a memorable portrait of Davis based on stories about him still current in the town. He was a charming but volatile man, North said, "a warm partisan of the federal school in politics, haughty to his political enemies, and gracious and condescending to his friends; highly choleric, provoking enmity by his irascible temper, which was easily excited but soon over." The man's crimes seem almost engaging in this account. Even the reputation for dueling is reduced to a comic coda. Yes, he had challenged Arthur Lithgow, the sheriff, to a duel, but his seconds, Moses Partridge and "Jemmy" Black, had loaded the pistols with butter balls, saving both the lives and the friendship of the two men. North removed all antagonism and conflict from his story. He even managed to inject some humor into an anecdote about Davis ripping a new silk coat to shreds after he daubed it with paint on the newly decorated stairs of his house. He had more difficulty with the story of Davis ordering his subordinates to kill a colt when it failed to pace to his liking.[3]

In North's history, Davis comes across as an eighteenth-century gallant—sans sex. That detail is provided by Martha's diary. Hers is the only surviving record of his alliance with Mehettable Pierce, Martha's account of the child's death the only confirming evidence that Davis acknowledged "his bastard son with apparent pride glorying in his shame."

Of all the couples in Martha's diary, Hitty and Davis come closest to characters out of eighteenth-century fiction, he a fashionable gentleman of dishonorable intentions, she a rural maiden. Davis was the descendant of prosperous Boston merchants; his maternal grandfather, John Vassall, Jr., built the famous Vassall-Craigie house, now known as the Longfellow House, in Cambridge, Massachusetts. Hitty's father, Eliphalet Pierce, was a Kennebec farmer of middling means. Davis had been a clerk in the East India Company, spent time in London, and with the support of his Vassall relations, who were shareholders in the Plymouth Company, come to Maine to pursue their claims and run a store leased from Judge North. Hitty was born in Canton, Massachusetts, and had come to the Kennebec with her parents in early childhood.[4] She was sixteen when he came to town, twenty-two when she gave birth to his child.

In fact, there was a novel of seduction published in Hallowell in 1797, a year before little John's birth. Though the plot was conventional and derivative, it was apparently written as well as published in the town. Entitled *Female Friendship; Or the Innocent Sufferer*, it was advertised as a "A Moral Novel." The plot consists of an interlocking maze of seduction stories, all presented as cautionary tales to young ladies. The opening pages introduce the upright Sir Henry Summers and his rakish friend Modish. When Summers, who has been widowed, finds a baby on his doorstep and vows to keep it, Modish is jubilant. Surely, the child is proof that the sober Summers is capable of indiscretion. "Egad, I'm glad to see any honest fellow, who has spirit enough to acknowledge his gallantry," Modish gloats. "I really began to fear, we were all reverting to the antideluvian state, when an amour was looked upon as a crime." When Summers coolly denies paternity, Modish is incredulous. Why would any man support a child not his own? Summers retorts that charity is a Christian value and chastity "as noble a qualification in our sex as in the female, though, to our shame be it spoken, in the present age it seems totally excluded from the catalogue of male virtues."[5] As for Modish, he valued neither chastity nor charity. Despite his praise of Summers, he abandoned his ill-gotten children.

This is a novel about morality but also about reputation, about the discrepancy between appearance and reality. The author of *Female Friendship*, Nathaniel Cogswell, unlike the anonymous letter writer, didn't look to public officials to uphold standards of morality but to young women. Courtship was a treacherous game. Only by better education—and the reading of "moral novels"—could girls learn to distinguish between a real-life Modish and Summers. Historians have taken a new interest in such stories, hundreds of which poured from American presses in the years following the Revolution. One scholar reads them as parables of republican politics (a too-trusting populace susceptible to seduction by disingenuous leaders); another finds in them an almost proto-feminist outcry against the sexual double standard.[6] That they were somehow connected to real events seems certain; Susanna Rowson, author of the best-seller *Charlotte Temple*, was not the only author to promote her story as "A Tale of Truth."

Unlike fictional rakes, however, Davis supported his son, and Hitty stayed healthily single, refusing to die in disgrace in the manner of Charlotte Temple or Eliza Wharton, the heroine of Hannah Foster's novel *The Coquette*. In a town where midwives still examined unwed mothers in labor, few gallants could deny their amours. Yet there *was* something new about this case. Most men who hoped to remain in credit in the town married their lovers. Davis neither married Hitty nor abandoned her. William Howard's affair, if Sewall's diary can be trusted, was at least ostensibly a secret. Davis's behavior was a double assault on community values because it was so open. "The Father of the Child Came to see them," Martha noted a few hours after the baby's delivery, adding that she had received a twenty-four shilling fee, four times her usual rate. If Davis had once attempted to deny his paternity, and so caused Hitty to initiate a suit, he had soon changed his mind.[7]

Martha did not know what to make of the affair. On November 5, 1798, four months after the delivery, she wrote, "Otis Pierce conducted his sister Hitty to see me. Tarries all night. Her Babe is with her." On November 7, she noted, "Mrs Pierce with me yet," and on November 12, "Mrs Pierce went from here attended by Mr Kimball in a shais." What the two women did during those ten days is a puzzle. Martha's comment that Hitty came "to see me," suggests a medical visit of some sort, but there is no confirmation of that in succeeding entries. Hitty might have come to spin and bake—it was not unusual for a single woman to bring her child with her when she came to work at the Ballards—yet there is no reference to any task performed. Nor was it usual for a hired helper to leave in a chaise. Perhaps it really was a social visit. Hitty was, after all, Sally's sister, almost a part of the family. Yet the subtle shift that led Martha at the end of the week to describe Otis Pierce's sister Hitty as "*Mrs* Pierce" is intriguing. Martha usually reserved "*Mrs*" for married women or for mature daughters of prominent men.[8] No other single mother had been given this honorific. Hitty's alliance with John Vassall Davis had given her a peculiar eminence.

Kennebec leaders might disapprove of Davis's behavior, but it was difficult to do so openly. He was a well-connected and powerful man. Despite the admonitions of the anonymous letter writer, he was confirmed as Justice of the Peace in the newly created Kennebec County, joining such other "leading characters" as William Howard, Joseph North, Henry Sewall, Samuel Dutton, and Daniel Cony.[9] Whether out of Christian charity or social deference, the Kennebec gentry hovered around his bastard son, as Martha's diary makes clear. Dr. Colman and Dr. Cony attended him. The Reverend Mr. Stone prayed for him. Joseph North witnessed the autopsy. The minister and a visiting member of the clergy attended his funeral. Without Martha's record we would know none of this, of course. In the official histories, John's name, like his life, went out as a candle.

February 1. I was Calld to see John Davis at my sons. The story of John Davis, Jr., offers grist for cultural or political commentary. Those issues are tangential to Martha's diary, however. In her account it is the daily realities that stand out. Whatever name she was called by, Hitty Pierce lived the life of an unmarried woman. That is, she floated from relative to relative. In July of 1800, Hitty and her child were at Sally and Jonathan's house. In

January they were living with her brother Asa Pierce. John Davis may have paid child support, but he did not provide a home. Little John played around the looms and hearths of other people's houses, joining his cousins' games, not quite part of any family, but never without playmates. On July 31, 1800, Martha went to Sally and Jonathan's house to see "how John Davis did. His Burns are all most healed." That is one of those casual entries that says more than it intends. Sally Ballard had five children under ten and was pregnant with her sixth. If her sister Hitty and her two-year-old son were living with her, the house was crowded indeed, though the extra pair of women's hands was probably welcome.

Eighteenth-century households were workshops. Mothers engaged in soapmaking, weaving, candle-dipping, slaughtering, and endless sewing relied on older children to care for their littlest siblings.[10] On December 30, 1800, Martha again rushed to Jonathan's house to "see little William. Ephraim let him fall this morning and Burnt his arm and Cut his Chin with a pott which was by the fire." Little Ephraim was four, his brother two. Three days later Martha wrote, "I was at home till 8 hour Evening when I was Calld to son Jonas to see John Davis who is scholt [scalded] and brot from Asa Pierces there. He had fitts. I tarried all night."[11] Like his cousin William, the little boy had been playing too near the fire. Despite the convulsions, his burns did not seem catastrophic, nothing like those that had taken little Polly Burtun three years before.[12] Martha stayed two nights at Jonathan's house, then on the third day noted that "Esquire Davis brot his miss and son here. We gave up our North room to them. Doctor Coleman sleeps here. Esquire Davis, son Lambard and famely allso. My husband and I lay by the kitchen fire."[13]

The next night the Lambards went to Jonathan's. Esquire Davis again watched with his son, who for a time seemed "cleverly." But the next day the child was so ill that Dr. Cony and Dr. Colman were both called. The doctors remained most of the day. "Drest the burns with pulltises of 3d part rhum, oinions, and indien meal," Martha wrote. "Colman and Mrs Duttun with him this night. I laid down a little while in my cloaths." Martha had help from the doctors, and from Mrs. Woodward, who came to watch, but the burden of the care fell on her. On January 8, John seemed better, but then unexpectedly a new symptom appeared. "I laid down in my cloaths after midnight. Doctor Colman came after that and tarried the remainder the night. I was calld up at 5 to help dress John. He pa[s]t 1 worm." On January 9, he passed nineteen.

"I have had a fatauging day," Martha wrote on January 10, grateful that Jane Herington had come in the evening to help her. But she had just settled herself in bed when her son-in-law Moses Pollard came to tell her Hannah was in labor. Martha rushed to the scene, welcomed the baby just after midnight, then sat up with her daughter until 5:00 a.m. When Dolly Lambard came to relieve her, she "went on the bed and had the finest nap I have had since the first in this year." By three that afternoon, she was in motion again: Sally Ballard was in labor. Ephraim hastened his mother back to the farm. The baby was born at 6:30. "I tarried with her till 10," Martha wrote, "then Came home and set up with John till midnight."

Little wonder that by the next day she was cross and irritable. "I have been at home. Don my house work and done for John," she wrote, "but am ungreatfully treated by his mother. May God forgiv her." The next day: "Hitty continues her ingrattitude. Esquire Davis Came and removd his son to son Jonas. Mrs Conry, Jason Pierce & wife, Son Jonathan and Sabery Price Came to assist. It is happy for me as I am allmost fataugd to Death by doing what I have." The following day: "I have had a day of grat Composier."

Martha's composure meant Sally's discomposure. With five rambunctious children and her sister Hitty's dying son in the house, she was trying to lie in with a new baby. It is hardly surprising that five days later, Martha found the afternurse, Mrs. Conry, "sick with the head aich." Martha herself suffered intermittent fits of colic throughout the next week. "I wrose before day," she wrote on January 19, "feel very unwell but had to do my work and bear other troubles. God giv me grace to bear it."

On January 24, she spent the night at the Lambards' house caring for a sick grandchild. On the way home, she "Calld at son Jonas. Find his wife setting up. John very restless."

For the next few days, Martha tried to anchor herself in her own work—but in vain.

[*January 27*] ... I washt Boards to Cover milk and washt my kitchin. Esquire Davis Came for me to administer Clisters to John. Colman and Page there. Mrs Springer allso. I went again at Eving. Olive Fletcher watched.

[*January 28*] ... I finisht removing my Turnips and did other matters. Mrs Conry here. Wisht me to go and see Jonathans infant. It is not so well as it has been.

She managed to stay at home, unwell, on January 29, 30, and 31, though on two of those days she cared for Sally's toddlers. Then on February 1 began the long vigil described in the diary passage you have read: "I was calld to see John Davis at my sons. He apears to have the symtoms of the near aproach of Death. . . ." Around this story churn many of the major themes in the diary—the communal rituals of healing and death, the close but problematic relations between doctors and midwives, the perennial trials of family life, Martha's tenderness and toughness.

Because Martha tells the story, it is her troubles that stand out, yet it is hard not to sympathize with Hitty, a woman without a home, and most of all with Sally, who, at thirty-three, was burdened with almost overwhelming cares—a new baby, a houseful of children, a temperamental husband, and a younger sister who needed constant attention. Sally was the middle of five Pierce daughters. Her older sisters, Hannah and Elizabeth, married respectably, delivering their first babies an ample ten months after marriage. The two younger sisters, like Sally herself, had a record of sexual misbehavior. Olive, the sister between Sally and Hitty, married a seaman, William Getchell, and was widowed young.[14] On June 21, 1805, Martha wrote, "I am informed that a man by the name of Dunphas is apprehended for abusing his wife. The widdow Getchel has been so imprudent as to liv with him." Her use of the term "imprudent" to describe Olive Getchell's behavior is characteristically reserved; a more zealous Christian might have said "wicked." The next day, she reported that "Jonathans wife Came home fatagued both in Boddy & mind. Her Sister Getchel was apprehended and brot down for Tryal, before Justice North. Shee was not found guilty on Tryal." Even though Olive escaped legal censure, her troubles, like Hitty's, were enough to exhaust Sally— physically and emotionally.

The family drama is real enough. So too is the graphic account of John Davis's death. The child lived a little more than a month after he was burned. Martha wrote something about his condition or care on nineteen of those thirty-five days. She herself nursed him on seventeen days, sometimes around the clock. Including the autopsy, she recorded eleven visits by Dr. Colman, five by Dr. Cony, and three by Dr. Page. Colman apparently had primary care of the boy. Interestingly, Page and Cony never appeared together. Presumably Page, who lived in Hallowell, was a substitute for Cony, whose house was just across the river near Fort Western. Other than Martha and Hitty, seven women were involved in John's care. Mrs. Saunders, presumably Mrs. James Saunders of Augusta, appears three times. She and Olive Fletcher were both with Martha when she dressed the child for burial. Perhaps they helped Hitty nurse her child after he was removed from Martha's care.

The doctors prescribed the poultice of corn meal, rum, and onions, but Martha was responsible for applying and changing the dressings. One of them recommended a clister. She administered it. Whether she or they, or all of them together, counted the worms the child expelled, we do not know. The sight cannot have been pleasant. John was probably infested with *Ascaris lumbricoides*, an intestinal parasite that produces an adult worm the diameter of a lead pencil and as much as fourteen inches long.

Ascariasis is a backyard infection, common to areas where little children defecate in dooryards and orchards or where human waste is used to fertilize vegetable gardens. Both practices may have been common in Maine. Eggs are spread through the soil by chickens, insects, pigs, winds, and rains, infesting adults as well as children. John's death didn't end the problem on the Ballard farm. On May 21, 1802, Martha wrote, "Daughter Ballard pukt up 6 long worms," and, on August 3, "Jack pukt 6 very Larg worms." The worms don't cause death, but they do deplete the bodies of young children. A twentieth-century estimate says that twenty worms harbored in a child's intestine can consume two to three grams of carbohydrates a day. Certainly, Martha considered them a serious threat to health. On September 29, 1801, she wrote, "Little Samuel Gill dies of dysentary & worms." Although there was no physiological relation between John's burns and *Ascaris*, the close monitoring which his illness required may have allowed Martha to discover them.[15] Certainly, they put an additional strain on his body.

On February 10, 1801, a week after John's death, Esquire Davis came to the Ballard house. Martha wrote that "He gave Mr Ballard 8 1/2 Dollars on account of the trouble we had with his son." The entry is curious. This is one of the very few times in the diary when Martha's economic activities were included in a family account. Since she was the one who nursed John, it is surprising that Ephraim would settle the account. Was she elsewhere in the house at the time? Or was Davis deliberately ignoring her? Probably what the entry reflects is an ongoing economic relationship between the two men; Ephraim did a great deal of surveying for Esquire Davis during this period. It may also be a consequence of John and Hitty's residence in the house (and presumably their consumption of fuel and food). This was a rare event in Martha's practice; her accounts could be independent of Ephraim's because she usually did her work at other people's houses without implicating him for any sort of expense.

Martha Ballard spent parts of seventeen days caring for John. If the $8.50 was for her work alone, she was paid an average of fifty cents a day. Contemporary physicians charged from fifty cents to a dollar for a visit, including medicine.[16] Presumably, all-night vigils cost more. For midwives as for physicians, autopsies were probably free.

February 4 . . . I was Calld to my sons to see the Desection of the Son of Esquire Davis which was performed very Closly. The left lobe of the lights were found to be much inflamed, the intestines allso in which were 4 intersections, an inflammation of the kidneys and Blather. . . . The opperation was performd by Doctors Colman and Page. Judg North, Son Jonathan, & myself were attendants. Martha's account of the "Desection" is a rare document in the history of early American autopsies, especially important because it was written by a woman. By Martha's time, dissections had become somewhat routine in New England. Cotton Mather and Samuel Sewall (Henry's Puritan ancestor) both described dissections performed in late-seventeenth-century Boston. By the second quarter of the eighteenth century, donating one's body to science was considered a public-spirited act. The *New England Weekly Journal* of February 10, 1736, reported that a young Dedham woman, dying of "Pulmonary Pthisis," had "earnestly desired, that her Viscera might be Anatomically inspected, for the Benefit of those, who may be afflicted with the like Disorders." At midcentury, newspapers sometimes reported the results of autopsies.[17]

Human dissection, like man-midwifery, was related to the growth of experimental medicine in seventeenth- and eighteenth-century Britain. Although a few anatomical works were published in the sixteenth century, the first major landmark came in the seventeenth century with the work of William Harvey, best known for his study of the circulation of the blood. Harvey not only made important contributions to anatomy but to embryology. The connection between anatomical dissection and obstetrics was affirmed in the work of William Hunter, the most famous London anatomist of the eighteenth century and also a renowned obstetrician.[18] British physicians sometimes invited midwives to observe dissections, as did their counterparts in rural Maine. Martha observed four autopsies in the period of the diary. Except for John Davis, all were of young women.

Kennebec doctors, like their British contemporaries, wanted to see rather than read about the interior of the human body. That Martha carefully recorded the details of each dissection suggests that she shared their curiosity. After Nabby Andros's autopsy, for example, she noted that the "complaint was in the Uterus. It contained one gallon water together with other substance. The weight of it after the water was taken out was 7 lb. The Liver weighed 3 1/2 lbs. The trunk of her Body contained a large quantity of water." Martha's interest in measurement returned in her description of Rachel Savage's dissection— "there was a Larg sustance which weighed 35 lb found in her."[19]

Martha's brief summaries record general results—"Her Lights were found to be very much ulcerated, & a skerrous utera"— rather than precise anatomical detail. In the John Davis case, she referred to the "left lobe of the lights," using the word "lobe" in much the way the young Cotton Mather did a hundred years earlier in describing the dissection of his infant sister: "When shee was opened, it was found, that the right Lobe of her Lungs was utterly wasted and not any thing but about three Quarters of a Pint of Quittor, in the room thereof."[20] A sophisticated physician-anatomist would, of course, have used more specialized vocabulary. Albertus Haller, whose works were republished in America in Martha's lifetime, explained that the lungs contained "two viscera, which are distinguished into right and left," noting that the structure of the organ "is a heap of lobes separated from each other by intermediate intervals, in which is extended a loose cellular substance."[21] That Martha used the term "lights" rather than "lungs" may be an indication of rural experience as much as rural education. Any woman who had cleaned and cooked organ meats would recognize the difference in weight between the lungs and the denser liver or heart.

For Martha, the human body had a recognizable geography. She could identify John Davis's lungs, intestines, kidneys, bladder, and gall bladder, noting they were all inflamed. Her reference to "4 intersections" in the intestines is curious, however. Did she mean that there were four blockages of some sort? That the "operators" had intersected or bisected the intestine in four places? Or was she referring to a kind of anatomy lesson in which the physicians pointed out the three divisions of the small intestine—duodenum, jejunum, ileum—and the colon, a sequence commonly described in eighteenth-century medical literature, much to the dismay of one physiologist, who complained, "Anatomists have usually reckoned three small intestines, though nature has formed but one."[22]

In her description of the February 4 autopsy, Martha carefully distinguished between those who "performd" and those who participated as "attendants." Among the latter she included herself, her son Jonathan, and Judge North. The men may have attended simply out of curiosity, but more likely they were official observers or witnesses selected by the parents. Jonathan, of course, was the child's uncle; North, a close business associate of the father. Martha's role was more complex. She was a witness of a special sort. At Rachel Savage's dissection on March 13, 1808, she had noted, "There were 12 Doctors present and 3 midwives." Whether there were other attendants on that occasion we do not know, but it is clear that midwives, like doctors, attended autopsies because of their calling as healers.

The practice was well established in England by the 1730s, when Sarah Stone wrote her treatise on midwifery. She cautioned women against men who saw their study of anatomy as giving them a claim to practice obstetrics, "for dissecting the Dead, and being just and tender to the Living, are vastly different." Not that women should disdain anatomy:

> I have seen several Women open'd; and 'tis not improper for all of the Profession to see Dissections, and read Anatomy, as I have done. But had I inspected into them all my life, and had not been instructed in Midwifery by my Mother, and Deputy to her full six years, it would have signified but little; nor should I have dared to have undertaken such a Profession, lest any Life should have been lost thro' my ignorance; which I am well assured, thro' the blessing of God, has never happened.[23]

In the long-term history of women's medicine, the routine presence of midwives at autopsies is an extraordinarily interesting phenomenon. As guardians of women and children, midwives presumably ensured proper reverence for the bodies. From the doctors' point of view, inviting midwives to observe was perhaps a professional courtesy, a way of including them in an important educational event. At the same time, it helped to validate the activity and perhaps to reassure anxious relatives. Later in the nineteenth century, however, as autopsies shifted from homes to hospitals, as medical education became more institutionalized, and as definitions of appropriate feminine behavior narrowed, that role ceased to be either necessary or possible.

In 1820, a professor at the Harvard Medical School published an anonymous treatise in which he argued that women should no longer be employed as midwives because their character would be destroyed by acquaintance with the dissections essential to thorough instruction in medicine.

> It is needless to go on to prove this; it is obvious that we cannot instruct women as we do men in the science of medicine; we cannot carry them into the dissecting room and the hospital; many of our more delicate feelings, much of our refined sensibility must be subdued, before we can submit to the sort of discipline required in the study of medicine; in females they must be destroyed; and I venture to say that a female could scarce pass through the course of education requisite to prepare her, as she ought to be prepared, for the practice of midwifery, without destroying those moral qualities of character, which are essential to the office.[24]

This was a classic double bind: Women could not qualify themselves to practice midwifery without mastering general medicine, but learning general medicine would disqualify them as women and therefore as midwives.

In Maine in the early nineteenth century, no one worried about the refined sensibility of Martha Ballard. She administered clisters, counted intestinal worms, prepared bodies for burial, and observed dissections, all the while recording appropriate religious sentiments in the pages of her diary. The Harvard treatise raises a larger question, however. The doctor's insistence that medical discipline subdue sensibility identifies him with the scientific effort to separate observation from feeling, to objectify and quantify experience.[25] Because that ethic, once praised as the source of scientific progress, has come under severe criticism in recent years, it is worth asking about Martha's sensibility. Was her ability to attend autopsies a sign of insensitivity? Did familiarity dull feeling?

In her account of John Davis's illness, there is just a hint of the distancing which some historians have associated with early responses to infant death.[26] The child had always been "John" in the diary, but on February 2, as death grew near, he became first "the patient" and then "it."

I laid down by the fire at 11, was Calld on at midnight when an alteration in the patients breathing took place. It was not able to swallow after that nor had it any great struggle. Its life went out as a Candle.

Still, there is a gentleness in that entry that suggests Martha was moved by the little boy's death. "He was [a] promising Child," she wrote. "How oft are our Expectations Cut off."

Her account of Nabby Andros's death also suggests awareness of pain, of both spirit and body. "Oh, how distresst a being shee is," Martha wrote. "May God be pleased to shine on her soall by the influence of his holy spirrit and giv her comphort before shee goes hence to be here no more." The day before Nabby's death, she reported finding the family "very distressed." She brought practical comfort: "Helpt remove Nabby. We put her Bed out and I made her as Clean as I could and tended her till Evening when I left Mrs. Cowen, Ingerham, & Cypher to watch." The next morning, she was called to put on Nabby's grave clothes and observe the autopsy.[27]

In Martha's account of Parthenia Pitts's last days, expressions of compassion alternated with the precise observations of an experienced healer. "I was at Shubal Pittses all day. She is very low

Exersisd with sever gripings, & loose stools. God only knows how it may turn out. I sent for my hors but find her so ill I tarried thro the night. Shee had Entervails of Paine & rest but weak indeed."[28] Each day Martha found a new reason for concern. Parthenia "had a distrest turn by Eating a little meat." "Her hands & feet cold." "Her mouth & throat very sor." She "was very much put to it for Breath." "Poor creature endures her illness with great patience."

In the entries describing Parthenia's last hours, the juxtaposition of facts and feelings is striking:

September 1. Old Mrs Pollard & Mrs Barton watcht till near day when I rose & they retired to take some rest. At 6 O Clock shee desird Mr Pitts & I to move her & fix her Bed. We did & laid her in again. She Expird in a very short space without a strugle Except distress for Breath. We have reason to hope our loss [is] her gain. I came home from Mrs Pitts' after we had performd our last ofice of friendship Except her interment. My son Ephraim went to inform her friends at Winthrop. It is four months this day since I was Calld to see my dear Neace who was seisd with this her last illness, which shee has born with Christian meekness and humility. She has manifested her regard to Christianity by an open profession of religion & receiving the ordinance of Baptism. We morn the los of her Company, but have the greatest reason to hope that shee has Changd this for a world in which shee will be free from all pain and sorrow, joind with glorified saints to sing Redeeming lov.

September 2. I walkt to Mr Pitts this morning, where I saw the operation of a dessection performed on his decesed wife. Her Lights were found to be very much ulcerated, & a Skerrous utera.

Martha moved from a simple record of Parthenia's last moments to quiet remembrance of the four-month vigil. Parthenia was both "Mrs Pitts" and "my dear Neace." By the end of the passage, she was a converted Christian ready to join the glorified saints. It is not the vision of heaven that closes the account, however, but a stark record of mortality. Eighteenth-century life allowed a combination of experiences rare in modern America. Parthenia had been Martha's niece, her surrogate daughter, her servant, her neighbor. Martha had been a watcher at her bedside, a nurse, spiritual supporter, and physician. She had lovingly dressed her for burial and was now prepared to observe and record the dissection of her body.

In witnessing autopsies, as in so many other ways, social healers connected illness and death with life.

A larger question that hovers over Martha Ballard's diary is how the eighteenth-century system of cooperation between midwives and physicians gave way to the medical exclusiveness exemplified in the Harvard professor's treatise. Why were women invited to observe dissections in 1800 in one setting and twenty years later deemed incapable even of practicing midwifery in another?

The professor's concern with female delicacy suggests that changing notions of womanhood played some role. More important is the emphasis in his treatise on a new kind of male professionalism based on the full-time practice of medicine and on a unified therapeutic system in which "ordinary" and "emergency" practice were merged. Such an approach demanded the elimination or further subordination of social healers. To allow women to continue to practice midwifery, or, by extension, any other form of independent healing, deprived male doctors of the experience they needed and at the same time perpetuated the notion that uneducated people could safely care for the sick.

One cannot assume, however, that such a view had prevailed even in Boston by 1820. The history of American medicine in the nineteenth century is the story of a long argument over just these issues.[29] As homeopaths assailed allopaths and Thompsonians attacked regulars, female healers went in many directions. Some persisted in traditional practice or pursued sectarian medicine. Others pioneered in the development of the nursing profession or in new voluntary societies. A few, including Martha's great-great-granddaughter, entered medical school. Each choice preserved some strand of eighteenth-century female practice. In Martha's world, herbalism and dissection, charity and account-keeping, independence and deference, seemed compatible. The nineteenth century did not so much destroy social medicine as unravel it.

The diary hints at how that happened. As we have seen, the new professionalism had very little effect on Martha's practice. Her deliveries declined after 1800 because she was ill, not because of any lack of demand for her work. Yet the aggressiveness of the new doctors may have discouraged other midwives. It was experience that made Martha a formidable competitor for the young physicians. A new or less popular midwife would not have had that advantage. The person who eventually succeeded to Martha's eminence was probably none other than the bungling Benjamin Page. Entering the full-time practice of medicine at the age of twenty-four, he had many years to learn his craft. Martha's decline gave his career a boost.

According to a nineteenth-century biography, Page "attended upwards of *three thousand females in their confinement, without the loss of a single life from the first year of his practice.*" (Emphasis in the original.) There were still midwives practicing in Hallowell at the time of Martha's death, but most of them probably slipped gradually into the role of assistants to men like Page. This was not because doctors had secrets that midwives did not, but because doctors, being less constrained by other obligations, could now add experience to the book learning that had always been theirs. Ironically, the new doctors both supplanted and imitated women. Judith Walzer Leavitt has argued that physicians who attended home births in the nineteenth century self-consciously conformed themselves to a female-centered environment, and the same laudatory biography confirms that point, describing Page as not only self-sacrificing and charitable but "so averse to notoriety and display, that he often manifested a shrinking and retiring modesty in society that was truly delicate and feminine."[30]

The diary also suggests how nineteenth-century conflicts between botanic and heroic medicine may have developed out of eighteenth-century gender divisions. In October of 1799, Ephraim suffered a frightening attack of colic. Martha sent for Dr. Cony.

> He arivd here at 10 hour Evening. Gave him phisic and accused me with going to Mr Dingleys in his sickness and objecting to his prescriptions and prescribing some of my own and seting Mrs Dingley Crying by giving my opinion of the disease and said this was one of many instances I had done so. Which I must deny till her or some other Can bring it to my recollection. This is a world of tryal. May those which I am Calld to meet with serve for my good.

On October 26, Dingley came to call. "I informd of what Doctor Cony had laid to my Charg Concerning my Conduct with him in his sickness," Martha wrote. "He declares no such thing mentioned by him or his wife as the Doctor represented to me. There was but quite the reverse. The mistake, if one, seems very strange."

In protesting her innocence, Martha acknowledged her duty to defer. She had no recollection of ever questioning Cony's advice. She was obviously dismayed and annoyed by his accusation, which, if the diary is any indication, was probably unjust. She had, after all, sent for him to treat her own husband. But one need not attack another person in order to undermine his advice. All she needed to do was go about her business, quietly offering her own opinions without reference to any other. What the incident shows is the power of her presence in the community. Cony was threatened by her intervention, presumed or real. It also shows the doctor's willingness to assert his authority against the claims of a presumably inferior practitioner. This was, of course, what the new medical societies were encouraging physicians to do.

In March of 1800, Hannah Pollard's youngest child, her only son, fell ill. Martha gave him the usual laxatives, rhubarb and senna, but the child remained very sick. Dr. Colman recommended castor oil; Dr. Cony confirmed the other doctor's prescription but also left snakeroot, camomile, paregoric, and another ingredient Martha did not know. They used it "according to his direction to a punctilio," she wrote, "but to no affect. The illness still increases." The next day Cony came again and gave the baby an emetic. The medicine "had a kind operation," Martha wrote, but again there was no improvement.

Her language in succeeding entries is oblique but suggestive. As the child's condition worsened, she grew less and less confident of the doctor's judgment. For the most part, his therapies were familiar enough, but his use of them seemed extreme. Perhaps she saw death approaching and wanted to avoid harsh remedies that might increase the baby's suffering.

March 4 ... He gave it Excesive washings with Brandy, order onions applied to the belly and feet. We followed his directions. Mrs Hayward and Polly Pollard sett up with the child. It was thot to be Expiring at 4 hour morning.

March 5 ... The babe is very sick indeed. Cony came. He proposed to put blister on the neck. He Cast very hard reflections on me with out grounds as I think. May a mercyfull God forgiv him. The Child faded away and gave up the ghost at 11 hour 55 minutes Evening with very little struggle. Mr Pollard brot all his daughters there to see their dear little distrest brother. May God Teach us to take the visitation as duty teacheth us.

The doctor's work was over, but Martha had one more duty. With the help of Sally Ballard, Sally Pitts, and another neighbor, she put on the grave clothes. "The Cofin was made by Mr. Gill," she wrote. "He put the remains therein. It lookt as pleasant as when in health and in sweat sleep. The Lord gave and he has recalld it to himself and may we be able to bless his holy name." The peaceful repose of the child was especially reassuring because, as she wrote in the margin of the previous day's entry, "the babe Expired ... with a frown in his Brow." The quiet ministrations of the women and of Charles Gill helped to salve the family's discomfiture. Martha added, "There were a number of friends Came in to Condole with my Children, which seems Comfortable when in trouble."

Whether consciously or not, Martha juxtaposed the "hard reflections" of Cony, and his excessive washings and troublesome blister, with the gentle care of the neighbors, the women who put on the grave clothes and the kind friend who made the coffin. Yet Cony's treatment hardly differed from her own: she had often applied onions to the feet of a patient or used an alcohol rub to reduce fever. Nonetheless, something new was happening in her relationship with the doctor and she did not quite understand it. The arguments with Cony were a consequence of tensions inherent in the system of social medicine. Yet they may also have stemmed partly from subtle shifts in the attitudes of local physicians. As new medical ideas infiltrated the region, even conservative doctors like Daniel Cony became acutely conscious of their authority. Here, the founding of the Kennebec Medical Society in 1797 was probably less important than the presence of Benjamin Vaughan, who had begun dispensing advice to Hallowell doctors from his grand house at the Hook. Vaughan's correspondence with Benjamin Page shows that he was aggressively promoting the three therapies we earlier identified as solidistic.

"I wish you would apply opium & the digitalis to the patient at Mr. Wests'," Vaughan wrote Page in September 1800, adding that he would send the doctor "some powders consisting of foxglove & opium. The former came to Dr. Jeffery's of Boston from Apothecaries Hall. The medicine was made up for Miss Hallowell, being the same which she had been in habit of taking with such palliative success."[31] For a patient suffering a "derangement," he recommended a compound containing camphor, ipecacuanha, opium, and calomel, though he noted in passing that the man was already an "eater of opium."[32]

Vaughan also urged a more vigorous use of bleeding, reminding Page that "Sydenham's rule is 40 ounces for the cure of pleurisy of an adult," though in this case he recommended only four ounces to begin. In a postscript to the same letter, he added, as if to overcome the doctor's reluctance and at the same time assure him of their own superiority to back-country practitioners:

> Did you ever know of a *single* instance of evil committed by our bleeding in fever; and on the contrary, have you not known evils, or at least delays, from procrastinating it? If you balance accounts with the lancet, you will I fear find yourself largely its debtor, even in the last year.
>
> They have had much sickness & mortality in the new townships from fever, which their best practitioners call *mixed*. You may judge of the practice by this appellation & the result.[33]

Vaughan may also have encouraged Page to make more frequent use of bloodletting in pregnancy and delivery. Obstetrical literature from the period was beginning to encourage bloodletting for various complications of pregnancy, but also, if Dr. Moses Appleton's commonplace book can be trusted, for "obstructed menses," a condition indistinguishable from early pregnancy. Bleeding was a "powerful emmenagogue," Appleton wrote, much more successful than other remedies.[34] A set of Dr. Page's accounts with a man named William Mathews survives. It includes 108 entries, thirty-nine of which specifically mention Mathews's wife. These include, in addition to four deliveries, a number of entries for bloodletting. Page bled the woman twice during her second pregnancy, once at 2 1/2 months, again at seven. He also tried the same remedy five months *after* one delivery, and thirteen months following another.[35]

Whether opium and bleeding were among the remedies Vaughan prescribed for Tabitha Sewall, we do not know. Henry noted on June 8, 1807, that his wife's mind was "considerably disordered" and, on June 9, that "Mr. Vaughan called, & prescribed physic." Tabitha died three years later, still in a distressed state, though leaving her husband hopeful of her salvation. Henry left a more extended description of the death of his daughter Mary in 1825. Mary was considered to suffer, like her mother, from mental illness. Her "derangement" took the form of running away to join the Shakers at New Gloucester, Maine. Her father and the attending physician, Issachar Snell, responded by confining her in a special chair (and later a bunk "with a lid to shut down"), reducing her food, and drawing blood to alleviate her nervous excitement. She died six months later, after expressing her love to all her family and begging their forgiveness.[36]

Not all Kennebec families were happy with the new therapies. Already in New England a powerful backlash was developing against academic medicine. In a letter to Page, Vaughan documented with evident exasperation the resistance of one parent to the new emphasis on bleeding:

> Please to give my compliments to Mr. Morse, and tell him, that if he refuses to allow the lancet to his child's mouth, I shall have no hesitation in saying, that he will have been the probable cause of the child's death, should it die; & that he has less courage or more prejudice than all the females that I have yet met with in Kennebec. I hold it *criminal* to pray publicly for a child on one hand, & refuse the approved & innocent means of care on the other. I wish all means may not now be too late.[37]

Vaughan was convinced that the new therapies, heroic blood-letting and the use of digitalis, usually in combination with opium, were essential to patient care. To his dismay, he had found a man who preferred the quiet operations of established remedies—and prayer. In Benjamin Vaughan's mind—and perhaps in Daniel Cony's as well—the lines were clearly drawn. It was a case of prejudice versus science and of "female" versus "approved" therapies.

Under other circumstances, the promoters of the new medicine were capable of promoting the cause of women. (It was not the female mind *per se* that alarmed them, but the stubborn and untutored female mind.) It was Henry Sewall who in 1800 placed sixteen young women at the head of a parade honoring George Washington. It was Charles Vaughan, the doctor's brother, who in 1805 urged the Kennebec Proprietors to open a female department in the Hallowell Academy. It was Daniel Cony who in 1816 provided the money to start a school for girls in Augusta.[38]

Educated women would value expert opinion; uneducated women might foolishly resist the "innocent means" offered for their care. This theme appears in comic form in the May 9, 1804, issue of the *Kennebec Gazette*. A short piece, reprinted from a London paper, entitled "Vulgar Prejudice," tells the story of a woman in Dublin, Ireland, who was suffering from "an acute and obstinate fever." A physician prescribed the most powerful medicines available, certain they would effect a cure. Returning to her house to ask how she did, he was astonished at being told she was dead. He entered her chamber and found several women washing the body for burial. "Casting his eyes towards the window, [he] observed in the casement of one of the shutters not only the bottles he had ordered that day in the state they came from the apothecary's untouched, but all the medicines he had prescribed for a fortnight before!" When he asked the nurse why she had not followed his instructions, she replied that she "thought it a sin to tease the poor lady with such nauseous trash, or to make a Potterkerry's shop of her belly." Inspecting the body, the doctor discerned a faint pulse and a slight warmth, whereupon he instantly put the woman into a warm bed, "and by the application of proper cordials, restored her to life in less than three hours, and to perfect health in less than a month, to the inexpressible joy of the lady's friends; but the poor lady had the mortification to find herself deprived of a most beautiful and luxuriant head of hair, which the witches of death had shorn off, in their hurry to fit her for the coffin."

Whether Martha read that paper, we do not know. Against its "vulgar prejudice" her diary is a quiet witness.

CHAPTER EIGHT

MARCH 1804

"what a scean had I to go at Evening"

14 4 *At home. Luke Barton ran over a sheep with his Sleigh.*
Cloudy morning. Clear afternoon. Luke Barton wriding in a sleigh ran it over a sheep and hurt it so it Could not stand. It was my Sons sheep. I have been at home very unwel.

15 5 *At home. James Hinkley Expired.*
Clear and Cloudy by turns. I have been at home very unwel. Ephraim & Burr got me wood.

16 6 *At home. Daughter Ballard here.*
Clear and Cool. I feel more Comfortable for which I wish to giv God praise. Have been at home. Daughter Ballard & Mrs Getchel here. 6 grand Children Dined here. 3 sleep here.

17 7 *At Shubael Pittss. Feel very unwel and what a scean had I to go at Evening. May the good God support me.*
Clear part of the day. Son & Daughter Pollard and part of their Children here. Shee went on to see her Father. I went afternoon Conducted by Lemuel Witham, a lad who is Com to work with son Ephraim. I returned at Evening very unwell. Lemuel went to take son Lambards hors and Sleigh to Joness for Jonathan and him to Come up in but not finding them ready to Come

returned with it. They Came up on foot and Jonathan Came here without his hat, took him from his supper, push him out a dors, Drove him home to his house, damning and pushing him down and struck him. Shaw and Burr went on after to prevent his being diprived of life. I followed on, falling as I went, till meeting Daughter Lambard was assisted by her. I reacht his house, find him Cursing and Swearing he would go and giv him a hard whiping. My Daughter Lambard desired Heman to go and Conducted him to Ephraim. He went and tarried all night. Son Lambard brot me home in his sleigh. O that the God of all Mercy would forgiv him this and all other misconduct.

18   1   *At home but in a situation of sorrow. Mr. Kinslys 3d son Born.* Snowd part of the day. Daughter Lambard and Pollard here. My Comfortors are much as Jobs were. O that my Patience may hold out and may I see good acording to the days in which I have been afflicted.

19   2   *At home. Daughter Pollard sleeps here.* Clear and Cool. I have been very unwel. Phebe Church Came at 9 hour. Son Pollard, his wife & Rhoda and Dolly here at Evening.

20   3   *At home. Daughter Pollard & Children went home. She De- livered me 7/6 on James Blacks acount.* Clear and Cool. Son Ephraim brot his wife here. His prentis Boy Conducted Daughter Pollard and Children home. Son Jon- athan was here this day. He spake very indecently to me. I pray God to forgive the ofences of all who do ingure my feelings. May they Consider they may be old and receiv like Treatment. Polly went to son Jonathans. His wife & Children are unwel.

21   4   *At William Stone's. Birth 1st. Received 6/ May 10.* Clear. I was Calld before morning to William Stones wife in Labour. Shee was Delivered at 9 hour morning of her 6th son and 8th Child. I returnd afternoon. *Birth. William Stone's son.*

22   5   *At home*
Cloudy and some rain. I have been at home. Done my work, Brewed &c. Am very much fatagud.

23   6   *At home. Jonathans wife Bakt here.*
Clear part of the day. Daughter Ballard here to Bake. Shee made Nutts for Ephraim.

24   7   *At home*
Clear part of this day. I have done my hous work and cleand the Chambers, mended stockins &c. I do feel very much fatagued.

Martha's fatigue grew deeper as she entered her seventieth year. Although there were fewer deliveries to take her from her bed in the night, there was enough work in the house and barn to keep her back stiff and her fingers sore. She knitted, brewed beer, dipped candles, made vinegar from pumpkin parings, colored old clothes in cornstalk dye, leached lye from wood ashes and made soap. "Have got three Barrils full and some more," she wrote on March 25, 1803.[1] Spinning was easier now that there was a wool carding mill at Winthrop (Martha called it "the masheen"), but there were still lambs to birth and fleeces to wash. The Ballards had more than twenty sheep, not counting the one Luke Barton ran over with his sleigh on March 14, 1804.[2]

More exhausting than all the work were the emotional upheavals. "What a scean had I to go at Evening," she wrote on March 17, after Jonathan, the worse for an afternoon at Jones's Tavern, had burst into her house in a rage. This was not the first family gathering that had ended in anger and despair. Two years before, on a similar occasion, she had written:

> Jonathans wife & Children supt here. He Came in Just as we sett down to Table in a great passion about his white

Mare being hurt. It overcame me so much I was not able to sett up. I Could wish he might see the folly and Evil of such Conduct and reform.[3]

Though the details in the two accounts are different, the underlying themes and images are the same—a peaceful supper, an impassioned man, an injured or unavailable horse. The first time, Martha felt her son's lack of control so deeply she was herself immobilized, psychologically struck down. The second time, fear for Lemuel Witham's safety propelled her into the middle of the fray, delaying her own collapse. "I followed on, falling as I went, till meeting Daughter Lambard was assisted by her. Son Lambard brought me home in his sleigh." Assailed by the bad child, she was uplifted and sustained by the good ones.

Yet when Hannah and Dolly came to visit her the next day, they only increased her sorrow. Like Job's comforters, they seem to have blamed her for the problem, or at least offered explanations or proposed solutions she could not accept. It was Jonathan who "spake very indecently" to her on March 20, but she used the plural when she prayed God "to forgive the offences of all who do ingure my feelings," adding, "May they Consider they may be old and receiv like Treatment."

Age surely had something to do with Martha's troubles. It wasn't just the physical process of growing old that made her life difficult, but a subtle passing of authority from one generation to another. The move to Jonathan's farm symbolized this transition. Martha and Ephraim were now old folks, living in semi-dependence on their son's land. If Jonathan had been a different sort of man, this might have been easier to bear. As it was, every outburst of temper was a deliberate assault on Martha's identity. "May the good God support me," she prayed.

In 1804 her problems were complicated by Ephraim's arrest for debt. That is why Daughter Pollard had come to the house on March 17 and then gone on "to see her Father," why Martha herself had gone to the town "Conducted by Lemuel Witham." Ephraim had been taken on January 2. As Martha described it:

My husband Came home at 4 p.m. Took a little food. Complains of feeling the pain in his stomach, but was Calld by John Sewal to answer an Execution of 800 Dollars. Was by him Conducted to the Jail in Augusta and Commited. Our two sons Jonathan & Ephraim were bound for the Liberty of the yard for him. I pray the great Parent of the universe to protect him and giv him Comfort in his present tryal.

The "Execution" which John Sewall carried was an order signed by a single justice of the peace. Like most debtors in this era, Ephraim had been taken through a mesne process that avoided jury trial. He had signed a promissory note, witnessed by a judge, acknowledging the right of his creditor to attach his goods or person if he did not pay his debt in time. Local judges kept books filled with such "Confessions" and their resulting "Executions." In each case, the sheriff or his deputy was instructed to seek goods equivalent to the debt and, if he found none, to take "the body" of the debtor. Since Ephraim's inventoried wealth in 1800 amounted to $684, there was nothing in his possession to satisfy an $800 execution.[4]

Ephraim's creditor was the town of Augusta. As Martha explained in the margin of her January 2 entry, "My Husband was this Evening Committed to Jail on account of the tax Collection." Eighteen months before, he and his sureties had signed a note binding themselves to collect $4,550, the town's combined total tax bill for the year 1803.[5] Although he had worked hard at collecting when he wasn't in the back country surveying for John Davis, and had turned in his proceeds to the town treasurer every two months as the law required, his accounting on November 17 had fallen short by $800.[6] The town had no choice but to imprison him. A Massachusetts statute of 1786 said that when a collector failed in his duty, and when his own property was insufficient to cover the deficiency, the sheriff or his deputy was "empowered *and required*" to take the body of the man. No sentimental regard for the man's age or for his years of service could abrogate the law. He would be treated like other debtors.[7]

A 1787 law "for relief of poor debtors" allowed indigent persons to leave prison after a month if they were willing to swear themselves incapable of paying their jail expenses. They were still liable for the debt, however, and any property they acquired after release was subject to seizure.[8] Ephraim chose a second option: by posting bond, he could leave the prison during the daytime to pursue his work. This is what Martha meant when she said her sons had been bound "for the Liberty of the yard for him."[9] A jail yard was not a yard at all, but an invisible boundary around the central part of the town. Ephraim had surveyed the very bounds that now confined him. They stretched inland from the river a quarter of a mile on both sides, as far north as John Jones's mill lot and as far south as the bend of Water Street.

"I went down to Mr Thwings," Martha wrote of her first visit to the settlement after Ephraim's arrest. "My husband Came and spent [the] afternoon with me. He dind and took Tea there but must go up the hill at night."[10] The jail stood in a new neighborhood at the top of a hill that rose breathlessly from the river, convenient to the courthouse and Timothy Page's hotel. As long as Ephraim returned to his debtor's quarters before dark, he could move about the town in the daytime, visiting his lawyer, attending church or court, dining with Esquire Cony, or chatting with friends at the wharves. Despite the embarrassment, such a confinement was hardly oppressive. For an old man exhausted from years of physical labor, it may even have been a kind of vacation. Martha didn't see it that way, of course. "May the Grat parent giv him patience and Composiur of mind," she prayed, a petition she might just as well have offered for herself.

In the abstract, imprisonment for debt seems a barbaric practice, something on the order of branding thieves or cutting off the ears of rioters. In reality, it put as much pressure on a man's connections as on the man himself. A form of coercion rather than punishment, it was a way of forcing a man to reveal hidden property or liquidate capital—social as well as financial.[11]

Martha's diary provides a classic illustration of how the system was supposed to work. On July 3, 1800, she reported that Jonathan was "in the Care of an ofiser or in prison for a debt."

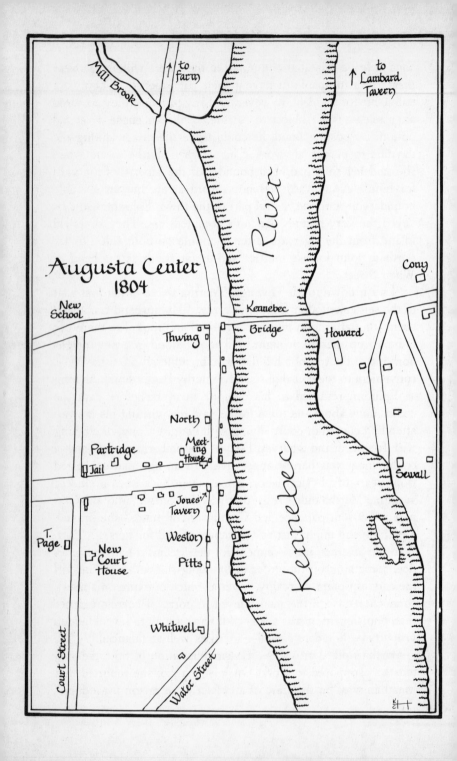

Two days later, Sally went "to see her husband and has allso been to try to Borrow money to help him out of his trouble but did not sucseed." On July 7, Ephraim, Sr., "went to son Pollards for money for son Jonathan who is Confind to the prison yard." The next day, Martha reported that Jonathan had "discharged the debt for which he has been Confined one weak and returned to his family." The combined efforts of the man's wife, father, and brother-in-law had ended his troubles—for a time.

On September 22, Martha added to the end of her day's entry, "Son Jonathan is gone to jaill again." This time Ephraim went to Esquire Haywood's at Winthrop to borrow money. "Did not succeed," Martha wrote, though in the margin of the entry added, "Son Jonathan returned from Jaill." Apparently, Sally or some other family member had been more successful.[12] Jonathan's experience was typical. The average incarceration for debt was only a few days, though as debt multiplied and more and more poor farmers from the backcountry were taken, the length may have increased.[13] Most men, however, either took the poor debtor's oath or, like Jonathan, discharged their obligation within a few weeks.

For others, the mere threat of jail was enough to enforce creditor demands. In the summer of 1804, while Ephraim Ballard was still in prison, Daniel Cony won a suit for debt against "Moses Pollard of Sidney, Innholder," Hannah's husband. The execution instructed the sheriff to attach the goods, chattels, or lands of Pollard to the amount of $279.20, with 20 cents damage, and failing that to "take the Body of the said Pollard and him commit unto Our Gaol in Augusta." Moses was not committed. Part of his farm at Sidney was "set off" to Cony, and a week later, for $520, he deeded the rest, including the "house I now live in," to his brother-in-law Jonathan. Apparently, Jonathan had rescued Moses as four years earlier Moses had rescued him.[14]

In Ephraim's case, however, the outcome was strikingly different. On February 11, six weeks after her husband was jailed, Martha noted, "Ephraim [Jr.] been down to trie to have his Father Liberated but did not suckseed." As the weeks passed with

no result—and seemingly with little effort on anyone's part—
the old man's condition must have seemed permanent. May 18,
1804: "My Husband has this day seen 79 revolutions of the Sun.
He has ended this and began the 80 year of his age in Augusta
jail." August 2, 1804: "It is 7 months since my husband went to
Jail." Perhaps Martha feared that her husband, like Mary Hussey's, would die in prison. The nature of Ephraim's debt in part
accounts for the problem. It was far better to let his sureties
complete the tax collection than to use his or his family's resources to settle the town's account. Although Moses Pollard
could do nothing to help his father-in-law, Barnabas Lambard
had the wherewithal to relieve him, as did Jonathan. That they
allowed him to remain in jail so long suggests a deliberate strategy. Ephraim was an old man. His future earning power was
not enough to gamble against the tenuous fortunes of young
men with families. Barnabas and Dolly had recently acquired
David Thomas's tavern on the east side of the river above Fort
Western. Jonathan was piecing together ownership of Daniel
Savage's mills nearby.[15] This was not the time to jeopardize
their futures. In fact, Ephraim may have deliberately assigned
some of his assets, including the farm, to Jonathan to avoid just
such an emergency. As town tax collector, he was in an extraordinarily vulnerable position. As a consequence, he spent one
year, four months, and twenty-seven days going up the hill to
Augusta jail at night.

The jail was a gaunt two-story structure of hewn timber, win-
dowless, with small apertures for light and air. Twenty-foot
pickets surrounded an exercise yard in the back. Seen from the
river, the jail looked impregnable. In reality, security was remarkably lax. A thief from Winthrop escaped by laboriously
enlarging an opening with his jackknife, then slipping through
naked, leaving some of his skin behind. For debtors, there were
hardly any barriers at all. The jailkeeper, Amos Partridge, seg-
regated them from felons, as the law required. It was as much
for his convenience as theirs that he left the back door of
the jail unlatched at night, allowing unattended visits to "the
necessary."[16]

Some judges and creditors thought debtor liberties had gone too far. The boundaries of the yard were one source of contention, an issue that may have provoked Amos Partridge's visit to the Ballard house on May 25, 1804. "Mr. Partridge here for the plan of the Jail yard," Martha wrote.

In June 1804, Augusta jail held seven debtors, including Ephraim Ballard, and three felons—one charged with theft, another accused of forgery and fraud, and a confessed murderer and local celebrity named Henry McCausland. McCausland, convinced that God had called him to save Maine for the Congregationalists, had set fire to the Anglican Church in Pittston in 1793. When he couldn't find the rector of the church, whose name was Warren, he killed a woman of the same name. Insanity saved him from hanging. For more than a decade, he had sat in his solitary cell, chatting with visitors through a wicket, his beard growing longer and more grizzled with each passing year, his manner more mild. To offset his jail expenses, the county allowed him to charge visitors a small fee.[17]

Thanks to Henry McCausland, the jail was a tourist attraction as well as a prison. Reading the *Kennebec Gazette*, one might assume it was also a special kind of tavern. In 1804, the paper reported that Independence Day had "been celebrated in this town by a number of persons, now confined in gaol." The men gathered at the prison, appointed necessary officers from among themselves, and then "moved into procession to the meeting-house and after attending to a well adapted Oration on the occasion, returned in order, where an elegant repast was prepared at the expence of the Hon. Daniel Cony." After dinner, they drank the requisite thirteen toasts, praising the president, the day, the "illustrious Washington," the Honorable Daniel Cony, the candor and impartiality of the judiciary, the "fair sex" and "Our Families: Tho' we are now confined from them, may peace and contentment await them while our return."[18]

Providing a July 4 or Thanksgiving "repast" was one way the Kennebec gentry proclaimed the impartiality and benevolence of the law. When such treats were not forthcoming, clever prisoners knew how to beg. In November of 1807, a poetic petition addressed to the sheriff of the county, signed by "Asa Emerson and twenty-five others," begged for a ration of alcohol.

> *Our minds are still noble, we never repine,*
> *Yet what a good thing is a bottle of wine;*
> *And a bet we would lay, if our cash was but handy,*
> *That a good Rum, Geneva, or Brandy,*
> *Our minds would enliven, our spirits would cheer,*
> *And then we would join in Thanksgiving sincere;*
> *Our dull cares would fly, and around we should jump,*
> *And what matter if a few of us chance to get drunk.*
> *Your Honor's good health we will certainly drink,*
> *And Sullivan's too, we assuredly think,*
> *Will ring thro' our cells with rapture profound,*
> *Our Sorrow, our cares, and our woes will be drowned.*

According to the town historian, "this epistle had its desired effect."[19]

Asa Emerson, the poem's author, was one of Ephraim's jail mates in 1804. A former resident of Augusta, now of Winslow, he was an ardent defender of the rights of poor farmers. Not all his literary efforts were so benign. In 1809, he and fifty others submitted a long petition to the General Court, arguing that Kennebec County judges were harassing debtors. Internal evidence suggests Emerson may also have been the author of *An Address to the Inhabitants of Maine, Showing a Safe and Easy Method of Extracting Good from Evil*, published in Augusta in 1805, an impassioned attack on the entire judicial structure of Kennebec County. "There are in the county of Kennebec, not less than twenty-eight Lawyers!!!" the pamphlet screamed, as though the number alone would convince any reasonable person of the absurdity of the system. Although the Court of Common Pleas in the year past had entered 2,100 actions at an estimated cost of $39,784, they had not settled more than $1,000 worth of disputed property—"a useful court this!" The only solution was to curb the power of a legal profession whose whole purpose was "to render the laws dark and ambiguous, in order to secure to themselves the privilege of twisting and turning them into ten thousand forms and meanings, at the expence of the ignorant." [20]

The same themes reappeared in the 1809 petition. "It costs your constituents near fifty thousand dollars per year to pay a general court and then they have to pay a Number of Judges Eight Dollars per day through the year to tell what the general court means, then an individual has to give a Lawyer ten dollars to know what a judge means." [21] The petitioners were especially distressed at the recent reinterpretation of customs that had long governed the county jails. "The greater part of the prisoners that is brought to goal in this county are simple honest men and they have no money and some of them Leave their children in the woods in want and they have nothing but their Labour to support themselvs and to pay their Large goal charges." For years, men with the liberty of the yard had been accustomed to working until nine o'clock at night, whatever the season, and without the supervision of the jailor. Now Judge Thatcher and others had begun to interpret the law narrowly, forcing them into the jail by sunset, insisting that the keeper bar the door. "If a prisoner put his body one foot from the gaol doors after dark, he broak his bond as much as tho he went one hundred miles." Even in the daytime, the judge demanded constant supervision by the jailor, an impossibility when some 400 men passed through the prison every year and as many as forty-five at a time had the liberty of the yard. "If a prisoner went into a private house, it was an Escape, or if he got over a fence out of the county Road he broak his bonds, or went into a feild to Labour for a man he broak his bonds." [22]

Probably it was that sort of ambiguity that lay behind Martha's diary entry for September 25, 1804: "Ephraim here. Informs his Father has Broke his Bonds and that he Expects his property will all be attached this day. Would the Parent of all mercy Enable me to support under all the tryals he is pleased to lay upon me and take me to him self in his own time." [23] In fact, Ephraim's property was not attached, nor were there any apparent changes in the terms of his imprisonment. Although he slept in jail, he took his meals at various houses along Water Street, eventually boarding with Shubael and Sally Pitts (Martha's helper, Sally Cox, had married Shubael after Parthenia's death). There was a comforting familiarity in sitting down to a dinner cooked by Sally, who had spent so many years living and working at the Ballard house. For Sally, friendship with the Ballards was only part of the motivation, however. She now had a small business boarding debtors. Even better, perhaps, that many of them happened to be friends and relatives.[24]

Ephraim also found work. Part of the spring he labored on the construction of a new grammar school with young Ephraim, who was now a housewright. He probably did some surveying as well (house lots were moving fast in this part of the town), and he gathered debts as he could. Writing to the Plymouth Company on February 2, 1805, after more than a year of imprisonment, he asked for some "reasonable compensation" for attempting to run the line at Balltown in 1802, even though he "did not perform the Business by reason of the outragious abuse and threatning which we received from the people in that visinity." He sent the letter, and an account of his expenses, with Benjamin Whitwell (the Augusta attorney who represented the town in its suit again him!), receiving $9.46 for his trouble, not enough to get him out of jail but enough to provide some of the small comforts he required while there.[25]

At home, Ephraim's imprisonment gave the small annoyances of life new meaning. "I wish to retain my reason if it be the wil of the great Parent of the universe," Martha wrote on January 25, 1804, after bringing snow into the house to melt for soap-making. When the bottom hoop of her soap barrel sprang, she managed a makeshift repair, complaining, "It was not so when I had a husband with me."[26] Throughout the spring and summer, absence made the pen grow fonder.

May 5, 1804. "Walkt to Shubl Pitts, saw my Dear husband there. Partook of a dish of Tea with him, then to my great mortification he left me and went to his place of destination where I wish him the presence of the Great Parent of the universe."

July 15, 1804. "Son & daughter Lambard, their babe, son Jonathan, his wife, Ephraim and his wife, Heman & Lemuel and James Purington partook of a Loin of Veal with me, but alas my husband is debard the favour."

The change in her vocabulary is subtle—the addition of the adjective "Dear," a more frequent use of exclamations ("Oh," "alas")—a limited range of expression to be sure, but real because so rare in this taciturn journal. Yet Martha expressed her love less frequently in words than in small services. She mended Ephraim's breeches, knitted his leggings and hose, did his laundry, and sent him small gifts—"some of the harslett of the Calf," the branch of a currant bush "very full of frute," "Plumbs and Apples" in season.[27]

A sequence of entries in January 1805 artfully juxtaposes her own and her husband's affliction. On January 29, she wrote simply, "I have partly mended a Coat for my poor Confined Husband who is suffering for want of it." The language here evokes the image of the old man, frail and cold, shivering in his debtor's cell, but when the entry is read in sequence with those immediately preceding it, the focus of sympathy shifts from him to her. She had traveled to see him a few days before, slipped on the Lambards' doorstep and broken her foot, and was now back at home, lame and ailing. "I have been very ill this night," she wrote on January 26. "Very ill with pain in my head & Back," she continued on January 27. On January 29, she wrote, "A severe snow storm. I have kept my bed the most of this day but thro God's goodness some Easier this afternoon. I have taken a little gruel with a small pice of Cracker." Then, on January 29, she recorded the entry about Ephraim's coat. For her and for him, each stitch was a small victory over adversity.[28]

Ephraim had no children "in the wood in want," nor was Martha one of those ragged debtors' wives the anti-Federalist pamphlets described, "with a child under one arm and a few quarts of begged or borrowed meal under the other."[29] She had a cow and pigs and enough potatoes in the cellar to pay Mr.

Wyman when he came to hoop her barrel. Her children brought her grain and butter, and from time to time Ephraim sent commodities—gin, sugar, "shushon Tea," "1 dozen crackers" —part of the payments he received for work.[30] In most respects, Martha's life continued at it had always done. She gardened, sewed, cared for her grandchildren, nursed the sick, laid out the dead, and delivered babies. Though her midwifery and nursing practice continued to decline, her own family helped to sustain it. In the year and a half Ephraim was in jail, she delivered five grandchildren, and helped to bury three.[31]

Yet she faced one seemingly insurmountable deficiency. Wood. Clearly, her husband's major contribution to their house-keeping had been fuel. It wasn't the daily tasks of chopping kindling or carrying logs to the fire that concerned her—she had long done that—but the larger labor of cutting and hauling logs and splitting them at the door. That was man's work. She could not do it. On January 25, Jonathan's man brought a sup-ply, but when that was exhausted, she was desperate for fuel. For some reason, young Ephraim, working in the nearby woods hewing house timber, didn't take the time to haul wood for his mother, even though she was cooking and baking for his crew. Perhaps he considered that Jonathan's duty.

April 18, 1804: "I have fatagued to heat my oven for want of wood sutable."

April 19, 1804: "I have gathered Chips South side of my gardin. Broke the old logg fence to pieces and kept fire to do my work."

Nor did Jonathan discover on his own that his mother needed wood, even though Sally or her servants usually did their bak-ing in Martha's oven. The real problem wasn't wood but Mar-tha's relationship with Jonathan. Never good, it had grown increasingly tense as her husband's incarceration tipped the axis of her life toward her son. The problem intensified when cold weather returned in the fall.

October 24, 1804. "Rainy. I have had to go thro the wet to feed my hoggs, milk my Cow, and pique my wood from the old loggs in the Gardin."

October 25. "Clear I have been getting wood and fatagued

much to do. I broke old loggs with an old hough and brot in the pieces in a baskett and O how fatagued I was.

October 26. "Clear part of the day. I have been giting wood and finishing my wash that I began last night after 9 hour Evng. Son Jonathans wife here to spin thread. I Brot a Burthen of Bark after sun sett which took me 300 & 50 steps. O that I might be patient."

October 27. "Snowd. I have had to go out to feed my swine, milk my Cow, get in wood &c. A Mr Spaldin who livs with son Lambd Calld in and got Stakes out of the snow for me to keep a fire this day."

Without wood she could not bake. On October 29, she wrote, "I Eat the Last bread I had for Breakfast and have sustained without the rest of the day." The size of her handwriting increased with her dismay. Although Jonathan's nephew, Luther Pierce, brought a little wood and cut it for her, it was still not enough. On October 31, a cold day, she finally "went to son Jonathans to git him to Cutt me some wood." He sent Luther Pierce. Asking for Jonathan's help only increased her feeling of dependency.

One particularly distressing encounter with Jonathan caused Martha an uncharacteristic slip in her command of events in the diary. The same entry exemplifies the peculiar mixture of self-righteousness and self-sacrifice that characterized her relationship with him, a pattern we saw earlier in her conflicts with Ephraim over Hepsy.

Son Jonathan been here this morn and treated me very unbecomingly indead. O that God would Chang his stuborn heart and Cause him to behave in a Cristion like maner to parents and all others. I Came home on Monday and past the above sien yesterday. I have brot wood from the old fence above here to boil potatoes for son Jonathans swine. He has 8 in my hogs sty.

Continuing to feed Jonathan's pigs was a way of attesting to his culpability and her own innocence. She, like Job, would endure. Reading such entries, one can be forgiven for concluding, with Hannah and Dolly, that Martha brought many of her problems on herself. She was a resourceful and independent woman, perfectly capable of predicting her need for wood and taking the steps necessary to get it. She had three grown sons and two sons-in-law nearby and several grandsons capable of helping. None of her children wanted her to freeze. Clearly, she was having trouble separating her practical need for wood from an emotional need for sympathy, for someone to listen to her, to understand her sorrows and acknowledge her burdens. Ephraim's imprisonment exposed her to a particular kind of neglect. Without a husband, she had no one on whom she had a first claim for care. A husband was one's "best friend," even if he did not always behave that way. Married children had competing obligations, wives and husbands of their own, and children, sometimes more children than a grandmother could comprehend. "I saw 13 of my grandchildren at son Lambard's," Martha wrote after one visit to the old Thomas tavern. She enjoyed her grandchildren, yet after all these years of struggle she felt an intense need for someone to lean on. There is a telling entry in the springtime, when she was struggling to put in her garden. "I have dug ground and planted Poland Beens," she wrote. "Feel much fatagued. The Childn helpt me some. Allin said he wisht to help me." [32] Martha only wanted the help her family *wished* to give.

Cyrus was a partial comfort, helpful when he was there but too frequently gone. He remained a peripatetic miller, spending a few weeks or months at one site, going on to another. He left for Lincolnville the March after his father's imprisonment (George Ulmer, the leading landowner of the town, had solicited his help) but was back for corn planting in May. In October, he was gone again. "Cyrus left here to go to tend mill for Mr Pullin at Watervil. I wish him health and prosperity but alas how shall I do without him," his mother wrote. The next day, Jack Ballard, age thirteen, "Came and Cutt wood for us. He brot me 2 turns of water." [33]

Ephraim, Jr., had married Mary Farwell on February 5, shortly after his father's imprisonment. On February 21, Mary's widowed mother (Martha now called her "Sister Farewell") came to tea. Ephraim and Mary followed local tradition by living apart after their wedding, though occasionally they spent a day together. "Ephraim's wife assisted me to do my housework," Martha wrote on one of those happy days. "I roasted a goos for supper which Son Town gave me." Mary followed another tradition by giving birth to a baby girl, at her mother's house, four months after her marriage. She and Ephraim went to housekeeping in a rented house in the center of Augusta in July.[34]

After the young couple went to housekeeping, Widow Farwell and her younger daughter Sally moved in with Martha for a time, hardly a solution to the wood problem but at least a source of companionship. The two women cohabited happily until Jonathan and Sally decided that they needed the house.[35] On October 25, 1804, ten months after Ephraim's imprisonment, Sally Farwell returned from a visit to Jonathan's. "She informed me at Evng that my son was Determined to Come into this house within a fortnit and that I might tarrie here or go and liv in their house and see how good it was to bring water from this wel. O thou parent of the universe Cutt short thine aflictions and suffer me thine unworthy handmaid to see some Comfort before I go home."

To his mother, Jonathan's insistence on taking over his father's house appeared to be yet another instance of his impetuous and irrational behavior. To him it may have seemed like a practical and appropriate thing to do. His mother needed help; he and Sally needed a better house, a bake oven, and a decent well.

Jonathan was impulsive and perhaps given to hard drinking, but he was no ne'er-do-well. He had pieced together a 200-acre farm over a fifteen-year period, buying part of Lot #15 from Savage Bolton in 1787, the rest from William Howard in 1800, meanwhile acquiring the adjoining Lot #16 to the north. How much his father had to do with this, we do not know. By 1800, he had 348 acres of land in Augusta, more than three times as much as his father (though, as was typical of most farms in the town, only fifteen acres had been cleared and "improved").[36]

His steady rise on the Augusta tax list was impressive, though at least one of his neighbors found him crafty and mean-spirited. In December 1804, while his father was still in jail, Jonathan was indicted by the grand jury and in the subsequent trial convicted of "wickedly and unjustly devising and intending to defraud one William Stone, Junior." (The Stones were near neighbors; Martha noted the birth of their eighth child on March 21, 1804, in the diary entry at the beginning of this chapter.) According to the indictment, Ballard's hired hand, Cyrus Willson, had secured a horse from Stone by claiming he owned a farm in one of the back settlements and an acre of land in Hallowell, when he was, in fact, a mere laborer with no capacity to pay for a horse. Stone was not content to sue Willson alone, but pressed a charge of conspiracy against Jonathan. The jury was convinced. When Jonathan appealed the conviction, he again lost.[37] Of all the Ballards, Jonathan appears most frequently in county court records, both as a plaintiff and as a defendant.

Perhaps his acquisitiveness was another manifestation of the self-indulgent behavior that so distressed his mother. There is nothing to suggest he sacrificed in any way to help his parents during this period, though perhaps he would have argued that he was only trying to insure the survival of the next generation. In 1804–1805, he sold or mortgaged $551 in land but added an additional $1,635, some of it outside the town. In 1805, he finally acquired Daniel Savage's "homestead farm" with "buildings & saw mill," a property he had been purchasing piecemeal since 1798. Meanwhile, he was suing Noah Woodward, Jr., in the Court of Common Pleas and asking for executions of debt against John Robert and Savage Bolton. Such behavior was characteristic.[38] Between 1797 and 1803, Jonathan was a plaintiff in nineteen cases before the Kennebec County Court of Common Pleas, a defendant in ten. He won fifteen of the twenty-nine cases and lost the rest. His record before the Supreme Judicial Court was less impressive; he lost four of the five cases tried there. His one success was a token $3.33 1/2 for reporting Benjamin Palmer for selling a pint of rum and half a pint of brandy without a license. Jonathan was not only involved in conflicts with his neighbor William Stone but with old friends like Theophilus Hamlin and with his mother's cousin Hains Learned.

Now, it appeared, he had decided to take over his father's house. "This is 50 years since I became a housekeeper," Martha wrote on December 19. "I went to the Jail to see my husband." The next day, Ephraim came to young Ephraim's house, where Martha and Sister Farewell were staying. "He Exprest a wish for me to keep possision of this hous at present." But when she returned from Sidney where she found Hannah already "safe delivered by Old Mrs. Savage of her 3d son and 7th child," Jonathan and Sally had moved in.

Ephraim's imprisonment now became her imprisonment. She became a lodger in her own house, taking one room as her own, giving over the rest to her son's family. She tried to preserve her independence, keeping her own fire, cooking her own meals, and shutting her door when she had to. Diary entries during this period refer to taking tea with her children or inviting them to "partake" with her, as though they lived across the fence instead of in the same house. Even with carefully drawn boundaries, however, cohabitation was difficult. Sally was "an inconsiderate or very impudent woman to treat me as shee does," Martha complained, adding that if her daughter-in-law couldn't "shew more maners and discretion," she should "hold her peace for the future." Did she deliver these sentiments vocally, or only in her diary?

Martha could have taken comfort in an English treatise on marriage published in 1624, which argued that: "The mixing of governours in an household, or subordinating or uniting of two Masters, or two Dames under one roof, doth fall out most times, to be a matter of much unquietness to all parties." [39] In fact New England families rarely combined two married couples in a single household. It was common, however, for men to assign their widows a room in a house inherited by a married son. When Ephraim's father, the first Jonathan Ballard, died in 1754, he had left his wife all his "indoor moveables and one cow" and "the use and improvement of the east end of my present dwelling house." In addition, his oldest son was to provide an annual allotment of Indian corn, rye, malt, cider, beef, pork, firewood, sheep's wool, flax, and the use of a horse and furniture "when she has occasion to ride and good and suitable attendance in sickness and health." [40]

Martha was experiencing a kind of pseudo-widowhood, but without the usual allotments of food and fuel. As the second year of Ephraim's imprisonment began, she complained, "I have sufered for fire but must bear it." She did a little washing on January 5, melted snow and brought two pails from the well, but on January 6 wrote, "slept in my cloaths this night [the entry spilling into the margin]. I was oblidged to sleep in my Cloaths or freas, unhappy Mother I am."

She responded in the way hundreds of women must have done before—and since, seeking refuge with another married child. Unfortunately, when she arrived at Lambard's tavern on January 7, she found as much noise and confusion there as at home. Since winter was the season for traveling, with a frozen river making sleighing easy, there was "a great deal of company" in the tavern the entire time. When a Mrs. Emerson from "Deryfield" fell into fits on January 11, Martha sat up with the patient after Dr. Winship left. On January 18, there were fourteen lodgers in the tavern. The next day, Martha noted, with some relief, "The famely that slept here sett out at noon."[41]

Throughout the winter Martha rotated from the farm to the Lambards' to young Ephraim's. Spring work kept her at home, gardening, helping with the housework and baking, caring for a collection of grandchildren that grew and diminished as Ballard, Lambard, and Pollard cousins mixed with the Pierce and Getchel children, who still frequented Sally's house. The patterns of visiting and trade that had been so important during her years at the mills and at the Howard farm were being replicated in Jonathan's and Sally's family, but now she was at the fringe rather than the center of the activity. She still made small trades with neighbors, often paying in potatoes, but her resources and energy were limited.

Between March 14 and April 14, 1805, in addition to the twelve regular inhabitants of the Ballard house, twenty-one other persons dined, took tea, or slept there one or more times. Sally's sister-in-law, referred to in the diary only as Mrs. Pierce, frequently washed, baked, or spun, sometimes for herself, sometimes for Sally. The Pierce family may have been living in the old house Jonathan and Sally had vacated when they moved in with their mother. On March 14, Martha returned from delivering Hitty Babcock (John Davis's former mistress) to find Hannah Pollard and two of her children at the house. They stayed the night. Martha's diary entry for the next day suggests the changing composition of her world:

Mr Lambard sent Joseph S Spaldin for Daughter Pollard. Shee and children went. Daughter Ballard, Lafaett, and Martha went to Mr Babcocks. Ebenezer Trask and wife dined here and sett out for Mr Babcocks. I went to Mr Pierces. Helpt dress the child's Burns. Came home, finisht washing.

In addition to the "children," eleven persons are mentioned in this entry. Ten were relatives or relatives of relatives. Martha's web now included in addition to her own family (Pollards, Ballards, and Lambards), Sally's kin (the Pierces, Trasks, and Babcocks). Even more important, there had been a shift in generations. All the families mentioned in this entry were relatively young and as a consequence had scores of children among them. "I have felt very unwel but have had the nois of Children out of 5 famelys to Bear," Martha wrote on April 14. "Some fighting, some playing and not a little profanity has been performd. My son and his wife have spent a part of the day at Jason Pierces."

On April 19, Sally gave birth to her sixth son and ninth child. Her next-youngest child, two-year-old Martha, "past 7 worms" on April 23 and three on April 25. On April 26, Martha summarized what had become the pattern of her life, "I have Nurst some, workt some in the door yard, Cleand the Chambers and washt some. It is 9 weaks and 4 days since I saw my husband but hear he is wel for which I would Bless God."

Then, on May 7, without elaborating, she wrote, "Mr. Partridge here to see my son. O that he would make a settlement with his Dear Father without A Law Sute." Apparently the debt to the town had been paid. Now Ephraim was liable for sheriff's fees and his jail expenses. Probably he expected Jonathan to pay them. Why a lawsuit was threatened we do not know; perhaps

Ephraim had turned over the house in compensation and his son had failed to follow through. On May 25, Martha "went to the Jail and slept with my Husband." Three days later, he was still "not Liberated yet." Finally, on May 29, Election Day, "My Husband was sett at Liberty."

Together at last, Martha and Ephraim celebrated with a dinner of new greens and vinegar and made peace with daughter Ballard by inviting her to tea. But if Martha thought her husband's release would remove Jonathan's family from the house, she was mistaken. On June 7, "Daughter Ballard told me if I wanted the privaledge of my house I should not have it this sumer. I Coald wish to see peace." On July 27, "Jonas wife has shewn her tantrums. I could wish it might be the will of God that I might see other treatment." On August 11, "I could not sleep for noise in Jonathans famely. I rose lit my Candle & wrote this."

On August 27, the summer almost over, Martha reported that a man had come to dig a cellar by the shop and that men were "giting timber for a hous phraim." Jonathan and Sally had decided to build a house of their own, though not soon enough for their mother's comfort. She began going to their old house, now vacant, to work and think. On September 11, she wrote, "Jonathans wife Calld me a liar &c May God forgiv her. It would make a heathen Blussh to read the whole she said if I should write it." The next day, she went to the old house to twist yarn, "Have been insulted, the door fastened upon on me twice &c. I have need of Patience and Grace to bear it." The conflict had probably become as difficult for Sally. On September 14, Martha wrote, "Son Jonathan's famely removd from here to his old house." She celebrated by cleaning her bedroom and buttery and moving furniture.

On September 22, she "attended divine service." The Reverend Mr. Parker preached from the Book of Acts, and, to her great comfort, "he allso shewed the Duties we ought to perform and shew they would be our Comfort in this life and our Everlasting happiness in that which is to Com. I Could wish it might have been the lot of all my Children to have heard him, but God is able to teach the heart. I pray he might."

* * *

Most historians have studied imprisonment for debt as an aspect of economic and legal history. Martha's diary shifts the focus from mortgages and lawyers to wood boxes and sons, showing how family history shaped patterns of imprisonment in an era of political and social transformation, and, conversely, how a volatile economy shaped family relations. The first half of Martha's diary, written when her family's productive power was at its height, portrays a self-confident and vigorous woman managing a household, acting autonomously, and trading with her neighbors. The second half shows how illness, fatigue, and an unlucky move could shatter such a world, expose a woman's dependence, and force her to lean on the uncertain arm of family affection.

Martha referred to the family tumults of 1804–1805 as "scenes." "What a scean had I to go at Evening," she wrote on the day Jonathan attempted to whip Lemuel Witham. "It was yesterday this sien past," she wrote in the margin of the entry regarding the pig's potatoes. A scene was a wrenching event, a break in the flow of life. Unlike a day of accomplishment in which one could list tasks performed, some part of the world overcome and brought into order, it was over in a moment; yet it brought a fatigue deeper than any journey across the river or sojourn in the garden, a fatigue so draining that one did not want to lift one's head from the pillow.

In the next year, "the most shocking scene that was ever seen in this part of the world" convulsed Martha's neighborhood and all the country around. Shocking because it was so complete in its horror and so totally unexpected. There was nothing at all in Martha's quiet entries for the spring of 1806 to presage a mass murder, nothing to distinguish the Purrintons from any of the other neighbors on Belgrade Road.

CHAPTER NINE

APRIL 1806

"Polly Purington here"

1   3   *At home*
Clear and spring like. Grew cold at Evening. Snowd some. I
have been at home. Irond my cloaths &c.

2   4   *At home*
Clear and very Cold. Mr Ballard been to the meddow Lott.
Finds treaspas has been made thereon. He went to the settlement. Ben & Lafaett got up some wood for us. I have wound
3 skeins hoes yarn, wound & doubled 3 ditto.

3   5   *At home. Son Lambard sleeps here. Mrs Hartwell calld in this
day.*
Clear and not so Cold. Mr Ballard to meeting. It [is] Fast day.
Cyrus Came home and went to meeting. Sons Jonathan & Lambard Came here at Evening. The Latter sleeps here. Informs that
his Famely are wel Except Barny who has had the misfortune
to hurt one of his Eyes by a fall.

4   6   *At home. Mrs Wiman to see me.*
Clear and more moderate. Jason Pierce, William Cypher & John
Pierce workt for us this forenoon giting wood. Mrs Wiman

made me a visit afternoon. I have not felt so well as I could
wish.

5   7   *At home.*
Clear. I have been at home. Mr Ballard to the settlement to be
shaved.

6   1   *At home*
Clear. Mr Ballard & Cyrus to meeting. Reverend Mr Stone Discoarsed from John 5 Chapter 9th vers. Mrs Heartwel here with
her Babe.

7   2   *At home. Mr Ballard to Town meeting.*
Cloudy the most of the day. Mr Ballard to Town meeting. I
have twisted 11 knots hoes yarn and mended 3 pair hoes for my
husband and done other matters. Mr Ballard bot 2 lb sugar.

8   3   *At home.*
Raind all day. Mr Heartwel in here. I have been mend[ing] hoes
for my husband & Cyrus.

9   4   *At home. Mr Ballard made new tinnants to a Bedsted*
Snowd all day. I have done my houswork and knit a mitten for
Cyrus Except the thumb. Betsy Wiman brot 6 knots wik yarn
her marm has spun for me. Meriah here. Says her marm is unwell. Hannah Ballard here for Tanzy for Samuel. Says he is very
unwell. Pukt up a worm.

10   5   *At home. Hannah here. Says Samuel is very unwell yet.*
Clear some part of the day and very Cold. Mr Ballard went to
son Jonathans. Made a head bord for the Beadsted he fixt yesterday. I took down that in my Bedroom and put that which he
has altered. Finisht the mitt I began yesterday and knit part of
another. Polly Purington here for herbs for her marm who is
unwell. Meriah here. Says her marm is some better.

11   6   *At Mr Heartwells. His wife unwel.*
Clear forenoon. Cloudy afternoon. Very cold. Mr Ballard been
to the settlement. Bot 1 bushel Corn for the sheep, price 6 s. I
went to see Mrs Heartwel. She is unwel. Funeral of Mr Childs
youngest Child.

12   7   *At home. Did my washing.*
Clear part of the day and very cold. I have done my washing
and other matters. Mr Ballard been to the settlement. Brot home
1 gn spirit, 1 qt Jinn, 4 lb pork, 2 ditto Butter & 1 skein Black
silk.

13   1   *At home.*
Clear and cold. Mr Ballard & Cyrus went to meeting. Reverend
Mr Stone delivered a discoars forenoon on the death of Mr
Childs youngest child from 2nd Samuel 12 Chapter 23 verse. I
have been at home. Mr Heartwel here. Says his wife is better.

14   2   *At home*
Clear and not so cold. I have washt and fixt my old gownd
waist. Mr Ballard took Care of the Barn and cut wood. Mrs
Smith here. Wanted herbs. Her Babe has the Canker.

The April 1806 entries show how a small neighborhood was
developing around the crook of the road on the Ballard farm.
When Jonathan and Sally moved into their new house, they
leased the old one to the Hartwells. "Mr Hartwell began a
school this day at the house where he resides, where Jonathan
formerly lived," Martha wrote on December 31, 1805. About
the same time, Jonathan sold Dean Wyman a still older house
at the south end of his property, perhaps the one he and Sally
had lived in when they first moved to the farm.[1] The Wymans
and Hartwells were good neighbors, ready to send small presents or exchange work. "Betsy Wiman brot 6 knots wik yarn

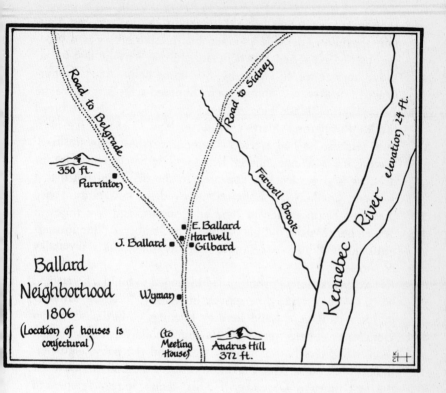

Road to Belgrade

Road to Sidney

Fatwell Brook

Kennebec River elevation 24 ft.

350 ft.
Purrinton

• E. Ballard
J. Ballard • • Hartwell
• Gilbard

Ballard
Neighborhood
1806
(Location of houses is
conjectural)

Wyman •

(to
Meeting
House)

Andrus Hill
372 ft.

her marm has spun for me," Martha wrote on April 9, adding that "Meriah," one of the Hartwell girls, had also been there. Because the Hartwells lived so close, they were frequent callers, coming more often than Jonathan or Sally, who now lived down the road a way. There were others in the neighborhood as well, a family named Gilbert who did not appear very promising to Martha, though she looked forward to getting to know the Purrintons, who lived up the road toward Belgrade.

James Purrinton first appeared in Martha's diary in the spring of 1803. "Mr. Purington here," she wrote on April 13, as though he were an old and familiar neighbor. Perhaps she *had* made his acquaintance earlier. He had come from Bowdoinham, a town at the mouth of the Kennebec that had contributed many settlers to Augusta, including her old neighbors the Densmores. Captain Purrinton (the title signified his militia rank) was a prosperous and respected Bowdoinham citizen. Why he decided to move upriver we do not know. Sometime before 1803, he purchased Lot #17, an "unimproved" hundred acres just above the Ballard farm. "Made Flower Bread for my self & Brown bread for Mr Purington," Martha wrote on May 6, 1803. Like most new settlers, he had erected a temporary shelter on his land, leaving his wife and children behind while he cleared space for a house and garden. He appeared in the diary ten times that summer. On May 21, Ephraim surveyed the new farm. Twice that month, once each in June and August, and five times in September, Martha did his baking. On October 4, "Mr Purington Paid me 6/7 for Bakeing for him this sumer and 2/ for stalks & shock."[2]

Two years later, Purrinton had managed to build a house and barn. In August 1805, he moved his family. "Two of Mr Purington's daughters Calld here at Evening," Martha wrote on October 21. There were eight Purrinton children, four sons and three daughters big enough to work, and the baby, eighteen-month-old Louisa. Mrs. Purrinton came to the Ballard house for the first time on December 13. She didn't appear again until May, though the visits from the children continued.

"Captain Purington's little sons [here] for herbs for their marm, shee being unwel," Martha wrote on February 18. On April 20, nineteen-year-old Polly, the oldest daughter, came on the same errand. The mother's illnesses may have impeded her ability to move around the neighborhood, yet they were not severe enough to demand a house call from Martha. Perhaps Mrs. Purrinton was simply too busy to visit. She had work enough to engage her at home—there were two spinning wheels and tackling for weaving in the house, though the old loom was still in Bowdoinham. Ten lambs, seven piglets, and several calves were born that spring, and the garden needed planting. Seventeen-year-old James came to the Ballard house with his friend Peter Wyman on May 3 "for Balm Giliad, apple trees, & Curent Bushes." On May 7, Mrs. Purrinton once again stopped in at the Ballards' for tea. Two days later, the Captain took time from his own work to carry Martha to and from a delivery. Gradually, the new family was taking its place in the neighborhood, weaving in and out of Martha's diary with other near neighbors—the Hartwells, Wymans, and Gilberts. As new families settled in the area, it seemed less isolated, less limited to Ballards and Pierces, than before.

On the town tax inventory for 1805, James Purrinton is credited with 100 acres of unimproved land. A year later, he had cleared six acres—two of tillage, four of pasture—a respectable ratio in this part of the world. Jonathan Ballard still had only three acres of tillage, four of mowing, and ten of pasture on his 200-acre farm.[3] By all accounts, the Captain was a sober and industrious man, if a bit taciturn. He had a modest wife, strong sons and daughters, a sturdy house, good oxen, and a reliable horse. To all appearances, his farm was one more patch of civilization in a neighborhood dark with trees.

Then came that terrible day, July 9, 1806:

Clear and warm. My Husband & I were awake at 3 hour this morning by Mrs Heartwel and Gillbard who brot us the horrible tydings that Captain Purington had murdered all his famely Except his son James who must have shared the same fate had he not been so fortunate as to make his Escape after an attempt was made to take his life. He was wounded with an ax. He fled in his shirt only and alarmd Mr Wiman of the horrid scein who immediately ran to son Jonathans. They two went to house where the horrid scein was perpetrated. My son went in and found a Candle, which he lit and to his great surprise said Purington, his wife, & six Children Corps! and Martha he perceived had life remaining who was removd to his house. Surgical aid was immediately Calld and she remains alive as yet. My husband went and returned before sunrise when after taking a little food he and I went on to the house there to behold the most shocking scein that was Even seen in this part of the world. May an infinitely good God grant that we may all take a sutable notis of this horrid deed, learn wisdom therefrom. The Corps were removd to his Barn where they were washt and Laid out side by side. A horrid spectakle which many hundred persons Came to behold. I was there till near night when Son Jonathan Conducted me to his house and gave me refreshment. The Coffins were brot and the Corps Carried in a Waggon & deposited in Augusta meeting hous.

Martha's account is vivid yet compact. As in the best folk narrative, a few details speak for the whole—James fled "in his shirt only," Jonathan "found a Candle, which he lit," the bodies were laid out "side by side" in the barn. Even the religious gloss is brisk. God is "infinitely good" regardless of what his children do. Good Christians can "learn wisdom" even from terror.

The economy of Martha's telling contrasts with the more self-conscious narrative published (and probably composed) by Peter Edes, editor of Augusta's *Kennebec Gazette*. Edes titled his broadside "Horrid Murder," embellishing the margins with a ring of dark coffins. Like Martha, he described Jonathan lighting a candle at the scene, a detail that must have been repeated over and over in the telling of the story, but he went further. Where Martha had been content with the single exclamation "Corps!," Edes went on to describe the dimly lit scene, body by body. The father lay in the outer room, "Prostrate on his face, and weltering in his gore," the bloody razor with which he cut his throat lying on a table by his side. "In an adjoining bed room lay Mrs. Purrinton in her bed with her head almost severed from her body; and near her on the floor, a little daughter about ten years old, who probably hearing the cries of her mother, ran to her relief from the apartment in which she slept, and was murdered by her side."[4]

In the "outer room" with Purrinton lay two little boys, one eight, one six. A third brother, age twelve, was found in an adjoining room, fallen on the hearth, with his trousers under one arm. "On the breastwork over the fire place, was the distinct impression of a bloody hand, where the unhappy victim probably supported himself before he fell." The boy apparently slept with his brother James, age seventeen, who had heard his mother's cries and rushed to the door of his room, where "he was met by his father with an axe in his hand." In "another apartment" were found the two oldest daughters and the youngest, the first "dreadfully butchered; the second desperately wounded, reclining her head on the body of the dead infant 18 months old, and in a state of horror and almost total insensibility."[5]

Edes's account discloses Martha's restraint. There are no severed heads or sheets soaked in blood in her story, though, having helped to lay out the bodies, she knew as well as any what condition they were in, and certainly she was one of the first to hear Jonathan tell what the candle revealed. With remarkable economy, her account composed the raw reality into a few telling images.

Her description of the funeral, held on July 10, has the same qualities. She began as in any other funeral entry in the diary, by naming the minister and the text; but as she wrote, the details quickly overwhelmed her form, drawing forth another tightly constructed narrative.

Cloudy, raind afternoon. My husband and I attended at the sollom funeral of James Purington & his famely which he murdered. There was a prayer made by Reverend Mr. Stone, a discoarse delivered by a Mr Taylor from Proverbs 25 C 28 V—he that hath no rule over his own spirit is like a city broken down and with[out] walls. There were a vast number of people attended. The performance was on a stage which was Erected before the meeting house. The houses near were Crowded, the street Crowded & the tops of Buildings Covered with people. Said Puringtons remains were Lodged in the Porch with the ax & raisor which he made use of to deprive his famely & himself of life on his Coffin, his Dear wife & 6 Childrens remains laid in the ally before the Boddy Pews. A sollom specttacle to behold. May we all learn a profitable lesson from this dreadful scein

and may it pleas the God that rules [to] Sanctify this affliction to the surviving relatives and to us all. The funeral
proseeded from the meeting hous, went over Kenebeck
Bridg, then turned and went up the hill south and down
second street, turned at the Jail, & went to the grave yard.
He was interd without the wall.

Martha's prayer that God might "Sanctify this affliction to the
surviving relatives and to us all" no doubt echoed Mr. Taylor's
sermon—and hundreds of others she had heard in her seventy-
one years. It wasn't the sermon, however, but the pageantry of
the occasion that impressed her most powerfully, the ritualistic
arrangement of the bodies, the funeral march, and the hundreds
of people crowded in nearby houses, in the street, on the tops
of the buildings. There had not been an event like this in Augusta since the commemoration of President Washington's
death six years before. Martha had attended that ceremony, too,
had noted the presence of the militia and a "larg concoarce of
people," but, unlike Henry Sewall, who had devoted two pages
of his diary to the parade, had felt no need to describe it. This
time she marked the route of the parade with great precision,
carefully noting the march down Second Street to the jail, a
purposeful and highly symbolic digression.

From the meeting house, past the wharves and stores, across
the bridge, past the courthouse and jail, to the grave, the funeral
procession recapitulated all the emblems of social order—ecclesiastical, commercial, and civil. Edes's broadside gave the order
in which the marchers were arranged:

Senior Marshal,
The Coroner, and Inquest,
Rev. Mr. Haskell, Rev. Mr. Stone,
The Corpse of Mrs. Purrinton,
And her six children, according to their ages,
supported by bearers attended by pall holders,
followed by the surviving Son
and other relations.

Other relations, selectmen, clergy, sheriffs of the county,
judges of the courts, military officers, magistrates,
citizens and marshall.
A cart bearing the body of Captain Purrinton.

Everything about the procession reaffirmed the principle of order. Even the bodies of the children were ranked "according to
their ages." The coroner and jury of inquest—citizens charged
with establishing the cause of death—led the procession, followed by victims, close relatives, and, in Edes's phrase, "various
classes of citizens properly arranged." The parade, like the arrangement in the church and the burials themselves, placed Purrinton outside the civil community. He lay in the porch of the
church, his family within. Their coffins were borne by their
neighbors, framed in the protective custody of clergy, magistrates, militia, and citizenry; his lay, untouchable, on a cart at
the rear of the parade. They were buried within the yard; he
was "interd without the wall," literally dumped from the wagon
into the waiting hole. The ritual was impressive because the
need for it was so intense. The ordering of the procession transformed a horrid scene into a solemn spectacle, an event from
which one might take instruction.

What was there to learn from the Purrinton murders? For
contemporaries, the most accessible mode of analysis was religious. Martha used much the same language in commenting on
this event as on any other unexpected and troublesome death in
the diary. When her little grandson, Samuel Adams Ballard, died
on November 28, 1806, she wrote, "May the God of mercy
sanctyfy his Chastisements for our Everlasting good." That is,
God as the controlling power in the universe allowed death and
sorrow but also provided ways to transform those events into
good. She expressed much the same sentiment regarding the
Purrinton murders: "May an infinitely good God grant that we
may all take a sutable notis of this horrid deed, learn wisdom
therefrom," or, on the day of the funeral, "May we all learn a
profitable lesson from this dreadful scein and may it pleas the
God that rules [to] Sanctify this affliction to the surviving rela-

tives and to us all." The essential point was that God was in control, that he had the power to "sanctify" as well as to destroy.

For some of her contemporaries, the lessons were more complex. By 1806, religious dissent in the region had increased. New sects were growing surprisingly strong, making the old divisions among Congregationalists seem tame. In 1780, all the churches in Lincoln County, whatever the differences among them, had been Congregational; by 1800, in the by then two counties of Lincoln and Kennebec, sectarian churches—Separate Baptist, Free-will Baptist, Methodist, and Universalist—outnumbered orthodox congregations by almost three to one.[6] Henry Sewall was not entirely pleased with the ecumenical element of the Purrinton funeral. "The funeral of those unhappy victims was attended from the meetinghouse by a vast concourse of people," he began.

A sermon &c was performed on a stage in front of the meeting house *by a Methodist* [added above the line] & the funeral service performed at the grave by Rev. Mr. Haskell & after the procession had returned to the Meeting house, the scene was closed by an appropriate prayer from Rev. Mr. Gillet. The murderer was distinguished from the other victims in the manner & place of his burial—being drawn on a horse cart, & buried in the highway without the burying yard.

Sewall's account is the only one to give prominence to Mr. Gillet, whose prayer Martha (and others who did not take the long trek back to the meeting house) may have missed. Eliphalet Gillet was, of course, the single local minister of whom Sewall fully approved. The interpolation "by a Methodist" suggests he did not know—or care to know—Joshua Taylor. Martha did. She showed no interest in the Methodist movement herself, though several members of her family were attracted to it. Even Jonathan had occasionally attended Methodist meetings at Mr. Ingraham's barn, and Dolly Lambard and an Oxford cousin had attended the Methodist quarterly meeting held in Augusta in 1804.[7]

It was inevitable that the Purrinton murders should feed into the growing anxiety over religious dissent in the region. Congregationalists along the Kennebec continued to squabble among themselves while Methodists, Free-Will Baptists, Universalists, and even Shakers took their members. Martha's neighbors were among those affected. "There were 6 persons Baptised by imertion at Sidney," she wrote on August 4, 1805. "Mrs Andrus was one." James Purrinton, it was said, had dabbled in more than one heterodox creed.

Edes's broadside had noted that the murderer was "a warm believer in the fatal doctrine of universal salvation," but made no effort to exploit the fact. Within days, Edes had accumulated enough additional information to amplify this explanation into a twenty-page pamphlet giving a more detailed account of the murder, a sketch of the life of Captain Purrinton, and "Remarks on the fatal tendency of erroneous principles, and Motives for receiving and obeying the pure and salutary precepts of the gospel." This version of the Purrinton story transformed it from a "Horrid Murder" in the penny-dreadful style into an object lesson in the dangers of religious dissent. "Unbelief in the superintending providence of God, and human accountability, is a principle which opens the door to every vice," the author argued. In a footnote, Edes quoted "a respectable gentleman in Bowdoinham" who affirmed that

about twenty years ago, he (Capt. P.) joined the (Calvinistic) Baptist Church in Bowdoinham, and continued in their fellowship several years; till he imbibed the sentiments of the Freewill Baptists; for which he was cut off from the church. He was not a Universalist till some years since. I have conversed with several of his former neighbors, who unanimously testify that he was a Fatalist.[8]

If Edes's account is correct, Purrinton's life recapitulated the religious history of the region. In towns like Bowdoinham, already split by Baptist and New Light revivals, the heterodox teachings of Free-Will Baptists and Universalists found fertile soil. Both groups challenged the central Calvinis God predestined some souls for salvation, others The Free-Will Baptists believed sinners chose to Christ's atonement; the Universalists argued th children would be saved. The emphasis of b "a benevolent God, human perfectability, univ atonement, and free grace for all believers" al liberal Arminians in New England's urban c pamphlet associated Purrinton's universalism with "the fearless impiety of a Paine and the unrestrained licentiousness of a Godwin"—yet both groups were evangelicals rather than rationalists. They were powerful precisely because they grafted their optimistic doctrines onto the experiential, charismatic religion familiar from earlier revivals. In the light of the Free-Will challenge, Bowdoinham's Calvinist Baptists described themselves as "a fold in the midst of wolves, or a defenceless flock surrounded with ... prowling multitudes."⁹

Of the two groups, the Universalists appeared most threatening because they undermined the socially useful distinction between the saved and the damned. (They were also the newest and least numerous of the sectarians.) How could society survive once the doctrine of an eternal judgment was destroyed? In a sermon preached at Bowdoinham ten days after the murders, Timothy Merritt argued that the first and moving cause of Purrinton's murders was disbelief in the Providence of God: "Though he died seizened of a large estate, he was under apprehensions that his family would come to want." But second only to his lack of faith in God's superintending care was his belief in the doctrine of universal salvation.

> You all know, that for some years past, he has professed to believe firmly that all mankind, immediately upon leaving the body, go to a state of the most perfect rest and enjoyment: and to my own certain knowledge he denied the doctrine of a day of judgment and retribution. Of course it was no question with him whether his family

were regenerate, or born again, or in other words, whether they were prepared for so sudden a remove from this world. It was, therefore, natural, and what any one would do under the same circumstances, to endeavour to prevent the anticipated trouble of his family, and make them all for ever happy. There is every reason to believe that this was his real motive.[10]

The Universalist explanation resolved the major contradictions in Purrinton's character—his presumed love for his family and his violence. Blaming *ideas* made the murders seem "natural," accessible to human comprehension: Purrinton did "what any one would do under the same circumstances." The moral was clear: sectarian teaching was an instrument of Satan. It could transform positive human attributes into heinous sins.

As a good Calvinist, Merritt could not let his congregation rest there, however. Purrinton's sins were natural because they mirrored the fundamental errors of humankind. Gently, he led his listeners from comfort to discomfort, from calm reassurance in the face of evil to jolting reminders of their own culpability. The murders forced Purrinton's neighbors to recognize the depravity of human nature, the frailty of life, and the folly of trusting in any earthly thing, including their nearest and dearest relations. "We may bolt our doors at night against thieves and robbers; but bolts are no security to life;—the assassin is within."

This is not said with a view to excite jealousies and fears between friends and connections; nor to destroy that subordinate confidence which husband and wife, parents and children, reasonably repose in each other; but merely to shew you your real circumstances, and bring you to put your highest trust in God alone, where it ought to be placed.

Merritt urged his listeners to become fathers and mothers, brothers and sisters, to young James Purrinton, the sole survivor, but he also warned James to put his first trust in God. Nor did he fail to remind him that now that his father, mothers, and brothers and sisters were all dead, he would soon come into possession of a considerable estate. "I entreat you to consider your danger . . . let it never be said that, the oldest son, and only surviving member of Capt. Purrinton's family has become a *rake*." [11]

If given the opportunity to answer Merritt's accusations, the Universalists surely would have argued that the doctrine of universal salvation nurtured righteousness rather than sin, that their teachings were no more to blame for Purrinton's murders than Congregationalist doctrine for Henry McCausland's slaughter of Abigail Warren thirteen years before. Universalists would have disdained Calvinist efforts to breed fear in the hearts of their listeners; surely a true knowledge of God's love was a more powerful motive for good than an erroneous fear of God's wrath. [12] Despite differences in emphasis, however, the arguments of both groups began at the same point—predestination—and ended with the same consolation—an ultimate trust in God's goodness.

The oral history of Universalism contains an account of a triumphant sermon preached by Father Barnes of Poland, Maine, when all the Congregational ministers in the region refused to officiate at the funeral of a suicide. The theme of Barnes's sermon— "when all the designs of God in apparent ills are seen through, and his benevolent purposes understood, all that is now dark will become light"—is ultimately indistinguishable from Merritt's argument—"When we see that God has suffered these evils, which he could have prevented, to come upon us, we are to conclude that he has acted upon some wise and benevolent principle, worthy of himself." [13] God is all powerful and all good. We must submit to his judgments. It is that theology which underlies the religious sentiments in Martha's diary: "May an infinitely good God grant that we may all take a sutable notis of this horrid deed, learn wisdom therefrom."

The Purrinton tragedy is a grotesque, an outlandish distension of the ordinary. Timothy Merritt understood how to reconnect the bizarre and the commonplace, how to read through the sensational to dark—but common—truths about human nature. James Purrinton committed horrid sins: without God all of us are depraved. Mrs. Purrinton and her children died violently: all of us are subject to sudden death. A husband turned on his wife, a father on his children: all natural relations are secondary to the relation with God.

Merritt's method transcends his content. Interpreted with a different set of first principles, the Purrinton murders yield different lessons. Suppose the overarching concern was not the relation of believers and God but that of men and women. A feminist gloss on the murders might read: a man murdered his wife and children: in the patriarchal family all members are subject to the will of the father. Elizabeth Pleck has argued that "The single most consistent barrier to reform against domestic violence has been the Family Ideal," a constellation of ideas that affirms the privacy of the individual household, the hierarchical orderings of relations among family members, and the indissolubility of marriage. Although the family ideal enjoins mutual obligations, as well as rights, it allows forms of tyranny more comprehensive than those exercised by the state. Even today, she explains, "in many areas of law a stranger is entitled to more legal protection than a family member." [14]

To sustain this interpretation of the murders, one need not imagine a long chain of physical abuse leading up to the final slaughter, though such a pattern is possible. Purrinton's steadiness, his prosperity, his regard for his family, also fit the argument. The primary obligation of a father was to provide economic support; the primary obligation of a wife and children to love, honor, and obey. A wife went where her husband beckoned—even in death. Among the end notes to Edes's pamphlet is the text of the suicide note Purrinton allegedly wrote on the Sunday before the murders:

Dear Brothers: These lines is to let you know that I am going a long journey, and I would have you sell what I have, and put it out to interest, and put out my boys to trades, or send them to sea.

I cannot see the distress of my family—God only knows my distress—I would have you put Nathaniel to uncle Purrinton, to a tanner's trade—I want James to go to school, until sufficient to attend in a store—Benjamin to a Blacksmith's trade, or to what you think best—But to be sure to give them learning, if it takes all—Divide what is left, for I am no more. James Purrinton [15]

Abandoning his sons, Purrinton cannot abandon the obligation (or need) to shape their destinies. He is compassionate and loving (their distress is his distress) and at the same time too focused on his own misery to endure. Delegating responsibility to his brother is apparently his solution to the dilemma. What is astonishing about the letter is his utter disregard for his wife and daughters. "My family," as he defined it, consisted of Nathaniel, James, and Benjamin, the three male children over the age of eight. Even five-year-old Nathan is ignored. Purrinton must have known the law would allow his wife the use of a third of his estate and some sort of support for the other children, yet his only acknowledgment of their existence is that terse last sentence, "Divide what is left."

According to Edes, it was the discovery of the suicide note by the daughter that led to the murders. When she asked her father what he was writing, "He replied nothing, and immediately asked for his butcher knife, and said he wanted to sharpen it." When she brought it to him, he "made it very sharp," then stood with it before the looking glass, seemingly preparing his throat for the knife. She was so alarmed by the incident, she reported it to her mother, who searched for the note. The Captain calmly explained that he had no intention of contemplating suicide but simply "a presentiment that his death was near." Edes concluded that it was the expression of "terror and alarm" on the part of the women that caused Purrinton to change his original plan, which was only to kill himself. "Seeing their distress, and anticipating how poignant it would be on his death, he no doubt determined to take them all with himself; believing they would thus lose their sorrows, suffer but a momentary pang, and be with him eternally happy." [16]

Edes's reconstruction of the event is shaped at every turn by the Family Ideal. No hint here that Purrinton deliberately terrorized his daughter by asking her to bring him the knife, that he wanted his wife to find the letter, that he deliberately used the threat of suicide to manipulate and control her. In this account, he appears as a loving, if deluded, father. Presumably, he resolved to move his family to Heaven, just as he had recently moved them from Bowdoinham to Augusta. Ironically, Edes made the mother and daughter responsible for their own deaths. It was their dismay—not Purrinton's inability to separate his will from theirs—that motivated the murders.

What James Purrinton believed or felt we will never know. He may have been propelled by Universalism, by an overweening patriarchy, by an unresolvable conflict between family obligation and personal despair—or by other motives we can only dimly glimpse. Curiously, none of the commentators made anything of the fact that at the time of the murders his Bible was open to the ninth chapter of Ezekiel:

> He cried also in mine ears with a loud voice, saying, Cause them that have charge over the city to draw near, even every man *with* his destroying weapon in his hand.... let not your eye spare, neither have ye pity: Slay utterly old *and* young, both maids, and little children, and women: but come not near any man upon whom *is* the mark.[17]

After all the lessons, neatly argued, we are left with a dark apocalyptic vision and an inexplicable slaughter.

"Polly Purington here." Martha's casual entry of the spring takes on a Gothic quality in light of the horror that followed. The name "Polly Purington" has an almost comic coziness, as though it belonged to a housewifely cat in some children's tale. It is not pleasant to think of Polly dead in bed with her wounded and murdered sisters. She was the oldest of the Purrinton daughters, the one who accompanied her mother to church while her father sharpened his ax. The neighbors believed she had at least some awareness of what was happening on that terrible night. As Edes explained it, "The oldest daughter and second son received many wounds in various parts of the body, which were probably caused by their resistance."[18]

Martha Purrinton, who shared a bed with Polly that night, lived long enough to describe the murder. She said she was awakened by the blows on her sister. Winding herself in the bedclothes, she felt blows on her head and arm. "Her father then left her, though at this time she did not know or suspect who it was. She remembers laying her head over the edge of the bed, and hearing (to use her own expression) the blood run like a brook upon the floor—that she felt the blood from her sister's wounds, and was convinced she was dead." When she heard Jonathan Ballard approaching, she cried, "Glory to God! Do kill me again."[19]

Martha was taken to Jonathan's house, and as the diary explained, "Surgical aid was immediately Calld." There seems to have been some hope of her recovery. When the appraisers came to inventory the estate on the day after the funeral, they reserved a dozen pair of stockings, five skirts, three "womans Gowns," four "short loose Gowns," four pockets, a short cloak, two shawls, four linen and one silk handkerchief, an overcoat, a pair of silk mitts, two pair of mittens, three woman's bonnets, a blue petticoat, and a gold ring for her, with a chest to keep them in.[20] She lay at Jonathan and Sally's house for three weeks. Her grandparents, Benjamin and Anna Clifford, offered what help they could, though Sally was probably responsible for nursing.[21]

Martha Ballard assumed a different set of responsibilities. The day after the funeral, she summarized her work of that day: "Mr. Purington, his two daughters, & James P took Breakfast. He [& *James* crossed out] dind. He & James supt and sleep here." The careful accounting was necessary since she and Ephraim would eventually make a claim on the estate for "boarding." Mr. Purrinton was the Captain's brother, Hezekiah. The whole group was back the next day. Martha got dinner for them and "then was allmost or rather quite giving up for a time," though she recovered enough to go to Jonathan's, where she received a pair of sheets and two shifts to replace those "which I Carried to Lay out the Dead." It was a clear day and hot enough to make cooking or walking uncomfortable. The Purrinton deaths had taken most of Martha's time now for four days and would continue to drain her energy for several more to come. Hezekiah and James slept at her house again on Sunday. She prepared supper for them and breakfast the next morning, after which they "left here Bound for Bodinham." She spent the rest of that day catching up on her dairying, churning three and a half pounds of butter, and making a cheese.

On Tuesday, she went to Jonathan's house. "Found Martha in a Low situation. Old Mr. Clifford there. I feel very feeble but have put a Barril of water to my plants." While the vigil continued at Jonathan's house, Martha and Ephraim tried to resume their lives. He went to the mill "to see about Boards to fens his Corn field"; she did her housework and "Bakt brown & flower Bread." He went to see a ship launching; she cleaned her cellar. Her lack of involvement in Martha Purrinton's care is striking. This disengagement was probably a mark of Sally's growing competence as a nurse as well as the continuing coolness between the two women. On July 23, after returning home from a delivery, Martha again went to her son's. Her comment—"I saw Martha Purington's wounds Dresst"—is ambiguous. Does the verb *saw* describe the role of an observer or an overseer?

She did not return. Her account of the young woman's demise was secondhand: July 28, "We hear that Martha is no better." July 29, "We hear that Martha Purington is near the Close of Life." July 30, "Martha Purington Expired at 3 hour this morning." July 31, "I have felt very unwel but went to son Jonathan's to see the Corps of Martha Purrington. Patty Town went & helpt my daughter sew. Mr. Purington & Son took supper and Lodging here. Paty slept up Chamber." Then, on August 1, the day of the young woman's funeral:

Mr. Purington took Breakfast. They & Mr. Cliford, Getchel and a young man who lives with Mr. Getchel dind. Daughter Pollard and Patty & Jonathan Ballard Junior dind also. We all attended the funeral of Martha Purington. Mr. Merrit discoarsed from Job 1st C 20–21 vers. Then Job arose and rent his mantle and shaved his head and fell down upon the ground and worshiped and said, Naked Caim I out of my Mothers womb, and Naked shall I return thither, the Lord gave and the Lord hath taken away. Blessed be the name of the Lord.

For Martha the minister's text bore a deep resonance. As a midwife, she understood both the coming forth and the returning.

For most of the town, the Purrinton story ended there. For Martha's neighborhood, however, there would be a long forgetting. Although Edes's writings had made public all there was to tell about the family, codified the neighborly discussions in Bowdoinham and Augusta, and settled the Captain's story, it would take longer for the women who knew them to forget the quiet man and his family, to reconcile the terrible murder with the ordinariness of their outward behavior in the months before. A single, taciturn entry, written two weeks after the murders, while Martha Purrinton still lay dying at Jonathan's house, suggests the anxiety and guilt many must have experienced: "Mrs Heartwell calld over for some one to run, for Gilbard had allmost killd his wife. I went but did not find any one killd or hurt with any thing but spirit which is often the Case there."[22]

Mrs. Hartwell and Gilbert had come together on July 9 to tell the Ballards of the Purrinton deaths. Now one woman had begun to fear for the other. Martha's brisk dismissal of the problem suggests she was unwilling to generalize, little disposed to translate a tragedy in one house into potential danger in another. "There was a great noise at Gilberts," she had written on June 10, a month before the murders. Drunken fights were one of the annoyances of the neighborhood. But the larger record of the diary, the quiet succession of comings and goings during the next few months, suggests she was more affected than she knew.

Mrs. Wyman and Mrs. Hartwell had been the most frequent visitors to Martha's house in 1805–1806. In contrast, there are only five entries for any member of the Gilbert family in the entire year before the murder. In the five months after, however, there are twelve. Before Mrs. Hartwell summoned her on July 24, Martha had herself never been to the Gilberts' house. In the next few months, she went twice. Even more important, she found ways to encourage the other woman to visit her. What is especially striking about the two visits to the Gilberts' is that Martha seems to have gone, not on a medical call, her usual reason for leaving home during this period of her life, but simply to sit and stay. "I went afternoon to help Mrs Gilbard quill," she wrote on September 26, mentioning an activity she hadn't been engaged in for years. Whether consciously or not, Martha helped to weave the troubled woman into the neighborhood. "Mrs Gilbard Came and took my Black Cloak home. Shee mend it [blot] and brot it home. Her Demand was 1 shilling. I gave her 1.6."[23] Little wonder that on December 6, "Mrs Gillbard made me a present of an Oring, some Cakes & Chees." As usual, Martha revealed less in what she said than in what she did.

On December 19, 1806, Martha wrote, "This day is the anaversary of my Marriage 51 years since. O the seins which have past since that time. I lay museing thereon and slept but little." In half a century, she had experienced many tumultuous scenes —the throat distemper that had taken her little girls, the removal to the Kennebec in the midst of revolution, the troubling journey to Pownalboro for the trial of Judge North, the attacks on Ephraim, and more births, illnesses, deaths, hailstorms, blizzards, and floods than she could remember. Now, in her own neighborhood, this "horrid scene."

There would be more. On March 15, just eight months after the Purrinton slaughter, Martha was called across the river in haste:

We were informd about 10 hour this morn that our friend Charles Gill had Cutt his Throat with a Shave in so horrable a manner that no hopes of his life remain. May God of his infinite goodness support his wife and all connections in this dreadful tryal. I went to his hous about 1 o Clock, found he was Expired. He had his sense & wrote some lines. Mrs Gills Tryal is all most insupportable.

Mrs. Gill was Betsy Barton, the niece who had married Charles Gill ten years before at the Ballard house. Betsy had nine children, two by her first husband and seven by Gill. He died insolvent. Yet Martha made no effort to condemn the man. Her major concern was for Betsy. "Her trial is *all most* insupportable," she wrote, unwilling to give up on Betsy's faith or her own.

Henry Sewall, who was a near neighbor, described the event this way:

> About 8 in the morning the neighbourhood was alarmed with a cry of murder! It proved to be Mr. Charles Gill, who had cut his own throat in a shocking manner with a draw shave. I saw him after the horrid deed was committed—& was astonished at his composure—or rather stupidity—which continued to the last. He died about 1 o'clock, without manifesting any signs of repentence.

Martha stayed with her niece all night, then came home, bringing her own grandchildren Barney and Lucy Lambard with her. "Grammer School house Consumed by fire," she wrote in the margin of that day's entry. On March 17, Sewall reported "Mr Gill was buried. The verdict of a Jury of Inquest on his body was wilful & premeditated murder." Martha wrote, simply, "Son Cyrus Came home. His Father & he & Allin Lambard attended funeral. I did not feel able to attend myself."

The next day brought more bad news, enough to overwhelm her already overworked stock of religious sentiments. "Mr Heartwel informed me that Benjamin Petty was dead. His death was ocationed by Nathaniel Dinglys Strikeing him with an adds. What are we cuming to in this Eastern world?" That is a question she might have asked again and again in the next five years. And yet, as her own life drew to a close, Martha found an eye of peace in a heroic commitment to her neighbors and in a passionate, almost lyrical devotion to the small patch of earth for which she was responsible.

CHAPTER TEN

MAY 1809

"Workt in my gardin"

1 2 *At John Shaws. Birth 2nd. June 16th receivd 7s and 6d of Mr Shaw.*
Clear. I was Calld about midnight to John Shaws wife who is in Labour. Shee was safe delivered at 8 hour this morning of her 2nd Child and daughter. I returned home about noone. Mr Ballard went to Town meeting. Magr Samuel Howard was Chosen to represent the Town in general Coart.
Birth John Shaws daughter [illegible]

2 3 *At home. Feel unwell. Patty T Came here.*
Clear. I have been doing work about my soap. Feel very feeble. My husband been to Hallowell. Patty Town Came here at Evening.

3 4 *At home. Daughter Ballard sent us 4 1/4 lb. chees.*
Clear and warm. I have helpt do my hous work. Patty washt and Cleand bed rooms. We removd Cyrus Bed and Chest up Chamber. Mrs Smith & Brooks Calld here. Inform me Mrs Mosier is very sick.

4 5 *At Daughter Lambards and Mr Mosiers.*
Cloudy and some rain. I went to Daughter Lambards. Calld to see Mrs Mosier. Find her very sick.

5   6   *At Daughter Lambards. To Lecture & son Ephraims.*
Rained part of the day. I went to Lecture from daughter Lambards. From there to son Ephraims. Sleep there.

6   7   *At Son Ephraims & Mr Hamlins. Hear Mrs Mosier is wors*
Clear. I am at Son Ephraims and Mr Hamlins. Mrs Farewell & Daughter Lambard, Theophilus Hamlins wife, her daughter Sally & Mrs Carter took Tea there. I slept at son Ephraims.

7   8   *At son Ephraims. Mrs Pipers & daughter Lambards. Birth 3d. Receivd 9 shillings at Babcocks, 24 instant.*
Clear part of the day. I was Calld from son Ephraims to Mr Pipers Early this morn. His wife in Labour. Shee was delivered of a son, her 5th Child at 12 O Clock. We took dinner & I left them. Went to Daughter Lambards. Tarri all night. Henry had a very sick night. I did not undres but slept some. Sophia Gill slept there. My daughter been to see Mrs Mosier. Finds her very sick.
Birth Mr Pipers son & 5th Child. X X

8   2   *At Daughter Lambards, Son Jonathans, & Mr Pipers.*
Rainy. I was at dagter Lambards forenoon. Had a hors brot and went home. Call into Son Jonathans. Took Tea. Mr Ballard allso. Ephraim & William slept here. Jack Came after we were in bed. Slept here.

9   3   *At home. Workt in gardin. Sophia & Dolly sleep here.*
Clear part of the day. I have sett Turnips & Cabbage stumps. Daughter Ballard here. Her son Jonathan Came & informd he had shipt for Liverpoole. Setts out tomorrow. Sophia Gill & Dolly Lambard sleep here.

10   4   *At home. Mrs Emry here. Girls went home after breakfast. Jonathan Ballard sett out to go to sea.*
Cloudy the most of the day. I have done hous work. Planted Cucumbers & three kinds squash. Removd Banking from the house &c. Knit some. Mrs Emry to see me. The girls left here this morn.

Mrs Emry, two of William Stones daughters had gardin seeds of me. Mr Ballard workt at son Jonathans. Jack sett out for sea.

11   5   *At home. I brewed.*
Cloudy. I have done houswork. Brewed. Mr Ballard workt at son Jonathans forenoon, went to sett hoops for Daughter Lambard afternoon. Informs Patty is very Lambe in her hand.

12   6   *At home. Bakt & planted squash & Cucumbers.*
Cloudy the most of the day. I have done hous work. Bakt brown Bread. Have not felt well. Mr Ballard mending fence round the gardin. Ephraim & William sleep here.

13   7   *At home. Mr Ballard to Hallowell. Had of Mr Lad 1/2 lb Tea, 2 lb Sugar, & 6 alwives. Deaths.*
Cloudy the most of the day. I have fixt a bed, planted squash seeds and removd part of the Banking from East side the hous. Mr Bullin here, informed that his son Jessy buried his youngest Child yesterday. Rhoda Pollard sleeps here. Informed that Old Mr Bisbee is dead. Patty Town is very Lambe. Hannah Ballard & William sleep here.

14   1   *At home. Rhoda left here after dinner.*
Cloudy part of the day. Raind some. Mr Ballard to meeting. Reverend Mr Stone discoarst from Romans 1st Chapter 28th vers. Hannah Ballard & Getchel Calld here. Ephraim & William sleep here.

15   2   *At home. Jonathan Junior returnd. Could not get a Chance to go to sea.*
Clear part of the day. Showers afternoon. I have dug ground west of the hous. Planted squash, Cucumbers, musk and water mellons East side house. Began and finisht a Large wash after 3 O Clock. Feel fatagued. Son Jonathan ploughing our field. My husband workt with him.

17   4   *At home. Son Town left here this morning. Mr Ballard is 84 years this day. Death Mr Hains.*
Clear, warm and spring like. I have workt in my gardin. Planted long squash by the hogg pen, sowd pepper grass, sett sage and other roots. Mr. Ballard mode Bush & dugg gardin. I washt his & Cyrus's old over Coats, my gound & other things. Son Jonathan had 6 Oxen taken by Execution and drove away. I do feel for but am not able to help him. Ephraim & William Sleep here.

18   5   *At home. Hear that Mrs Mosier is no Better.*
Clear. I workt in my garden. Sett Parsley & 3 quins trees by the pigg pen. Knit some &c. Mr Ballard diging gardin & setting hop poles. Ephraim sleeps here.

19   6   *At home. Mr [blot]*
Clear & warm. I have workt in the gardin, knit some, boiling soap. Jonathan Junior sleeps here. Mr. Wiman made us a present of 12 fish.

20   7   *At home. Company here. Jonathans wife gave us Butter.*
Clear. I have ironed & workt in gardin. Daughter Lambard sent me 3 Lb. pork. Mrs Farewell, Daughter Ballard & 3 Children, Patty Town took Tea here.

21   1   *At home. Son Ephraims wife and Patty Town here.*
Clear & warm. Mr Ballard went to meeting. Walkt. Son Ephraims wife Came here before noone. Shee & Patty Town took supper with us. We are informd that Mrs. Mosier is more Comfortable. Pattys hand is better. The text from Hebrews 12, 3 vers, afternoon Psalms 62nt, 8 vs.

22   2   *At home. Washt & workd in gardin.*
Cloudy & some rain. I have washt & workt in gardin. Sett 2 quins trees and 1 apple tree. Planted some of Luke's potatoes, set Leutis plants & strawberries. I have squash & Cucumbers Come up in the bed East side the hous.

23   3   *At home. Sowd string peas.*
Cloudy morn. Sun shine the most of the day. I have done houswork and some in my gardin. Mrs Jones here forenoon. I sowed
string peas N end of my gardin. Mr Ballard had 1/2 lbs Butter
at son Jonathans. Jonathan Junior sleeps here.

24   4   *At home. Workt in my gardin.*
Clear. I have done my hous work and dug gardin. Sowd pees
&c. Mr Ballard went to son Ephraims. He sent me 7 1/2 lb.
fresh pork. Son Jonathan sent me a piece green Chees & some
rice. Ephraim sleeps here.

25   5   *At James Catons. Birth 4th. Fell from the hors on my way*
home. Received 9/ at William Babcok.
Clear. I was Calld by Mr Caton at 2 hour 30 m this morning to
go and see his wife. I arivd there at sun rise. Found her delivard
of a son, her 11th Child, but not safe. I performd what was
necessary and left her as Comfortable as Could be Expected.
Arivd home before ten and sent herbs and other matters.
At James Caton's Birth. His 11th child, 5 son. X X.

26   6   *At home. Planted Beans.*
Clear, cool & windy. I have done houswork and workt in my
gardin. Planted Crambury, Brown, & hundred to one beens
south of the hous. Jonathan Ballard Junior sleeps here.

27   7   *At home. Brewd & workt in gardin.*
Clear and windy. I have transplanted Cucumbers and done
other work in my gardin. Mr Ballard to Hallowell. Calld at
Daughter Lambards. Brot 6 lbs 3/4 veal from her. Lefaett
ploughd the S end of our field.

28   1   *At son Pollards. Birth 5th.*
Clear part of the day. I was Calld by Son Pollard at 2 hour 30
m this morning to go and see his wife. We reacht there before
5 and my Daughter was delivered at 6 of a fine Daughter, her

ninth Child, and is Comfortable. The Babe weighed 11 pounds. Sally Cleark & Preuda Snow Came at Evening, there all night. *Birth Son Pollards Child. Daughter, the 6th.*

29   2   *At ditoes.*
Raind. My Daughter & infant Comfortable. Pruda helpt wash, Sally assisted. Shee tarried all night. All Cleverly. Son Pollard went to Watervill.

30   3   *At ditoes and Son Jonathan's.*
Clear part of the day. I got my Daughter up, Changed her Lining &c and left her at 8. Reacht home at 11 a.m. Find my hous [without] any person in it. Daughter Pollard gave me Cake & 2 3/4 lb pork. I went to son Jonathan's. Carried herbs & other matters for Patty Town to Carry to Daughter Pollard. Sett squash plants East side the Gardin.

31   4   *At home. Workt in the gardin. Mrs Mosier is no better.*
Clear. I have done hous work & sett out squash plants & Cucumbers. Capt Smith & Lefaett ploughing our field. Cyrus Shearing sheep. Allin Lambard here for potatoes and Beens. Daughter Ballard sent us 13 oz Butter.

Without intimate knowledge of Martha's diary, it would be difficult to discover anything unusual, any evidence of change in the May 1809 entries, other than the slow turning of the seasons. The month began, like so many others, with a birth: "I was Calld about midnight to John Shaws wife." That entry could have been written—in fact, was written—in 1788: "I was Calld to Leut John Shaw's Lady who is in travil." Or 1812: "I was calld to John Shaws. His wife delivered of her second son, 4th Child at 9 hour Evening."[1]

Yet beneath the recurring cycles of the seasons, each year the same seeds, the same words, the same shifts in weather, old lives were passing away and new lives beginning. The John Shaw who welcomed his second child on May 1, 1809, was not the same man whose wife delivered her first in 1788 or her fifth ten years later. The "Magr Samuel Howard" elected state representative at the town meeting on the day of the Shaw birth was the third Hallowell leader of that name. Samuel's uncle and great-uncle, the first Samuel Howards, were long since dead. His father, Colonel William Howard, though still living, had been declared *non compos mentis* by a probate court.[2]

"Jonathan Ballard set out to go to sea," Martha wrote on May 10, using her grandson's full name rather than the familiar "Jack." This Jonathan, like his father and his great-grandfather (both named Jonathan Ballard), was ready to try his fortune in new places. The granddaughters, too, were growing up. Patty Towne, a toddler when her grandmother's diary began, now "washt and Cleand bed rooms" the way her aunts Hannah and Dolly had done fifteen years before.[3] Dolly's Dolly, Hannah's Rhoda, and Jonathan's Hannah moved in and out of their grandmother's house in early May, as did little Ephraim Ballard, Jonathan's son.

New faces, old names. New names, old patterns of behavior. Ephraim Ballard, eighty-four years old, still going off to town meeting. Martha Ballard, seventy-four, still getting up in the middle of the night to nurse the sick and deliver babies, still struggling with her own housework. "Began and finisht a Large wash after 3 O Clock. Feel fatagued," Martha wrote on May 15, adding, "Son Jonathan ploughing our field. My husband workt with him."

In such a record, one might discover that conservative, kin-oriented, rural quietude that many scholars associate with early New England. "Sett Parsley & 3 quins trees by the pigg pen," Martha wrote on May 18. Martha raised parsley and pork for the winter and quince for the next generation. Yet this apparently seamless world was neither changeless nor secure. "Son Jonathan had 6 Oxen taken by Execution and drove away," she continued her entry for May 17. "I do feel for but am not able to help him." The pastoralism of her entries is a reflection of her circumstances as well as her values. She could do nothing for Jonathan, but she could order her own small universe.

"Planted some of Luke's potatoes, set Leutis plants & Straw-berries," she wrote on May 22. "I have squash & Cucumbers Come up in the bed East side the hous."

The apparent timelessness of Martha's entries contrasts sharply with public histories of the period. Measured by the space devoted to it in James North's *History of Augusta*, 1809 was one of the three most important years in the history of the town, more significant than 1796 when Augusta separated from Hallowell, or 1797, when the Kennebec Bridge was completed, and only slightly less notable than 1827, when Augusta became the capital of Maine, or 1865, the year a disgruntled lobster peddler set a fire that de-stroyed all the banks, dry goods stores, and lawyer's offices in the central business district of the town.[4] Eighteen hundred and nine was the year Kennebec County had its own insurrection, or would-be insurrection, an affair historians call the Malta War, for the small Maine town where it began. One of the leaders of the in-surgents was Martha's nephew Elijah Barton.

The Bartons wavered in their commitment to Maine. As we have seen, Stephen and Dorothy Barton left Vassalboro in 1788 to return to Oxford, leaving their oldest daughters, Pamela, Clarissa, and Parthenia, in Maine.[5] In 1801, they were back. "Brother and Sister Barton & Luke go to housekeeping at Mr Crages Shop," Martha wrote on May 18. By fall the Bartons were in Vassalboro once again, though they soon moved further west to Malta (now Windsor), an unsurveyed settlement on contested Plymouth Company lands. In a letter dated October 14, 1802, Stephen Barton encouraged his oldest son, Stephen, who was still in Oxford, to join them:

We are Getting some Land and Expect to move five Miles from the next week where we shall have No Neighbours in Less than a Mile Saving Owls &c but if the boys are well they may make a farm if they will work. I wish you would write as soon as you can by the Post or some other way and inform us wheather you think of Going to the

Mohawk to Live or not. If you do Not I dont know but you would do well to come and see Kennebeck.[6]

The "boys" were Elijah, age eighteen, and Gideon, age sixteen, both born in Maine and named for brothers who had died in the Oxford diphtheria epidemic of 1769–1770.

On October 21, 1804, Stephen Barton died. "May God be with his Berieved wife, Children and other Connections and may we all be ready allso," Martha wrote. According to family tradition, the doctor was buried beside a great rock he and his sons had found on their first journey to Malta. In Gideon's notebook is a confirming phrase, "Dr. Stephen Barton and his two sons, Gideon and Elijah accepted the hospitality of this rock, beside which, at his own request he now lies in Christian repose."[7]

In 1806, the Augusta law firm of Williams and Bridges reported on their efforts to identify trespassers on undivided lands east of Augusta. They found that great quantities of pine had been cut, some oak timber, red oak staves, and a few mill logs. "We find about 60 persons engaged in this plundering, some of whom are able to pay what may be recovered against them & others of them are entirely destitute of property & means to pay for their misdoings." (In the settlers' view, of course, they were not plundering timber but clearing land, making farms for themselves in the wilderness. They believed that their labor gave them a better claim to the land than the paper claims of absentee proprietors.) Some of the trespassers were mere rascals, the lawyers continued, adding that there was a group of settlers "of a less mischievous disposition, & more likely to make improvements on their possessions." Among these were "the heirs of Doc Barton."[8]

Tensions between the proprietors and the settlers intensified in 1807–1808, when French and British harassment of American shipping brought a fourteen-month embargo on trade, referred to with disdain among Federalists in Maine as "Jefferson's embargo." While piles of lumber grew and traders and merchants, to forestall their own bankruptcy, began to demand immediate payment in full, the Plymouth proprietors began to issue ejectment suits. Despairing of any relief from the law, settlers organized to resist the surveyors, writ servers, and sheriffs sent to enforce the proprietors' will. Attacks on land agents and their sympathizers escalated, from twelve in the years 1805–1806 to thirty-six in 1807–1808. The rituals of terror grew more elaborate. The resisters not only adopted Indian garb, they parodied the military rituals that had become an increasingly important part of the male culture of the region.[9]

In Augusta, leading men had long used their militia titles—*Colonel* Howard, *Lieutenant* Shaw. In 1798, as Henry Sewall explained it, they began "wearing the uniform dress on Sundays and on other public occasions."[10] Women, too, were drawn into martial pageantry. In 1806, in a ceremony staged at the new courthouse in Augusta, several "patriotic ladies" presented the town's newly organized Light Infantry Company with an elegant standard of white silk, emblazoned in red with the motto "Victory or Death." In a speech presenting the flag, Sarah Williams, the daughter of one of the militia captains, likened the women to "the matrons of Rome," who in their nation's peril encouraged their men toward victory. "Should the dread hour arrive that threatens to immolate your country at the shrine of foreign ambition or internal faction—fly to this standard—protect it with your lives—let retreat and capitulation be terms known to you only by name—and swear by the avenging spirit, you will adhere to the emphatic motto here inscribed." The military exercises were followed by a "splendid ball."[11]

Training under Captain Solomon Vose's own version of Steuben's manual, the men yearned for action. When, in September of 1807, President Jefferson requested the governors of the various states to raise 100,000 men in case of war, Vose wrote Henry Sewall, Major General of the Kennebec regiments, that his officers "do not wait for a cold and formal detachment of their men; they hasten to tender their unanimous services in the cause of their country; they are ready for action; they seize the first instant to enter into engagements with arms and equipments complete, at a moment's warning to march under the orders of their superiors."[12] Sewall soon found an opportunity to respond, though it was not "foreign ambition" but "internal faction" that provided the occasion.

In the early winter of 1808, rumors of a planned squatter attack on Augusta reached the Kennebec County sheriff, Arthur Lithgow. On January 19, Sewall, "On the written request of the sheriff ordered 400 of the militia in the vicinity to be ready at a moments warning, to assist him in the due execution of his duty." Rumors reached the town that settlers were mustering in the back country for an attack on the county seat. On January 28, Deputy Sheriff Pitt Dillingham rode into the Sheepscot country to negotiate with the settlers. As he stood before an immense crowd gathered near Broad's Tavern in Fairfax, seventy-five masked and armed men appeared at the top of a nearby hill. In good military order, they marched in single file behind "an elegant standard" toward the tavern. Firing a deafening salute into the air, they formed a half-circle around him. The men were dressed in blankets and moccasins with caps three feet high and masks of bearskin or sheepskin, "some stuck over with hog's bristles." Dillingham spoke in conciliatory terms ("Their savage appearance would strike terror in the boldest heart," he later wrote), promising that no sheriff would serve proprietary writs without posting prior notice at the tavern, a strategy that would presumably allow the object of the writ to flee. Maintaining their charade to the end, the settlers promised to consider the Sheriff's terms, returning an hour later with the report that "All injun like very much your talk, all injun agree as you say."[13]

In Boston, Governor Sullivan was less concerned about white Indians than about the possibility that Lithgow and Sewall had exceeded their authority. Not only did circumstances not warrant the raising of troops, the county magistrates had failed to follow the procedures outlined in the Massachusetts Riot Act of 1786. On February 5, Sewall wrote in his journal, "General Orders of the 1. inst. recd. by Express, for disbanding the sheriff's detachmt. Added Division Orders & distributed them by Major Howard thro' the Division."

Denied troops, the Augusta gentry organized a voluntary patrol, taking as their motto *Custodia est Clypeus,* "The Watch Is Our Protection." Concerned about continuing rumors of an invasion, they circuited the center of the town from 11:00 p.m. to daylight each night, starting at Burton's Inn on the west side of the river, going past the courthouse, meeting house, and jail, beyond Judge Bridge's house and across Kennebec bridge, past Cony's, Lithgow's, and Sewall's residences, then around Fort Western and back across the bridge. (Charles Hayden's map shows the impressive houses that now stood near Fort Western.) Despite the watch, the Augusta jail burned to the ground on March 16, 1808. "Fears are entertaind it was disinedly done," Martha wrote. Sewall added, "In the night a military guard, being requested, was supplied by Capt. Vose's light company, to protect the prisoners & the Courthouse which was also attempted to be fired." The next day the leading "magistrates and gentlemen" of the county gathered at the courthouse, agreed that Sewall was right in ordering a military force to secure the records and prisoners, and requested that Joseph North, Thomas Fillebrown, and John Davis, Esquire, inform the Governor of the fact.[14]

Meanwhile, violence increased in the back country as the proprietors pressed their claims. In April, settlers led by a religious mystic named Nathan Barlow surrounded a constable in the woods near Fairfax, seized the writs he was attempting to serve, then carried him to a nearby house, tore off his clothing which they shredded into rags, beat him, and turned him naked into the night. Barlow was arrested and brought to Augusta. "The troops on gard this night thro the Indians so called," Martha wrote on May 31, 1808, and, on June 2, "Mr Ballard & Cyrus to hear tryal of Barlow. He was found gilty." Despite fear that the resisters might march on Augusta to rescue their leader, Barlow was sentenced to thirty days' solitary imprisonment and two years of hard labor at the state prison in Charlestown, Massachusetts.[15] Barlow's imprisonment brought only temporary quiet. "Cyrus informd that a Collectors hors was shot at Belgrade this weak and that Mr Dillingham has been fired at by men in disguise," Martha wrote on June 18.

Martha's descriptions of these troubles, like her earlier record

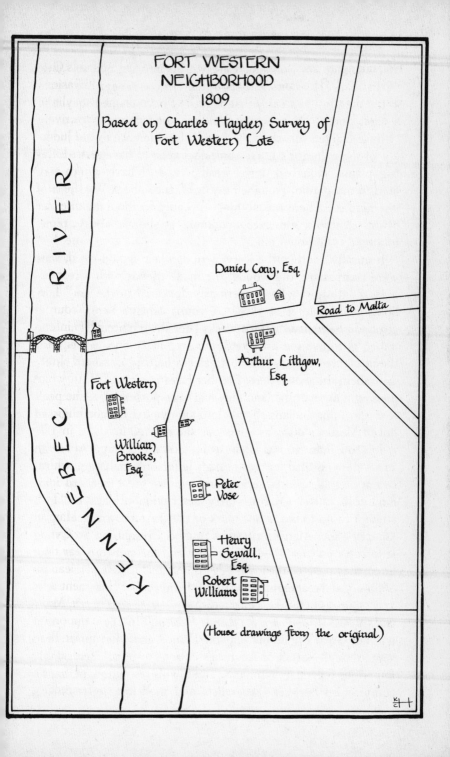

FORT WESTERN
NEIGHBORHOOD
1809

Based on Charles Hayden Survey of
Fort Western Lots

RIVER

KENNEBEC

Daniel Cony, Esq.

Road to Malta

Arthur Lithgow,
Esq.

Fort Western

William
Brooks,
Esq

Peter
Vose

Henry
Sewall,
Esq.

Robert
Williams

(House drawings from the original)

of the assault on Ephraim, were woven into the quieter fabric of the diary. Her comment about the "troops on gard" appears in the margin of an entry that begins, "I have planted squash of several kinds." The report of Barlow's conviction is followed by "I have planted squash in the field." Her reference to the shooting of the collector's horse comes between "I have sett 60 Cabag plants. Houghed down weads," and "I have workt very hard in my gardin. Houghed my corn, cucumbers. Wed part of my oinions." There was nothing she could do about the disorder of this eastern world, except continue, as she had always done, to attend to her own plot.

Ironically, during the very period when would-be Indians were compassing the woods, she made friends with a real Indian, a little girl who mysteriously appeared in the neighborhood in the winter of 1809. "A young Squagh here," Martha wrote on February 13. Two weeks later she reported, "The little indien girl gave me a basket," then regularly once a week for the next three weeks, "Elizabeth sleeps here"; "Elizabeth here"; "Elizabeth the indien here. I let her have potatoes." With white men fighting over the land they had once possessed, Kennebec's few remaining Indians slipped into anonymity. Elizabeth passed out of Martha's diary as quietly as she entered it.

In 1809, international affairs again took center stage. Although some shipping had leaked through Jefferson's embargo, the restraint on trade created serious problems for great men and common folks alike. (Martha's wry description of Jack Ballard's attempt to go to sea is one mark of that.) At a town meeting in January 1809, Augusta's leaders drafted a resolution protesting Jefferson's policies. Predicting civil war if the embargo were not lifted, they pledged the town's determination "to defend the cause of liberty and real republicanism" and prayed that "Massachusetts may again, as in the days of '75, *dash in pieces the shackles of Tyranny and Oppression, and open the door to Freedom.*" In 1809, the tyrant was not Great Britain but imperial France, and what appeared to some though not all of Augusta's citizens to be an increasingly imperious federal government. The town's resolution, perhaps a compromise between Federalists and moderate Jeffersonians, passed by a vote of eighty-six to twenty-three. It was in the hand-writing of John Vassall Davis.[16] In the back country, settlers were less concerned about national politics than about the proprietors who persisted in their attempt to expel men from their lands. They, too, thought of the days of '75.

Martha didn't notice the January meeting, though on June 10, 1809, she reported drily, "They had a great day down at the Settlement on the removal of the imbargo." During that week of celebration, she was far more concerned with a painful swelling in her left knee than with men's affairs. Whether caused by her fall from the horse on May 25 or by the continued exertions of the garden, it was a terrible annoyance. "Hannah Ballard brot me spirrit to Baith it with. I applied black wool allso," she wrote on June 7, but the next night her leg was so painful she could not sleep. "I am still lame," she wrote the next morning, "but have workt in my gardin all day." Life in a free land required more than one kind of courage.

If the May 1809 diary tells us little about the political and economic turmoil of the times, it is a brightly colored limning of spring. The ground froze hard on April 28, 1809, but on May 9 Martha "sett Turnips & Cabbage stumps." The warm weather and gentle rain of the past week made it possible to plant the roots of last year's cabbage (wintered over in the cellar) into the ground and to begin planting cucumbers and squash. Year after year, cabbage stumps, not hyacinths, were the first harbingers of spring. Martha began setting roots as early as the ground would allow. In 1801, she began her work on April 18, setting 165 cabbage stumps into the ground. In 1806, she planted on May 4 and had the first yield two weeks later, mixing the young shoots with wild plants from the field. "I have cookt pork, patience, Cabage sprouts, yerrow, & shepherds sprouts," she wrote. Meanwhile, she planted corn, cucumbers, pumpkins, squash, and melons, "set" sage and beet roots, "brot manure from behind the out house," and did "other matters in my gardin." Cabbage, turnips, and other roots would not yield mature vegetables in their second year, but in addition to greens, they produced seed for another crop. For old-fashioned gardeners like Martha, planting was a self-perpetuating cycle, like leavening bread with dough saved from an earlier batch, an interlocking chain in which fragments of one yield helped to assure another.

Historians have written a great deal about field agriculture in early America but not enough about the intricate horticulture that belonged to women, the intense labor of cultivation and preservation that allowed one season to stretch almost to another.[17] Martha was proud of being able to gather a milk pan full of "Poland King" beans as early as July 11 of one year, of having green peas, from a fall planting, on October 4 of another, of having parsley "fresh and green from my gardin for to put in my gravy" on December 17, and of serving stored cabbage from her cellar on March 13, only six weeks before she began the whole cycle anew.[18]

On May 10, Martha noted selling as well as planting seeds, reporting that Mrs Emery and two of William Stone's children "had gardin seeds of me."[19] There were more ambitious seed dealers in the town. Each spring Augusta's newspapers advertised "A general Assortment of GARDEN SEEDS for Sale by Joseph North."[20] A petty account book listing North's seed transactions survives from this period.[21] Martha's home-grown seeds were a bargain. When she was selling an ounce of parsnip seed for two shillings, roughly forty-five cents, he was charging seventy cents for one-half ounce. His were no doubt imported seeds, produced by commercial growers. His terse account book gives no indication of varieties, however. Most entries simply say "garden seeds," though a few specify "Yallow Turnip," "Redish," "peper," "millin," or "Cuwcomber," North's spelling being as various and imaginative as Martha's. North also sold apple trees (he charged one customer $1.80 for thirteen young trees) and "Lambar popels," presumably the Lombardy poplars that were becoming popular among the gentry.[22]

There is a single entry under Ephraim Ballard's name in North's book, a purchase on May 29, 1807, of garden seeds worth twenty-five cents. Martha made no mention of the seed purchase, but on May 30 she wrote, "Mr. Ballard planted beens in the gardin. He planted Corn and pumpkins yesterday." If the seeds Ephraim got from North were indeed beans, corn, or pumpkin they must have been an unusual variety, something not already available in the family seed stock. The only thing unusual about the entry is Ephraim's involvement in the garden. Though he sometimes helped to dig it, it was almost always Martha who did the planting.

She dropped her first seeds into raised beds on the sunny side of the house, transplanting the young plants into the big garden when the ground was warmer.[23] A methodical and serious gardener, she showed concern for the soil, adding manure in the early spring (some of it shoveled from behind the outhouse) and lime in the form of ashes or plaster.[24]

Her gardening entries are far more descriptive than other Augusta sources for the same period. Henry Sewall mentioned planting corn and wheat but seldom had anything at all to say about gardening, perhaps because that was Tabitha's work. Daniel Cony, who left a fragmentary diary from this period, used gardening references to mark the passing of the seasons: On April 5, 1808: "Dug asparagus bed. First vessel came up. Farmers ploughing." On May 5, 1808: "Plumb trees in bloom," On July 4: "Green pease, plenty."[25] As a record of the actual contents of his garden, however, the doctor's diary is useless.

Martha grew beans, cabbages, lettuce, parsnips, carrots, turnips, beets, cucumbers, radishes, onions, garlic, peppers, "pepper grass," "French turnips," squash, "sugar and string peas," muskmelon, watermelon, pumpkins, and medical and culinary herbs (sage, saffron, coriander, anise, mustard, marigolds, camomile, parsley, and many more), though she did not mention asparagus. In her diary, even those old staples, beans and squash, came in several varieties. "Planted Cucumbers & three kinds squash," she wrote on May 10, 1809, and, on May 17, "Planted long squash by the hogg pen." The diary lists "Bannybiss Beans," "Crambury, Brown, & hundred to one beens," "yellow Bush Beans," and "wild goos Beens."[26] One year Ephraim planted "8 kinds of Beens at the South End of the Corn field,"[27] and on July 9, 1801, perhaps in a stroke of whimsy, Martha planted one "yellow-eyed bean *on the rock*," the rock presumably a large granite outcropping, common in glacial New England, with a declivity or crevice filled with dirt. Corn and potatoes both came in two varieties, distinguished by color. Martha planted "purple" as well as "sweet" corn, and on June 16, 1807, reported that "the Blue potatoes I first planted are coming up."

By July, her currant bushes were bent to the ground with fruit, jewel-like globules of a brilliant red and an astringent tartness. She used them fresh, in pies or tarts, in sauces, and medicinal syrups.[28] Some of the fruit trees on the farm were already bearing when the Ballards moved there. On July 10, 1801, in the second year at the farm, Martha wrote, "We have Bakt apples, Cherry, Currant tarts, Custard and Wheat Bread," Eventually, she added English gooseberries to her garden, and, in May of 1806, set out young plum and apple trees in the orchard. Her shrubs and trees not only added variety to her table but provided additional commodities for trade. "Marshall Edson's wife here for cherries," she wrote on July 21, 1806, and, four days later, "Mrs. Howards made [maid] and Mr Fuller here for Cherrys & Curents."[29] On July 27, 1811, the last summer of her life, she noted that "Warrin Stones wife Came and gathered our Cherries which were in the gardin 22 quarts. She is to have half," adding "He [presumably Ephraim] sold them for 6 cents per quart." Whether Ephraim took it upon himself to market the cherries or whether he was simply Martha's messenger, carrying the fruit to town, we do not know.

Ripe currants and cherries added color to a garden predominantly green. There was little intentional ornament.[30] Even Marigolds were planted for their medicinal properties rather than their hue, though the bright yellow must have been attractive. Yet, with its trailing squash vines and flourishing cabbages, Martha's was the sort of garden a traveler might have found "pretty," that is, pleasantly productive, an oasis of order amidst the savagery of woods. "The gardens were rare for so new a place," an itinerant minister wrote of one Kennebec settlement, adding by way of explanation that "onions, beets and parsnips were excellent."[31]

According to one descendant, Joseph North had "a remarkable floral taste," introducing into his garden "almost every flower which would bloom in our climate." But there is little evidence of that in his seed book. Daniel Cony at least noticed flowers. "Good hay weather," he wrote on July 25, 1808. "Roses in full bloom from 20th of June to the 15th of July. Season continued wet—very wet 'till 14th July, great crop of grass." For him roses, like asparagus, were emblems of the season. The one fully documented ornamental garden in the Kennebec was that of Dr. Benjamin Vaughan of Hallowell.

According to a family memoir, the doctor cultivated "a large garden of several acres tastily laid out, with broad paths and numerous alleys, whose borders were adorned with flowers shaded with currant bushes, fruit trees and shrubbery. The whole under the care of an English gardener."[32] Timothy Dwight, who visited Hallowell on one of his famous journeys through New England, concluded that:

A more romantic spot is not often found, than that on which stands the house of Mr. V. a descendant of Mr. Hallowell, from whom this town took its name. . . . In the rear, as you recede from the river, but at the side of the house . . . lies a handsome garden, furnishing even at this time of the year ample proofs of the fertility of the soil. Behind the garden is a wild and solitary valley; at the bottom of which runs a small mill stream. . . . on either side, the banks, which are of considerable height, and sometimes steep, formed of rude forested grounds, and moss-grown rocks, are left absolutely in the state of nature. Along the brook Mr. V. has made a convenient foot-way, rather appearing to have been trodden out by the feet of wild animals, than to have been contrived by man, and winding over a succession of stone bridges, so rude and inartificial, as to seem the result of accident, rather than the effect of human labour.[33]

The gardens people cultivated—and described—revealed their aspirations. For Daniel Cony, "farmers ploughing" was an economic forecast. Good crops meant prompt payment of rents and suits. Interspersed among his agricultural entries for 1808–1809 is a cryptic history of the settler war. "Goal burnt," he wrote on March 16, 1808, without further comment or explanation. The only hint that he, as a representative of the Plymouth Company, was involved in pressing for settlement with the squatters is his entry for August 5, 1809, "Sent by Major Cony 27 contracts and deeds to T. L. W. Esquire. . . . Also sent duplicates Chas. Hayden plans and field notes." (T.L.W., Esquire, was Thomas L. Winthrop of Boston, one of the Plymouth Proprietors, Charles Hayden a surveyor.) His account of the Malta War was even more clipped: "Armed men came into town to liberate the prisoners."

In North's account book, politics, like agriculture, was reduced to sums. He debited Kennebec County for repairs to the jail after an attempted break, itemizing charges for "Iron pikets," "percuring cedar posts", hauling "plank & Joyc from the shore," and "1 day about the valt," as well as for "gittin shurt for McCauslan," who was still the most visible prisoner.[34] Cony and North would have found congenial a poetic tribute to Augusta published in 1810. In the "salubrious" air of the county seat, so the poet argued, law and justice reigned.

> *There native Industry, with noble toil,*
> *Improves his field, or yokes his patient team*
> *To send the produce of his labors forth.*
> *There, too, the Merchant deals in ten per cent,*
> *All mindful of his gain; and vends his goods*
> *For useful cash, that solace of our woes;*
> *That sweet companion through the storms of life.*[35]

"Useful cash" was Augusta's best crop.

Benjamin Vaughan's vision, at least as reported by Timothy Dwight, was more utopian. The gate between his well-ordered flower beds and "the wild and solitary valley beyond" symbolized a romantic harmony between art and   and by extension, perhaps, the hoped-for reconciliation between English gentility and the Maine woods. "This is the haven of the lover, of the saint and of the philosopher!" gushed an English visitor. Unfortunately, the real woods were inhabited by squatters and quacks.[36]

In contrast to the crisp records of Cony and North and the effusions of Kennebec travelers, Martha's far more expansive record focused on the mundane *work* of gardening, the daily, incremental tasks that each season exacted. In May of 1809, she "sowed," "sett," "planted," and "transplanted" in at least half a dozen places, digging ground "west of the hous" on May 15 and starting squash, cucumbers, muskmelons and watermelons on "East side house" the same day. She planted "by the hogg pen" on May 16 and 18 on May 23 sowed string peas "N end of my gardin," and on May 26, planted "south of the hous." The plots she defined by the three points of the compass were no doubt raised beds, rich with manure, used for starting seeds in cool weather. The garden proper had a fence, which Ephraim mended on May 12. Whether it included the plot near the "hogg pen" we do not know. All of these spots, managed by Martha, were distinct from the "field," which Jonathan plowed on May 15, and DeLafayette and Mr. Smith on May 27 and May 31.

Martha's was an ordinary garden, a factory for food and medicine that incidentally provided nourishment to the soul. "I have workt in my gardin," she wrote on May 17, the possessive pronoun the only hint of the sense of ownership she felt in her work. The garden was hers, though her husband or son or the Hallowell and Augusta Bank owned the land. "I have squash & Cucumbers Come up in the bed East side the house," she wrote on May 22. The garden was hers because she turned the soil, dropped the seeds, and each year recorded in her diary, as though it had never happened before, the recurring miracle of spring.

In May of 1809, as Daniel Cony cut his asparagus and Martha turned over the soil in her garden, Paul Chadwick of Malta, enticed by the promise of 100 free acres, volunteered to assist

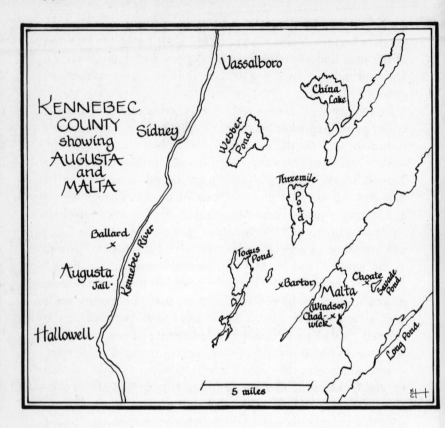

KENNEBEC
COUNTY
showing
AUGUSTA
and
MALTA

Vassalboro

China
Lake

Sidney

Webber
Pond

Threemile
Pond

Ballard
x

Kennebec River

Togus Pond

Augusta
Jail.

x Barton

Malta
(Windsor)
Chad- x
wick

Choate
x

Savade
Pond

Long Pond

Hallowell

5 miles

the Plymouth Company in its survey of the town. Elijah Barton's white Indians were able to stop the first attempt in mid-June; but by August, ejectment suits had been commenced against five settlers and the surveyors were back. On September 8, in midafternoon, Chadwick was working as chainman on Paul Choate's land when eight masked men burst from the woods. "Damn you, how came you here? This is good enough for you!" one shouted. Three others discharged their muskets at close range. Chadwick lived three days.

Martha's account of these events, written on September 12, is breathless:

Hear that Elijah Barton has gone away being acused of shooting Mr Chadock which hapned 9th inst when he was asisting a surveyer in running out land in [blank, she apparently intended to name the place but couldn't remember or didn't know]. There were three guns fired. The men who Cummited the crime were in disguise. A woful afair.

On September 16, she learned that "Elijah Barton & 7 others are in Jail on acount of Chaddocks Death. O my Dear Sister how I feel for her." Martha's initial reaction to the news of the Chadwick murder was colored by her experience as the wife of a surveyor who had himself been attacked in the woods. The news of her nephew's involvement deepened her dismay. But when she was told that Elijah and the others were in jail, her first thought was for Dorothy. Having wept herself over the impulsive behavior of a hot-tempered son, she could identify with her sister's sorrow. She had only to think of that distressing scene of March 17, 1804, when Jonathan drove young Lemuel Witham from the house, "damning and pushing him down," two hired hands running after them to prevent the boy "being deprived of life."

She could think, too, of all those earlier episodes when Jonathan had been in trouble for vandalism, fighting, and drinking. Her sister's son was twenty-five years old in 1809, about the same age Jonathan had been when Amos Pollard, the tavern keeper, had thrown him out of his house. "It is very strange that men cannot behave like rationall beings," Martha had written, a comment she might easily have repeated now.[37] The circumstances of the Chadwick murder—the adoption of mock Indian garb, and the surprise attack on a surveyor—place it within the theater of squatter resistance, the dramatic but seldom violent demonstrations long used by back-country settlers to frighten and intimidate their would-be landlords; but the emotional content of the encounter mirrors the passionate, and perhaps drunken, scenes Martha had so often witnessed and deplored.

One witness testified that shortly before the attack, Elijah Barton had told him, "Chadwick has crooked eyes: and damn him, we mean to straighten them." David Leeman, Chadwick's father-in-law, said that soon after the murder he saw Elijah Barton and Jabez Meigs at John Lynn's, going from the barn to the house. Later, he "heard a carousing in the house: they were jumping on the floor, and halooing. They appeared to make a noise like men in liquor; and I heard one say, 'by God, I meant to fetch him,' and immediately after, 'by God, I thought I should fetch him;' and then, "God, I did fetch him." The profanity, however common in ordinary life, was an important part of the evidence against the men. The felony indictments in the case, still following ancient forms, ascribed the defendants' crime to their "not having the fear of God before their eyes, but being moved and seduced by the instigation of the Devil."[38]

Chadwick's mother testified that there had been trouble between Jacob Meigs, one of the defendants, and her son for three years past. The defense attorney ridiculed her evidence. "To what does this mighty controversy amount?" he asked.

> What, that about three years ago, there was a dispute at the raising of a barn frame; and when the witness found that this was going too far back, she attempted to tell you something more recent; but after puzzling herself some time, she can only remember that Meigs took away a sled, the joint property of him and the deceased, and to which it is obvious he had an equal right with him. Other witnesses tell you, that there was a good understanding between them; and even the mother allows, that they were to have stoned a well together, had not the fatal accident intervened.[39]

This was skillful psychology. Dismissing the killing as a "fatal accident," the defense attorney subtly reminded the jurors that the defendants were men like themselves, given to fits of passion perhaps, but not capable of premeditated violence. Here he reversed the method used by Timothy Merritt after the Purrinton murders to connect the bizarre and the ordinary. Instead, he reassured the jury that common quarrels, fights at barn-raisings, disputes over joint property, or disagreements between men who otherwise depended on one another could not lead to such a heinous crime as murder. No one could deny that the killing occurred, but since the assailants were in disguise it was impossible for anyone to know for certain who actually fired the shots. Referring to the killing as a terrible "accident," he assured the jury that the men seated before them, common farmers like themselves, could in no sense be criminals.

The prosecutor took the opposite tack, painting the defendants as wild men, uncivil and out of control. He did not use traditional religious arguments, however, but neoclassical notions about the relation between human and outdoor nature. The murder had occurred in the woods on a day when "the mild temperature of the air, and the green foliage of the forests invite man abroad to view and contemplate the works of nature." The setting exposed the true character of the assailants:

> The effect of this natural scenery is to move the mild, the tender, and the benevolent affections. But this effect was not produced in the savage bosoms of those who sought the life of poor Chadwick; nothing would assuage the rancor of their hatred but his blood.—Barton and his party had, by a sense of their guilt and a fear of punishment, been driven from the haunts of men to assume a savage life among the beasts of the forests.[40]

It is hard to know how that argument affected the jurors. The pastoralism of the rhetoric probably seemed as unconnected to their own lives as Benjamin Vaughan's garden. These were men who dealt daily with timber and mosquitoes and the realities of the merchant's "ten percent." The allusions to "savage life" were even more problematic, since there was much sympathy in the country for white Indian attempts to harass writ servers and surveyors.

"It is muster day. They parade at the forks of the roads," Martha wrote on September 22. If rumors racing through the town could be believed, Malta's Indians were also mustering. On October 2, a man sent by the Sheriff toward Malta to gather information reported that men were assembling there and "that a beef creature had been driven into the woods and killed for their support." On October 3, another man, working on the road to Malta, reported seeing fifteen or twenty men armed with muskets and nine or ten others on foot. On October 4, Abner Weeks, patrolling the road in Augusta on the east side of the river, discovered armed men supposedly coming from Malta. He was taken into the woods eight miles, as he thought, pricked with a bayonet, and told to go to Augusta and tell the court to release the prisoners or they would burn the town.[41] That day Martha got home at dusk, after staying up all night at a delivery. "The Town was in an up roar by those who are Calld indiens makeing their apearance," she wrote. Fear of violence in the center of the town sent Dolly Lambard home to her mother on October 5. "Daughter Lambard, Lucy, William & Henry & Sarah sleep here," Martha wrote. "May that Great being who rules over the univers subdue our Enemies in bringing them to a right sence of their Duty." Characteristically, she placed her faith in God rather than the militia.

On October 6, having spent the night at Samuel Livermore's house waiting in vain for labor to begin, Martha went to her son Ephraim's to rest. "Sister Barton, Benjamin Porter, his wife & son-in-law there," she wrote. "They went to the Jail to see Elijah. Sister & I were Calld to Livermores again. Shee was delivered of a son at 5 hours 30 minutes this morning and of a Daughter at 6 hour 20. Her illness severe but thro Gods mercie there [they're] Cleverly." It must have been a poignant, yet familiar, experience for the two sisters, sharing the work of nursing while violence broke out around them. Thirty-five years before, they had brewed tea for the sick in Oxford while Dorothy's husband rallied his neighbors against British taxes. In that year, too, young Bostonians disguised as Indians had mustered in the night. For both women, then, as now, the needs of the sick and the obligations of kinship superseded political allegiances.

The Barton relatives came and went through October, sometimes staying with young Ephraim or the Lambards in town, sometimes stopping at the Ballard farm.[42] Meanwhile, Martha harvested her Poland King beans, gathered hops and damson plums, spun wool, made pickles, baked bread with the first flour from the year's crop, and put cider into the cellar. "Sister and Patty washt," she wrote on October 10, and, on October 21, "Sister Barton & I went to Mr Hodges. Find his wife and Daughter very sick."

On November 16, the court opened. "Mr Ballard went to hear the trial of the prisoners. The Jury were paneild & ajourned," Martha wrote. The two lawyers opened their arguments on November 18, testimony continuing through Saturday, when Elijah's brothers Gideon and Stephen and their brother-in-law, Benjamin Porter, came in from Malta and slept at the Ballards'. The court recessed for the Sabbath, testimony resuming on Monday and continuing through Thursday, when the jury began to sit. "I have finisht makeing my apple sauce," Martha wrote on Saturday. "Am informd the jury brot the prisoners in not guilty. May their Conciencies do the same." On December 3, Dorothy Barton and her four sons took supper with Martha and Ephraim. Elijah spent the night. To all appearances, he was just another relative, just another visitor.

Martha's dismissal of the Malta resisters as "enemies" and her simultaneous welcoming of Elijah Barton to her home were consistent with her view of life. She might deplore her nephew's behavior, and at the same time serve him, just as she had done so often with Jonathan. She may or may not have discussed the political ramifications of the Malta affair with her sister Dorothy or offered her own opinions on the matter in the letters she wrote to Brother Collins and Sister Waters in Oxford soon after the trial, but for her the duties of friendship were clear. She had seen enough fighting, swearing, and dying in her time. In her own realm, at least, she could cultivate peace, leaving the ultimate verdict to God.[43]

Martha had passed through her own wars, had survived the continuing battles with hired helpers, the troubling estrangement from Ephraim, the struggle with Jonathan over possession of her house, and had come to a period of reconciliation. Age was a great teacher. "I feel very feeble," she wrote on August 3, 1807. "My husband complains also. We seem to be a feeble couple. May the Great parent support us thro life and may we be conformed to his will is the desire of me his undeserving hand maid." The reference to herself as "undeserving" is conventional, of course, yet the fervor of her religious sentiments was heightened in the years after the Purrinton murders, a response less to the terror of those events than to her own growing awareness that her end was near. "Now I have lived to see this year end and may I reflect on the time past of my life and strive to amend my ways," she wrote on New Year's Eve 1807. The diary made it easier to "reflect on the time past," and Martha must have done so. Perhaps the extremes of passion she had witnessed in her own neighborhood and the growing cry of war in the country, the embargoes, the mustering of troops, the continuing harassment of surveyors, had helped her put her family problems in perspective.

Jonathan and Sally's new house relieved the immediate source of conflict with her children. The May 1809 entries reflect a new accommodation between the two families. Almost every night, one or more of the grandchildren slept at Martha and Ephraim's house, a strategy designed to relieve the crowding at home but also to provide help and support for the aging couple. But circumstances alone do not account for the shift in the diary. A telling entry for April 2, 1808, during a difficult period when Dolly and Barnabas Lambard and their six children were living with their parents, suggests that Martha deliberately excluded family quarrels from her entries. "I have been to son Jonathans to help her quilt her Bed quilt," she wrote, adding, "What elce I have endured I wish not to write." Earlier she would have elaborated on her dismay if not on the immediate cause of the argument. A week later, in the margin of an entry mostly devoted to knitting, she wrote, "A trying scein hapned." No more.

Martha took command of the one thing that was hers to shape —her diary, creating in its pages the order and restraint so often missing in life. "I have more trouble to see other ways than I know how to indure," she wrote on May 11, 1808, "but God is able to giv me strength and Fortitude." She did more than excise from her entries the arguments that so distressed her; she substituted other scenes more pleasant to read and remember.

May 5, 1808: "I have workt in my gardin. Mr. Ballard and I dind at son Jonathans. We had Beautiful rice puding and Calvs head & harslett [organ meats]."

On October 18, 1808: "Daughter Ballard sent us a quarter muttun. Shee brot me bread on Sunday. They are very kind." Whatever her faults, Sally was a good cook.

On March 19, 1809, a different menu: "Son Jonathan sent for his Father & I to dine with him. We had moos meet stakes."

On March 12, 1810, pastoral unity: "Daughter Ballard came here. I went to the barn with her. Performd 2 Extractions for the Cows."

On June 19, 1811, genuine sympathy for Jonathan's continuing troubles: "Son Jonathan was put in jaill for debt, an unfortunate thing for him at this time as the freshet is rising and his Lumber up river in a precarious situation. May all thing work together for his good here or hereafter is the wish of me his affectionate mother."

Martha never developed an intense and daily intimacy with Jonathan and Sally. The grandchildren are far more visible in the diary in these years than either of the parents. But she did learn to appreciate and accept the small gifts of love and care they were able to offer. Sally's burdens too, though immense, were lightened as Hannah and the boys grew old enough to help.

In these years of renewal, God gave Martha an unexpected gift, the strength to begin her work anew. As we have seen, her midwifery practice declined rapidly after the move to the farm. Between May 1, 1801, and April 30, 1809, she averaged less than one delivery a month; in 1808, she performed only three deliveries in the entire year. Suddenly in May 1809 the trend reversed. The Shaw delivery that began the segment you have read was only her second of the year (the first had been to Daughter Ballard on April 1), but by the end of the month she had attended three more deliveries, by the end of the year twenty-one.

The reason for the sudden shift is revealed in the May segment, though it takes a little work to find it. On May 3, Mrs. Smith and Brooks called at Martha's house: "Inform me Mrs Mosier is very sick." Martha went to see the woman the next day. For the rest of the month, she followed the progress of the illness: May 7, "My daughter been to see Mrs Mosier. Finds her very sick." May 18, "Hear that Mrs Mosier is no Better." May 21, "We are informed that Mrs Mosier is more Comfortable." May 31, the false hope corrected, "Mrs Mosier is no better."

On June 1, Mrs. Mosier was still "very sick." When Martha went to see her on the Sabbath, she was "yet living," but on June 5, at 1:00 p.m., she died. "The remains of Mrs Mosier were Carried to Sidney and there interd this afternoon," Martha wrote the next day.

Only careful sifting backward through the diary reveals that Ann Mosier was a midwife. Born in Dartmouth, Massachusetts, in 1743, she had lived for a time in Winslow before coming with her husband and family to the Augusta section of Hallowell sometime before 1795.[44] She first appears in the diary on August 24 of that year, when she helped Martha dress a child for burial. Four years later the first midwifery entries appear.[45] She would then have been fifty-two years old. On March 15, 1800, the wife of one of the ubiquitous John Shaws was "delivered of a daughter by Mrs. Mosier," and on June 9 of the same year, after Martha left another woman after a bout of false labor, she heard that Mrs. Mosier had been called there in the evening. Ann Mosier is not a strong presence in Martha's diary, but every mention, except for the May 1809 entries, describes her as a midwife or nurse.

Ann Mosier, like Martha, moved to Augusta in midlife. She may already have had some midwifery experience, enough so that she was an obvious substitute for Martha, as on May 30, 1799, when a man came to the Burtun house, where Martha was attending a delivery, and when he could not get her, "went after Mrs. Mosur." As Martha's practice declined, Mosier's increased. Benjamin Page was surely active at the Hook after 1800, and in Augusta Dr. Cony was joined by Dr. Ellis, but Ann Mosier, a woman who otherwise left no record in Augusta's history, was probably the person who assumed most of Martha's work.[46]

Her unexpected death created new problems and opportunities. On June 25, 1809, a few weeks after the funeral, Martha wrote:

I was Calld by son Ephraim at 3 hour 30 minutes this morning to go and see my Dear Daughter Lambard who was delivd of her 8th child and 3d Daughter before he Came for me. No one present at the Birth of the Child but Mrs Piper. Doctor Ellis performd the remainder of her Labour and through the great Goodnes of God I found her as well as Could be Expected. Son Ephraim shew a brotherly kindness, went and brot accessories and then went to Son Pollards and brot Polly Town to Nurs her aunt. I returnd home before night and did my household business.

Since Dr. Ellis lived nearer to the Lambards' than Martha, it is not surprising that he was called when the baby came faster than expected, but it does suggest that there was now no other midwife in the center of the town. Mrs. Piper was apparently a helpful neighbor rather than an experienced practitioner.

Ann Mosier's death gave Martha a reason for resuming her work. Though other midwives may eventually have picked up some of the slack—Martha's deliveries declined in 1810 and 1811 —she never dropped back to her low of 1808. In fact, she delivered almost as many babies in the last four months of her life as in the first years of the diary. Since hard times continued, the extra income was probably welcome. On February 13, 1810, she wrote, "Mr Petengail took our Cow for Taxes. What we are to do God only knows." Joseph North's account book explains how that problem was solved. On February 17, he noted under Ephraim Ballard's name, "let a cow to him I Bought at Vendue of Benj Petingill for $12.50. Agreed to pay 5.00 a year for the use of her." Three deliveries would just about pay for the rent of the cow.

Martha was needed. There were no doubt other women in town with experience in nursing, but after Ann Mosier's death there was no one else with a clear claim to eminence in the field. The logical heirs of an old midwife were her own daughters or daughters-in-law, but Hannah, Dolly, and Sally were all still too encumbered by young children to take up the work. On November 14, 1810, Martha was accompanying Ebenezer Hovey to his wife's delivery when she "met Joel Savage on the same arand." She was relieved sometime later to hear that Mrs. Savage "was delivd by Mrs

Carter and comfortable." Mrs. Carter was apparently a new midwife. In some families, a doctor was the first one called. On August 6, 1811, Martha delivered Moses Partridge's wife of her second son. "Mr P had been after 3 doctors. Could not obtan neither of them before he Calld me."

Martha pushed herself to keep up with the demand. In the first four months of 1812, she delivered fourteen babies, her yearly total for the year before. Her description of a delivery on March 27, 1812, suggests a peculiar kind of competition between her and the doctors:

I was Calld at 10 hour AM by Edward Savage to go and see his wife who was in Labour. I had a fall on my way but not much hurt. Found the patient had Calld 2 midwives & Doct Ellis before shee saw me. I found her mind was for Doct Cony. He was Calld and as Providence would have Shee Calld on me to assist her. I performd the Case. Shee was delivered at 8 hour 30 m pm of a son and is as wel as can be expected. I slept at Mr Jery Babcocks. Had an aguish turn in the night.

That the woman summoned three midwives and two doctors suggests that female practitioners were still important. In naming the doctors but not the midwives, Martha revealed continuing habits of deference as well as a subtle pride that she was the person chosen to attend the mother.

Such strenuous activity was taking its toll, as Dr. Cony may have recognized. He stopped to see her later. "Gave me hirapicra & Camphr. I went to bed & slept some afternoon." She felt very unwell the next day and for most of the week following, but on April 4, she got out of bed at one o'clock in the morning to attend Mrs. Clark. "I wrode on horsback without a pillion. Felt very much fatagud. The patient was safe delivered at 3 hour pm of her fifth son. I tarried all night."

She attended Sally Foy's delivery on April 18, and, though she suffered "two ague fitts" the next day, went in a rainstorm to deliver William Saunders's wife of her third daughter and fourth child. "I laid down & slept some," she wrote, then took breakfast with the Saunders, stopped to see another patient, and came home, and "did my ironing and some mending but feel feeble." She was called to see Mrs. Heath on April 24, stayed with her all day and night and into the next day: "We have slept a little. I have had ague fitts yesterday & to day." Mrs. Heath's illness increased after midnight on April 26, and after a "very severe" labor she was safe delivered at 4:30 a.m. Martha left her before noon in the care of her mother.

"I have been very ill," Martha wrote the next day—and the next and the next. On May 4, "Clear. Mr Ballard to Town meeting. Dolly Lambard came to help me." On May 5, "Snowd and very Cold. I have felt very feeble." On May 6, "A very stormy day. I do not fel any better." Spring was very slow in coming. This year for Martha there would be no planting. On May 7:

> Clear the most of the day & very Cold & windy. Daughter Ballard and a Number of her Children here. Mrs Partridge & Smith allso. Revered Mr Tappin Came and Converst swetly and mad a prayer adapted to my Case.

So the diary ends. Martha probably lived another three weeks, but the life she recorded closes here, as she would have wished, with a roomful of visitors and a prayer. "Funeral of Mrs. Ballard at Augusta," Henry Sewall noted on May 31. On June 6, Joseph North inadvertently documented her death by transferring the rented cow from Ephraim Ballard to Barnabas Lambard, a paper transaction between three men documenting and at the same time obscuring the passing of a stewardship from mother to daughter. On June 9, the *American Advocate* printed its one-sentence obituary: "Died in Augusta, Mrs. Martha, consort of Mr. Ephraim Ballard, aged 77 years."

If the Reverend Mr. Tappin preached a sermon at Martha's funeral, it has not survived. He could have done no better than repeat the eulogy written in 1739 by Jared Eliot, a Connecticut minister, for Mrs. Elizabeth Smithson, an aged midwife of Killingworth. Eliot began by debunking the "false Light & wrong Notions" of greatness extant in the world. Why is it, he asked, that "troublers of others Peace have been Celebrated in History, have been Extolled and Admired" while "Real worth has been disregarded"? The deceased, he continued, was a true light upon a hill.

> She was a person of Humility, Affability, Compassion, and on whose Tongue was the Law of Kindness; Her Ear was open to the Complaints of the Afflicted, and her Hand was open for the Supply of the Needy.
>
> If others were so Unhappy as to divide into Parties, and to burn with Contention, yet she remained'd a Common Friend to all. . . .
>
> She was a Person Useful among the Sick, and ready to minister to them to the utmost of her Power.
>
> As a Midwife, she was a Person of Superior Skill and Capacity; as was found by Experience in the most difficult Cases. . . .
>
> She regarded the Poor as well as the Rich. . . .
>
> She denied her self both Sleep and Rest, and spared neither Skill nor Pains for the Relief of those that were Afflicted and Distressed.
>
> At last, when her Powers were broken, and Strength almost Exhausted, in one of the last instances of her Improvement; it being an Uncommon and seemingly a Desperate Case, her usual Dexterity and Success did not fail her.
>
> Those Mothers in Israel, who are in these Towns usefully imployed as Midwives, will suffer me to Apply those words, Prov. xxi.29, I may say of You, Many Daughters have done Vertuously; but of the Deceased I may say, But Thou Excellest them all.[47]

The ideals that permeate Eliot's sermon, old at the time of Martha's birth, shaped her life—and her diary. Her restraint in recording the sins of her neighbors, her humility in acknowledging her own, her charitableness, even her martyrdom and self-pity, were molded by this ethic of caring. But unlike the thousands of midwives and ordinary Christians who have always lived by these standards, Martha Ballard ensured that she would not be forgotten.

There was nothing in Christian tradition that said a midwife ought to keep a diary. In fact, most people, including Eliot, assumed that the works of women would be hidden from the world, though known to God. For some complex of reasons, probably unknown even to her, Martha felt an intense need to re-create her own life day by day in her diary. As a consequence, she left a eulogy more powerful than any New England pastor was capable of preaching.

She not only documented her prayers, her lost sleep, her deeds of charity and compassion, she savored and wrote down the petty struggles and small graces of ordinary life. The diary is a selective record, shaped by her need to justify and understand her life, yet it is also a remarkably honest one. Through it we know her as a Daughter of Zion who shoveled manure and bled cats, a pious midwife who religiously collected her fees and even treated herself, once in a while, to a new teapot or dress, a self-sacrificing neighbor who took naps while her girls washed, scolded her servants when they misbehaved, and occasionally quarreled with her husband. The diary tells us that Martha was a devout Christian and humble nurse whose intelligence sometimes made it difficult for her to attend church or to defer to her town's physicians, a loving mother who fought openly for possession of her house and sometimes felt abandoned and unappreciated. She was a gentle woman with a sense of duty and an anatomical curiosity that allowed her to observe autopsies as well as cry over the dead, a courageous woman who never quite learned to stay on her horse, a sharp-eyed and practical woman who kept faith in ultimate justice despite repeated encounters with suicide, murder, and war.

To celebrate such a life is to acknowledge the power—and the poverty—of written records. Outside her own diary, Martha has no history. Although she considered herself "the head of a family," a full partner in the management of a household, no independent record of her work survives. It is her husband's name, not hers, that appears in censuses, tax lists, and merchant accounts for her town. She is not listed in Hallowell's poor relief records, though we know she relieved the poor, nor in the earliest records of the Augusta First Church, though she was a member. Nor does any extant court record acknowledge the testimony she took from unwed mothers in delivery. Her name appears on a list of witnesses at the North rape trial, but no one, except she, preserved a record of what was said. Henry Sewall mentioned her five times in his diary, four in relation to births and once when she died, but he never explicitly identified her as a midwife or acknowledged paying a fee.

Without the diary, even her name would be uncertain. Although Oxford records note the baptism of "Martha," daughter of Elijah and Doratha Moore," Martha lost her given name as well as her surname at marriage.[48] For 58 of her 77 years, she was known as "Mrs. Ballard." Even Benjamin Tappin, the minister who "conversed sweetly" with her just before her death, was unsure of her name. Sometime after 1830, he took it upon himself to correct the early records of Augusta First Church. "It does not appear that any record was made of female members," he wrote, "but there is sufficient evidence that several females were considered members of the Church. I have taken the liberty, therefore, to add their names." Beside Ephraim's name, he wrote "Dorothy Ballard."[49] James North, Augusta's nineteenth-century historian, referred to her as "Mrs. Ephraim Ballard" in the body of his work and as "Hannah" in his brief genealogy of the Ballard family.[50] Fortunately, she had the good sense to write firmly at the end of one of her homemade booklets, "Martha Ballard Her Diary."

Ephraim Ballard left Oxford in 1775 to establish a patrimony in a land of wood. He eventually succeeded. Although the site of John Jones's mill is lost in the congestion of twentieth-century Augusta, and the old Howard farm, cut through by the railroad in the nineteenth century, is now the location of a city water treatment plant, Ballard's corner survives, the road running today almost on the line Ephraim marked in his first maps of the town. Near the spot where Jonathan and Sally built their house in 1805 is an early-nineteenth-century dwelling built by their grandson, an Augusta selectman named Ephraim Ballard.

Martha's Ephraim died in 1821, at the age of ninety-six, surrounded by three generations of descendants. Into the 1830s, his
sons and grandsons were still assembling mill sites in the neighborhood and the women of the family were still struggling to
maintain their autonomy. When Jonathan died in 1838, Sally received "in leiu of dower," a portion of the dwelling house with
"exclusive occupancy and control of the West door leading out of
said house," DeLafayette's widow and her second husband to
have the rest. Whether Sally adjusted to joint occupancy more
easily than Martha we do not know, though an addendum to the
record suggests otherwise: "The said Sally Ballard surrenders all
right and control of the south door and entry."[51]

Martha did not leave a farm but a life, recorded patiently and
consistently for twenty-seven years. No gravestone bears her
name, though perhaps somewhere in the waste places along
Belgrade Road there still grow clumps of camomile or feverfew
escaped from her garden.

EPILOGUE

That Martha Ballard kept her diary is one small miracle; that her descendants saved it is another. When her great-great-granddaughter Mary Hobart inherited it in 1884, it was "a hopeless pile of loose unconsecutive pages"—but it was all there. The diary had remained in Augusta for more than sixty years, probably in the family of Dolly Lambard, who seems to have assumed custody of her mother's papers along with the rented cow. At Dolly's death in 1861, the diary descended to her daughters, Sarah Lambard and Hannah Lambard Walcott. James North no doubt consulted the diary at Sarah Lambard's house on Chapel Street in Augusta, extracting the few passages he included in his *History*.

Mary Hobart was ten years old when her great-grandmother Dolly Lambard died. She was thirty-three and a recent graduate of medical school when her great-aunts Sarah and Hannah gave her the diary. "As the writer was a practising physician," she later explained, "it seemed only fitting that the Ballard diary, so crowded with medical interest, should descend to her." In 1930, Hobart gave the diary to the Maine State Library in Augusta. In a letter written at the time, she summarized her own life in a few brisk sentences, referring to herself in the third person:

The doctor, who likes to believe that the mantle of her gifted ancestor fell on her shoulders, was born in Boston, 1851. She graduated from the Woman's Medical College of the New York Infirmary, in 1884, and carried on her medical work in Boston until 1913, when she retired to private life and took up her residence at Needham Heights, Mass. During the thirty years of her professional life, she was associated with the New England Hospital for Women and Children of Boston.[1]

It is not surprising that Mary Hobart found inspiration in her ancestor's life. She was herself a pioneer.

Hobart began her professional life at the famous New York Infirmary for Women and Children, founded by Dr. Elizabeth Blackwell, the first woman in the United States to graduate from medical school. Blackwell had hoped that other women might follow in her footsteps, but when established medical colleges, including her own alma mater, Geneva College, closed their doors to female students, she was forced to open her own. Thanks to Blackwell's efforts and those of others like her, female physicians comprised about 5 percent of the profession in the late nineteenth century, a figure that changed little until the 1960s.[2] Mary Hobart spent the remainder of her professional life at another landmark institution: the New England Hospital, founded in 1862 by Dr. Marie Zakrzewska, was the second hospital in the United States run by women for women. Unabashedly separatist, it survived into the middle of the twentieth century, simultaneously committed to high professional standards and to female control.[3]

The year Mary Hobart received the diary was an important one for the female physicians of Boston. On June 10, 1884, after more than thirty years of debate, the Massachusetts Medical Society voted (63 to 47) to admit women as members. Marie Zakrzewska had first petitioned for membership in 1852. After repeated rejections (male leaders felt it was improper for men and women to discuss medical matters together), she gave up trying, vowing that if ever the society did open its rolls to women, she would ignore it. Still, when the opportunity finally became available, she did not discourage her young colleagues from applying.[4] Mary Hobart lost no time.

On June 16, less than a week after the society's vote, Charles Green of the Suffolk District Medical Society wrote to Dr. Francis Goss of the state society informing him that two women, one of whom was "Mary F. Hobart, M.D.," had applied for membership. "Before I can Examine into the Credentials of these women I shall need instructions as to what diplomas to recognize," he continued, adding, "Of course there are no women's colleges on the authorized list." He closed the letter, "Yours truly & in disgust."[5]

Conscious of her own place in history, Mary Hobart was drawn to her ancestor's diary. Her cousin Lucy Lambard Fessenden arranged the scrambled leaves of the diary in order and bound them in homemade linen covers. Mary had a mahogany box made in which to keep the now two-volume diary. "During her practice, it has been a source of vital interest to her colleagues as well as to her family," she told the state librarian. One can imagine the doctors of the New England hospital turning the pages of the old diary during the troubling decades at the turn of the century, a time when old traditions of separatism were being challenged by the gradual opening of male colleges and hospitals to women. What lessons did they glean from the faded pages?

Mary Hobart did not say. But some sense of the complex attitudes of nineteenth-century women toward the past can be gained by comparing Hobart with one of her relatives, Dorothy Barton's granddaughter Clara Barton. In 1882, while Mary Hobart was studying at the New York Infirmary, Barton was lobbying Congress to support the Treaty of Geneva, making possible the establishment of the American Red Cross, a success, as her biographer proclaims, "to be measured not only against the goals of humanitarians—where it stands as a stunning achievement—but also with the work of diplomats."[6]

Unlike Hobart, Barton was old enough to have known her Maine progenitors personally. Her grandmother, Dorothy Barton, had spent the last years of her life in Oxford during Clara's childhood. Clara was intrigued with her grandmother's feistiness and rebellion. She identified, too, with her father's and grandfather's stories of war, which may help account for her own battlefield adventures. During the Civil War she fled her Patent Office clerkship in Washington, D.C., for the fields of Fredericksburg, Harper's Ferry, and Bull Run, collecting bandages and candles for military physicians, assisting with nursing, and, when no doctor could be found, standing in pools of blood and extracting bullets with her pocketknife. She may have been thinking of herself as well as her ancestors when she wrote a colleague who proposed compiling a history of American women, "From the storm lashed decks of the Mayflower . . . to the present hour; woman has stood like a rock for the welfare and the glory of the history of the country, and one might well add . . . unwritten, unrewarded, and almost unrecognized."[7]

Barton rebelled against the genteel femininity of her own generation by joining men in their own arena, proving her heroism in wholehearted commitment to her country's glory. Despite her public reputation as a self-sacrificing "angel of the battlefield," she was a conscious feminist, a lifelong supporter of women's rights and women's suffrage. At the same time, she was also somewhat conventional in her acceptance of male values. She remembered her grandmother's resistance to the pre-Revolutionary tea boycott, but she never questioned her father's and grandfather's commitment to war. She was the sort of woman who would have gloried in a "storm swept" canoe ride along the Kennebec but might have grown tired of the narrow theatre of birth.

In contrast, Mary Hobart was attracted less to the heroism than to the professionalism of her great-great-grandmother's life. To her, Martha was a "gifted" woman, a skilled practitioner, careful about her fees and sure of her methods. In some ways, Mary Hobart *had* assumed the mantle of her ancestor. She and her great-great-grandmother were both independent and resourceful women. Both specialized in the care of women and children. Both had problematical relations with the medical establishments of their time. Yet there were also important differences between them. Martha was a skilled practitioner in an ancient female craft, Mary an early entrant in a once exclusively male profession. Martha derived her authority from a local community of women.

Mary owed her profession and her identity to a new feminist sisterhood. Martha ministered to women of all social classes in their own homes. Mary cared for the poor in a public hospital. Martha was married and the mother of nine children. Mary was single, by choice and perhaps by necessity as well. Unlike women of her great-great-grandmother's generation, she was able to support herself independently, yet was expected to choose between marriage and a career.[8]

Mary Hobart cherished her ancestor's diary. Only a desire to make it "more accessible to a wider circle of antiquarian workers," combined with a fear that it was not quite safe in her wooden house, prompted her to donate it to the Maine State Library in 1930. The library promised to give her, in exchange, a typewritten transcription of the original. She never received such a transcription, though two years later the library presented her with offprints of Charles Elventon Nash's abridgment of the diary. Nash's version of the diary had been completed sometime before 1904 as part of a proposed two-volume history of Augusta. At his death most of the first volume had been printed but not bound or published. For almost sixty years the uncut signatures sat in wooden crates in a descendant's house. The state librarian apparently got wind of their existence and secured a print of the diary portion for Dr. Hobart. He apologized for not having provided the full typescript promised, but he assured her that Mr. Nash had "copied the most important parts of the Journal and also made a great many important and valuable footnotes."

Hobart was gracious in her acknowledgment of the gift, though obviously disappointed.

> I am greatly indebted to your untiring zeal in obtaining and sending this reprint to me. Of course in its modern setting I miss the old-time paper, the quaint penmanship and especially the marginal notes which stated the various 'rewards' my great-great-grandmother received from her patients. Also, I shall never feel certain about the completeness, as much material is doubtless omitted. But I consider my self and my descendants—or, more properly speaking,

my heirs—fortunate in the possession of so good a copy
&, as you say, Mr. Nash's introduction & footnotes will
add to its value.[9]

Much of importance had indeed been omitted from the diary.
As we have seen, Nash preserved about a third of the original.
He recorded the dramatic journey across the Kennebec in 1789,
the passage with which we began this book, most of Martha's
account of the Purrinton murders, and many of her casual references to public affairs. But he provided only an edited version
of the births, salvaging genealogical but deliberately excising
sexual content. He mentioned autopsies, but excluded her detailed descriptions of them, gave representative samples of her
work entries, but cut or muted all references to family troubles.
He omitted her description of the North rape trial and reduced
to a minimum her lists of visitors, purchases, journeys, household work, gardening, and textile production.

Still, it took genuine commitment for a busy man to copy by
hand hundreds of pages of an obscure diary, traveling to Boston
to do so. Given the circumstances, Nash can certainly be forgiven
for dropping generic references to weeding cucumbers or bleaching cloth. That he wished to preserve his own good name in the
town by omitting scandal is also understandable. Unlike his nineteenth-century predecessor, he knew Martha's name and he gave
her diary the prominence in his work that it had long been denied.
His footnotes and index *are* useful, though the latter might have
been more so had it included women's names as well as men's.

Nash's work deserved a better fate than it received. Although
most of the first volume had been typeset and printed at the time
of his death, no person then or for fifty years thereafter thought it
worth completing and binding. In 1958, one of his descendants
contacted the Maine State Library. The sill of the barn where the
old crates were kept needed replacing. Did the State Library want
to store them? Edith Hary had a better idea. With the help of two
other women, she sorted through Nash's papers, collated the signatures, found a printer willing to experiment with binding the old
paper, and in 1961 published *The History of Augusta: First Settlements*

and Early Days As A Town Including The Diary of Mrs. Martha Moore Ballard. "Mrs. Ballard made the difference," she explained.[10]

Through Hary's work, a new generation of schoolchildren, scholars, and readers have discovered the diary. Still, the promise made to Mary Hobart is yet unfulfilled. Martha Ballard's diary rests safe in a vault at the Maine State Library, a monument to a remarkable life and a testimony to the fragile web that connects one generation with another.

Appendix:
Medicinal Ingredients Mentioned in Martha Ballard's Diary

Since the majority of Martha's medicinal entries are nonspecific ("made a syrup," "administered a clister," "gathered herbs," "used means"), it is not possible to develop a complete pharmacopoeia. The difficulty is compounded by the fact that in her lifetime many common garden vegetables or household staples had potential therapeutic uses. I have included here every ingredient for which she gave an explicit medicinal reference as well as others known *primarily* as medicinal plants and for which clear references to growing, gathering, or purchasing appear. I have included onions, for example, because she clearly used them medicinally, but not beans or radishes, even though herbals sometimes give medical uses for them. Where Martha mentioned growing or gathering a medicinal herb but did not indicate how she used it, I have given possible applications from contemporary sources.

There is not enough information in the diary to distinguish wild from cultivated herbs. Martha noted planting camomile and coriander in her garden and digging cold water root in "a field," but when she wrote that she "Cut up" catmint and tansy, we cannot be sure where she got them. Both are English plants, often cultivated in gardens, but in some places they had also become naturalized. Usually, however, I can distinguish local plants from imported ingredients on the basis of her descriptions.

I. LOCAL PLANTS

Agrimony For her niece Parthenia Pitts, she made a syrup of "comphry, plantain, agrimony & Solomon Seal leaves," June 5, 1794.

Anise "Planted pepers, anis, coriander," May 26, 1787. Martha also mentions purchasing "annis seed," which she used with manna and senna as a laxative. See also Anise seed and Rhubarb in Part II below.

Balm "Gathered my Balm flowers," July 29, 1801. This could be the "Balm" listed in Culpeper as an herb for inducing perspiration and suppressing menstruation. It could also be a shortened reference to Balm of Gilead, below.

Balm of Gilead "I sett Current Bushes & Balm Giliad," April 22, 1802. "I have been drinking a beer made of hops and Balm Gilliad," April 5, 1805. Meyer (p. 82), mentions cough syrup made with Balm of Gilead. See also Southernwood.

Balsam "His Child very unwell. He Came to me and had syrip of Balson for it," August 14, 1803. Not clear whether this is local or imported.

Basswood "I applyd a poltis of Basswd to Manlys foot it being sweld," June 1, 1789.

Buckthorn root "Mr. Gill Came to bring some Buckthorn roots for my daughter" (Lucy Towne, who was dying), July 6, 1798.

Burdock "Was directly Calld to son Lambards, his little Daughter being in a fitt but was revid before I reacht there, but seems to be in a high feavor. We applied Burdoc leavs to her stomach and feet and gave her a syrrip of mullin and shee had some rest," August 26, 1799.

Burnet "I removd parsley and Burnet roots," May 12, 1797. Culpeper says it will "staunch inward or outward bleedings" including "too abundant women's courses," among other uses: Potterton, p. 35.

Camomile "I sett Cammomile roots," July 18, 1791. "I gathered my Cammomile, the second gathering," October 4, 1792. "My daughter Hannah is very unwell this evening. I gave her some Cammomile & Camphor," November 30, 1791. See also Mugwort.

Catnip, catmint "We made a bed by the fire & gave him some catnip tea," October 5, 1787. "Cut up herbs to drie, catmint and tansey," August 2, 1811.

Cold water root "Went to the field & got some Cold water root. Then Calld to Mr Kenydays to see Polly. Very ill with the Canker. Gave her some of the root," August 7, 1787. Name not found in early herbals. Meyer, p. 286, identifies it as *Aster puneceus*. Thacher, p. 214, says that the plant favored by the common people for canker and sore throat was marsh rosemary, which he identified as *statice Limonium*. See Vitriol.

Comfrey "Applid a plaster of Comphry to his ancle," June 25, 1786. Also used internally. See Agrimony.

Coriander See Anise. Hannah Smith added coriander and annis seeds to a "gripe water": p. 266.

Currants During Lucy's last illness, "sent a bottle of current syrup," August 31, 1798. "I eat Curant saus with Tea about 2 hours before sun sett and in 3 hours it found its way thro me and I find relief," July 14, 1802. "H-S & Martha Ballard here for Curents for old Mrs Dunpha. Her grand childn have the hooping cough," July 8, 1806.

Dock root "Mrs Nason Calld in to get some Dock root for the itch," May 5, 1807.

Feverfew "Cut sage & feaverfue," June 11, 1802. "I made a decoction of feaverfue, peneroial [pennyroyal] & Cammomile for my self & daughter," September 16, 1793. After childbirth, Martha found Hannah Pollard "Exercised with a severe pain in her head. We applied feaverfue to her temples and gave a Clister," October 24, 1795. See also Mugwort.

Gold thread "Old Mrs. Kenny advised to giv her a syrup of vinegar and onions, and a decoction of gold thread and shumake berries. It was done and shee seemed revived," March 29, 1797.

Hops "I have gathedd part of my hops," September 24, 1805. "Cyrus to Son Lambards. He Carreid 3 lb hops and my daughter sent me 3/ 2/1 oz. sinamon," December 24, 1805. Culpeper claimed that hops would kill worms, bring down women's courses and expel urine: Potterton, p. 99.

Hyssop "Cut hyssop," July 31, 1787. For complications following childbirth, "applyd ointment & a Bath of Tansy, mugwort, cammomile, & Hysop, which gave Mrs Cragg great relief," April 5, 1790.

Lily "Lidia Braly got yellow lilly roots to apply to Mrs Pollards Breast. It seemd to giv her more pain," February 15, 1801.

London pride For a grandson "ill with pain like a Collic we administred a Clister and gave him the decoction of the flowers of London pride," June 30, 1801.

Lovage "Gave my daughter some Lovage Tea which relievd her of faintness," May 9, 1790.

Maidenhair "Nabby Jackson here for some maidenhair for Mrs Bent who Remains poorly," October 22, 1786. Gave Jonathan "a Tea of mullin & maidin hair which gave relief," August 17, 1791.

Mandrake "I planted sumer squash, Crambery Beens, musk mellons & Mandrake seed," May 16, 1797. According to Culpeper, a powerful purgative and emetic: Potterton, p. 119.

Marigolds "Gathered Cucumbers, Camomile, merigolds, and pikt some wool," August 24, 1798. Hannah Smith included marigold flowers with Virginia snakeroot and other ingredients in a "water" used to "deliver a woman of a dead child,": p. 261.

Melilot "Mrs Pollard Came here with her son Amos who had a Lame knee. I Bathd it with Camphor & mellolot ointment, applied a plaster of my salv," December 1, 1787. "Have made mellolott Ointment for myself and son Jonathan's wife," July 10, 1811.

Mugwort "Put oinions to her feet and gave her a decoction of mugwort and Feaverfue," February 7, 1800. See also Hyssop.

Mullein "Calld at 2 hour morning to see Mr Black's infant, who is unwell. It was a little revivd before I arivd. I gave it a Syrrup of mullin which gave it relief," June 14, 1791. See also Maidenhair.

Mustard "Gathered mustard seed. Shelld some that was dried," August 31, 1809. "Bot . . . a mustard sallt," November 24, 1792. Used for poultices or, following Culpepper, to "bring down the courses": Potterton, p. 131.

Onions Usually applied to the feet, e.g., "Jonathan was very violant siesd with feavor and universally pained. We put him to Bed, appld onions to his feet, gave him tees to promote sweting, set up to him till 1/ O Clok," September 5, 1786. See also Indian meal under Miscellaneous Ingredients.

Parsley Many entries for cultivation. Smith added parsley to many syrups and also included it with oil of turpentine and sulfur in a remedy for piles: pp. 256, 268, 323.

Patience "Cookt pork, patience, Cabage sprouts, yerrow, & shepherd's sprouts": May 18, 1806. Used as a pot herb here.

Pennyroyal See Feverfew. Thacher, p. 157, says it had "long been esteemed as an aperient and deobstruent, particularly in hysteric and other female complaints."

Peppers "Had Collic symptoms. Took some pepper pod steept which remoovd it," September 1, 1786. "[She] was seisd with pukeing. I gave her the tincture of red pepper. Shee soon revivd and went to rest," February 26, 1797.

Plantain See Agrimony.

Rhubarb   Martha grew rhubarb in her garden ("Ephraim had Currint Bushes, rhubarb & other roots," May 1, 1810), but the rhubarb mentioned most frequently in her diary was probably an imported laxative. See Rhubarb under Purchased Medicines.

Rue   "I removd my Rhue and Camomile," November 3, 1797. "Planted Rheu, safron, marigolds," May 26, 1806. Used to promote menstruation: Potterton, p. 160.

Saffron   Many entries for planting and harvesting. Usually prescribed for infants. Sent "honey and safron" when Son Pollard's youngest child was "unwell with a soar mouth," October 14, 1798. See also Snakeroot.

Sage   "Set out 100 young sage roots," October 28, 1800. "Cut 14 1/2 lb sage from the two beds next to the house," July 29, 1801. "Sally Ballard is unwell. I made her Sage Tea," December 23, 1811.

Sanicle   "Betsy and I went to the field and got sennakle root," July 21, 1785. According to Culpeper, it helps to "stay women's courses, and all other fluxes of blood": Potterton, p. 164.

Shepherd's-purse   Might be the "shepherd's sprouts" Martha cooked with cabbage. See Patience. Like so many other herbs on Martha's list, it was credited with stopping "the terms" in women: Potterton, p. 171.

Snakeroot   "They gave me a decoction of snake root & saffron," October 11, 1801.

Solomon's seal   See Agrimony.

Sorrel   "Dolly lame. Poultist her foot with Sorril roasted," October 11, 1787.

Southernwood   A stranger came to Martha's house, "requested me to giv her some buds of Balm Gilead and some suthernwood. Shee took what shee wisht for and went on for Capt. stackpoles at Winslow," December 14, 1801.

Sumac berries See Gold thread.

Summer savory "Sowed summer savory," May 1, 1794. Culpeper said it "expels tough phlegm from the chest and lungs" and was useful in easing pain from bee stings: Potterton, p. 166.

Tansy "Hannah Ballard here for Tansy for Samuel. Says he is very unwel. Pukt up a worm," April 9, 1806. See also Catnip, Catmint, and Mugwort.

Tow "Eunice had a very severe pain in her teeth & face. I aplyd some scorcht Tow & hett her face & shee got Ease," March 4, 1789.

Turnip "Elisa very unwel. We aplyed Turnip poltis to her bowels which gave relief soon," August 4, 1810.

Wormwood "I gave Dolly a Decoction of the two wormwoods," March 18, 1792.

Yarrow See Patience. Still used medicinally. Culpeper considered it effective in stopping bleeding and "running of the reins in men and whites in women": Potterton, p. 204.

II. PURCHASED MEDICINES

Martha bought most of the imported ingredients she used from Dr. Colman, though she occasionally bought or borrowed ingredients from Dr. Cony.

Aloes Mrs. Black "had a small Tumbler full of my aloctic Tincture. Paid me /9," September 10, 1794. Gave aloes to a child who was "Cutting her Eye teeth," January 10, 1788. See also Bravux, Myrrh.

Anderson's pills "Mr Ballard got me a Box Andersons Pills. I took 2 at night," October 18, 1806.

Anise seed "To Doctor Colmans, bought ... 1 oz annis seed /4," August 5, 1793.

Bravux   "I gave my daughter three pills prepared of myrr, Alloes and a grain of Bravux," November 5, 1795.

Camphor   Usually used externally, e.g., "Ephraim was Choping & a Chip struck my face which hurt me much. I applyd camphor," September 20, 1791. See Myrrh, below, and Camomile and Mugwort under Local Plants.

Dragon's blood   "Bought 1 oz. Dragon's Blood for 1/6," October 5, 1793. "Gave his wife Dragons Blood which abated her Complaint," September 5, 1795. See also Spermaceta.

Elixir proprietas   "Gave the Lady some senna & manna with seeds and left her an ounce of Elixer propt," February 7, 1791.

Galbanum   She bought 1 oz. from Dr. Colman, October 6, 1794.

Hartshorn   "Dr. Coney here. Let me have half oz. hartshorn & 2 stiptic Powder, pric 1/," September 18, 1786.

Licorice   "Gave her son urin & honey & some Liqurish, put a plaster to her stomach," September 23, 1786. Joseph North sold licorice as well as garden seeds.

Linseed oil   "Made ointment of Lintseed Oil, Bees wax & resin" (for a child who was "scalt"), April 6, 1792.

Manna   "Dolly very unwell. I gave her senna & manna with annis seed and Rheubarb. It opperated kindly," February 1, 1791.

Myrrh   "At Dr. Colman's, 2 oz. spermaseta, 2 oz. manna, 1/2 oz. myr, ditto alloes, 1/2, Vial & salts, Camphr 1/2 oz," July 3, 1794.

Niter   "I was Calld out of Bed at 10 hour Evening to go and see Mr Pillsbury's Child. Its Complaint was obstruction of urin. I recommended giving a little Niter which relievd the patient," July 11, 1795.

Oil, British oil, sweet oil   "I made a syrrup for Mrs Weston and for Mrs Porter & some oil a mulge," October 23, 1786. "I had a sever pain in my left Ear. I applied some british Oil and a warm Brick. Went onto the Bed and got Easier," March 6, 1799. "I find Hepsy unwell by being poised in her face and hands. I washt her with spirit and ointed her with Sweet Oil," August 16, 1799.

Pepper "I find Patty very sick. I put Black wool wet with Brandy & pepper in her Ears which gave her present relief," December 6, 1798. This could be either black pepper, which would most likely be purchased, or red—see Peppers under Local Plants.

Pink root "To Doctor Colmans. Bot ... 1/2 oz. pink root /4 1/2" August 5, 1793. "Son Jonathan's son is better. Has had a Number of Large worms past from him, after takeing the Pink root, & senna after it," August 12, 1793.

Rhubarb "Dolly is very unwell. I gave her senna & manna with annis seed and Rhubarb. It opperated kindly," February 1, 1791.

Scraped horn "I drest Manlys wound. Aplyd an Egg cataplasm & scraped horn," June 2, 1789.

Senna "I gave her senna and it opperated twice with the assitance of Clisters," November 3, 1795. See also Elixir proprietas, Manna.

Spanish flies "Sister is very unwel. I sent for flies to draw a blister," April 18, 1810.

Spermaceta "Went to Doct Colmans. Bot 1/2 lb. spermaseta @ 2/, 1 oz Dragons Blood 1/6; 2 oz. of manna 2/; 1 nutmegg 1/. Paid 6/ in Cash," October 5, 1793.

Styptic powder "Mr Wicsom here the morn for advise, his wife being in Dangerous circumstances. I sent her a steptic powder which he gave her, it gave relief. I went myself, left her some things to take," January 10, 1791. See also Hartshorn.

Turpentine "An ox trod on Mr Ballard's foot & Lamd it very much. I Batht it with Camphor & turpentine," September 1, 1787.

Vitriol　"I was at Mr Densmores to see his Daughter Dorcas, who has a soar throat. We gave her Cold Water root Tea & a fue drops Viteral," June 14, 1794.

III. MISCELLANEOUS INGREDIENTS

Beeswax　Dressed burns with "an ointment of Lintseed Oil, Bees wax, & resin," April 6, 1792.

Brandy　Used internally and externally. "Very unwell. I tried to take a swett Last night but could not. This night went into a warm Bed, Drank some hott Brandy tody. Swet a little," November 8, 1785. "Calld Lydia up in the night. Shee applyed poultises to my feet and warm Brandy to my head with hot flannell," April 11, 1803. See Pepper.

Broth　"I gave him a Portion of Rhubarb. We kill a Chikin, made some Broth," September 24, 1786.

Cat's blood　"He has the shingles. We bled a Catt & applid the Blood which gave him Relief," October 13, 1786.

Cow's milk　"Mrs. Pitts rose about an hour by sun in the morn, went out & milkt the last milk from the Cow into her mouth & swallowed it," July 23, 1794. See also Salt.

Egg　James Andrews "has a swelling on his right side. Applied a Cataplasm made of the yolk of an Egg, Honey & flower," June 29, 1789.

Flour　See Egg.

Honey　"Ephraim's Mare is Lambed. Put honney & Camphor onto the wound," January 30, 1802. See also Egg, Licorice under Purchased Medicines, and Saffron under Local Plants.

Indian meal (cornmeal)　"Dresst the burns with poullises of 3 pt rhum, oinions, and indien meal" January 6, 1801. (May have been prescribed by Dr. Cony or Dr. Colman).

Linseed oil   See Beeswax.

Lint   "Mr Chamberlin Calld me to see a wound his daughter Polly had on her right Legg. I dresst it with lint & spirrit," October 14, 1790.

Resin   See Beeswax.

Rum   "At my sons. His little son Burnt his head. We applied Rhum & salt," January 30, 1793. See also Indian meal.

Salt   In a postpartum case, Martha "administered a clister of milk, water & salt" and, the same day, "Calld at Mr. Savages. Gave Nancy a dose of salt & water which Causd her to puke. Shee threw up two worms and seemd Easier," April 5, 1790. See Also Rum.

Soap   "[She] was seisd with pukeing & a disentery attended with severe pain in her stomach. I gave her some annis seed decoction with manna dissolved therein and afterwards 4 soap pills which Expelld thee wind & gave relief," August 8, 1790. Thacher believed soap should only be used as a vehicle for other ingredients, noting that common people had "erroneous notions of its medical virtues."

Spirit   See Lint.

Urine   See Licorice under Purchased Medicines.

Vinegar   "Doctor Emerson calld to see it [a dying child]. We rubd it with vinegar. Gave blisters," May 31, 1788. See also Golden thread under Local Plants.

Wool   "My left knee is sweld & painful. Hannah Ballard brot me spirrit to Baith it with. I applied black wool allso" June 7, 1809. See also Pepper under Purchased Medicines.

BIBLIOGRAPHY

Meyer, Clarence. *American Folk Medicine*. New York: Thomas Y. Crowell, 1973.

Potterton, David, ed. *Culpeper's Color Herbal* (New York: Sterling, 1983).

Smith, E. *The Compleat Housewife: or, Accomplish'd Gentlewoman's Companion*, 15th ed. (London, 1753, fascsimile, London: Literary Services, and Production Limited, 1968).

Thacher, James. *The American New Dispensatory* (Boston, 1810).

Notes

ABBREVIATIONS

ATR   Augusta Town Records, Maine State Library, Augusta

HS   Diary of Henry Sewall, 1776–1842, Massachusetts Historical Society, Boston

HTR   Hallowell Town and Vital Records, I, 1761–1812. II, 1797–1824. Microfilm, Maine State Archives, Augusta.

KCCCP   Kennebec County Court of Common Pleas, Records and Files, Maine State Archives

KCCGSP   Kennebec County Court of General Sessions of the Peace, Records and Files, Maine State Archives

KD   Kennebec County Deeds, Kennebec County Court House, Augusta, Maine

KPR   Kennebec County Probate Records, Kennebec County Court House, Augusta, Maine

LCCCP   Lincoln County Court of Common Pleas, Records and Files, Lincoln County Court House, Wiscasset, Maine

LCCGSP   Lincoln County Court of General Sessions of the Peace, Records and Files, Lincoln County Court House, Wiscasset, Maine

LCD   Lincoln County Deeds, Kennebec County Court House, Augusta, Maine

LCSJC   Lincoln County Supreme Judicial Court, Records and Files, Office of the Clerk of the Supreme Judicial Court, Suffolk County Court House, Boston

MMB Diary of Martha Moore Ballard, I (1785–1799), II, 1800–1812. Maine State Library, Augusta
MSA Massachusetts State Archives, Boston
MHS Massachusetts Historical Society, Boston
MeHS Maine Historical Society, Portland
MeSA Maine State Archives, Augusta
MeSL Maine State Library, Augusta
MeSM Maine State Museum, Augusta
Nash Charles Elventon Nash, *The History of Augusta: First Settlement and Early Days as a Town, Including the Diary of Mrs. Martha Moore Ballard (1785–1812)*. Printed by Charles Nash and Sons, 1904, bound and published 1961 by Edith Hary
NEHGR *New England Historic and Genealogical Register*
North James W. North, *The History of Augusta*. Augusta, 1870; rpt. Somersworth, N.H.: New England History Press, 1981
WMQ *William and Mary Quarterly*, Third Series

INTRODUCTION

1. William Avery Baker, *A Maritime History of Bath, Maine, and the Kennebec River Region* (Bath, Me.: Marine Research Society of Bath, 1973) I, pp. 120, 154–155, 177, 179; North, pp. 240–241, 274–277; *The Tocsin* (Hallowell, Me.), February 26, 1796, December 31, 1796; MMB, May 6, 1785, August 3, 1785, November 24, 1785, February 7, 1786, April 20, 1786, June 13, 15, 1785, July 15, 1786, August 7, 1786, November 16, 1786, December 13, 1786, May 6, 1787, July 19, 1787, April 27, 1789, February 12, 1791, September 28, 1791, October 21, 1789, August 11, 1795.

2. MMB, November 25–26, 1790.

3. MMB, April 22–30, 1785, and May 3–6, 1785; North, pp. 90–91, 198, 884; and on the general importance of the river opening and closing, MMB, March 18–21, 1786, November 23, 1786, April 7–8, 1787, December 15–17, 1789, April 17 and 29, 1790, April 1–3, 1791; John Sheppard to Charles Vaughan, November 18, 1791, John Sheppard Letter Book, I:1, New England Historic Genealogical Society; Deposition of Solomon Park, Files, LCSJC, 912:60.

4. MMB, April 10–13, 1797, April 24–25, 1785.

5. MMB, December 2, 1792, December 30, 1787, December 16, 1789, April 1, 1791.

6. Franklin P. Rice, ed., *Vital Records of Oxford, Massachusetts, to the End of the Year 1849* (Worcester, Mass.: 1905), pp. 13, 14, 268; North, p. 804; *American Advocate* (Hallowell, Me.), p. 3.

7. "Narrative of the Captivity of Mrs. Mary Rowlandson, 1682," in Charles

H. Lincoln, ed., *Narratives of the Indian Wars, 1697–1699* (New York: Charles Scribner's Sons, 1913), pp. 130–131; "A Narrative of Hannah Swarton," in Cotton Mather, *Humiliations Follow'd with Deliverances* (Boston, 1697), p. 59.

8. A useful source for exploring the folk dimensions of early diaries is Marilyn Ferris Motz, "Folk Expression of Time and Place: 19th-Century Midwestern Rural Diaries," *Journal of American Folklore*, 100 (1987): 131–147. Martha's diary is similar to the diaries Motz studied in its hewing to chronological order and in its compression. In other respects, it is more complex and varied.

9. North, p. 297; Nash, p. 234; Richard W. Wertz and Dorothy C. Wertz, *Lying-In: A History of Childbirth in America* (New York: Schocken, 1977), p. 9. The Wertzes relied on the Nash abridgment, as has every other contemporary author of whom I am aware. June Sprigg has made the greatest use of the Nash version of the diary, interspersing quotations from Martha Ballard and six other eighteenth-century women with her drawings of household implements in *Domestick Beings* (New York: Alfred A. Knopf, 1984). Those who have used brief selections include Nancy F. Cott, *The Bonds of Womanhood: "Woman's Sphere" in New England, 1780–1835* (New Haven: Yale University Press, 1977), pp. 19, 29; M. Lelyn Branin, *The Early Potters and Potteries of Maine* (Middletown, Conn.: Wesleyan University Press, 1978), pp. 208; 234; Lee Agger, *Women of Maine* (Portland, Me.: G. Gannett, 1982), pp. 115–119; and Judith Walzer Leavitt, " 'Science' Enters the Birthing Room: Obstetrics in America Since the Eighteenth Century," *The Journal of American History* 70 (September 1983): 281–304.

10. Ebenezer Learned Estate, Worcester Country Probate Records, A:36615, and Elijah Moore Estate, A:41335, Worcester County, Court House, Worcester, Mass.

11. George F. Daniels, *History of the Town of Oxford, Massachusetts* (Oxford: 1892), pp. 257, 619–620; Clifford K. Shipton, *Sibley's Harvard Graduates: Biographical Sketches of Those Who Attended Harvard College*, 15 (Boston: Massachusetts Historical Society, 1970), 80–82; Jonathan Moore Papers, Houghton Library, Harvard College, Cambridge, Mass. Jonathan Moore's will (at Harvard) mentions "interlev'd Almanacks," but I have not been able to locate them.

12. We know too little about female education in early New England. Early work on literacy focused on the ability to sign one's name. More recent work emphasizes that girls were often taught to read but not to write. For a summary of that point, see David D. Hall, *Worlds of Wonder, Days of Judgment: Popular Religious Belief in Early New England* (New York: Alfred A. Knopf, 1989), pp. 32–34. Gloria Main, who has done the most sophisticated work on female signatures, sees a significant improvement in writing ability in the second quarter of the eighteenth century. "Female Literacy in New England," unpublished paper, University of Colorado, Boulder.

13. Rice, *Vital Records of Oxford*, pp. 15–16; Elizabeth Brown Pryor, *Clara Barton: Professional Angel* (Philadelphia: University of Pennsylvania Press, 1987), p. 3. Oxford baptismal records between 1761 and 1772 show the rarity of such names. There is one other "Tryphene," a "Luranna," and a "Bialeta," but old favorites like Abigail, Elizabeth, Hannah, Sarah, and Mary predominate: Church Record Book, MS, First Congregational Church, Oxford, Mass., pp. 222–230. On the uses of the names "Pamela" and "Clarissa Harlowe," see Leslie Dunkling and William Gosling, *The Facts on File Dictionary of First Names* (New York: Facts on File, 1983, pp. 51, 217, and on neo-classicism, David W. Dumas, "The Naming of Children in New England, 1780–1850," *NEHGR* 132 (1978): 196–210.

14. Daniels, *Oxford*, pp. 619, 390. Stephen Barton's account book, MeSL, contains medical entries, especially during the years he lived in Vassalboro, Maine. Daniels says Barton "studied with Dr. Green of Leicester," and that he was also one of "the leading organizers of the 'Social Library' " in Oxford, a fact that may account for his daughters' literary names.

15. Anonymous Barton Family History, typescript, Clara Barton Papers, American Antiquarian Soceity, Worcester, Massachusetts.

16. Clara Barton to Bernard Vassal, November 22, 1890, quoted in Pryor, pp. 4–5.

17. MMB, e.g., April 14, 1785 (salves), July 23, 1787 (syrups), August 19, 1786 (pills), May 27, 1786 (teas), April 6, 1792 (ointment), October 23, 1786 (oil emulsion), October 8, 1785 (poultice), August 19, 1785 (burns), October 11–17, 1785 (dysentery), September, 13, 1786 (sore throat), November 28, 1786 (frostbite), January 15, 1791 (measles), November 13, 1791 ("hooping Cough"), September 4, 1792 ("Chin cough"), August 1, 1793 (St. Vitus's dance), June 15, 1789 ("flying pains"), April 17, 1788 ("salt rhume"), March 17, 1786 ("the itch"), February 1, 1786 (tied tongue), October 9, 1785 ("clister"), August 4, 1788 (abscessed breast), November 14, 1786 (blisters), April 5, 1790 (vomiting). On the effectiveness (or ineffectiveness) of eighteenth-century medicine, see J. Worth Estes, "Medical Skills in Colonial New England," NEHGR 134 (October 1980): 159–175.

18. In addition, her mother and mother-in-law were both alive when she left Oxford; her Grandmother Moore lived until 1760: Daniels, *Oxford*, pp. 618, 587.

19. Sarah Stone, *A Complete Practice of Midwifery* (London, 1737), p. xiv.

20. *Boston Evening Post*, October 16, 1769; Rice, *Vital Records of Oxford*, pp. 268, 297–298; Ernest Caulfield, "Some Common Diseases of Colonial Children," *Publications of the Colonial Society of Massachusetts*, 35 (1942–1946): 24–36.

21. MMB, June 17, 1789.

22. There is just the barest hint in the family history that their children's deaths may have encouraged Martha and Ephraim to leave Oxford. Fifty years

earlier Jonathan Ballard, Ephraim's father, had left Andover, Massachusetts, after an unknown illness had taken his mother and three of his sisters within eighteen days. Charles Frederic Farlow, comp., Charles Henry Pope, ed., *Ballard Genealogy* (Boston, 1911), p. 72; *Vital Records of Andover, Massachusetts to the End of the Year 1842* (Topsfield: Topsfield Historical Society, 1912), pp. 382–383; Daniels, *Oxford*, p. 379.

23. The Ballards were among the families included in Philip Greven's now classic study of Andover, *Four Generations: Population, Land, and Family in Colonial Andover, Massachusetts* (Ithaca, N.Y.: Cornell University Press, 1970). See pp. 47, 84–85, 146, 162–3, 186.

24. Samuel Howard sold land to Nathan Moore "of Kennebeck River above Ft Western" in May of 1768, LCD, I:323;

25. Daniels, *Oxford*, pp. 122, 587–589, 619–620, 725; Ira Thompson Monroe, *History of the Town of Livermore* (Lewiston, Me.: 1928), pp. 24–25; "Journal of Thomas Fish," in [Israel Washburn, Jr.], *Notes, Historical, Descriptive, and Personal of Livermore, Maine* (Portland LCD, 1874), pp. 141–143;

26. LCD I:321, 322, 323, 325, 345; LCCGSP, Records, I: 143; Alma Pierce Robbins, *The History of Vassalborough, Maine* (n. pub., n.d. [1971]), pp. 15, 16; North, p. 146; Daniels, *Oxford*, pp. 619–620, 725.

27. Alan Taylor, *Liberty-Men and White Indians: Frontier Migration, Popular Protest, and the Pursuit of Property in the Wake of the American Revolution*, Ph.D. dissertation, Brandeis University, 1986, pp. 53–70. On the colonial background, see Gordon E. Kershaw, *The Kennebeck Proprietors, 1749–1775* (Portland, Maine Historical Society, 1975).

28. James Phinney Baxter, ed., *Documentary History of the State of Maine* (Portland, Maine Historical Society: 14:242; North, *Augusta*, pp. 45–47; "List of lands to be sold," Gardiner, Whipple, & Allen Papers, MHS, 2:29, Boston. Gardiner gave Ephraim Ballard a letter introducing him to John McKechnie, who had earlier been responsible for certifying land petitions from prospective settlers. Perhaps if the Revolution had not intervened, Ephraim would have assumed this post. John Jones, whose land at Fort Western, Ballard later rented, performed a similar function at Hallowell from 1773 until June of 1776. See Petitions for Grants, 1751–1818, Kennebec Purchase Company Papers, Box 1, MeHS.

29. Mary DeWitt Freeland, *The Records of Oxford, Mass.* (Albany; N.Y.: Joel Munsell's Sons, 1894), pp. 370–387; LCCGSP Records I:143. Learned was something of a hero though his brother Jeremiah, like Ephraim Ballard, was hesitant about supporting the Revolution. Jeremiah Learned said that as he held several commissions under the king he could not violate his oaths of office: Daniels, *Oxford*, p. 590.

30. John Joseph Henry, "Campaign Against Quebec," in Kenneth Roberts, ed., *March to Quebec: Journals of the Members of Arnold's Expedition* (New York: Doubleday, Doran, 1940), pp. 303–305.

31. James P. Baxter, ed., *Documentary History of the State of Maine,* 24 vols. (Portland, Me.: Maine Historical Society, 1869–1916), 24:407–410 (hereafter *Doc. Hist. Me.); Acts and Resolves, Public and Private, of the Province of the Massachusetts Bay, 1775–1776* 19:793 (Boston: 1918).

32. North, p. 140; HTR, I, p. 19; Records, LCCGSP, I:158–161; LD, I:255, II:525–526, 574–576. Jones bought the mill lot from Jonathan Bowman of Pownalboro in 1772; he deeded it with all his other land in Hallowell to his father-in-law, Joseph Lee, of Concord, May 29, 1779, the description of the lot granting all privileges except "Ballards Lease." That same month Jones chose Ephraim Ballard to appraise his real estate in a Concord court action involving his brother-in-law Jonas Lee. Jones's father-in-law had his own trou bles with the Concord Committee of Safety. See Robert A. Gross, *The Minutemen and Their World* (New York: Hill and Wang, 1976), pp. 138, 168.

33. *Doc. Hist. Maine* 18:45; HTR, I:30–32, 33, 35, 36; North, *Augusta,* p. 156. In 1777, Jonathan Ballard, Ebenezer, Levi, and Collins Moore, and Thomas, Edward, and Solomon Towne, all relatives of Martha and Ephraim Ballard, were accused of being "inimical to the Rights and Liberties" of the United States, but their cases were dropped. See LCCGSP Records, I; 154, 155, 159–161, and (for a highly colored description of the trial) William S. Bartlet, *The Frontier Missionary: A Memoir of the Life of the Rev. Jacob Bailey* (Boston: Ide and Dutton, 1853), pp. 263–264.

34. MMB, October 14, 1797.

35. A Register of Marriages Intended, HTR, I: 17.

36. The letter, mentioning "your father Ballard," was addressed to Ephraim Towne, the Ballards' son-in-law, who rented the lower farm after Ephraim and Martha went to the mills: Towne Papers, 6:2, MeSM.

37. MMB, November 15, 1785. Jones first appeared on a Hallowell tax list in 1794: Invoice of the rateable property in possession of the Middle Parish in Hallowell, 1794, MeSL.

38. Interview with Miss Della Towne by Edwin Churchill, October 25, 1972, Towne Papers, 2:39, MeSM.

39. MMB, May 22, 1790, June 13, 1786, July 17, 1790, July 27, 1786.

40. MMB, January 27, 1786, June 5, 1785, July 12, 1788, May 18, 1786, March 17, 1791, June 29, 1788, July 12, 1788, April 2, 1788, November 25, 1787.

41. MMB September 29, 1789, April 28, 1786.

42. MMB, e.g., July 15, 1786, October 24, 1788, July 7, November 9, 1789, April 26, 1790.

43. MMB September 29, 1789, April 28, 1786, November 17, 1785, October 6, 1789, May 12, 1786; Edward P. Hamilton, *The Village Mill in Early New England* (Sturbridge, Mass: Old Sturbridge, Inc., 1964), pp. 3, 15; R. W. Dyer, "Weare Saw Mill, Hampton Falls, N.H.: Historic American Buildings Survey,

N.H., 34D, typescript, Dimond Library, University of New Hampshire, Durham.

44. *Collections and Proceedings of the Maine Historical Society,* 2nd Ser., 4 (1893): 217–218; *Vital Records of Nantucket, Mass.,* 5: 185–192. (Boston: New England Historic Genealogical Society, 1928).

45. Baker, *Maritime History,* p. 92.

46. I have been unable to find any surviving court record describing Obed Hussey's imprisonment, though in 1792 his creditors took 564 pounds from the widow. By 1800 she had recouped her losses and was one of the wealthiest taxpayers in Hallowell: LD, II:72; III:393, 481; VI:34; VI:35, III:369–370, 385; Mary Hussey Estate File, KPR.

47. MMB, June 28, 1787; Ebenezer, Hewins and Zilpha Comings Marriage Intentions, March 31, 1787, Marriage June 28, 1787, HTR, I, n.p.

48. Recent works that explore these themes include Judith Walzer Leavitt, *Brought to Bed: Child-Bearing in America, 1750–1950* (New York: Oxford University Press, 1986), chapter two; Ruth Bogin, "Petitioning and the New Moral Economy of Post-Revolutionary America," *WMQ,* 45 (1988): 391–425; Alan Taylor, " 'A Kind of Warr': The Contest for the Land on the Northeastern Frontier, 1750–1820," *WMQ,* 46 (1989): 3–26; Jan Lewis, "The Republican Wife: Virtue and Seduction in the Early Republic," *WMQ,* 44 (1987): 689–721; and Cathy N. Davidson, *Revolution and the Word: The Rise of the Novel in America* (New York: Oxford University Press, 1986), Chapter 6.

49. Mary Beth Norton, *Liberty's Daughters: The Revolutionary Experience of American Women, 1750–1800* (Boston: Little, Brown, 1980), and Linda Kerber, *Women of the Republic: Intellect and Ideology in Revolutionary America* (Chapel Hill: University of North Carolina Press, 1980). Norton's and Kerber's books revised the conclusions of Nancy Cott, who located the origins of this new ideology of domesticity somewhat later and attributed it to religious revivalism and to the emergence of a market economy. See Cott, *The Bonds of Womanhood,* pp. 58–62, 157–159, 197–206.

50. North, p. 4; Jeremiah Barker, "History of Diseases in the District of Maine," chapter two, MeHS. Daniel Cony to Joseph Whippe, November 1, 1801, Francis A. Countway Library of Medicine, Boston, Mass.

51. James Thacher, *American Medical Library* (Boston, 1828), p. 45.

52. Daniel Cony, An extraordinary case in Midwifery, Read April 1788, File No. 47, in Documents Illustrative of the Early History of the Massachusetts Medical Society, II:22, Countway Library of Medicine.

53. North, pp. 86–90, 883.

54. Samuel and William Howard Account Book, 1773–1793, MeHS. (The only other extant volume of Howard accounts now at the Maine State Library dates in the 1770s and carries Samuel's name only.)

55. MMB, e.g., September 22, 1786, May 14, 1791, March 14, 1785, May 19, 1786, March 9, 21, 26, 1788 (male activities); June 16 (weeding) 1788;

August 10, 1786 (pulling); May 11–14, 1785 (combing); August 17, 1785 (spinning and bleaching); April 8, 15, 1786 (doubling and twisting); March 23, 1786 (boiling); November 17, 1786 (winding); June 23, 1791 (quilling); April 29, 1788 (spooling); October 26, 1787 (bucking).

56. MMB April 5, 19, 25, 1786, June, 9, 1786, July 1, 1786.

57. MMB April 20, 24, 1786.

58. North, p. 934.

59. HS, April 23, 1787. Sewall's description of the inaugural festivities continued through April 30.

60. MMB, March 6, 1790.

61. MMB and HS, December 31, 1786, April 2, 1788, November 13, 1790, May 11, 1792, April 5, 1794, January 17, 1797, March 26, 1798, October 23, 1799, and contiguous entries. On bonnet-making, MMB, March 6, 1790. Interestingly, in 1789 William Howard credited Henry Sewall with pasteboard and buckram (two materials used in bonnet-making). See Howard Account Book, p. 156.

62. HS, February 22, 1800. Nash, p. 203, identifies the girls.

63. North, pp. 86–90.

CHAPTER ONE

1. For different assessments of the recent social history of medicine, see Gerald N. Grob, "The Social History of Medicine and Disease in America: Problems and Possibilities," *Journal of Social History* 10 (1977): 391–409, and Ronald L. Numbers, "The History of American Medicine: A Field in Ferment," *Review in American History*, 10 (1982): 145–163. Both studies show the dearth of studies on early America. Two notable recent efforts show the promise of the field and the amount of research left to be done: Robert I. Goler, *The Healing Arts in Early America*, issued in conjunction with an exhibition of the same name at the Fraunces Tavern Museum, New York City, 1985, and *Medicine in Colonial Massachusetts, 1620–1820*, ed. Philip Cash, Eric H. Christianson, J. Worth Estes, Publications of the Colonial Society of Massachusetts, Vol. 57 (Boston: 1980). For an incisive bibliography on midwifery, see Judy Barrett Litoff, "Midwives and History," in Rima Apple, ed., *Women and Health in America* (New York: Garland, forthcoming). I would like to thank Litoff for sharing her essay with me.

2. According to one medical historian, every state from Maryland to Maine suffered a sizable scarlet fever epidemic between 1783 and 1791: Ernest Caulfield, "Some Common Diseases of Colonial Children," *Publications of the Colonial Society of Massachusetts*, 35 (1942–1946): 24–36. See also Hall Jackson, *Observations and Remarks on the Putrid Malignant Sore Throat* (Portsmouth, N.H., 1786), pp. 8–10; J. Worth Estes, *Hall Jackson and the Purple Foxglove: Medical*

Practice and Research in Revolutionary America 1760–1820 (Hanover, N.H.: University Press of New England, 1979), pp. 124–125; and W. Barry Wood, Jr., *From Miasmas to Molecules* (New York: Columbia University Press, 1961), pp. 32–37. A mortality of 6.9 percent in an epidemic of 1794 was considered "very mortal" by one contemporary observer. Also see William Baylies, "An account of the Ulcerated Sore Throat, as it appeared in the Town of Dighton, County of Bristol, in 1785 and 1786," in *Medical Papers Communicated to the Massachusetts Medical Society*, I (Boston, 1790): 41–48.

3. HS, June 9–19, 1787.

4. HS, July 28, 1787; MMB, July 14, 30, 1787.

5. MMB and HS, August 4, 1787.

6. MMB, June 3, 1787, August 4, 1787, May 24, 1787. Of James Howard's death, she wrote: "A sudden change. He was well and dead in about three hours."

7. Martha's comment on the mother's death allows us to add the 177 deliveries completed before the diary opened (the number arrived at from retrospective totals later in the diary) to the eighty-one deliveries recorded between January 1785 and August 1787. That is, Martha had lost one mother in 258 births, a remarkable record. Such good fortune would not continue. In 1789 she saw another patient and her newborn infant die, and in 1790 a third. While her lifelong record was excellent (one death for every 200 births), her statistics for the period 1787–1790 are dismal, one death for every forty-five deliveries.

8. Leonard G. Wilson, "The Historical Riddle of Milk-Borne Scarlet Fever," *Bulletin of the History of Medicine*, 60 (1986): 322. The timing of the deaths—five days after delivery—suggests infection. Puerperal fever, the most important cause of maternal deaths in childbed, can be caused by any of a variety of organisms.

9. As for Mrs. Clayton's baby, even in the twentieth century, babies born to mothers with infections are at especially high risk, though their symptoms are typically vague and generalized rather than specific: Erna Ziegel and Carolyn Conant Van Blarcom, *Obstetric Nursing*, 6th ed. (New York: Macmillan, 1972), pp. 524–525, 736–737. The relation of puerperal fever to other seemingly unrelated forms of infection is also suggested in the 1784 records of Dr. Jeremiah Barker of Gorham, Maine, who reported (without noting the connection) parallel "epidemics" of childbed fever and what he identified as "unusual appearances ... in wounds & bruises": Barker, History of Disease in the History of Maine, chapter three, MeSM.

10. Susanna Cowen and John Clayton filed marriage intentions October 14, 1786, HTR, I: n.p. Ephraim Cowen lived on part of Lot #4, East Side, Robert Kennedy on Lot #3, LCD 2:312, 7:123, 7:187.

11. There were ten deaths in 1785, nine in 1786, sixteen in 1787, twelve in 1788, nine in 1789, and fifteen in 1790, a total of seventy-one deaths. I found references to sixty-eight Hallowell deaths in the diary in the same period, only

some of which identified causes. (Hallowell had 1,119 persons in the 1790 census.) On mortality in other places, see J. Worth Estes, *Hall Jackson*, pp. 96–97, and J. Worth Estes and David M. Goodman, *The Changing Humors of Portsmouth: The Medical Biography of an American Town, 1623–1983* (Boston: Francis A. Countway Library of Medicine, 1986). pp. 27–31, 326–327. On the significance of scarlet fever, see John Duffy, *Epidemics in Colonial America* (Baton Rouge: Louisiana State University Press, 1953), pp. 239–240. On twentieth-century death rates, see John Ross, *International Encyclopedia of Population* (New York: Free Press, 1982), vol. 2, p. 462.

12. Carolyn Merchant, *The Death of Nature: Women, Ecology, and the Scientific Revolution* (San Francisco: Harper & Row, 1980), p. 153. William Sermon, *The Ladies Companion, or the English Midwife* (London, 1671), p. 3. Here my argument differs slightly from earlier historians who have emphasized only the negative connotations of midwifery. The connection between midwifery and witchcraft was first introduced by Thomas Rogers Forbes in the title essay of his collection, *The Midwife and the Witch* (New Haven, Conn.: Yale University Press, 1966), then analyzed in feminist terms by Barbara Ehrenreich and Deirdre English, *Witches, Midwives and Nurses: A History of Women Healers* (Old Westbury, N.Y.: Feminist Press, 1973). For feminist scholars the theme has enormous resonance, not only for what it reveals about Western misogyny but because it suggests that women in past times had occult knowledge of sex and reproduction that was suppressed by physicians and the Church. See, for example, Adrienne Rich, *Of Woman Born: Motherhood as Experience and Institution* (New York: W. W. Norton, 1976, pp. 128–139) and Linda Gordon, *Woman's Body, Woman's Right: A Social History of Birth Control in America* (New York: Penguin Books, 1977), pp. 29–32. Two historians of New England witchcraft have found suggestive references to healing activities by suspected witches, though no strong correlations between witchcraft and midwifery per se: John Putnam Demos, *Entertaining Satan: Witchcraft and the Culture of Early New England* (New York: Oxford University Press, 1982), pp. 80–81; Carol Karlsen, *The Devil in the Shape of a Woman: Witchcraft in Colonial New England* (New York: W. W. Norton, 1987), pp. 142–143. I would argue that healing was such a pervasive female activity that *any* sample of women, including deviant women, would turn up a few healers. Midwives, like all women, were susceptible to the witchcraft slander, but most were highly respected in their communities. Merry E. Weisner makes a similar point in her study of Nuremberg midwives, "Early Modern Midwifery: A Case Study," *International Journal of Women's Studies*, 6 (1983) 1:26–43.

13. Wertz and Wertz, *Lying-in*, pp. 8–9.

14. Hall, *Worlds of Wonder, Days of Judgment*, pp. 140, 100–101. I Timothy 47, Exodus 1:15–19.

15. T. Dawkes, *The Midwife Rightly Instructed* (London, 1736), and John Maubray, *The Female Physician* (London, 1724), quoted in Robert A. Erickson, "Mother Jewkes, Pamela, and the Midwives," *ELH*, 42 (1970): 508, 514, n.15.

16. Erickson, "Mother Jewkes, Pamela, and the Midwives," pp. 500–516.

17. Charles Dickens, *Martin Chuzzlewit*, ed. Margaret Cardwell (Oxford: Clarendon Press, 1982), pp. 315–316.

18. Mrs. S. J. Hale, *Northwood: A Tale of New England* (Boston, 1827), II, 182.

19. *Short Fiction of Sarah Orne Jewett and Mary Wilkins Freeman*, ed. Barbara H. Solomon (New York: New American Library, 1979), pp. 48–49.

20. J. Worth Estes has observed that doctor's account books from the region show a preponderence of entries for adult males; "Therapeutic Practice in Colonial New England," in *Medicine in Colonial Massachusetts*, pp. 296, 303.

21. MMB, September 18, 1786, February 5, 1791, November 5, 1793, July 3, 1794; MMB, September 9, 1791; John B. Blake, "The Compleat Housewife," *Bulletin of the History of Medicine* 49 (1975): pp. 30–42; George E. Gifford, Jr., "Botanic Remedies in Colonial Massachusetts, 1620–1820," in *Medicine in Colonial Massachusetts*, pp. 263–288.

22. Martha Ballard makes no reference in the diary to any medical book. American women did, however, use Culpeper, and old editions were passed on from generation to generation. An inscription in a copy of Culpeper's *Pharmacopoeia Londinensis* illustrated in Gifford, "Botanic Remedies," Fig. 68, is inscribed, "Rachel Martin Her Book Given Her by Her Mother Jest before her Deth March 13th day 1765."

23. MMB, October 5, 1787; Gifford, "Botanic Remedies," pp. 263–267.

24. MMB, November 20, 1788; *Culpeper's Color Herbal*, ed. David Potterton (New York: Sterling, 1983), p. 74.

25. Herbert Leventhal, *In the Shadow of the Enlightment: Occultism and Renaissance Science in Eighteenth-Century America* (New York: New York University Press, 1976), pp. 27–47, and Bernard Capp, *English Almanacs 1500–1800: Astrology and the Popular Press* (Ithaca, N.Y.: Cornell University Press, 1979), pp. 64–65, 118–120. Daniels, *Oxford*, p. 666, says that Samuel Robinson, who married Hannah Learned of Oxford in 1748, was "a doctor, astrologer, and innholder" on the Oxford-Dudley line.

26. MMB, e.g., May 11, 1790, December 18, 1790, January 17, 1792; James Thacher, *The American New Dispensatory* (Boston: 1810), pp. 203–204, said that the "detergent property of soap ... has given rise to very erroneous notions of its medical virtues." Nathanael Low, *An Almanack or Astronomical Diary for ... 1787*, recommends castile soap pills for jaundice. In his earliest almanac Low advertised himself as a "Professor of Astronomy," in later editions as "A Student of Physic": Marion Barber Stowell, *Early American Almanacs: The Colonial Weekday Bible* (New York: Burt Franklin, 1977), p. 86.

27. E. Smith, *The Compleat Housewife: OR, Accomplish'd Gentlewoman's Companion*, 15th ed. (London, 1753, facsimile, London, Literary Services and Production Limited, 1968), pp. 267, 276, 304, 263, 256, 283. Smith's recipe for "Cock water" includes herbs, currants, raisins, and white sugar candy as well as an old rooster. Martha used rabbits as well as fowl, as on April 10, 1791,

when "Jonathan killd a rabbit & sent it Mrs Nabby Hodskins who is unwell." Smith's book was first published in London in 1727. For a survey of early English cookery books containing medical receipts, see Blake, "The Compleat Housewife," pp. 30–32.

28. For a similar use of urine, see *The Diary of Matthew Patten of Bedford, N.H.* (Concord, N.H., 1903), p. 13 (March 30, 1755): "our son John was taken very bad in the forenoon so that we almost Dispaired of his life he was easier in the afternoon by Giving him Chamber Lie and Molasses sweet oyl and neatsfoot oyl." On cow dung, see Rose Lockwood, "Birth, Illness and Death in 18th-Century New England," *Journal of Social History* 2 (1978): 120, and on the general use of excreta, Fanny D. Bergen, *Animal and Plant Lore: Collected from the Oral Tradition of English Speaking Folk* (Boston and New York: Houghton Mifflin, 1899), pp. 70–71.

29. MMB, October 13, 1786. On the widespread use of this remedy, see Bergen, p. 68, and Wayland Hand, *Magical Medicine* (Berkeley: University of California Press, 1980), pp. 189–190. Ebenezer Parkman used a cow-dung poultice for toothache, and killed a cat and applied the blood to a child's burns: Lockwood, "Birth, Illness, and Death," pp. 119–120. (Note that Parkman's daughter married Jonathan Moore, Martha Ballard's brother.)

30. MMB, July 23, 1794. On the importance of the sun in magical cures, see Hand, *Magical Medicine*, pp. 2–5. The necessity of going to the barn and establishing intimate contact with the cow also relates to British and American traditions that prescribed inhaling the breath of a cow or horse for respiratory disorders; Hand, pp. 378–379. On the difficulties of identifying magical cures, see Neil C. Hultin, "Medicine and Magic in the Eighteenth Century: The Diaries of James Woodforde," *Journal of the History of Medicine & Allied Sciences*, 30 (1975): 348–366.

31. I have taken the ingredients and their applications from the diary, MMB, July 12, 1792, June 25, 1786, August 11, 1788, December 1, 1787, June 1794, the details of preparation (brown paper, wool cloth, etc.) from [Nicholas Culpeper], *The English Physician Enlarged* (Exeter, N.H., 1824), pp. 315, 320.

32. One eighteenth-century American botanist, Mannasseh Cutler, worried about the medical consequences of applying English names to "plants that are entirely different, belonging to other classes, and possessed, no doubt, of different properties," yet his lists of "native" plants include many that may have escaped from the gardens of early settlers and include many of the English plant names also found in Ballard's diary, herbs like mullein, plantain, golden thread, Solomon's-seal, wormwood, tansy, and burdock. He was uncertain, for example, whether comfrey was truly indigenous, though like Martha Ballard he found it useful for treating sprains: Cutler, "An Account of Some of the Vegetable Productions, Naturally Growing in This Part of America," *Bulletin of the Lloyd Library*, Reproduction Series No. 4 (1903), pp. 398, 419, 437, 459, 414, 410, 427, 434, 457, 476, 479; MMB, June 25, 1786.

33. MMB, July 21, 1785, October 11, 1801; Potterton, *Culpeper's Color Herbal*, p. 164; Cutler, "An Account," p. 426; Marilyn Dwelley, *Summer & Fall Wildflowers of New England* (Camden, Me.: Downeast Enterprise, 1977), p. 40. To "deliver a woman of a dead child," Smith recommended a "water" that included Virginia snakeroot and marigold flowers.

34. Clarence Meyer, *American Folk Medicine* (New York: Thomas Y Crowell, 1973), p. 286, identifies "cold water root" as *Aster puneceus*. He also identifies two other of Martha Ballard's plants that do not appear in English herbals, balm of Gilead (*Populus balsamifera*), p. 283, and basswood (*Tilia americana*), p. 284.

35. [Mary Hall Leonard], *Mattapoisett and Old Rochester, Massachusetts* (New York: The Grafton Press, 1907), pp. 118–119.

36. Lawrence W. Levine, *Black Culture and Black Consciousness* (New York: Oxford University Press, 1977), pp. 63–66; Jon Butler, "The Dark Ages of American Occultism, 1760–1848," in *The Occult in America: New Historical Perspectives*, ed. Howard Kerr and Charles L. Crow (Urbana: University of Illinois Press, 1983), pp. 59–61; Smith, *The Compleat Housewife*, p. 378.

37. Thacher wrote, p. 232, "However disparaging to medical erudition, it is but justice to confess, that we are indebted to the bold enterprize of illiterate pretenders for the discovery of some of our most active remedies." He urged "patriotic physicians and citizens" to unite in identifying and testing indigenous plants.

38. MMB, November 30, 1791, September 5, 1786, October 9, 1785, November 30, 1791.

39. Moses Appleton, Medical Recipe Book, Countway Library of Medicine, Boston. The inscription inside is dated "Waterville, 1791." Appleton displayed his sophistication in an elegant display of "chemical characters," including graphic emblems for fire, air, earth, water, quicklime, *talk*, sand, and other fundamentals. On the common assumptions of empirical and academic medicine, see Richard Brown, "The Healing Arts in Colonial and Revolutionary Massachusetts: The Context for Scientific Medicine," in *Medicine in Colonial Massachusetts*, pp. 41–42. Also see Samuel Curtis, *A Valuable Collection of Recipes, Medicinal and Miscellaneous* (Amherst, N.H., 1819), a publication by Daniel Cony's mentor, and, on the general education of early physicians, Eric H. Christianson, "The Medical Practitioners of Massachusetts, 1630–1800: Patterns of Change and Continuity," in *Medicine in Colonial Massachusetts*, pp. 56–57, and Joseph Kett, *The Formation of the American Medical Profession: The Role of Institutions, 1760–1860* (New Haven: Yale University Press, 1968), pp. 9–14.

40. "Births from Hallowell Records," *Collections of the Maine Historical Society*, 2nd Ser., 3 (1892): 332. The fullest expression of an interest in lunar influence is in the "Reverend Seaborn Cotton Commonplace Book," New England Historic Genealogical Society, Boston. The section entitled "the nature and dis-

position of the moone in the birth of children" was apparently written by
Dorothy Cotton, the minister's wife, who was a daughter of the poet Anne
Bradstreet.

41. J. Worth Estes, "Medical Skills in Colonial New England," *NEHGR*,
134 (1980): 265–266. The North Andover Historical Society owns an oak
instrument case said to have belonged to Dr. Thomas Kittredge, 1746–1818,
a highly respected surgeon and early member of the Massachusetts Medical
Society. His instruments included a key-form tooth extractor, a trephine (with
interchangeable bits) for making holes in the skull, a periosteome for scraping
tissue from bone, a tripod bone elevator for lifting depressed bone fragments
in skull injuries, a wrench used to change surgical saw blades, forceps and a
vectis for use in obstetrics, and a tourniquet. Dr. Kittredge trained Dr. Benjamin Page of Hallowell. As Charles Rosenberg has observed, even in the
middle of the nineteenth century there was little technical difference between
"professional" and "domestic" practice: "A flushed face and rapid pulse, a
coated tongue and griping diarrhea would be apparent to laymen just as to
physicians; and grandmothers as well as senior consultants could and did make
reasoned prognoses." *Care of Strangers: The Rise of America's Hospital System*
(New York: Basic Books, 1987), p. 70.

42. Such an attitude was not a quirk of frontier medicine. Roy Porter has
argued from his study of medical receipts in the *London Magazine* that even in
England, "doctors still saw it as good policy to share medical learning." It
was possible to do so because physicians, lay healers, and patients still shared
"overlapping, if not identical, cognitive worlds": "Introduction," in *Patients and
practitioners: Lay perceptions of medicine in pre-industrial society*, ed. Roy Porter
(Cambridge, Eng.: Cambridge University Press, 1985), pp. 14–15.

43. MMB, March 10, 1791; Estes, "Therapeutic Practice," pp. 318, 374, 377;
Thacher, *The American New Dispensatory*, characterizes manna and rhubarb as
mild laxatives that might safely be administered to children, invalids, delicate
women, and the aged.

44. MMB, July 8, 1789, January 30, 1787.

45. Leventhal, *In the Shadow of the Enlightenment*, p. 202.

46. MMB, August 1, 1788; Charles E. Rosenberg, "The Therapeutic Revolution: Medicine, Meaning, and Social Change in Nineteenth-Century America," in Charles E. Rosenberg and Morris J. Vogel, eds., *The Therapeutic
Revolution: Essays in the Social History of American Medicine* (Philadelphia: University of Pennsylvania, 1979), pp. 8, 23.

47. MMB, September 27, 1789. In seventeenth-century Massachusetts, savine boiled in beer was the recognized abortifacient: Roger Thompson, *Sex in
Middlesex: Popular Mores in a Massachusetts County, 1649–1699* (Amherst: University of Massachusetts Press, 1986), pp. 25, 46, 107, 183. Today's Maine
midwives consider tansy dangerous, as does Potterton, *Culpeper's Color Herbal*,
pp. 166, 189. On traditional English use of savine, pennyroyal, tansy, and

other herbs as contraceptives, see Angus McLaren, *Reproductive Rituals: The Perception of Fertility in England from the Sixteenth Century to the Nineteenth Century* (London and New York: Methuen, 1984), pp. 73–75, 89–106.

48. MMB, October 4, 1791; "Bleeding Implements and Drug Chests of Colonial New England," *Medicine in Colonial Massachusetts*, Appendix II, p. 380. On the use of bloodletting by contemporary physicians, see Estes, "Therapeutic Practice," and Whitfield J. Bell, Jr., "Medicine in Boston and Philadelphia: Comparisons and Contrast, 1750–1820," in *Medicine in Colonial Massachusetts*, pp. 301–303, 175–176. The New Hampshire physicians Estes studied bled between 5 and 6 percent of their patients. Since children were usually bled from the tongue, the one reference in the diary to cutting an infant's tongue might indicate therapeutic bleeding. Since it is a unique entry and since the baby was very young, I have interpreted it literally, as cutting a too short frenum.

49. Erwin H. Ackerknecht, *Therapeutics: From the Primitives to the 20th Century* (New York: Macmillan, 1973), p. 81; Rosenberg, "Therapeutic Revolution," p. 9.

50. Rosenberg, "Therapeutic Revolution," p. 6.

51. J. Worth Estes, "Patterns of Drug Usage in Colonial America," paper presented at the Fraunces Tavern Museum, April 18, 1986, to be published in the *New York State Journal of Medicine*. That solidistic notions had penetrated lay practice is clear from Smith's *Compleat Housewife*, which recommended an emollient for its ability to "sheath and soften the asperity of the humours in general" and "relaxing and suppling the solids at the same time," p. 287.

52. Jackson, *Putrid Malignant Sore Throat*, p. 14. He also recommended a fermenting cataplasm of milk, beer grounds or yeast, and oatmeal, p. 24.

53. MMB, March 26–31, 1797.

54. MMB, October 12, 1789, February 9, 1786, October 27, 1795.

55. HS, July 19, 1787.

56. MMB, August 11, 1785, December 30, 1789; North, pp. 828, 836, 817.

57. Benjamin Wait to George Thatcher, February 14, 1788, George Thatcher Papers, Boston Public Library.

58. Daniel Cony to George Thatcher, 12 March 1789, Thatcher Papers, Boston Public Library.

59. LCCGSP Records, 2:79. On Williams's political involvement, see Daniel Cony to George Thatcher, June 16, 1789, Thatcher Papers, Boston Public Library. A book list in Williams's probate inventory suggests his divided interests. In addition to a Bible, a dictionary, a copy of *King Lear*, and five unidentified pamphlets, he owned four books: *The Laws of Massachusetts, The Trial of Atticus* (a legal satire), *The Practice of Physic*, and *The Institution of Medicine*: KPR, 1: 210–212. It is impossible to identify Williams's medical books from the short titles. Among books owned by northern New England physicians that might fit the description are Richard Brooks, *The General Practice of*

Physic, 2 vol. (London, 1754); John Allen, *Synopsis Medicinae: or, a Summary of the Whole Practice of Physick*, 4th ed. (London, 1761); William Cullen, *First Lines of the Practice of Physic* (Philadelphia, 1781).

60. MMB, e.g., December 13–14, 1785, August 26–27, 1788, October, 30, 1791, November 5, 1793, July 3, 1794, June 11, 1796; *Kennebec Intelligencer*, May 26, 1797.

61. Moses Appleton Day Book, March 20, 1806, Waterville Historical Society. The Historical Society has Appleton daybooks, ledgers, dockets, and medical notes dating from 1794 to 1839, as well as a diary kept by Appleton when he was in medical training in Boston. These records deserve systematic study. My cursory survey suggests that medicine was more important in the early part of his career than as he grew older and more prosperous.

62. *Collections and Proceedings of the Maine Historical Society*, 2d ser., 9 (1898):428; *The Tocsin* (Hallowell, Me.), July 1, 1796.

63. North, pp. 171–173; "Memoir of Benjamin Page," *The Boston Medical and Surgical Journal*, 33 (1845), 176; Massachusetts Medical Society Documents, Miscellaneous, vol. 1, Countway Library of Medicine. *The Massachusetts Register and United States Calendar* (Boston: annual) lists members and officers, e.g., 1804, pp. 49, 71; 1805, pp. 39, 75; 1811, pp. 41, 42; *Collections of Maine Historical Society*, 1st ser., 5 (1857):xviii. For general background, Kett, *Formation of the American Medical Profession*, pp. 14–15.

64. MMB, June 10, 1797.

65. The term "social childbirth" first appears in Wertz and Wertz, *Lying-In*, p. 2. For a useful survey of the literature and a discussion of the issue of professionalization, see Barbara Melosh, *"The Physician's Hand": Work Culture and Conflict in American Nursing* (Philadelphia, Pa.: Temple University Press, 1982), pp. 15–35.

66. Florence Nightingale, *Notes on Nursing: What it is, and what it is not* (New York: D. Appleton, and Company, 1860; Dover reprint, 1969), p. 3.

67. MMB, March 23, 1788.

68. Cf. Lockwood, "Birth, Illness and Death," pp. 118–120.

69. Carroll Smith-Rosenberg, "The Female World of Love and Ritual: Relations Between Women in Nineteenth-Century America," *Signs: A Journal of Women in Culture and Society* 1 (1975): 1–29.

70. William Smellie, *A Collection of Cases and Observations in Midwifery* (London, 1764), vol. III, p. 410.

71. William Buchan, *Domestic Medicine* (New York: 1815), pp. 337–338. This edition purports to be an accurate copy of Buchan's 1798 revision.

72. Charles E. Rosenberg, "Medical Text and Social Context: Explaining William Buchan's *Domestic Medicine*," *Bulletin of the History of Medicine*, 57 (1983), pp. 22–42.

73. Gifford, "Botanic Remedies," p. 276.

74. North, pp. 87–88.

75. James had had an older son named James, who probably died in the 1760s: "Who was Captain James Howard's Son James," *The Kennebec Proprietor* I (1984): 22.

76. Buchan, *Domestic Medicine*, p. 183. According to Portsmouth, N.H., bills of mortality, bilious fever accounted for 1.5 percent of deaths between 1801 and 1843, and scarlet fever for 2.24 percent; Estes, *Changing Humors*, pp. 321–322.

77. MMB, October 7, 1786.

78. The term "present" appears elsewhere in this period. On September 26, 1787, "Mr Foster made me a present of a silk hankerchief," and, a month later, "Capt. Savages Lady here. Made me a present of 2 handkerchiefs." Only careful sifting backward through the diary exposes the reciprocity in these transactions—Martha's nursing of the minister during the scarlet fever epidemic in July and her patient administration of "physick" to Mrs. Savage in August 1786: MMB, July 28, 1787, August 14, 15, 17, 25, 1786, and September 3, 1786.

CHAPTER TWO

1. Yarn destined for but not yet attached to the loom could also be called a web, e.g. MMB, June 7, 1785.

2. MMB, April 23, 1788, October 16, 1790, June 26, 1788, June 4, 1787, November 29, 1791, December 15, 1788, August 20, 1788, May 3, 1788, November 28, 1794, October 9, 1788.

3. For an excellent summary of the literature, see Linda K. Kerber, "Separate Spheres, Female Worlds, Woman's Place: The Rhetoric of Women's History," *Journal of American History* 75 (1988): 9–39.

4. Edward M. Cook, Jr., *The Fathers of the Towns: Leadership and Community Structure in Eighteenth-Century New England* (Baltimore: Johns Hopkins University Press, 1976), pp. 23–24. Ephraim Ballard served four terms as selectman in Oxford and another five in Hallowell. (In 1788 he was filling out a vacancy left when Henry Sewall went to New York.) In Cook's terms, he qualified as a "town leader." Half of the forty men who served as selectmen in Hallowell between 1771 and 1800 served only one year; only 15 percent filled four or more terms. The average length of service was 2.1 years, lower even than for Hanover, N.H., the most fluid of the seventy-three New England towns Cook studied. See *Fathers of the Towns*, pp. 53–59; Oxford Town Records, II 91, 101, 114, 128, 135, Office of Town Clerk, Oxford, Massachusetts: North, pp. 972–973; HTR I: 147–166.

5. HTR, I: 155–156.

6. I have elaborated this point in "Martha Ballard and Her Girls: Women's

Work in Eighteenth-Century Maine," in Stephen Innes, ed., *Work and Labor in Early America* (Chapel Hill: University of North Carolina Press, 1988), pp. 83–86, and "Housewife and Gadder: Themes of Self-sufficiency and Community in Eighteenth-Century New England," in Carol Groneman and Mary Beth Norton, eds., *"To Toil the Livelong Day": America's Women at Work, 1780–1980* (Ithaca: Cornell University Press, 1987), pp. 21–34.

7. In parts of America and in certain textile-producing regions of England, weaving was a male occupation. In Oxford, early in the century, this may also have been so; Martha's uncle, Collins Moore (d. 1749), listed himself as a weaver: Daniels, *Oxford*, p. 618.

8. The three fibers are interspersed in diary entries from April-December 1786; e.g., March 23, 31, April 14, 21, July 25, 29 (linen), April 1, 4, 8, 10, 11, 19, 25, 27, May 4 (tow), June 24, July 3, 4, 10, 11, 12, 13, 18, 21, 24, 25, 26, 27, 29, August 18, 2, 8, 16, (cotton), September 12, 19, 24, October 25, November 15, 17, 25, December 9 (wool).

9. MMB, May 19, 24, 26, 28, 1787, June 4, 6, 25, 1787. Later, Ephraim helped with the cultivation of flax, as on May 15, 1788, when he harrowed it.

10. MMB, May 25, 1787, June 4, 1787, July 5, 18, 1787.

11. MMB, July 15, 1791, July 4, 1791, January 3, 1791, January 7, 1791, December 15–19, 1787, September 12, 1788, September 13, 1788, January 9, 1790, April 7, 1790, October 10, 1792, October 15–17, 1792, May 1, 1788.

12. Ruth Schwartz Cowan, *More Work for Mother: The Ironies of Household Technology from the Open Hearth to the Microwave* (New York: Basic Books, 1983), p. 38. Cowan follows earlier historians in seeing a basic transformation from an integrated family economy in the preindustrial era to a nineteenth-century "separation of spheres." For more than a decade, historians have been engaged in debate over the nature of the eighteenth-century New England economy, some emphasizing market relations, others the importance of neighborly interdependence. Clearly, both kinds of transactions were important in Hallowell. For a discussion of some of the broader implications of this argument see Innes, *Work and Labor in Early America*, pp. 34–47.

13. Daniels, *Oxford*, pp. 390–391; Stephen Barton Account Book, MeSL, has its first Maine entry in 1775, shifts to Oxford in 1788.

14. Throughout the early years of the diary, Clarissa came and went, e.g., November 6–7, 1786, April 16, 1788, January 25–28, 1790, July 28, 1790. She married Richard Foster of Winthrop on October 20, 1791. Pamela lived with the Ballards from October 24, 1786, until July 21, 1787. She married Benjamin Porter on July 18, 1787. Parthenia was with them continuously from May 1788 until the spring of 1791, when she began to leave intermittently for several weeks at a time, usually to work for "Mrs. Foot." She was gone from January until the end of July 1792 and was married at the Ballard house in November of that year (see Chapter Four).

15. MMB, August 27, 1785, September 17, 1785, May 29, 1789, June 4, 1789, July 1, 1789, July 2, 1794.

16. In the 1780s, the town provided long-term support for an unidentified "Black child" who seems to have moved back and forth between Nathaniel Tyler's household and the Widow Coy. The town orders for July credited Tyler, "for keeping the Black child," though Martha's diary for July 2 notes, "*Mrs.* Tylor Brot the Black Child here," apparently for some sort of medical advice. A loose piece of paper in the Abby Manley Sewall Scrapbook, MeSL, dated July 25, 1790, indentured Mary Kelly, a poor child, age seven, with no parents or other relatives able to support her, to Joseph North, Esquire, until the age of eighteen.

17. MMB, April 27, 1785, April 17, 1786 (bed moving). In connecting the remodeling to the introduction of the loom, I am making a logical inference; Martha Ballard offered no explanation for the improvements to the house, nor did she ever indicate where the girls were doing their weaving. After 1787, however, she referred to the upstairs rooms not as "chambers" but as "bedrooms."

18. North, pp. 820, 876, 934; MMB, March 27, 1785, April 24, 25, 1785. On December 15, a Thanksgiving, he "supt" at the Ballards. He also boarded for a short time with Henry and Tabitha Sewall, HS, June 20, 1787, July 7, 1787.

19. MMB, September 17, 1789 [emphasis added].

20. On another occasion, Woodward Allin subtracted from Martha Ballard's midwifery fee three shillings "due to him from Mr Ballard for his cooper ware" MMB, October 28, 1788.

21. MMB, October 19, 1789, August 24, 1789, September 29, 30, 1789.

22. MMB, October 28, 1786, July 10, 1787, June 21, 1787, May 5, 1787, October 18, 1787, November 14, 1786, June 27, 1789, April 6, 1787, May 22, 1790, January 17, 1792, December 31, 1787, November 10, 1785, June 13, 1786, July 14, 1788.

23. MMB, April 22, 23, 1788, May 9, 12, 13, 15, 1788, June 27, 1788, July 6, 1788, August 5, 21, 22, 23, 1788. Other entries refer to gardening, to general household work, and to flax, and one implies a medical treatment for *Mr.* Savage (whose name was Isaac) rather than for James, whose "phisick" was listed in the reckoning.

24. LD, 1:386.

25. LCCCP Files, Box 313 (1783).

26. Appropriately, this story was passed to me orally (via telephone) by Arlene Gilbert, who got it from Maud Mosher, who got it from Ethel Riccius King, who wrote down the words of Parthenia Porter Folsom, Pamela's daughter. For a discussion of some of the reasons behind the range of accounting skills in early America, see Patricia Cline Cohen, *A Calculating People: The Spread of Numeracy in Early America* (Chicago: U. of Chicago Press, 1982), pp. 27–28, 140–142.

27. Quoted in William S. Bartlet, *The Frontier Missionary: A Memoir of the Life of the Rev. Jacob Bailey* (Boston, 1853), p. 190.

28. E. E. Bourne, "The Bourne Family" (1855), typescript. Brick Store Mu-

seum, Kennebunk, Maine, pp. 222–223; David Thurston, *A Brief History of Winthrop* (Portland, Me., 1855); pp. 20–21.

29. Hale, *Northwood*, II, pp. 178–190.

30. Tabby to Henry Sewall, Hallowell, March 3, 1789, Abby Manley Sewall Scrapbook, MeSL.

31. *Heads of Families at the First Census of the United States Taken in the Year 1790, Maine* (Washington, D.C.: Government Printing Office, 1908), pp. 38–39.

32. Significantly, the one woman to appear in the William & Samuel Howard Account Book in the 1790s was Jane Welch, a poor widow. Before 1791 her husband paid for rye, molasses, and beef by rafting boards, mending shoes, and making "Bear Skin Mogissans." When he died, the credits shifted to spinning, but the widow's work was never enough to support her family. She was apparently pregnant when her husband died. On February 3, 1791, Martha delivered her of a daughter, "Dead born." Concerned about the woman, who had recently been widowed, she returned several times in the next few days. Finally, on February 8, she sent Ephraim "to see that Mrs. Welch had wood." Martha, and probably other neighbors as well, continued to help the widow as they could, usually by paying her and her older daughters for spinning, weaving, or housework. In 1792, the town began to pay their rent and provide some supplies.

33. HS, November 13, 1790.

34. MMB, November 13, 1790.

35. Nash, pp. 527–530.

36. County Tax #3, Hallowell, 1790, Hubbard Free Public Library, Hallowell, Maine.

37. "Memoir of Dr. Vaughan," *Collections of the Maine Historical Society*, Ser. 1, 6 (1859): 85–90. Charles was apparently more disdainful of the "Kennebeckers" than Benjamin. See Benjamin Vaughan to Charles Vaughan, December 15, 1797, Vaughan Papers, Bowdoin College. John Sheppard, who was once Charles Vaughan's agent in Hallowell, referred to Charles' wife, Francis Apthrop Vaughan as "the Lady at the Mountain," adding that the Vaughans picked their friends according to their financial circumstances. John Sheppard to Sarah Sheppard, December 8, 1799, Sheppard Papers, New England Historic Genealogical Society, Boston.

38. This group included William Howard's son Samuel and Samuel Howard's son William, as well as Cyrus Ballard, and sixteen men who may truly have been unattached laborers.

39. Jared Eliot, *The Blessings Bestow'd on them that Fear God* (New London: 1739), pp. 26–27.

40. MMB, 6 March 1792, June 1, 1793, August 2, 1793, February 2, 1795; Nash, p. 533. Fortis may have been the same man who in 1794 was convicted of raping and murdering a young Vassalboro woman. Martha mentioned the

murder and the execution, but did not draw any connection to the earlier delivery. She referred to Fortis as "a Negro" in one entry and "a black man" in another, but made no further comment other than to pronounce the crime "a shocking sein." May 20, 21, September 25, 1794. Her reserve is in sharp contrast to Nash's characterization of the man, apparently based on late-nine-teenth-century oral tradition: "Fortes was a negro of ebon blackness and giant stature; his face was hideously repulsive, and he was feared and hated by all the pioneers who knew him," p. 336.

41. MMB, May 12, March 24, 1787.

42. Eliot, *Blessings* p. 22; Cotton Mather, *El Shaddai* (Boston, 1725), p. 21.

43. Commonwealth of Massachusetts, *An Act for Regulating and Governing the Militia* (Boston: 1786), pp. 4–5, 9, 16.

44. North, pp. 71, 209, 220; William Willis, *A History of the Law, The Courts, and The Lawyers of Maine* (Portland, 1863), pp. 40–41.

45. Joseph Williamson, "Capital Trials in Maine Before the Separation," *Maine Historical Society Collections*, Second Ser., I (1890): 159–171, lists only eleven capital trials, four of which resulted in executions. He somehow missed the Edmund Fortis case, LCSJC Files, 920: 140970.

46. HTR, I:149–150.

47. MMB, March 16, 1795.

48. MMB, May 30, 31, 1792 [emphasis added].

CHAPTER THREE

1. Shipton, *Sibley's Harvard Graduates* 15:81; LCSJC Files, 143360.

2. Jotham Sewall, [Jr.], *A Memoir of Rev. Jotham Sewall of Chesterville, Maine* (Boston, 1853), pp. 20–21.

3. HS, June 5, 1785, October 30, 1785.

4. HS, November 13, 1785.

5. Nash, pp. 145–146, North, pp. 203–204.

6. HS, July 24, 1786, August 6, 13, 1786.

7. HS, March 5, 1786.

8. Frederick Clifton Pierce, *Foster Genealogy* (Chicago, 1899) p. 247; Bethuel Merritt Newcomb, *Andrew Newcomb and His Descendants* (New Haven: privately printed, 1923), pp. 75–76. Rebecca's father, said to have been "the stoutest man ever born in that town," for a time owned land in Stafford, Connecticut, where Isaac Foster's father preached.

9. Martha Brewster, *Poems on Divers Subjects* (New London, 1757); Subscrib-ers to Indian Charity School, Papers of Eleazar Wheelock, microfilm edition, Dartmouth College Library, Hanover, N.H., 765124.2. A number of letters in Wheelock's papers show the involvement of women in parish affairs and in the school, e.g., an angry letter (written in verse!) from Hannah Dunham. At

least ten girls from various tribes were among the students at the school, though most may have been placed as domestic servants in local homes: Wheelock Papers, 765690, 768624. Also see James Dow McCallum, *Eleazar Wheelock* (1939; rpt. New York: Arno Press, 1969), pp. 54–62, and James Axtell, *The Invasion Within: The Context of Cultures in Colonial North America* (New York: 1985), pp. 204–210.

10. Nash, p. 281; MMB, 2, February 1790.

11. MMB, September 17–21, 26, 1787.

12. MMB, April 17, 1788.

13. The next day, "Mr. Smith, having proposed a lecture at my house; on the invitation of Mr. Foster, had it in the meetinghouse." Sewall attended: HS, March 1–2, 1788. Smith was having his own trouble with dissidents, mostly Quakers, and would be dismissed in 1790: Calvin Montague Clark, *History of the Congregational Churches in Maine* (Portland: The Congregational Christian Conference, 1935), vol. II, pp. 107–108.

14. MMB, May 1, 1788; HS, April 26, 1786, May 1, 1786.

15. HS, June 6, 8, 1788.

16. MMB, June 22, 1788.

17. Report of an Ecclesiastical Council in the First Precinct in Rochester, November 1791; Suffolk County Supreme Judicial Court Files, 143360, Suffolk County Court House.

18. Nash, p. 147; Clark, *Congregational Churches*, pp. 101, 359, 103, 380.

19. *The First Laws of the Commonwealth of Massachusetts*, comp. John D. Cushing (Wilmington, Del.: Michael Glazier, 1981), p. 251.

20. Barbara S. Lindemann, "'To Ravish and Carnally Know': Rape in Eighteenth-century Massachusetts," *Signs* 10 (1984): 68–73.

21. Henry Sewall to George Thatcher, January 27, 1790; George Thatcher Papers, Boston Public Library.

22. Richard Welsman, *Witchcraft, Magic, and Religion in 17th-Century Massachusetts* (Amherst: University of Massachusetts Press, 1984), pp. 14–20, and *passim*.

23. Interestingly, eighteenth-century literature became obsessed with rape and seduction at the very time legal standards for prosecuting such crimes were changing. See Davidson, *Revolution and the Word*, pp. 101–109; Anna Clark, *Women's Silence, Men's Violence: Sexual Assault in England, 1770–1845* (London: Pandora, 1987), pp. 52–53. That such issues were connected with a larger argument over the nature of American political culture is clear from Jan Lewis, "The Republican Wife: Virtue and Seduction in the Early Republic," WMQ, 44 (1987):689–721.

24. Pownalboro Minute Book, LCSJC. All other material in the discussion that follows comes from this source unless otherwise noted.

25. LCCGSP Record, II, September 8, 1789; Clark, *Congregational Churches*, p. 146.

26. *Literary Diary of Ezra Stiles*, ed. Franklin Bowditch Dexter (New York: C. Scribner's Sons, 1901), III, p. 475. The notes to this entry incorrectly identify the minister as Isaac Foster, Sr.

27. Robert Bolton, *The History of Several Towns, Manors, and Patents of the County of Westchester* (New York, 1881), I p. 53.

28. Newcomb, *Andrew Newcomb and His Descendants*, p. 76; *The Eastern Shore Churchman* 5 (August 1927):1–3; F. Edward Wright, Maryland Eastern Shore Newspaper Abstracts, I, p. 58; photocopy, Somerset County Library, Princess Anne, Maryland. I have found no evidence that Baltimore ships were sailing to the west coast of South America in the early nineteenth century, but some were involved in the Spanish trade; see Stuart Weems Bruchey, *Robert Oliver, Merchant of Baltimore, 1783–1819* (Baltimore: Johns Hopkins University Press, 1956), pp. 261–263. Travel literature described Peru in terms that might have appealed to an adventuresome woman (in Lima, it was said, even Negro women wore Flanders lace). See Don George Juan and Don Antonio de Ulloa, *A Voyage to South America*, 4th ed., trans. John Adams (London: 1806), vol I, pp. 455–456, vol. II, pp. 29–66.

29. Martha attended church 18–19 times each year during Foster's tenure and after Stone was installed. She was never as regular in her attendance as Ephraim.

30. MMB, May 3, 7, 15, 1791.

31. MMB, May 18, 19, 1791. Her first cabbage harvest at the Howard farm was disappointing, however. "Got in our cabbages, had but 20 heads," she wrote on October 14. The year before, at the mills, she had gathered more than 200.

32. All diary entries are from 1791, MMB, May 28, 31, June 1, 24, August 9, 10, 11, 12, 15, 18, 19, 30 (farming); June 3, 4, 18, 21, 25, 29, 30, July 1, 2, 5, 6–10, September 3, 6, 7, November 9–22, December, 20, 1791 (surveying), July 12–13, 1791 (rafting), May 30, June 15, 16, 22, 23, August 5, 6, 7, 29, September 13, 15, 1791 (visits, community work).

33. MMB, October 6, 8, 13, 15, 17, 1791, November 6, 1791.

34. MMB April 5, 30, June 1, 2, 18, 30, August 15, 22, September 2, 11, 1791.

35. MMB, June 2, 12, 24, 26, 1791; July 11, 21, 25, 1791.

36. The year before, he had been "taken with a warrant" and then fined for "pulling Westons old rack down": MMB, June 4, 5, 1790.

37. MMB, October 15, 17, 1792.

38. MMB, November 10, 1794, January 7, 1791. See also January 9, 1790, December 16, 1790, November 10, 1794, February 15, 24, 1796, November 1, 3, 4, 5, 1796. I have found no discussion of rag *coverlets* in the secondary literature on New England textiles, though Nancy Dick Bognodoff says that rag *rugs* were "very common and most easily made, requiring no special designing or weaving skill," in *Handwoven Textiles of Early New England: The*

Legacy of a Rural People, 1640–1880 (Harrisburg, Pa.: Stackpole Books, 1975), p. 177. There is some evidence of the use of rag-filled textiles as bed coverings in early Quebec. See Harold B. Burnham and Dorothy K. Burnham, *"Keep me warm one night": Early Handweaving in Eastern Canada* (Toronto: University of Toronto Press, 1972), pp. 97–99. On the general method of rag weaving, see Dorothy K. Burnham, *The Comfortable Arts: Traditional Spinning and Weaving in Canada* (Ottawa: National Gallery of Canada, 1981), p. 125, and Geraldine Niva Johnson, *Weaving Rag Rugs: A Women's Craft in Western Maryland* (Knoxville: University of Tennessee Press, 1985).

39. Mrs. Welch warping, July 15, September, 3 November 29, 1791; Mrs. Wickson combing wool, September 10, 1791; borrowed a reed from Chamberlains, October 15, 1791; Mrs. Livermore weaving handkerchiefs, July 4, 1791.

40. MMB, August 29, 31, 1792, July 14, 1791.

41. KD 5:288.

42. MMB, June 1, 21, 28, 1791, July 25, 1791.

43. MMB, May 3, 1792, October 10, 1792.

44. MMB, June 1, 4, 1791, September 10, 1791, December 13, 1791, March 8, 1794. The Ballards had bought four sheep December 8, 1790, "the first we have ownd this 14 years."

CHAPTER FOUR

1. For England, Lawrence Stone, *The Family, Sex and Marriage in England, 1500–1800* (New York: Harper & Row, 1977), describes the rise of what he calls the "affectionate nuclear family." Alan MacMarlane, *Marriage and Love in England, 1300–1840* (Oxford, Eng.: Basil Blackwell, 1986), emphasizes the existence of a "Malthusian Marriage System" from the fourteenth century onward. Mary Beth Norton, following Lawrence Stone, emphasizes the restraints on young women in the mid-eighteenth century and the common recognition of a need for parental involvement in the formation of marriages, but believes women were granted greater freedom in the post-Revolutionary period, in Norton, *Liberty's Daughters*, pp. 51–60, 229–231. For New England, the most influential argument for a shift toward affective individualism is Daniel Scott Smith, "Parental Power and Marriage Patterns: An Analysis of Historical Trends in Hingham, Massachusetts," *Journal of Marriage and the Family* 35 (1973): In family law there seems to have been a shift in the early nineteenth century from a notion of marriage as a property contract between father and son-in-law to a romantic personal contract between a man and a woman: Michael Grossberg, *Governing the Hearth: Law and Family in Nineteenth-Century America* (Chapel Hill: University of North Carolina Press, 1985), pp. 35–38.

2. Persons residing in a town that had neither a minister nor a justice of

the peace could go to the nearest neighboring town: *The Perpetual Laws of the Commonwealth of Massachusetts, from the Establishment of its Constitution to the First Session of the General Court, A.D. 1788* (Worcester, 1788), pp. 253–256.

3. MMB, December 16, 1792. Actually Martha's dates fail to match Sewall's. He said the certificate was issued December 12 and that Joseph North married the couple on December 16. The marriage may have followed rather than preceded the delivery.

4. Based on marriage lists extracted from HTR, I. Also, see Nash, p. 582.

5. Except for the mention of a psalm, Henry Sewall's description of his own wedding is almost identical: "Was married to Miss Tabby Sewall about two o'clock," he wrote. "Mr. Ezekiel Emerson performed the ceremony. Her sisters with their husbands & Thomas were the only guests besides the family. Sang the 48 hymn of the 2 book": HS, February 9, 1786.

6. MMB, November 8, 11, 19, 1792.

7. MMB, March 14, 1795. Charles Gill and Betsy Barton had been married March 1, had made a brief trip to Winslow apparently in the company of "son and daughter Pollard," and had returned on March 7. The new bride lived at the Ballards until April 12, Mr. Gill coming and going just as in the other cases: MMB, March 15, 16, 18, 22, 1795, April 8, 11, 12, 1795. Sarah Parsons of Newburyport, Massachusetts, noted that after her marriage to Charles Porter Phelps of Hadley on January 1, 1800, she remained in Newbury while he went to Hadley. He came for her "the last of March," they visited in various places for the rest of the spring and summer, sometimes together, sometimes apart, "and went to housekeeping the first day of September": Sarah Parson Phelps Journal, Phelps Papers, Amherst College Library, Amherst, Mass.

8. Ellen Rothman, *Hands & Hearts: A History of Courtship in America* (New York: Basic Books, 1980), pp. 175–176.

9. MMB, October 26, 1792.

10. This statement is based on my own analysis of ten detailed household inventories from Hallowell, 1790–1796, using transcriptions of Lincoln County probate records at the Maine State Museum in Augusta. Six of the ten inventories listed frying pans or skillets, nine of them had kettles or pots. Only two households had more than four pieces of cooking equipment; most had from one to three. On the broader question of household amenities, see Gloria L. Main and Jackson T. Main, "Economic Growth and the Standard of Living in Southern New England, 1640–1774," *The Journal of Economic History* 48 (1988): 27–46. Living standards are, of course, relative. While the Mains found a sharp rise in household consumption in the third quarter of the eighteenth century, household possessions were still very limited. Less than 60 percent of households in the richest third of the population had forks, for example, less than a quarter had fine earthenware.

11. In describing a quilting held at Lucy Towne's house in Winslow just before the birth of a baby, Martha mentioned that she "helpt break the wool"

that was used to fill the quilt and that a neighbor came to "Chalk" or mark the design to be stitched: MMB, September 23, 24, 25, 26, 1795. In the Ballard diary quilting entries seem to cluster in the autumn. For other examples, see September 5, 9, 13, 23, 1791; and November 17, 1790.

12. Anna Tuels Coverlet, Maine, c. 1785, Wadsworth Athenaeum, Hartford, Conn. The quilt is illustrated or described in Patsy and Myron Orlofsky, *Quilts in America* (New York: McGraw-Hill, 1974), Pl. 76, p. 216; Carleton L. Safford and Robert Bishop, *America's Quilts and Coverlets* (New York: Dutton, 1972), Fig. 148, p. 112. The Wadsworth Athenaeum now lists this as a "Coverlet" rather than a "Marriage Quilt" because there is no documentation for the former title.

13. MMB, May 8, 1795, December 23, 1794.

14. MMB, February 27, 1786, March 1, 5, 6, 14, 24, 1786, October 6, 17, 1786, March 26, 1790.

15. MMB, July 23, 1792, October 3, 15, 1788.

16. MMB, October 7, 1794, February 25, 1788.

17. MMB, August 25, 1793.

18. William E. Nelson, *Americanization of the Common Law: The Impact of Legal Change on Massachusetts Society, 1760–1830* (Cambridge, Mass.: Harvard University Press, 1975), pp. 110–111; LCCGSP, Books 1–2.

19. The three points of view are exemplified by Nelson, *Americanization of the Common Law,* pp. 110, 251–253; Daniel Scott Smith and Michael Hindus, "Premarital Pregnancy in America, 1640–1971: An Overview and an Interpretation," *Journal of Interdisciplinary History* 5 (1975): 537–570; and Davidson, *Revolution and the Word,* pp. 106–109. For an excellent summary of the literature on eighteenth-century sexuality, see John D'Emilio and Estelle B. Freedman, *Intimate Matters: A History of Sexuality in America* (New York: Harper & Row, 1988), pp. 42–52.

20. *Province and Court Records of Maine,* IV, ed. Neal W. Allen, Jr. (Portland: Maine Historical Society, 1958), pp. 47–50; VI (1975), pp. 150–153. Metherell was whipped rather than fined because of the unusual circumstances of her case.

21. Mary Beth Norton, "Gender and Defamation in Seventeenth-century Maryland," WMQ, 44, (1987): 3–39, and "Gender, Crime, and Community in Seventeenth-Century Maryland," revision of a paper prepared for the Conference in Honor of Bernard Bailyn, Harvard University, October 30–31, 1987, pp. 28–36.

22. Cornelia Hughes Dayton, *Women Before the Bar: Gender, Law, and Society in Connecticut, 1710–1790,* Ph.D. dissertation, Princeton University, 1986, is a model of what needs to be done. There are differences in law and procedure in New Haven, but the general trends are similar to those in Massachusetts. Also useful for understanding the history of the courts themselves is Hendrik

Hartog, "The Public Law of a County Court: Judicial Government in Eighteenth-century Massachusetts," *The American Journal of Legal History* 20 (1976): 282–329.

23. *The Perpetual Laws, of the Commonwealth of Massachusetts, from the Establishment of its Constitution to the First Session of the General Court A.D. 1788* (Worcester: 1788), pp. 245–247.

24. MMB, March 1804. In thirteen of the fourteen entries the verb is "declared"; in the one exception she wrote, "Shee *says* William Sands is the father."

25. MMB, June 20, 1789.

26. Reverend Eliphalet Gillet marriages, September 20, 1794: HTR, I, n.p.

27. Rice, *Vital Records of Oxford,* pp. 14–15, 112–113; Daniels, *Oxford,* pp. 379–380, 618–619; *Ballard Genealogy,* pp. 82–83; Porter-Barton Notes copied by J.J. Haskell and Notes on Barton Genealogy by Edith Riccius King, Mosher and Barton Family Records, MeSL. It is difficult to know how Stephen and Dorothy Barton construed Richardson's novels. Clarissa's character was apparently more impressive than her unhappy history; by the early nineteenth century there were at least four Clarissa Harlowes among Dorothy and Stephen's descendants. The most famous of Clarissa's namesakes may have had an intimate relation with a married man during the Civil War: Pryor, *Clara Barton: Professional Angel,* pp. 112–115.

28. American novels of seduction include [Sally S. B. K. Wood], *Julia and the Illuminated Baron* (Portsmouth, N.H., 1800); Susanna Rowson, *Charlotte Temple,* ed. Cathy N. Davidson (New York: Oxford University Press, 1986 [1794]); and Hannah Foster, *The Coquette: or, The History of Eliza Wharton,* Intro. Herbert Ross Brown (New York: Columbia University Press, 1939 [1797]).

29. Susan Staves, "British Seduced Maidens," *Eighteenth Century Studies,* 14 (1980–1981), 109, 120.

30. Mary Gillpatrick, Sheepscott Great Pond, single woman v. Elisha Parkhurst, New Milford, Brick maker: LCCCP Records, 8:216.

31. She had written "Jonathan was married to Sally Pierce" in the margin of the diary on January 11, an obvious error if Sewall was correct in giving their publication date as February 11. Did Jonathan tell his mother he was married before he actually was? Or did she turn to the wrong page to record the entry in the margin when she heard the news after the fact? In the town records, Henry Sewall's handwriting is perfectly clear. He does not, however, give the actual marriage date.

32. Edward Cook believes the "humorous custom of electing newly married men to the office of hog reeve" devloped late in the eighteenth century, *The Fathers of the Towns,* p. 218, n. 14. In Hallowell 85 of the 124 hog reeves elected between 1785 and 1797 appear in the lists of marriage intentions for the year

or two immediately preceding. Moses Pollard and Shubael Pitts were both elected in 1794. Lois K. Stabler has discovered an even stronger pattern in Keene, New Hampshire. See Laurel Thatcher Ulrich and Lois K. Stabler, "'Girling of It' in Eighteenth-century New Hampshire," *Families and Children,* ed. Peter Benes, Proceedings of the Dublin Seminar on New England Folklife, 1987, pp. 24–36.

33. In addition to the Pitts vessel, a brig was being built at the Fort landing across the river: MMB and HS, October 30, 1793, November 6, 1793.

34. MMB, October 14, 1793, March 4, 1795. Once in a great while she would slip, as on April 1793, when she wrote, "Hannah & Parthenia here."

CHAPTER FIVE

1. "Bulah" was probably the Beulah Ephraims who married Laban Prince in June of 1793, shortly after her child was born. In the town records Henry Sewall described Bulah and her husband as "molattos, both of Hallowell." "Black Hitty" may have been the Hitty Slocum who appeared with Nicholas Wilson ("both Negroes") in the marriage lists six months after Martha delivered her of a second son. HTR, I. These entries for non-whites were written crosswise at the bottom of a page giving town meeting minutes for September 2, 1782. Martha identified the father of that child as "a Portugues who was Brot here by Mrs. Hussey from Nantucket" MMB, August 2, 1793, February 2, 1795.

2. Part of the 1792 valuation list for Hallowell is in North, pp. 240–242.

3. MMB, 1793, March 31–April 1, August 13, 1791.

4. The population increased from 1,199 in the federal census of 1790 to 2,575 in the now two towns of Hallowell and Augusta in 1800.

5. MMB, January 7–14, 1795, February 11, 1795.

6. MMB, April 24, 1794, July 29, 1808, March 31, 1800.

7. Charles White, *A Treatise on the Management of Pregnant and Lying-in Women* (London, 1772; rpt. Worcester, Mass., 1793), p. 76. For two very different assessments of the literature of "natural" childbirth in the eighteenth century, see Adrian Wilson, "William Hunter and the varieties of man-midwifery," and Edward Shorter, "The management of normal deliveries and the generation of William Hunter," in *William Hunter and the eighteenth-century medical world,* ed. W. F. Bynum and Roy Porter (Cambridge, Engl.: Cambridge University Press, 1985).

8. An Edgecomb, Maine, jury called to investigate the death of an infant reported that the mother had been "left alone in her House, and [was] inturly destitute of any help in the Time of her traveling pains by which means it is supposed that the said Child came into the world a Corpse, and the mother (when found) was but just alive": LCSJC, Files, 923:109.

9. MMB, e.g., March 17, 1789, December 30, 1789, January 2, 1790, December 30, 1790, February 12, 1791.

10. Estes and Goodman, *The Changing Humors of Portsmouth*, p. 298. For more detail on this point, see Laurel Thatcher Ulrich, "The Living Mother of a Living Child: Midwifery and Mortality in Eighteenth-Century New England," WMQ 46 (1989): 27–48.

11. B. M. Willmott Dobbie, "An Attempt to Estimate the True Rate of Maternal Mortality, Sixteenth to Eighteenth Centuries," *Medical History* 26 (1982): 79–90; White, *Treatise*, pp. 236–240.

12. "A Copy of Records from an Original Memorandum kept by Mrs. Lydia (Peters) Baldwin ...," typescript, Special Collections, Dartmouth College Library; Worth Estes, *Hall Jackson and the Purple Foxglove*, p. 120.

13. Edmund Chapman, *A Treatise on the Improvement of Midwifery* (London, 1759, 1st ed., 1733), p. xx.

14. MMB, October 23, 1796, March 21, 1795.

15. Sarah Stone, *A Complete Practice of Midwifery* ... (London, 1737), p. 67; Chapman, *Midwifery*, p. 132; Henry Bracken, *The Midwife's Companion; or, a Treatise of Midwifery* (London, 1737), pp. 124–125. William Hunter attacked the method of manual extraction urged in Chapman and in Bracken. I used Dr. William Appleton's handwritten copy of Hunter's "Lectures on the gravid uterus," Appleton Papers, Waterville [Maine] Historical Society, pp. 57–58. See also White, *Treatise*, pp. 47, 87–88.

16. Hunter, "Lectures," Appleton in pp. 59–60.

17. Bracken, *Midwife's Companion*, pp. 175–178; Chapman, *Midwifery*, p. 159.

18. MMB, May 3, 1792.

19. Adrian Wilson concludes that man-midwifery in seventeenth- and eighteenth-century England "tended to be concentrated upon difficult births. Normal births were brought into male practice only via advance and onset calls, and even these calls were usually made because difficulty was *expected*." Class distinctions were important, advance and onset calls being most common among the nobility. "Man-midwifery," pp. 357, 362.

20. MMB, November 17, 1793.

21. MMB, July 8, 1796, August 14, 1796, June 14, 1798, July 15, 1798; HS, October 4, 1799.

22. Bracken, *Midwife's Companion*, p. 194.

23. North, p. 93, 814; HS, August 28, 1798. The Benjamin Vaughan Papers, MeHS, include an account with William Mathew, "debtor to Dr. Benjamin Page," for $115.76 in medical fees, including three charges for "delivery & attendance" at $6 and one at $4. There may have been unusual circumstances in these births, but it seems likely that doctors' fees were from twice to three times as high as midwives'.

24. Fifty-three percent of the heads of household in the combined Hallowell-Augusta federal censuses for 1800 appear on her birth lists; 47 percent of

the men listed as selectman, town representatives, or county officers between 1790 and 1796 do so. This does not mean that she delivered *all* of the babies born to these families, only that she delivered some.

25. George Thornton Edwards, *Music and Musicians of Maine* (Portland: The Southworth Press, 1928), pp. 22–23. On February 23, 1790, Margaret Belcher was delivered, in her husband's absence, of "a fine son shee calls Hyrum," giving him the distinction of being the only newborn infant in the diary with a name. Coincidentally, Sarah Sheppard was also a musician, a teacher of voice and piano.

26. MMB, October 21, 1794.

27. Chapman, *Midwifery*, pp. xvi–xviii; Stone, *Complete Practice*, p. 36.

28. Dr. Kittredge's forceps and his copy of William Smellie, *A Treatise on the Improvement of Midwifery*, 3d ed. (London, 1759), are at the North Andover Historical Society.

29. MMB, November 11, 1785.

30. MMB, May 19, 1792. Dr. Hubbard, a native of New Hampshire, is described by one Augusta historian as a "physician and farmer" in East Readfield. His son, Dr. John Hubbard of Hallowell, was governor of Maine, 1850–1853. Nash, *Augusta*, p. 403.

31. MMB, August 29, 1797, February 28, 1799, July 19, 1794.

32. MMB, March 29, 1789, June 20, 1798. See also April 15, 1797, October 20, 1810. In describing the latter case, she noted that the woman had "3 Doctors with her." Worth Estes, *Hall Jackson and the Purple Foxglove*, p. 120, believes that Hall Jackson may have been called to a disproportionate number of twin births (eight sets in 511 pregnancies). Lydia Baldwin delivered ten pairs of twins in 926 deliveries. Since Martha Ballard delivered fewer twins, proportionately, than Baldwin or Jackson, a few Hallowell women, knowing they were expecting twins, may have called a doctor at the outset, though, given Martha's success, that seems unlikely.

33. MMB, October 12, 1788.

34. MMB, November 26, 1796.

35. MMB, December 23–27, 1791.

36. MMB, December 24, 1796, March 11, 1790, April 3, 1795, May 27, 1795, July 31, 1795.

37. MMB, April 7, 11, 1796. Nicholas Culpeper, *A Directory for Midwives* (London, 1651), is full of herbal recipes for use during labor, as we might suppose. Charles White assumed that midwives administered hot drinks and alcohol during labor and after delivery.

38. MMB, April 25, 1798, June 4, 1794, November 13, 1790.

39. Bracken, *Midwife's Companion*, pp. 117–118.

40. MMB, March 12, 1789: "I returned at 12 [midnight] precisely by our time piece. Left my patients cleverly." Sarah Stone disapproved of delivering a woman "standing on her feet," a method "too commonly practis'd in the country": *Complete Practice*, p. 55.

41. MMB, April 1, 1798.

42. MMB, March 5, 1801, October 8, 1790.

43. MMB, June 17, 1792. At Tabitha Sewall's third delivery (November 23, 1790), Mrs. Brooks, Belcher, Colman, Pollard, and Voce assisted.

44. MMB, May 4–7, 1793.

45. MMB, March 22, 1797, March 9, 1796, March 16, 1810. Thomas Densmore was the baby's grandfather; the birth probably took place at his house.

46. MMB, February 2, 1812, March 18, 1801, February 27, 1797.

47. MMB, June 21, 1798, January 2–February 4, 1801. Understandably, the town history is silent concerning Davis's alliance with Hitty Pierce, who later married someone else. For more on Pierce and Davis, see Chapter Seven.

48. HS, April, 10, 26, 1974, May 10, 1794, January 28, 31, 1795.

49. Charlotte may have been a sister of Hannah Cool, who was Martha's helper in 1787 (see Chapter One). The diary refers to at least four women with the surname Cool: Peggy, Polly, Hannah, and Katherine (the Mrs. Williams of Chapters One and Two). Miscellaneous entries in Moses Appleton's papers refer to Hannah and to Jane Coole, who apparently had a child; Moses Appleton Day Book, 1796, Waterville Historical Society, pp. 4, 8, 9, 10, 38, 45, 144, 146.

50. MMB, November 26, 1790, October 20, 1795, June 15, 1796, April 14, 1800, December 31, 1795, March 6, 1798.

51. MMB, November 27, 1795.

52. MMB, January 27–28, 1794, February 1, 1794.

53. MMB, May 31, 1799, November 28, 1787, August 24, 30, 1797.

54. John Rynier to Henry Knox, February 19, 1798, quoted in Alan Taylor, "*Liberty-Men* and White Indians: Frontier Migration, Popular Protest, and the Pursuit of Property in the Wake of the American Revolution" (Ph.D. diss., Brandeis University, 1985), p. 209; MMB, March 11, 1795; Bracken, *Midwife's Companion*, p. 176; White, *Treatise*, p. 93.

55. MMB, April 17, 1800, February 15, 1790, July 23–24, 1796.

56. MMB, October 21, 1787; HS, October 23, 1799, November 3, 1799.

57. MMB, e.g., March 26, 1789, October 20, 1789, June 8, 1793, May 22, 1788.

58. Leavitt, *Brought to Bed*, p. 165, discusses a case in which the husband did have sexual intercourse with his wife on the third and fourth days after delivery.

59. MMB, October 18–19, 1802, February 26, 27, 1789, March 1, 2, 4, 1789; Siegel and Van Blarcom, *Obstetrical Nursing*, pp. 208–213, 522–526; Wertz and Wertz, *Lying-In*, pp. 119–128; Leavitt, *Brought to Bed:* pp. 154–155. See also Dorothy I. Lansing, W. Robert Penman, and Dorland J. Davis, "Puerperal Fever and the Group B Beta Hemolytic Streptococcus," *Bulletin of the History of Medicine* 57 (Spring 1983): 70–80; and a comment by Leavitt, *Brought to Bed*, p. 166.

60. MMB, March 31, 1790, April 4, 5, 10, 11, 12, 13, 15, 16, 1790.

61. MMB, November 26, 1790. If this is Mrs. Hodge's fifth delivery, someone else must have attended the third. There are only three previous deliveries in the diary, September 1785, September 1786, and October 1789 (and two others in November 1792 and June 1794).

62. MMB, February 18, 1791, September 1, 1791.

63. MMB, May 18, 1790.

64. MMB, October 1, & 5, 1794, November 14, 19, 22, 23, 24, 30, 1794, December 3, 4, 1794.

65. North, p. 954; HTR, Marriage Intentions, January 31, 1791.

66. MMB, November 16, 1791.

67. MMB, December 12, 1791.

68. The illness apparently had no long-term effect on either mother or child. Mrs. Weston died in 1831 at the age of eighty-five, her youngest son in 1870 at the age of eighty-nine.

69. MMB, May 1–June 2, 1789.

70. MMB, August 1, 4, 1788, February 11, 14, 15, 17, 23, 26, 1801.

71. In 1793, only four birth entries fail to record some sort of fee. One of those was for "Daughter Town," who delivered her ninth child on October 3. The others may have been the result of oversight. In twenty-seven of the fifty-three entries she specified six shillings; ten other entries indicate a fee exceeding six shillings, some specifying additional amounts for "medicine and horse hire." Eight others simply say XX, presumably meaning "fee paid." Two mention commodities without giving cash values. The 1793 entries are typical of the diary as a whole, though fees rose slightly toward 1800. Of 385 midwifery entries specifying cash values, 374 are for less than ten shillings. Most are between six and nine shillings. Only seventy-five entries list commodities alone.

72. MMB, December 15, 1791, March 17, 1795.

73. MMB, September 5, 1792, December 3, 1789.

74. MMB, February 3, 5, 6, 8, 1791, March 20, 1796, May 3, 1797.

75. MMB, December 30, 1789, December 17, 1793, November 15, 1795, May 5, 1799, October 21, 1794, August 22, 1796, March 15, 1797, October 22–23, 1799, HS, October 4, 22, 23, 1799.

76. MMB, January 24, 1794, April 2, 1794, December 19, 1794, July 13, 1794, February 20, 1794, April 5, 1794.

77. That payment by fathers was the norm is suggested by the entry for June 1793, "I received 6/ of Mrs. Brown. Her husband is gone down the river."

78. KCSJC Files, Box 68.

79. I searched the Minute Books and File Papers for Lincoln County, 1785–1797, then at the Office of the Clerk, Supreme Judicial Court, Suffolk County Courthouse, Boston. I found twelve divorce "libels" in Lincoln County between 1785 and 1797, six in which the wife charged adultery, two in which the husband did so, four in which the wife charged cruelty, and two in which the husband charged desertion. The maritime theme is dominant

from the beginning, as is the charge of intemperance. North, p. 834, says that John Molloy "died," after which his wife married Samuel Prescott of New Sharon. Edward McCarron, who is doing research on Irish migration into Maine in this period, believes that Molloy may have been Irish, though the number of John Molloys who appear in country records makes sure identification difficult. McCarron has found that John Molloy of Hallowell was admitted as a retailer in 1790, was in jail for debt in 1796, lost land to satisfy a debt in 1797 (Ephraim Ballard as surveyor), and was presented by a grand jury, though acquitted, for some unspecified crime in 1797.

80. MMB, April 24, 1794.

81. MMB, March 31, 1785.

82. MMB, January 19–25, 1792.

83. MMB, April 27, 1791, April 18, 1795, September 17, 1789, July 10, 1797. See also April 21, 1786, March 6, 1792.

84. MMB, July 13, 1791. On the side saddle, see July 22, 1786, and February 25, 1791.

85. MMB, April 12, 1785, June 20, 1799.

86. MMB, October 26, 1797.

CHAPTER SIX

1. MMB, January 27, 1795, February 4, 13, 27, 1795, April 21–May 4, 1795, June 8–12, 1795; Plan of Hallowell, March 1795, Maps, 1794 Series, 13; 1361, p. 20; Plan of Vassalboro, January 1795, Maps, 1794 Series, vol. 3, 1385, p. 19, MSA.

2. MMB, January 29–February 7, 1795.

3. The diary mentions Sarah Neal at least eleven times between July 29 and December 15, when Martha wrote: "I paid her 3/ in Cash. Shee has done 4 weaks work for me since I setled with her." She came back again in May for a few days, then "went to Capt. Blunts to live": MMB July 29, 1795, August, 17, 1795, September 9, 15, 16, 21, 1795, October 10, 17, 1795, November 26, 30, 1795, December 15, 1795, May 16, 1797, May 12, 1797.

4. "Journal of Thomas Fish," pp. 132–139. Fish was related by marriage to Martha's cousin Ebenezer Learned; Daniels, *Oxford*, p. 500.

5. Daniel Cony to Ephraim Ballard, August 14, 1790, Eastern Lands Papers, 13:18; Ephraim Ballard to Daniel Cony, June 5, 1792, Eastern Lands Papers, 18:21, MSA.

6. MMB, January 12, 1795; Ephraim Ballard to Gentlemen, Eastern Lands Papers 17:35, MSA.

7. Ephraim Ballard Deposition, November 20, 1795, Kennebec Proprietors Papers, MEHS; KD 8:461; Instructions to Ephraim Ballard, June 24, 1795, Eastern Lands Papers, 13:31B, MSA.

8. MMB, November 30, 1795.

9. Alan Taylor, "The Disciples of Samuel Ely: Settler Resistance Against Henry Knox on the Waldo Patent, 1785–1801," *Maine Historical Society Quarterly*, 26 (1986): 80–82.

10. MMB, January 9, 12, 13, 1796.

11. MMB, November 17, 1794.

12. MMB, January 4, 1793.

13. MMB, January 22, 1790, April 28, 1795.

14. MMB, September 30, 1794, December 25, 1794, January 6, 1794, December 22, 1793.

15. MMB, January 26–27, 1796.

16. KD 9:400; Instructions to Ephraim Ballard, Eastern Lands Papers, 13:33, MSA.

17. MMB, September 1, 3, 4, 5, 1796, October 15, 17, 18, 19, 1796.

18. MMB, July 2, 1799.

19. *The Book of Abigail and John: Selected Letters of the Adams Family, 1762–1784*, ed. L. H. Butterfield, Marc Friedlaender, and Mary-Jo Kline (Cambridge, Mass.: Harvard University Press, 1975), p. 123.

20. Charles William Janson, "Stranger in America," in Gordon S. Wood, *The Rising Glory of America, 1760–1820* (New York: Braziller, 1971), p. 123.

21. MMB, July 18, 24, 1798.

22. North, pp. 278, 312–313, 315–316.

23. MMB, May 12–13, 1800.

24. Stephen Barton Account Book, MeSL, December 1769, MMB, October 1, 1801; *The English Dialect Dictionary*, ed. Joseph Wright (New York: Putnam, 1900), vol. II, p. 264; *The Scottish National Dictionary*, ed. William Grant and David D. Murison (Edinburgh: Scottish National Dictionary Association, 1952), vol. III, p. 252.

25. MMB, May 19, 1800.

26. MMB, August 28, 1801.

27. Taylor, *Liberty Men*, pp. 586–587, n. 10. Ephraim resigned his commission. Three subsequent attempts to complete the survey were also repelled.

28. MMB, August 28–29, 1802.

29. Luke 10:38–42.

CHAPTER SEVEN

1. Anonymous letter to Governor Increase Sumner, January 7, 1799, MeHS.

2. Anonymous Letter to Governor Sumner, January 7, 1779.

3. North, pp. 674–677.

4. North, pp. 674–675; Clifford K. Shipton, *Biographical Sketches of Graduates of Harvard University*, vol. IX, pp. 229–234. In the estate inventory taken at his death, Eliphalet Pierce is described as a "yeoman." He owned fifty acres of

land, a house and barn, and the usual assemblage of farm tools and household furnishings: Transcript of Lincoln County Probate Records, VIII:64, MeSM. I would like to thank Danny D. Smith of Gardiner, Maine, for helping me with the Pierce genealogy.

5. *Female Friendship; Or the Innocent Sufferer. A Moral Novel* (Hallowell, Me.: printed by Howard S. Robinson, for Nathaniel Cogswell, 1797), pp. 10–13. *The Tocsin* for February 4, 1797, has an advertisement from Nathaniel Cogswell, who "has taken the store, lately occupied by Captain John Molloy." In addition to textiles, hardware, crockery, tea, and coffee Cogswell sold a predictable selection of books—spelling books, singing books, testaments, works by Watt, Bunyan, and Goldsmith, "Edwards on Affections," "Berlamaque on Law," "Boyle's Voyage," and a few works of English fiction including *Clarissa Harlowe* and *Robinson Crusoe*.

6. Jan Lewis, "The Republican Wife," 689–721; Davidson, *Revolution and the Word*, pp. 140–150.

7. MMB, June 26, 1798.

8. Judge North's daughter, Hannah, for example, was sometimes called *Mrs.* Hannah North. After another visit, Martha simply noted, "Hitty and her son sleep here": MMB, February 3, 1800.

9. If church membership was the measure, only two of the new judges were "exemplary Christians," and they were on opposite sides in the ecclesiastical fights in the town. Henry Sewall, as we know, had affiliated with the maverick Chester church. Daniel Cony was a recently admitted member of the regular Congregational church: Church Records of the First Church in Augusta, vol. 1, South Parish Congregational Church, Augusta, Maine. This is apparently a copy of the early record kept by Daniel Stone with additions by Benjamin Tappan. A letter dated March 3, 1827, says the remains of this book were found by a Roman Catholic unbound in a pile of junk, bound by a Unitarian, and presented to the church by an "innocent (interested) bystander."

10. The diary suggests the sort of accidents that often resulted. MMB, January 28, 1791: "I was Calld at 8 to see Capt Burses little son who was scalt in his left arm yester morn. I drest the arm." August 21, 22, 1795: Martha called to "see Mr Burtun's infant who was scalt yesterday." On January 5, 1799, she was "called in hast to son Jonathan's; his oldest son Jack [who was seven years old] had drank spirrit and was apparently dead. We immersed him in warm water and put down oil. Doct. Cony was called and used some means and he recovered through the goodness of God. I tarried all night."

11. On January 2, 1801,

12. MMB, January 6, 1797. At the Burtuns', as at the Ballards', the mother was "Expecting soon to be sick." Accidents just before a lying-in may have been common. On March 9, 1791, "Mrs. Benjamins daughter Cutt her middle finger of her right hand off. They sent for me. I went twice to see her this afternoon." Two days later she went to Mr. Savage's "and Drest the Little

girls hand." She did it again the next day and again on March 15, in the morning, returning at night to deliver the child's mother of "a lusty son."

13. MMB, January 4, 1801.

14. Ethel Colby Conanti, ed., *Vital Records of Augusta* (Portland: Maine Historical Society), I, pp. 14, 177; Danny D. Smith of Gardiner, Maine, provided me with birth dates for Eliphalet Pierce's children from the parish records of Stoughton, Massachusetts, now at the Canton [Massachusetts] Historical Society. Arlene Gilbert of Windsor, Maine, also provided helpful information.

15. Benjamin D. Cabrera, "Ascaris: most 'popular' worm," *World Health* (March 1984), 8–9. I am thankful to Dr. Eli Chernin of the Harvard School of Public Health for diagnosing the ailment and for providing me with the article cited above.

16. Benjamin Page account with William Matthews, 1804–1819, Vaughan Papers, MeHS.

17. Albert Matthews, "Notes on Early Autopsies and Anatomical Lectures," *Publications of the Colonial Society of Massachusetts* 19 (1916–1917):280. The few accounts of early autopsies tend to be impressionistic and unfocused. E. B. Krumbhaar, "History of the Autopsy and Its Relation to the Development by Modern Medicine," *Hospitals* 12 (1938):68–74, begins with the Egyptians and Assyrians and assumes that there were few autopsies in colonial times. Worth Estes, who is compiling material on the topic, believes that they were far more common than has earlier been supposed. For an example of a newspaper account, see *Essex Gazette*, December 13–20 and 20–27, 1768.

18. K. F. Russell, *British Anatomy, 1525–1800: A Bibliography of Works Published in Britain, America and on the Continent* (Winchester, U.K.: St. Paul's Bibliographies, 1987), p. xxxii and Introduction. Michel Foucault argues for a fundamental shift in the early nineteenth century in the way autopsies—and therefore disease and death—were viewed. Dissections had been occurring in a rather matter-of-fact way long before this intellectual transformation occurred. It was not the autopsy but a particular way of seeing it that transformed medical views of the body and made possible the scientific fragmentation so many critics are discussing today; *The Birth of the Clinic: An Archaelogy of Medical Perception*, trans. A. M. Sheridan Smith (New York: Pantheon, 1973), pp. 124–148. Carolyn Merchant associates the anatomical explorations of Harvey with capitalist exploitation of nature and male domination of women, *The Death of Nature*, pp. 149–163. For an interesting portrait of English scientific curiosity at the local level, see Robert G. Frank, Jr., "The John Ward Diaries: Mirror of Seventeenth Century Science and Medicine," *Journal of the History of Medicine & Allied Sciences* 29 (1974):147–179.

19. MMB, September 16, 1800, March 13, 1808.

20. Matthews, "Early Autopsies," p. 277.

21. Albertus Haller, *First Lines of Physiology . . . Printed under the inspection of William Cullen, M.D.* (Edinburgh, 1786; repr. New York: Johnson Reprint, 1966), pp. 134–135.

22. He added that "The colon is an intestine altogether continuous." Haller, pp. 125, 138.

23. Stone, *The Complete Practice of Midwifery*, p. xiv.

24. [Walter Channing], *Remarks on the Employment of Females as Practitioners in Midwifery* (Boston: 1820), p. 7. This anonymous pamphlet has been variously attributed, though the Library of the College of Physicians and Surgeons, Philadelphia, has an autographed copy presented by Channing to an associate. As late as 1848, practical anatomy, which included dissection, was still taught in only a minority of medical schools in the United States, though some early women's colleges made it a point to include it in their curricula: William G. Rothstein, *American Medical Schools and the Practice of Medicine: A History* (New York: Oxford University Press, 1987), pp. 32–35; Regina Markell Morantz-Sanchez, *Sympathy & Science: Women Physicians in American Medicine* (New York: Oxford University Press, 1985), p. 80.

25. For a powerful recent discussion of that issue from the perspective of a twentieth-century nurse, see Sallie Tisdale, *The Sorcerer's Apprentice: Tales of the Modern Hospital* (New York: McGraw-Hill, 1986).

26. E.g., Lawrence Stone, *Family, Sex and Marriage in England, 1500–1800* (New York: Harper and Row, 1977), pp. 113–114. For a dissenting view, see Linda Pollock, *Forgotten Children: Parent-Child Relations from 1500–1900* (Cambridge, Eng.: Cambridge University Press, 1983), pp. 124–140.

27. MMB, September 6, 15, 16, 1800.

28. MMB, July 21, 1794.

29. Paul Starr, *The Social Transformation of America Medicine* (New York: Basic Books, 1982), gives the broad view; John Harley Warner, *The Therapeutic Perspective: Medical Practice, Knowledge, and Identity in America, 1820–1885* (Cambridge, Mass. and London, Eng.: Harvard U. Press, 1986), offers a detailed study of three locales, including Boston.

30. "Memoir of Benjamin Page," *The Boston Medical and Surgical Journal*, 33 (October 1, 1845), 173, 177; Leavitt, *Brought to Bed*, pp. 100–101.

31. Benjamin Vaughan to Benjamin Page, September 26, 1800, MeHS.

32. Benjamin Vaughan to Moses Appleton, April 22, 1812, Moses Appleton Letters, Waterville Historical Society, Waterville, Maine.

33. Benjamin Vaughan to Benjamin Page, March 14, 1802, MeHS.

34. Moses Appleton Commonplace Book, Waterville Historical Society, Waterville, Maine. The pages are unnumbered and undated. The most vigorous defense of bleeding during pregnancy and delivery is William Dewees, *An Essay on the Means of Lessening Pain, and Facilitating Certain Cases of Difficult Parturition* (Philadelphia: 1806). His notes on successful cases recommended drawing as much as 40 ounces of blood, or until the patient felt nauseous, bleeding "to sickness," and "bleeding nearly to fainting," pp. 63–89. His book was dedicated to a number of well-known physicians, including Benjamin Rush, a correspondent of Vaughan. The birth rate began to fall in New England sometime in the late eighteenth century, though we know very little

about how this occurred, or for what groups. Patent medicine ads with their veiled hints at abortion had already begun to appear in Augusta by the end of Martha's life. The October 9, 1810, issue of the *Herald of Liberty* carried an advertisement for "Dr. Rolfe's Aromatic Female Pills," concluding with the warning that "they are conducive to the health of married women, *unless when pregnant*, at which time they must not be taken as they would most certainly produce miscarriage." (Emphasis in the original)

35. William Mathews accounts with Benjamin Page, February 29, 1804, to March 18, 1819, MeHS.

36. HS, June 19–10, 1810; August 25–27, September 16–23, October 20, November 5, December 5, 20, 1824; January 10, February 18, 26, March 13–15, 1825.

37. Benjamin Vaughan to Benjamin Page, February 7, 1803, MeHS.

38. North, pp. 317, 422–423; Charles Vaughan to the Proprietors of the Kennebec Purchase, Feb. 13, 1805, Kennebec Proprietors Papers, Box 5, MeHS.

CHAPTER EIGHT

1. MMB, November 17–18, 1802 (pumpkin parings); September 12, 1808 (cornstalk dye); March 2, 1802 (leach for soap). The three barrels of soap on March 25, 1803, were the cumulation of many days' work: March 15, 16, 17, 18, 23, 24. In 1802 she mentioned soap-making on March 2, 3, 5, 6, 8, 9, and 10.

2. On carrying wool to the carding "masheen," MMB, August 15, 24, 1803; August 12, September 30, 1806; August 4, 10, 1810. The ease of processing may actually have increased the investment in sheep. Martha was very much involved in their care. On February 14, 1800, for example, Ephraim brought a frozen lamb into the house. On February 17, Martha went to the barn to care for the sheep. On May 30, 1806, Cyrus sheared the sheep. On June 3, two hired hands "washt the wool 20 fleases." On June 6, Martha "washt the rest of my wool." The women also integrated factory-spun yarn into their weaving operations. On November 9, 1805, "Cyrus carried 3 lb factory cottne warp to Daughter Lambard to weave." On July 6, 1806, "Olive Fletcher . . . took 1 3/4 facktory filling yarn to carry to Daughter Pollard."

3. MMB, April 4, 1802.

4. *Perpetual Laws*, 1788, pp. 112–114; "Confession Books" of Moses Appleton, Waterville Historical Society and Ephraim Towne, Maine State Museum, illustrate the process; Maine Valuation List, 1800, microfilm, Massachusetts State Library, Boston.

5. ATR, pp. 50, 51, 71, 108; Treasurer's Report, Town of Augusta, MeSL, p. 5.

6. MMB, February 1803, 28, March 4, 15, 1803, July 13, 1803, October 10, 13, 1803, November 15, 17, 22, 26, 1803, January 2, 1804.

7. *The Civil Officer; Or, the Whole Duty of Sheriffs, Coroners, Constables and Collectors of Taxes,* 2d ed. (Boston: 1814), pp. 26, 30. Because of the nature of the process by which Ephraim was taken, no record survives (except for a brief and cryptic entry in the town warrant for the next spring). Augusta's Town Meeting Warrant for March 1804 included an article asking "what length of time the Town will give the Sureties of Ephraim Ballard to pay his deficiencies." In February 1804, the town had initiated an additional Court of Common Pleas action against him and his two bondsmen, Benjamin Pettingill and David Thomas. The sheriff's return reported the attachment of "One Chair & two hats" for the men's appearance in court. (Presumably the sheriff found Ephraim in jail.) The case was entered as "a plea of Debt"; the defendants (by their lawyers Bridge and Williams) claimed "they owe the Plaintiffs nothing in manner & form as the Plaintiffs have declared against them," and the court ruled in their favor. The town lost its suit in August, and though it appealed to the Supreme Judicial Court (and lost again), that case wasn't tried until 1806. This must, therefore, have been an auxiliary suit, since Ephraim was imprisoned more than a month before it was initiated and remained in prison nine months after it was tried in the lower court. KCCCP, Records 3:497, Files, Box 4 (1804); KCSJC, Files, Box 72 (1806).

8. This altered an earlier Massachusetts law that allowed a creditor to keep a pauper in prison by paying his jail costs: Peter J. Coleman, *Debtors and Creditors in America: Insolvency, Imprisonment for Debt, and Bankruptcy, 1607–1900* (Madison: State Historical Society of Wisconsin, 1974), pp. 40–41.

9. William E. Nelson, *Americanization of the Common Law: The Impact of Legal Change on Massachusetts Society, 1760–1830* (Cambridge, Mass.: Harvard University Press, 1975), pp. 149–150.

10. MMB, February 2, 1804.

11. Coleman, *Debtors and Creditors,* p. 5; Ronald P. Formisano, *The Transformation of Political Culture: Massachusetts Parties, 1790–1840* (New York: Oxford University Press, 1983), pp. 187–190.

12. MMB, October 4, 1800.

13. An 1809 petition said that as many as forty-five debtors inhabited the jail at a time. Even at that rate, moving four hundred prisoners through the jail would mean an average incarceration of about forty days. Petition from Asa Emerson and others, Unenacted House Legislation, 6217, MSA.

14. KCCCP, Files, Box 261 (1804).

15. KD, 4:485; 6:132, 402; 6:260; 8:378.

16. North, pp. 248, 322–323; petition from Asa Emerson and others.

17. North, pp. 248, 323, 493–494; HS, August 10, 1803; KCSJC Files, Box 70 (June 1804) includes a List of Prisoners, signed by Amos Partridge: Henry McCausland for Murder, Timothy Hill for Theft, Moses Cilley, charged with

Forgery & Fraud. Debtors: Asa Phillips, Edmund Warren, Ephraim Ballard, Asa Emerson, George Lowell, John Robinson, Edward Savage. Of the debtors, only Savage and Ballard are listed on the Augusta Census for 1800.

18. *Kennebec Gazette*, July 12, 1804.

19. North, pp. 345–346. In 1809, during the so-called Malta War (see Chapter Ten), another Augusta versifier played on the image of the jail as a "jug" in describing the muster of two companies of militia from outlying towns:

> The reason of their coming here
> Is to keep Augusta snug,
> And keep the Malta Indians clear
> From breaking the stone jug.
>
> The great Stone Jug of Kennebec
> Has cost us many a crown,
> Yet Malta Indians do expect
> To tear the building down.
>
> Or else to drag the stopper out
> And liberate their friends,
> But they will find that we're so stout
> They'll not obtain their ends.

The poem, originally published in the *Kennebec Gazette*, is reprinted in North, p. 383. The *Oxford English Dictionary* gives the first citations for "jug" as slang for "jail" in the 1830s. This early association of jails with drinking suggests one possible origin of that usage. North also says that Joseph North's wife and later her daughter, Hannah Bridges, carried Thanksgiving dinners to the inhabitants of the jail, p. 510.

20. Anonymous, *An Address to the Inhabitants of Maine, Showing a Safe and Easy Method of Extracting Good from Evil* (Augusta, 1805), pp. 4–8.

21. Petition from Asa Emerson and others.

22. Petition from Asa Emerson, and others.

23. Coleman, *Debtors and Creditors*, p. 42, believes the "debt-collection system may have become more oppressive in the early nineteenth century." The bounds of prison yards were one source of contention.

24. MMB, November 6, 1803, January 19, 1804, February 2, 18, 1804, May 5, 29, 1804, July 1, 1804.

25. MMB, May 8–9, 31, 1804, July 3, 1804; Ephraim Ballard to Peleg Coffin, Kennebec Purchase Papers, Box 5, MeHS.

26. MMB, April 12, 1804.

27. MMB, February 8, 18, 1804, April 13, 22, 1804, May 5, 1804, July 15, 23, 1804, August 25, 1804, September 18, 22, 1804.

28. MMB, January 19, 22, 26, 27, 29, 1805, February 2, 1805.

29. *An Address to the Inhabitants of Maine,* pp. 4–5, 10.

30. MMB, e.g., October 19, 1804, February 9, 1805, March 10, 1805, April 13, 1805.

31. MMB, October 8–12, 1804, September 2–8, 1804.

32. MMB, May 4, 1804.

33. MMB, February 21, 1804, March 10, 1804, October 17, 19, 1804.

34. MMB, March 8, 1804.

35. MMB, August 16, 1804.

36. Massachusetts Tax Evaluation, 1800, Augusta, Maine, Massachusetts State Library, Boston.

37. KCSJC, Record, September 13, 1806, and KCSJC Files, Box 71.

38. KD, 4:56, 9:497, 6:64, 9:21. On the Augusta tax valuation, 1800, Ephraim Ballard has $684 total taxable wealth; Jonathan has $1,170 plus $340 in shares of the Daniel Savage estate (taxed for five shares).

39. William Whately, *A Care-Cloth or a Treatise of the Cumbers and Troubles of Marriage,* 1624, quoted in Alan Macfarlane, *Marriage and Love in England, 1300–1840* (Oxford, Eng.: Basil Blackwell, 1986), pp. 94–95.

40. Jonathan Ballard Will, 1754, Worcester County Probate Records A:3181, Worcester County Court House, Worcester, Massachusetts.

41. Edward Augustus Kendall, *Travels Through the Northern Parts of the United States* (New York, 1809), vol. III, p. 112. Kendall found the inn at Winslow where he stayed "as quiet as a private house.... Their season of business is that in which the snow is on the ground."

CHAPTER NINE

1. KD, 9:250, 9:497; MMB, December 31, 1805.

2. MMB, April 13, 1803, May 6, 16, 21, 1803, June 25, 1803, August 25, 1803, September 5, 8, 10, 14, 15, 1803, October 4, 1803. Purrinton appears in the South Parish tax book for the first time in 1804. On the 1805 tax inventory, he has a house, a barn, and 100 acres of unimproved land in the first mile. A probate inventory taken at his death identifies his land as Lot #17. Augusta Tax Valuation, South Parish, 1804, 1805, MeSA; Inventory of the Estate of James Purrington, Deceased, July 11, 1806, KCPR Files.

3. MMB June 16, 1804. Augusta Tax Valuation, South Parish, 1805, 1806, MeSA.

4. *Horrid Murder* [Augusta, Maine, 1806], broadside.

5. *Horrid Murder.*

6. Stephen A. Marini, "Religious Revolution in the District of Maine, 1780–1820," in Charles E. Clark, James S. Leamon, and Karen Bowden, *Maine in the Early Republic: From Revolution to Statehood* (Hanover: University Press of New England, 1988), pp. 120, 136, 137.

7. MMB, June 23, 25, 1804.

8. *Horrid Massacre!! Sketches of the Life of Captain James Purrinton* (Augusta, 1806), p. 18.

9. Stephen A. Marini, *Radical Sects of Revolutionary New England* (Cambridge, Mass.: Harvard University Press, 1982), pp. 46, 88, 136–137.

10. Timothy Merritt, *Discourse on the Horrid Murder of Capt. James Purrinton's Family* (Augusta, Me.: Peter Edes, 1806), pp. 9–10.

11. Merritt, *Discourse*, pp. 16–18.

12. Marini, *Radical Sects*, p. 145.

13. Eddy, *Universalism in America*, p. 519; Merritt, *Discourse*, p. 5.

14. Elizabeth Pleck, *Domestic Tyranny: The Making of Social Policy Against Family Violence from Colonial Times to the Present* (New York: Oxford University Press, 1987), pp. 7–9.

15. *Horrid Massacre*, p. 10.

16. *Horrid Massacre*, pp. 8–9.

17. Edes, who mentioned the Bible passage in note 2 to his *Horrid Murder*, could only comment, "By recurring to this chapter, it will be seen how strangely its true meaning must have been perverted, to influence the conduct of Purrinton.": p. 10. Neither discourse quoted or discussed the scripture. Edward August Kendall included a discussion of the McCausland and Purrinton murders in his description of Augusta in *Travels Through the Northern Part of the United States*, vol. III, pp. 115–117. For him, both were examples of religious fanaticism. He described Purrinton as a "predestinarian" without referring to any specific sect.

18. *Horrid Massacre*, p. 6.

19. *Horrid Massacre*, pp. 7–8.

20. Inventory of the Estate of James Purrington, Purrinton File, KPR. Seth Williams, Beriah Ingraham, and Lewis Hamlin were the appraisers.

21. "Old Mr Cliford" was at Jonathan's on July 15. Mrs. Clifford came to Martha's after water the next day.

22. MMB, July 24, 1806.

23. MMB, October 13, 1806.

24. On the broader issue of changing perceptions of suicide, see Michael MacDonald, "The Secularization of Suicide in England, 1660–1800," *Past & Present* 111 (1986): 50–97. The custom of burying a suicide outside the churchyard derives from ancient ideas about the diabolic origins of suicide; eighteenth-century neoclassicism and humanitarianism gradually altered traditional religious notions. Coroner's juries were concerned with maintaining local values as well as with protecting dependents. Gill's brother-in-law, Ephraim Towne, was involved in settling his estate, which was insolvent: Towne Papers, MeSM.

CHAPTER TEN

1. MMB, August 7, 1788, February 29, 1812. Among the more than 800 deliveries in the diary, eight appear under the name of John Shaw or some variant thereof. The other births to John Shaw, "Leut John Shaw," or "Mr. Shaw" were August 23, 1787, September 28, 1789, February 16, 1790, January 28, 1792, and March 27, 1798.

2. North, pp. 883–884; William Howard Estate, KPR.

3. *Vital Records of Winslow, Maine to the year 1892*, ed. Sarah Drummond Lang (Portland: Maine Historical Society, 1937), p. 103; Edwin Eugene Towne, *The Descendants of William Towne* (Newtonville, Mass.: 1901), p. 74.

4. North wrote his history in the form of annals, devoting four or five pages to most years. Eighteen hundred and nine received twenty-one pages; 1827, twenty-three; and 1865, twenty-two.

5. The Bartons moved around even in Maine. The accounts in the Stephen Barton Account Book are dated Oxford (1769–1773), Vasalboro (1775–1778), Winslow (1786–1787), Vasalboro (1787–1788), and Oxford (1788–1796). Martha's diary for May 24, 1786, confirms, "Doct Barton has Removd to Winslow."

6. A transcription of the letter is included in Herman Porter Riccin to Barton Lunt, August 8, 1932, copy in possession of Arlene Gilbert of Windsor, Maine, who kindly supplied me with the letter and with other Barton family material.

7. "A Lonely Mound in the Woods and the Story of a Maine Doctor," *Kennebec Journal*, no date, photocopy provided by Arlene Gilbert.

8. To the Proprietors of the Kennebec Purchase, March 20, 1806, Ruel Williams Papers, MeHS.

9. Taylor, "Liberty-Men," pp. 610–611.

10. HS, August 6, 1798.

11. North, pp. 339–340. For more on such ceremonies in other parts of Maine, see my essay " 'From the Fair to the Brave': Spheres of Womanhood in Federal Maine," in Laura Felych Sprague, ed., *Agreeable Situations: Society, Commerce, and Art in Southern Maine, 1780–1830* (Kennebunk, Me.: Brick Store Museum, 1987), pp. 215–225.

12. North, p. 344.

13. Taylor, "Liberty-Men," pp. 609–614. The quote is from Dillingham's report.

14. Copy of a vote of the magistrates in regard to the burning of the jail, March 17, 1808, House, Unenacted Legislation, MSA 6316.

15. Taylor, "Liberty-Men, pp. 609–610; "Nathan Barlow's Journey:" Mys-

ticism and Popular Protest on the Northeastern Frontier," in *Maine in the Early Republic*, pp. 100–117; North, pp. 344–369;

16. North, pp. 364–369.

17. On broad changes in the eighteenth and early nineteenth centuries, see Sarah McMahon, "A Comfortable Subsistence: The Changing Composition of Diet in Rural New England, 1620–1840," *WMQ* 42 (1985): 26–65. More work needs to be done on the gender division of labor in New England agriculture. Two exemplary studies for the Chesapeake and the Middle Atlantic are Lois Green Carr and Lorena Walsh, "Economic Diversification and Labor Organization in the Chesapeake," in Innes, *Work and Labor in Early America*, pp. 144–188, and Joan M. Jensen, *Loosening the Bonds: Mid-Atlantic Farm Women, 1750–1850* (New Haven, Conn.: Yale University Press, 1986).

18. MMB, July 11, 1791, October 4, 1789, December 27, 1800, March 13, 1791.

19. MMB, May 10, 1809.

20. For example, *Kennebec Intelligencer*, May 10, 1799; *The Kennebec Gazette*, May 7, 1804.

21. North, p. 179.

22. 1809 Account Book, MeSL, n.p. Because it gives no hint of his broader dealings, the account book was listed for many years as "anonymous." I have matched entries for pew rent and deed acknowledgments to corresponding records in the Kennebec County Court House, leaving no doubt that this is North's book. Like many contemporary records, including Martha's, it surely represents only a part of his enterprises. On seed dealers and Lombardy poplars, see Ann Leighton, *American Gardens in the Eighteenth Century: "For Use or for Delight"* (1976, repr. Amherst: University of Massachusetts Press, 1986), pp. 293–294, 468.

23. MMB, June 9, 1808, "transplanted cucumbers which I planted 10 May."

24. MMB, June 17, 1807, June 21, 1809.

25. "Daniel Cony's Diary," 1808–1810, reprinted in Nash, pp. 465–471. There are only two references to any medical activity, that for January 18, "Rode in my sulky to visit the sick in different parts of the town," and for March 20, "Six o'clock. P.M., Miss Catharine M. Weston born." The child was his granddaughter.

26. MMB, May 26, 1809, May 24, 1811, June 15, 1811.

27. MMB, May 28, 1808.

28. MMB,

29. Martha's curious reference to a maid (usually she knew the names of her neighbors' "girls") suggests that this Mrs. Howard, probably Samuel's wife, was somewhat distant, a consequence, perhaps, of her Boston upbringing and of Martha's infrequent visits to the town center after the move to the new farm: North, p. 884.

30. On the presence in Maine of the elegant country estates that one his-

torian has called *fermes ornées*, see Carolyn S. Parsons, " 'Bordering on Magnificence': Urban Domestic Planning in the Maine Woods," in *Maine in the Early Republic*, ed. Clark, Leamon, and Bowden, pp. 62–81.

31. Paul Coffin, "Missionary Tour in Maine, 1796," *Collections of the Maine Historical Society* 4 (1856), pp. 308, 312. The town being described was Starks, on the Sandy River.

32. *Vaughan Family*, p. 14.

33. Dwight, *Travels*, vol. II, pp. 238–239. Also see Kendall, *Travels*, p. 121.

34. "Daniel Cony's Diary," in Nash, pp. 465–471; 1809 Account Book.

35. *Truth and Falsehood: With Other Original and Fugitive Pieces* (Hallowell, Me: N. Cheever, 1810), pp. 35–36. Inside the copy owned by the Maine State Library is this inscription: "Miss Sally Louisa Williams, Boston. And should we never meet again/Till death shall seal our doom/Oh may that Friendship still remain/[illegible] o'er the tomb. Emily."

36. Kendall, *Travels*, pp. 122–123. Vaughan was probably responsible for the publication by Peter Edes of [Hans Kasper Hirzel], *The Rural Socrates* (Hallowell, Me.: 1800), a description of a rustic Swiss philosopher.

37. MMB, December 17, 1791, November 22, 1791.

38. John Merrick, *The Trial of David Lynn, Jabez Meigs, Elijah Barton, Prince Cain, Nathaniel Lynn, Ansel Meigs, Adam Pitts for the Murder of Paul Chadwick* (Hallowell, Me.: 1810), p. 10, and (an abridged version) *The Trial of David Lynn, et al.* (Augusta 1809), p. 9.

39. *The Trial of David Lynn* (1810), p. 93.

40. *The Trial of David Lynn* (1809), p. 36.

41. Depositions by John Morrill, George Marson, and Abner Weeks in Papers Regarding Troops at Augusta, 1809, House unenacted Legislation, #6795–6814, MA.

42. Elijah Barton had occasionally visited the Ballard house before the trial and continued to do so afterward. On March 11, 1806, for example, he had brought 1/2 bushel wheat and rye "as a present for us."

43. I do not mean to imply that all women were as estranged from politics. There is ample evidence that many women in the contested townships supported the struggle against the proprietors. See Taylor, *"Liberty-Men,"* pp. 619–622.

44. Mildred Chamberlain and Laura Clarenbach, *Descendants of Hugh Mosher and Rebecca Maxson Through Seven Generations* (published by the authors, 1980), pp. 20, 63. There are no Mosiers in the Hallowell census for 1790, though an Elisha is mentioned in Winslow and two others in Washington. Elisha Mosier is listed in Augusta in 1800 and 1810.

45. MMB, May 30, 1799.

46. Nash, *Augusta*, p. 451.

47. Jared Eliot, *The Blessings Bestow'd on them that Fear God* (New London, Conn.: 1739), pp. 24–26.

48. *Oxford Vital Records*, p. 82.

49. Church Records of the First Church in Augusta, South Parish Congregational Church, Augusta, pp. 100–101.

50. North, pp. 296, 804.

51. E.g., the complex deed including mill rights from Mary Dutton to Ephraim Ballard, November 10, 1830, KD, 71:114–115.

EPILOGUE

1. From Mary Hobart's typed history of the diary written on her personal stationery, embossed with "Dodona, Needham Heights, Massachusetts." Correspondence of Dr. Mary Forrester Hobart . . . concerning presentation of the diary, MeSL.

2. Regina Markell Morantz-Sanchez, *Sympathy & Science: Women Physicians in American Medicine* (New York: Oxford U. Press, 1985), pp. 47–49.

3. Virginia G. Drachman, *Hospital with a Heart: Women Doctors and the Paradox of Separatism at the New England Hospital, 1862–1969* (Ithaca and London: Cornell University Press, 1984); and Morantz-Sanchez, pp. 73, 81–84, 174–176. Both authors briefly mention Mary Hobart's efforts to strengthen clinical training at the hospital.

4. Drachman, pp. 129–131.

5. Charles Green to Francis Goss, June 16, 1884, Francis A. Countway Library of Medicine, Boston. Hobart first appears in the Boston street directory in 1889, at 16 Union Park. She had an office at 320 Marlboro Street by 1892 and a house at 157 Newbury St. in 1895, and had moved to 657 Boylston Street by 1902. *The Boston Directory* (Boston: Sampson, Murdock, and Co., 1885–1913).

6. Elizabeth Brown Pryor, *Clara Barton: Professional Angel* (Philadelphia: University of Pennsylvania Press, 1987), pp. 4–5.

7. Pryor, pp. 77–99, 368.

8. Hobart had strong ties with her relatives, but always maintained her own residence. The house she built in Needham sometime before 1915 is still standing, having recently been renovated by a couple who knew only that the builder had been a "woman doctor." They believe a small room off the front entrance may have been an examining room. The house is in Queen Anne style, with a romantic porch off the second-story bedroom. In the process of remodeling the present owners detected what seemed to them to be wheelchair marks on the doors, leading them to believe that the first owner was either disabled or very old. Hobart was still listed as the owner of the house in 1938, and seems to have died there on March 21, 1940, at the age of 88. *Annual Report of the Officers of the Town of Needham, 1915* (Brookline, Mass.: Riverdale Press, 1916), p. 357; *Town of Needham and Dover, Massachusetts Directory* (Bos-

ton: Harold Howard, 1934–1938); *Town of Needham, Annual Report, 1940* (New-
ton: Garden City Print, 1941), p. 68; Mary Forrester Hobart Will, 96297,
Norfolk County Probate Registry, Norfolk County Court House, Dedham,
Massachusetts.

9. Mary Hobart to H. E. Dunnack, September 27, 1931, MeSL.

10. Preface by Edith Hary to Nash, p. vi.

Acknowledgments

This book has had many midwives. My first debt is to the Maine State Library, custodian of the Martha Ballard diary. Bonnie Collins and other members of the library staff have answered my ordinary as well as extraordinary requests with courtesy and skill. The efficient and knowledgeable staff at the adjoining Maine State Archives also made visits to Augusta pleasurable. Their excellent job of microfilming the Ballard diary and their willingness to provide films of other documents made it possible for me to bring some of my research home.

Jeffrey Zimmerman of Fort Western Museum was generous with time and documents; Jay Adams, now the curator there, showed me through the restored Fort and offered helpful comments on Chapter Two. Edwin Churchill of the Maine State Museum introduced me to the byways of Kennebec history. Paul Rivard, director of the Maine State Museum, and Jack Larkin of Old Sturbridge Village shared their knowledge of eighteenth- and nineteenth-century sawmills. Jane Nylander, director of Strawbery Banke in Portsmouth, N.H., answered questions about everything from burying clothes to turkey feathers. Anne Masury of Strawberry Banke and Caroline Sloat at Old Sturbridge Village talked to me about gardening.

Danny D. Smith, Kennebec genealogist *extraordinaire,* wrote informative letters in answer to my many questions, and answered other queries over piles of books at the State Library. Janice Moore of Oxford, Massachusetts, provided valuable information on Moore family history and arranged for me to see the early Oxford church records. Arlene

Gilbert of Windsor, Maine, taught me about the Barton family and during a memorable meeting in Augusta showed me an intriguing photograph long thought to represent Martha Ballard. Although I ultimately decided that the "Granny Ballard" of the picture was not Martha (I suspect it is Sally, who died in 1858 at the age of 90), I very much appreciate her showing it to me. Perhaps someday the original, whether a photograph or a portrait, will be found.

Edith Hary, retired librarian of the Maine State Law Library, provided lodging for a night and, through her own example, inspiration to persist in telling Martha's story. William and Martha Vaughan showed me the Benjamin and Charles Vaughan papers, which they have since deposited at Bowdoin College. Ann Thomas talked with me about Kennebec deed research. Janet C. O'Brien drove from New Hampshire to meet with me at the eighteenth-century home of her parents. James and Patricia Alpin took time on a Saturday afternoon to show me Mary Hobart's house in Needham Heights, Massachusetts. Ralph G. Crowell shared geneological sheets.

Worth Estes has patiently guided me into the field of eighteenth-century medical history. Without his help I could not have made sense of much in the diary. I have also learned from conversations with Judith Walzer Leavitt and Nancy Tommes, who kindly read Chapter One of the book. Ann Weinraub, a member of Massachusetts Friends of Midwives and a historian, offered many helpful comments and alerted me to my own twentieth-century biases. Mari Patkelly, a practicing midwife in Portsmouth, N.H., read a late draft of the manuscript with extraordinary sensitivity and insight. Heather Stamler gave me a place to stay during one of my visits to Maine, told me about her own work as a midwife, and introduced me to other members of Midwives of Maine, whose questions, comments, and enthusiasm have helped sustain this book.

Alan Taylor helped me understand the significance of Ephraim Ballard's work and much more. His comments on an early draft of the book were crucial in helping to define it, and throughout the project he has generously shared research notes, ideas, and enthusiasm, very much in the spirit of the early economy he and I study. James Leamon, Charles Clark, Steven Innes, and Michael McGiffert, editors of essays in which portions of the Ballard material appeared earlier, also helped me to see my subject clearly, and they improved my presentations of it. I thank them for that. I am also grateful to Mary Beth Norton, James Henretta, Alfred Young, Elaine Crane, Nancy Grey Osterud,

Sarah McMahon, and Marcella Sorg for reading and commenting on these essays, and to Ross Beales, Howard Kushner, Randolph Roth, Richard Brown, and Patricia Cline Cohen for sharing their own work in progress.

In addition to Charles Clark, several colleagues at the University of New Hampshire have helped nurture this project. David Watters found the Jared Eliot sermon which I used in Chapters Two and Ten. William Harris and Robert Mennel offered thoughtful critiques of early chapters. Melody Graulich and Mara Witzling continually stretched my imagination through their own work in women's literature and art, and listened to my ideas about Martha. Janet Polasky offered astute comments, ice cream, and steady friendship.

Edward McCarron spent a very hot summer in the Kennebec County Court House transcribing deeds. Since then he has continued to enrich my work with his own research in eighteenth- and early-nineteenth-century Maine history. Karen Hansen gracefully turned Ed's research and my scrawls into maps. Edith Murphy helped make sense out of the footnotes, but neither she nor any of my other good helpers can be blamed for the errors that crept in while we all slept.

Participants in seminars and colloquia at the University of Delaware, the Winterthur Museum, Boston University, Brandeis University, Colby College, Harvard University, and the University of Pennsylvania have listened patiently and asked good questions. My own students, graduate and undergraduate, have simulated my thinking through their responses to Martha's diary and story. The book has also profited from comments made at meetings of local historical societies and women's history groups. The most difficult question was always, "When will the book be finished?" My editor, Jane Garrett, helped me to answer that. Like the good midwife that she is, she knew when to let me alone and when to offer direction.

For assistance and permission to use documents in their collections, I thank the Maine Historical Society, the Massachusetts Historical Society, the Countway Library of Medicine, the North Andover Historical Society, the Waterville Historical Society, the American Antiquarian Society, and the Hubbard Free Library in Hallowell, Maine. I have also used the resources of the Massachusetts State Archives, and the Registries of Probate and Deeds in Worcester and Norfolk counties, Massachusetts, and in Kennebec and Lincoln counties, Maine.

This project was supported by summer faculty fellowships and a year-long fellowship for independent study from the National Endowment for the Humanities, and by support grants from the Central University Research Fund of the University of New Hampshire. It was also supported and slowed down by my family. Thatcher Ulrich provided computer assistance and a critical reading of Chapter One. Amy Ulrich helped with deed research, Melinda Chiou gave advice on graphics, Henry Chiou tracked down an elusive printer wheel, Karl Ulrich and Nancy Bentley provided a place to sleep near Boston, and Nathan Ulrich tried to come up with a better title for the book. Gael Ulrich has patiently endured my long fascination with the eighteenth century and in the twentieth has given new meaning to what Martha called "the wedded state."

LAUREL THATCHER ULRICH

Durham, New Hampshire
June 1, 1989

Index

ABOUT THE AUTHOR

Laurel Thatcher Ulrich was born in Sugar City, Idaho, in 1938. She received her B.A. from the University of Utah in 1960, her M.A. from Simmons College in 1971, and her Ph.D. from the University of New Hampshire in 1980. She is currently a professor of history at the University of New Hampshire. The author of *Good Wives: Image and Reality in the Lives of Women in Northern New England, 1650–1750* and of various scholarly articles and personal essays, she received the 1990 Bancroft Award and the American Historical Association's John H. Dunning and Joan Kelly Memorial Prizes for *A Midwife's Tale*.